Contents

Preface   *page* vii

John Locke's conception of freedom, *by* RAYMOND POLIN,
   Professor of Philosophy, the Sorbonne, Paris   1

Locke, liberalism and nationalism, *by* M. SELIGER, *Associate*
   Professor of Political Science, the Hebrew University of Jerusalem   19

Locke and English liberalism: the *Second Treatise of*
   Government in its contemporary setting, *by* ESMOND S.
   DE BEER, *Fellow of the British Academy*   34

The politics of Locke in England and America in the eighteenth
   century, *by* JOHN DUNN, *Lecturer in History, King's College,*
   Cambridge   45

The family and the origins of the state in Locke's political
   philosophy, *by* GORDON J. SCHOCHET, *Assistant Professor*
   of Political Science, Rutgers University, New Jersey   81

The state of nature and the nature of man in Locke,
   by HANS AARSLEFF, *Associate Professor of English,*
   Princeton University   99

John Locke, the great recoinage, and the origins of the Board
   of Trade: 1695–1698, *by* PETER LASLETT, *Reader in Politics and*
   the History of Social Structure in the University of Cambridge   137

Locke, Newton and the two cultures, *by* JAMES L. AXTELL,
   Department of History, Yale University   165

The science of nature, *by* JOHN W. YOLTON, *Chairman of*
   the Department of Philosophy, York University, Toronto   183

Faith and knowledge in Locke's philosophy, *by* RICHARD
   ASHCRAFT, *Assistant Professor of Political Science,*
   University of California at Los Angeles   194

Contents

What is a nominal essence the essence of?, *by* w. von leyden, *Reader in Philosophy in the University of Durham* *page* 224

The essayist in his *Essay, by* rosalie colie, *Visiting Research Professor and Talbot Research Fellow of Lady Margaret Hall, Oxford* 234

Some observations on recent Locke scholarship, *by* hans aarsleff 262

Index 273

Preface

Locke's interests and activities covered a wide range of subjects: child-rearing and education, biblical exegesis, the economics of coinage, moral and political principles, knowledge, belief and understanding, science and religion. This list is of course not complete but it gives some idea of the scope of Locke's thought. One advantage of the collection of essays here assembled is that they have been written by persons from the different fields of Locke's interests. The polymath that Locke was in his own century may now be best revealed from the different perspectives of our academic disciplines. The cooperative effort of this volume (its contributors constituting most of those currently engaged upon Locke study and research) marks another step in the new understanding of John Locke.

The initial impetus for such a collection of essays came from a conference on the Thought of John Locke, held at York University, Toronto, Canada in December 1966. This conference was made possible through grants from the Humanities Research Council of Canada of the Canada Council and from the Faculty of Graduate Studies at York University.

Peter Laslett's essay is a revised version of an article which appeared in 1957 in the *William and Mary Quarterly*. All the other essays appear here for the first time.

Toronto   J.W.Y.
January, 1968

NOTE: Unless otherwise stated references to *Two Treatises* in the present volume refer to *John Locke: Two Treatises of Government*, ed. Peter Laslett (Cambridge, 1960).

John Locke's conception of freedom

by RAYMOND POLIN

The traditional interpreters of John Locke like to pretend that he professed simultaneously a theoretical philosophy of empirical style and a practical philosophy of innatist inspiration. People used to admit that Locke was able to publish, in the same year, his *Essay concerning Human Understanding* and the *Treatises of Civil Government* and could have been inspired in those two works, presented almost simultaneously, by two radically contradictory doctrines. Is it because of indifference to the ideal of a coherent philosophical system, derived from a poorly understood empiricism? Is it a desire to present *Two Treatises* as a work of circumstance, as a kind of pamphlet without any real doctrinal connexion with the whole of his philosophy? Anyway, the accusation of incoherence, which we would easily forgive, is very difficult to eradicate.

With respect to his theory of freedom, we would like to show that his metaphysics, morals, and politics are tightly interwoven and that the meaning of his political liberalism, a truly moral doctrine, can be understood only in the light of his philosophy considered as a really coherent totality.

PHILOSOPHICAL FREEDOM

If one follows the presentation of Locke's philosophy, one can directly, through one's own experience, arrive at an essential analysis of the idea of freedom. For Locke, freedom is a mode of power, power being in itself a simple idea which is given to us through sensation as well as through reflexion:[1] do we not observe within ourselves that we 'can' think, that we 'can' move the parts of our body at will? In a more general way, Locke tends to refer the changes we observe in the world to specific possibilities of changing or of being changed in ways characteristic of each thing.[2] While matter is essentially passive, and God its creator is truly purely active, man as an intermediary being shares with animals passive powers, such as perception, understanding and the passions, but shares

[1] *An Essay concerning Human Understanding*, ed. A. C. Fraser (Oxford, 1894), II, VII, §8.
[2] *Essay*, II, XXI, §1.

with God the privilege of possessing active power,[1] that is, the power of beginning to think or to move. We should not forget that Locke was the first to refuse to interpret these powers as distinct beings existing by themselves in the mind, as agents capable of existing and acting within us but beyond our control.[2] He thus in advance made a critique of the 'faculties', the theory of which is so freely attributed to him.

An active power is easily observable in the functioning of the mind, in the form of the will, which is the power to begin or interrupt the movement of a part of the body, or in the thinking of an idea.[3] It is the power the mind has of determining its thoughts and, through them, of determining the continuation, the completion or the cessation of an action. It is the power of preferring, of choosing. Freedom is also a power, the power of organizing one's thoughts and movements according to one's own preferences.[4] Consequently, we cannot speak of the freedom of the will, since it is absurd to speak of a power of a power; a power can be only the attribute of a substance; it can belong only to an agent. We can ask whether a certain man is free, but not whether a certain will is free.[5] It is the mind which has the power to be free, that is to say, the agent, considered as a whole, who has the power of accomplishing or not accomplishing an action according to his preference,[6] that is according to his judgment.

We can see now that for Locke the principle of freedom, as well as the principle of will, is located in thought. To be free is to think and act according to one's own judgment, that is, to 'the acquiescing of the mind':[7] the principle of freedom is a decision of the mind, a thought as such. In common with the Stoics, Locke discovered the efficacy of judgment in the *animadversio animi*: the judgment orients the thinking, the attention, and in so doing, drives thoughts and actions along a certain path. While the will is spontaneously determined by this properly human uneasiness, which tends to bind men to the vicissitudes of the present, of immediate existence,[8] in a constant and unreflective effort to dissipate that uneasiness, freedom on the other hand permits men to sever the pressure of uneasiness, to suspend the efficacy and the execution of desires that it engenders, and makes possible the examination, at length, through reflexion and with the light of reason, of the object of the desires and of the practical problems which the given situation creates.[9] 'Man has a power to suspend all determinations. This seems to me the source of all liberty.'[10]

Locke is perfectly aware of the rationalist orientation of his doctrine.

[1] *Essay*, II, XXI, §2.
[2] *Essay*, II, XXI, §6.
[3] *Essay*, II, XXI, §5.
[4] *Essay*, II, XXI, §8.
[5] *Essay*, II, XXI, §16.
[6] *Essay*, II, XXI, §15.
[7] *Essay*, IV, XVII, §16.
[8] *Essay*, II, XXI, §47.
[9] *Essay*, II, XXI, §48.
[10] *Essay*, II, XXI, §51.

Locke's conception of freedom

For him, not only is it the judgment which initiates a free act, but the more reasonable the judgment, the more perfect is the liberty of the act. Far from limiting our freedom, the determination of it through good reasons and reasonable motivation exemplifies it. The freedom of an intelligent being consists in this:[1] the end of our freedom is the achievement of the reasonable good we have chosen. It would be absurd to imagine that liberty would consist in acting according to whim, to shrug off the yoke of reason and not to submit to the constraint of reflexion and judgment.[2] The *Second Treatise* emphasizes this condemnation of freedom as 'caprice'. Freedom is not, as Filmer maintained, 'a liberty of every man to do what he lists'.[3] This is the reason why Locke does not hesitate to present the power of freedom as associated with the power of reason. Men have been created, he says, 'capable of freedom and capable of reason. We are born free as we are born rational.'[4] Since reason constitutes the comprehension of the world order and is identified with it in the end, it is evident that, for Locke, freedom acquires meaning only when it is related to an order, to the order of the world itself, which is the order of reason.

This is why Locke's theory of freedom finds itself torn between two poles, the first one, a very classical one, the other, much more modern. On one hand, liberty tends to be identified with the necessary order established by the Creator; it is thus that beings superior to us are determined, much more strictly than we ourselves are, by their preference for that which is good. As for God, he can choose only what is good; the freedom of the Almighty does not prevent him from being necessarily determined by the best.[5] Freedom then, as the ancients used to think, in God's case is nothing but the accomplishment of a potential order. It consists in accomplishing what he is.

On the other hand, for man, frail, fragile and imperfect by nature,[6] liberty works differently. Considering his pravity, the function of liberty takes a radically different meaning. The first manifestation of human freedom is the disruption of man's natural determination by the good and the abandonment of his judgment to the pressure of his passions. Liberty is therefore, first of all, the mark of man's imperfection and pravity. It is not excessive to say that, for Locke, between the Stoics and Kant, freedom represents a freedom for evil, the principle of *ein Urböses*, of a fundamental evil.

It is true, indeed, that we can often say, with Ovid, *video meliora proboque*,

---

[1] *Essay*, II, XXI, §49.   [2] *Essay*, II, XXI, §51.
[3] *Two Treatises on Government*, ed. Peter Laslett (Cambridge, 1960), II, §22.
[4] *Two Treatises*, II, §61.   [5] *Essay*, II, XXI, §50.
[6] *Essay*, II, XXI, §54.

Raymond Polin

deteriora sequor.[1] The fact is that our will is ordinarily determined by our constant lack of satisfaction, by the state of 'uneasiness'[2] which is an insatiable desire, which simultaneously keeps us from excessive consideration of the immediate and present, and maintains in us a permanent longing for absent goods and prevents us from estimating their worth. Values of the present and values of the future are not weighed with the same scales. The intervention of time falsifies their appreciation: the more distant the future moment is, the greater is the possible error. Judgment errs because of ignorance, precipitation and especially of 'inadvertency', i.e. that wrong orientation of attention, too easily attached to the present, unable to take into consideration the distant future, that so important future which is the location of eternal bliss. Errors of judgment lead men, fascinated by the proximity of present pleasures and pains, to a wrong use of their freedom and condemn them to misery and unhappiness. 'Without liberty, the understanding would be of no purpose; and without understanding, liberty (if it could be) would signify nothing.'[3]

How, under these conditions, is the right use of freedom possible? These formulas teach us clearly that liberty has no meaning outside the right use of the understanding, and we must even acknowledge that the very existence of the understanding, the fact that men have been endowed by God in his providence with an understanding, finds its end, its final cause, in the right use of liberty. In such an imperfect, frail and weak being, a permanent prey for any error and any passion, freedom, in its wrong use as well as in its right one, finds its meaning in the very end of the existence of men in this world, which consists in the quest for true happiness, I mean for eternal bliss.

The metaphysical and even theological dogma of eternal salvation constitutes indeed the foundation and the right justification for the existence of freedom.[4] Moreover, it is the consideration of eternal salvation, of eternal happiness, which makes actual freedom possible. Through faith in eternal happiness, our freedom acquires the power of suspending the course of our desires, of interrupting the determination of the will by that permanent uneasiness produced in us by the flight and disappearance of everything present and immediate. By suspending in such a way the pressure of our desires, we become able to examine and judge by ourselves in an impartial and loyal manner.[5] That negative intervention of our freedom, born from the destination of man to eternal happiness, allows our judgment to choose the better or the more reasonable, no force being

---

[1] *Essay*, II, XXI, §35.   [2] *Essay*, II, XXI, §§29 and 31-2.
[3] *Essay*, II, XXI, §69, fourth edition.   [4] *Essay*, II, XXI, §52.
[5] *Essay*, II, XXI, §53.

any longer opposed to it by our passions, to determine our will and provoke the achievement of actually free action.

But man, in his imperfection, is not necessarily led to eternal bliss. Only beings superior to men are necessarily bound to it. For man, it is only an obligation. 'The inclination and tendency of [human] nature to happiness is an obligation.'[1] From this affirmation it can be deduced that freedom itself is part of human nature, not as a necessary element of its essence, but as an essential function of obligation. Liberty, as a power or as an inclination to good, finds its source in obligation, in duty as such, inscribed in the very nature of man, a duty to search for eternal salvation and to merit it. Any desire, which is essentially by itself a desire for satisfaction and happiness, in such a way is but a secondary and corrupted form of that obligating inclination towards the unique and true and eternal happiness. Freedom, through this longing for eternal salvation, becomes able to master any human desire. Corresponding to an absolute obligation for happiness, it constitutes a decisive moral power, it accomplishes a moral function. A Kantian formula would almost be appropriate for it, something like: since you are obliged to search for the true happiness, you can. Understood in such a fashion, Locke's conception of freedom would find its real meaning: it is the very principle of a truly human existence, the means through which man can develop and achieve his real nature in a human world and for other men. Our freedom is indeed, as we have seen, a freedom of beings capable of reason, in a world organized in such a way that, with the power of reason and freedom given to us by God, we are capable of accomplishing a meaningful duty, that obligation for eternal happiness which happens to be the motive of our creation and the principle of our temporal existence.

POLITICAL FREEDOM

As soon as the human power of freedom has been determined in its meaning and function, the achievement of a moral human existence, the formation and even the salvation of a moral person do not represent for Locke philosophical problems any more so far as individuals are concerned, each of them being considered in his own peculiar destiny, in that pursuit of an eternal bliss in which his personal freedom alone is in question. That achievement is just a matter of practice, of application, of education, either of education of the understanding, of maturation of judgment, or of practice of the will.

On the other hand, if we consider the particular individual, i.e. the

---

[1] *Essay*, II, XXI, §53.

individual just as capable of becoming a social animal as he is essentially capable of freedom and reason, a new philosophical problem appears, a problem of political philosophy.

The state of natural freedom in which men live in the state of nature is precisely that state in which each man disposes of his power of liberty according to his own will and pleasure, in his relations with other men who are endowed like himself with a power of freedom of the same nature. 'All men are naturally in...a state of perfect freedom to order their actions and dispose of their possessions and persons as they think fit.'[1] This power of freedom is a specific power, so that all men 'who are creatures of the same species' are as such equal by nature: 'it is a state of equality, wherein the power is reciprocal, no one having more than another'.[2]

The characteristic of that equal power of freedom between men is that it does not manifest itself in society *in foro interno*, but that it presents external forms, it affects the existence of the others: it consists in the liberty of disposing of one's own body and limbs and, generally speaking, of everything that can be owned and that one owns. Property (as Hegel later explicitly explained)[3] is the external manifestation of freedom, its expression and its very concrete existence for others. Conversely, Locke calls one's own property everything which becomes an object for somebody's freedom: his life, body, liberties and estates.[4] By nature, a man is free to dispose of his property, independently 'from any superior power on earth'.[5] Every man, being equal to every other, manifests his liberty by the domination, the ownership of his property: 'he is the absolute lord of his own person and possessions'. As Locke puts it, 'his freedom is his empire'.[6]

Locke acknowledges the fact that man, as a work of God, remains always not only God's servant, but forever God's property.[7] However, the sovereignty of that divine Master, in spite of being absolute, does not hamper the liberty of man, since it is God himself who created man capable of freedom and capable of intelligence, so that he might search by his personal efforts for eternal bliss and eventually merit it. The only external limit to the reasonable usage of human freedom springing from this relation of Creator to creature consists in the fact that man, as the property of God, has been created to last as long as the Creator wishes and not according to his own good will and pleasure. That is the reason why man

[1] *Two Treatises*, II, §4. [2] *Two Treatises*, II, §4.
[3] Hegel, *Philosophie des Rechts*, ed. Hoffmeister (Hamburg, 1955), §§44-5.
[4] *Two Treatises*, II, §§87 and 123. [5] *Two Treatises*, II, §23.
[6] *Two Treatises*, II, §123. [7] *Two Treatises*, II, §6.

is not free to dispose either of his life or of the life of others, even if he has the desire, power and opportunity to do so.[1] Anyway, this external limit to liberty corresponds also to an internal one: would it not be absurd that, being created to accomplish their temporal existence in order to merit eternal salvation, men would be able to use their liberty to interrupt their own existence or the existence of any other man and, renouncing their own natural end, able to refuse reasonably the obligation inscribed in the very nature of their freedom?

Freedom indeed consists in ordering one's own actions and disposing of one's own property as each one thinks fit within 'the bounds of the law of nature'. The obligation essential to human freedom is expressed through a natural law,[2] which lets the voice of God be heard in man. There are two points to note here: on the one hand, natural law lets us hear the voice of God in man,[3] that which confers a special power of obligation in the order established by the Creator; on the other hand, and this point is peculiarly important for Locke, this law is a law of reason,[4] because reason is the proper way through which God speaks to man (instinct being the way he speaks to animals). Through reason only, man is able to interpret the data of the senses and discover the law of nature, which expresses the obligation through which human freedom receives its intention and meaning. To achieve this interpretation, man has to develop a state of maturity which allows him to be not only capable of reason, but also actually and efficiently reasonable.[5] Man's freedom is at last 'grounded upon his having reason'. Reason teaches him that law according to which he is at last able to govern himself as a free being.[6] Reason, like liberty, appears in him in the form of an obligation, in the form of a law: to be obliged to be free in conformity with the law of man is to be obliged to be reasonable, to act freely in a reasonable way.

Freedom is for Locke inseparable from law; the concept of law determines the proper means to lead an intelligent and free being towards his real interest. The end of any law—it is true of the law of nature and of any positive law, when it has been established according to reason—is not to abolish or to restrain, but to protect and enlarge human freedom.[7] The laws only, indeed, are able to guarantee our freedom against the violence of others. For all beings created 'capable of laws', 'where there is no law, there is no freedom'. Law as such alone allows us, *in foro interno*, as the law of nature, or *in foro externo*, as the positive law, to depend upon our own will only, to be actually free. Since freedom implies an essential

---

[1] *Two Treatises*, II, §6.
[2] *Two Treatises*, I, §86.
[3] *Two Treatises*, I, §86.
[4] *Two Treatises*, I, §101.
[5] *Two Treatises*, II, §59.
[6] *Two Treatises*, II, §63.
[7] *Two Treatises*, II, §57.

obligation to human nature, the very law of human nature, nature and obligation being one and the same thing, it does not depend upon man himself to renounce his own power of liberty, any more than it could depend upon him to renounce his own nature. 'Nobody can give more power than he himself has.'[1] 'Nobody has an arbitrary power over himself.'[2] Among men, that power—which is also an obligation, natural, reasonable and imposed by God to exercise that power—happens to be a legitimate power, a right in the presence of any other man, even in the state of nature. Locke acknowledges that right as an inalienable one, since it is a part of human nature and since, in the last analysis, man as a natural being belongs to God, as his property.[3] Nobody owns the right to renounce and suppress his own life; in the same way, nobody has the right to renounce and abandon or alienate his own freedom.

It follows as a direct consequence that every contract through which a man would abandon his life or his freedom to the arbitrary power of any other, would be properly void and vain. Nobody has either the power or the right to consent to his own servitude; no master can justify his domination by claiming that consent was received from his slave. It follows also that the man who lives actually as a slave lives like a wild brutish beast; not exercising his freedom any longer, he makes the worst and most inhuman use of it. Since he is not 'a free man',[4] he is not a man at all: he cannot be indeed a 'moral man', an actual human being. The slave has in reality excluded himself from the human condition. For Locke, it is not possible, as it was for Aristotle, that a man could be a slave by nature. It is not even possible that a man could be a slave by right—and this doctrine is a very new one—but he admits however that there may in fact exist, such is the weakness, the frailty and the pravity of mankind, a slavery *de facto*, actual human beasts consenting to their slavery. This situation corresponds to the principle that, for Locke, men are born with capacities and under a specific obligation, but that they have to mature and to develop themselves, and that they can remain undeveloped or can destroy and corrupt what they have been able to achieve. Consequently, human creatures happen to exist who, not being fully developed, having failed to make a reasonable and constant use of their liberty, live below the level of mankind, at the level of brute beasts.[5]

In the state of nature where social relations bind individual to individual, the meaning of the relation is still moral, not political. The solution of the

[1] *Two Treatises*, I, §23.   [2] *Two Treatises*, II, §135.
[3] *Two Treatises*, II, §6.   [4] *Two Treatises*, II, §60.
[5] Raymond Polin, *La Politique morale de John Locke* (Paris, 1960), pp. 40–3 and p. 41, n. 1.

8

conflicts necessarily developing between them, when each one acts for his own interest according to his own natural freedom, belongs to each individual as such and depends upon his personal and private view of the law of nature. Each person being both judge and member, the agreements with others are precarious and jeopardized by the inevitable partiality and the essential pravity of human nature; it depends upon the private good or bad judgment of anyone at any moment, upon the good or bad use of each one's freedom.

The formation of the body politic transfers the determination and protection of freedom as well as the control of conflicts to the public. 'The community comes to be the umpire.' It receives the exclusive right to judge and to let its judgments be executed, according to the positive laws it establishes, to interpret and make explicit the law of nature in terms universally valid for the whole community.[1]

A political obligation is developed from the publication of civil laws and takes its meaning from the law of nature and the reasonable order which it teaches in the form of a moral obligation. The law of nature frees man *in foro interno* from the arbitrary pressure of the passions; the positive laws free man *in foro externo* from the external restraints enforced by the arbitrary violence of the others. In the former case the interpretation of the law of nature and its execution depend without mediation upon the judgment and freedom of each individual. In the latter, a necessary and exclusive mediation interferes: the rulers are acknowledged to possess the exclusive right to interpret the law of nature through universal positive laws and to compel the members of the community to strict obedience, even with the threat and help of public force that they control. Could it be pretended that, under this rule and control, political freedom would still be a true freedom? that the mediator who judges and decides for others, whose freedom deals for them with all the most important problems of their civil life, does not abolish, for the others, through his presence and action, the very principle of freedom, the very fact of freedom, the capacity of judging by one's self and of actually acting according to one's own judgment?

The consideration of political freedom introduces indeed a new kind of problem. As soon as the political community is instituted, the external manifestation of freedom no longer opposes individuals to individuals, but individuals acting as citizens to the community as such on the one hand, and to the rulers on the other hand.

The same type of problem will be met later by Rousseau and he will solve it by affirming that when an individual has once given himself to

[1] *Two Treatises,* II, §135.

the whole, he gives himself through the whole to himself and, when he agrees to obey the subsequent laws, he obeys only himself and he remains as free as he has ever been.[1] Rousseau even pretends that, in the society founded upon the social contract, when the sovereign makes use of the public force according to the laws, he is able 'to force' legitimately the citizens 'to be free', to be actually free indeed.[2]

This answer was in fact more or less anticipated by Locke when he declared that the freedom in a community consisted in being 'under no other legislative power but that established by consent in the common-wealth, nor under the dominion of the will or restraint of any law, but what that legislative shall enact according to the trust put in it'.[3]

In its relation to the community as well as to the rulers, freedom consists, in its external manifestations, in acting in conformity with the laws and under their protection. The moral obligation, grounded upon reason and its expression through the law of nature, is reinforced by a political obli-gation, sustained by eventual public restraints. But the principle and the ground of political obligation is the very principle and ground of moral obligation, that is to say, the reasonable use of freedom according to the law of nature. This reasonable use of freedom is concentrated here in the 'consent', either explicit or implicit, given by the natural individual to the institution and existence of a political community, consent which is the expression of natural and reasonable freedom, and which takes place when the civil society is instituted or when an individual becomes a member of a civil society. This consent is permanently implied in all the events of its political life and in all the acts of the public authority. Each one of these acts is transformed into free acts *de jure* consented to by each one of the citizens.[4]

The initial consent, which was so strongly stressed by Hobbes, under the form of a social contract, does not appear so explicitly in Locke's doctrine: it is clear he is interested only in the principle of the contract, of the 'compact', as he prefers to call it, in that act of natural freedom through which each one personally institutes the political community or enters into it, by renouncing the use of his 'private judgment' and by transmitting the power to interpret the natural law and to enforce its application to 'the hands of the community', to the common authority, to the public.[5] Everyone authorizes the society to make laws for him. Everyone quits 'his executive power of the law of nature' and resigns it to

---

[1] Jean-Jacques Rousseau, *Contrat social*, ed. Halbwachs (Paris, 1943), book I, chapter VI.
[2] Rousseau, *Contrat social*, book I, chapter VII.
[3] *Two Treatises*, II, §22.   [4] *Two Treatises*, II, §87.
[5] *Two Treatises*, II, §87.

Locke's conception of freedom

the public.[1] But the real role of the public authority is to be the umpire,[2] who makes the law, who lets it be executed, the citizens remaining at any rate the agents as well as the 'authors' (those who authorize) of the law. 'That which acts any community' is only the consent of the individuals.[3] Nothing but the consent of the individuals can make anything be the act of the whole.[4] Besides, the permanent presence underlying the public life of the consenting citizens manifests itself through the permanent appeal to public authority, in case of conflict. The very sign and criterion of the existence of a civil society lies in the possibility and right belonging to any citizen to appeal to the justice of the sovereign.[5]

In the last analysis, the consent remains, even in the frame of a constraining civil society, a permanent act of natural freedom and the living principle of political obligation.[6] It is indispensable to the constitution of an obligation, even if it is interpreted as an obedience to a temporal power. Each man is born free by nature and nothing can subject him to any temporal power, if he does not consent.[7] Nobody is born by nature a subject or a citizen of any commonwealth, *that* principle is taught by an evident law of right reason. Since consent is an act of natural freedom, nobody can accomplish it for any other: nobody can consent for any other, particularly for children, who by nature are as free as their fathers,[8] so that their fathers cannot consent for them. A free man only, when he becomes an adult, when he comes to the 'age of discretion', is capable of giving for himself this consent which makes him a member of a civil society and of choosing the political community in which he prefers to participate. To make himself 'a perfect member of the society', he has to give an explicit consent: freedom only is able to commit itself 'in a positive commitment'.[9] If this consent is implicit only and comes from the fact that a man possesses property and lives in a commonwealth under the protection of its laws, it engages the obedience of this man, but does not make a full citizen of him. This obligation of obedience, however, begins and ceases with the enjoyment of this protection as soon as he alienates the property he owns in this state. An implicit consent does not imply any permanent political obligation; those who have given it once are always allowed to become members of another state or to go and institute a new community *in vacuis locis*.[10] On the other hand, those who explicitly consented to be members of a certain state, become citizens of this state for ever. They cannot be freed from their political obligation, at least so

[1] *Two Treatises*, II, §89.
[2] *Two Treatises*, II, §87.
[3] *Two Treatises*, II, §96.
[4] *Two Treatises*, II, §98.
[5] *Two Treatises*, II, §89.
[6] *Two Treatises*, II, §97.
[7] *Two Treatises*, II, §119.
[8] *Two Treatises*, II, §73.
[9] *Two Treatises*, II, §122.
[10] *Two Treatises*, II, §121.

long as the state lasts, if they are not excluded by the decision of the rulers.

We see that, in the determination of the relations between individual freedom and political community, Locke has two concerns: to preserve and guarantee individual freedom, and to protect the state against any danger or risk of corruption or destruction. He answers to the first by requiring that every new member of the community, even the children of its members, give an explicit consent, as a free and reasonable man's commitment. And he answers to the second one by ruling that the political obligation so contracted, being born from a free compact, must be an irrevocable and indestructible one. Emigration, even life emigration, does not free anybody from that indestructible commitment. As always with Locke, freedom finds its meaning through the obligations it implies and the limits to which it consents.

We have finally to consider the problem of the freedom of the people and of the citizens as members of the people, in their relations with those among them who exercise public authority, either as a body, the government, or as individuals, the rulers as such, the magistrates—as Locke very often puts it.

By constituting itself, the political community in effect makes the collection of citizens a people, with its unity, its common good, its will.[1] When Locke describes its action, its powers and its capacities of judging and willing, he proposes in fact a theory of its freedom. We shall limit ourselves to the definition of its philosophical meaning and of its principles.

For Locke indeed, the public good is something more than safety and security in peace and prosperity, as Hobbes described it: it implies also the enjoyment of the freedom of the people, which constitutes for it as well as for the individual the very principle of existence. Freedom constitutes 'their original right',[2] the right to be the supreme principle of its own decisions, of its laws, of its acts. A people as a community possesses and keeps the supreme power and right to preserve itself and to protect itself against the attacks of any other power, including even the power of those to whom it had previously delegated the authority to represent it.[3] Peoples, like individuals, necessarily obey the fundamental and ineluctable principle of conservation and, for peoples as for individuals, it behooves each one to try to preserve itself in its peculiarity. To preserve one's self consists in the preservation of one's own freedom against any arbitrary

---

[1] Polin, *Politique morale de Locke*, pp. 155–62.
[2] *Two Treatises*, II, §§166 and 239.
[3] *Two Treatises*, II, §149.

domination, any enslaving conditions, any servitude. A people, in a given community, not only disposes of specific liberties and rules by positive laws; not only does it found the political community by an act of freedom —a commonwealth is grounded only upon the consent of the people[1]— but it also continues to keep the freedom of safeguarding itself by its own decisions and means, if it should happen that it considers its common good endangered by those it once trusted to secure and promote it.

For Locke, peoples and individuals are alike: the people's freedom is a true freedom only if the people are reasonable. Locke is opposed explicitly to the traditional opinion of those who accuse the people of being inconstant, uncertain, ignorant and permanently passionate and confused.[2] He notices, on the contrary, that the people are attached to their ancient constitutions and traditions (this could be observed very clearly in England, in spite of its revolutions). 'The people is capable of weighing reason on all sides', to reflect and choose and decide, even in a more reasonable manner than do most individuals depraved by their weaknesses and passions. Locke does not hesitate to proclaim that 'the people have the sense of rational creatures'.[3] In other words, the people as individuals are capable of reason and capable of freedom and they play their part in political life by consenting and refusing, as do individuals.

Consequently, we should not be surprised if the compact through which the people bind themselves to a body politic as a government, and which constitutes a true *pactum subjectionis*, is of a moral nature: it constitutes the famous trust, which would not be comprehensible if it did not bind by their moral commitments beings similarly capable of intelligence and freedom, the people and the rulers. A trust as such binds beings capable of committing themselves, capable of promising—in a word, capable of freedom. The freedom of those who participate in the compact finds its expression, its rule, its limits, in the trust itself. It institutes for all an end for their liberty, an obligation towards the very object of the trust, the common good, the good of the people. All the powers transferred through the trust are ordered towards a certain end in conformity with a teleological reckoning.[4] According to the trust, the rulers' freedom is bound by the obligation of acting towards its end; the conservation of the people's freedom, by the obligation to obey the magistrats in the frame of the trust. But anyway, in this kind of compact, relations are not reciprocal, they remain in fact unequal; first, because the magistrates dispose immediately of a greater power than the people; secondly, because the people, on the contrary, keep only a decisive *de jure* power, since they

---

[1] *Two Treatises*, II, §§ 134 and 175.
[2] *Two Treatises*, II, §223.
[3] *Two Treatises*, II, §230.
[4] *Two Treatises*, II, §149.

give the trust, they fix its limits and they remain the witnesses and even the judges of its achievement.[1] They keep the freedom to appreciate in the last resort the adequacy of the rulers' actions for the 'good of the people'.

In case of a breach of trust, indeed, as he did in the frame of the *pactum societatis*, Locke introduces also the procedure of appeal. But he acknowledges the people's right to appeal and, because an impartial judge separate from the two parties in conflict is lacking, he acknowledges the actual power of the people to appeal to itself: it is the people as such which 'shall be judge'.[2] The body of the people shall be judge.[3] The people only can be the umpire, and not because they are impartial, but because their will, their free decision, is the principle of trust, the spring of supreme power. Even if the expression itself is not employed by Locke, it is anyway the sovereignty of the people, of the body of the people as a free and reasonable person, which he affirmed. The people's freedom consists in the fact that it is the supreme principle and foundation of any political power. Its liberty and its sovereignty are one and the same thing.

The free will of the people does not manifest itself only when the community is instituted through the founding affirmation of its unanimity. From that moment on, indeed, the totality of those who consented to constitute a unique political community, 'that whole', consented that, in the political body, the will of the majority would have the right to rule, to command and to act for the whole.[4] The free will of the people manifests itself permanently through the free will of the majority.[5] With majority rule, the freedom of the people acts effectively and efficiently at any moment in the political life of the community.

We shall omit here the technical means proposed by Locke to allow the people's will, in conformity with this principle, to be respected by the magistrates and to control the accomplishment of the trust they committed themselves to obey: representation of the people and of its will by delegates elected at short intervals, supremacy of the legislative power, immediate expression of the people's will, obligation to obey the law of nature in the enactment of any positive laws, expression of the magistrates' will under the exclusive form of 'established and promulgated laws', limited exercise of the 'prerogative' of the rulers, exclusively in case of peril and urgency, if the laws are silent, and only to secure the preservation of the common good. One could gather the whole of these technical dispositions in a single formula: the trust must be expressed under the

[1] *Two Treatises*, ii, §240. [2] *Two Treatises*, ii, §240.
[3] *Two Treatises*, ii, §242. [4] *Two Treatises*, ii, §95.
[5] *Two Treatises*, ii, §96.

form of a constitution, of fundamental laws, which determine the nature of the common good and the ways through which it is to be achieved.

But what will happen, in spite of all these precautions and in case of a 'breach of trust', if the rulers refuse to submit themselves to the people's will and do not recognize it as the necessary principle of their own power and as the supreme judge of any conflict concerning the trusteeship? As a last step in their defence, the people have but 'to appeal to heaven' and run the risk of a trial by force, by resisting and by beginning a civil war, with the hope that God's justice will secure the triumph of Right, of the people's right.[1] But, beyond that traditional interpretation, we can see, in the appeal to heaven, the supreme manifestation of the people's freedom coming back to its own initial source, expressing itself, no longer as a political freedom inside the community, but as a natural freedom again, according to the reasonable law of the state of nature, through violence. In this state of war, in this state of nature, the people, as a free being, appeals to heaven to establish or re-establish the necessary conditions of a constitutional government. For Locke, in the last analysis, political freedom is located for the citizens in the political body, for the people facing their rulers, between the extreme of violence and the extreme of a reasonable compact and trust; it is inseparable from both of them. With such a view, has Locke not made clear the very essence of any political reality, a permanent compromise between freedom and violence?

But the political society, the state, concerns only the affairs of this world: its object and goal is to preserve the security of persons and properties, the respect of any external manifestation of liberty in the frame of established laws. The justice of the political community is exclusively a temporal justice.[2] Its means, public force and restraints, its sanctions, belong to the temporal world and are efficient in it only.

The manifestations of *in foro interno* freedom do not depend upon the state: they do not belong to the same order of things. Human understanding is of such a nature that it cannot be compelled by any kind of violence or restraint to judge or to engender a belief in a certain direction.[3] Torture itself can perhaps impose the verbal expression of a judgment, but not the judgment itself, whose freedom remains beyond the grip of any violence. As far as judgment is concerned, each one is, in the last resort, the supreme and absolute authority.[4] To this principle inherited from the Stoics, Locke adds the affirmation of a modern individualism,

---

[1] *Two Treatises*, II, §241.
[2] *Epistola de Tolerantia*, ed. Klibansky and Polin (Paris, 1963), Latin text, p. 10.
[3] *Epistola*, p. 12.   [4] *Epistola*, p. 72.

the individualism of the free social man, rooted in this freedom of judgment.

How could it be otherwise, especially when judgment deals with the problems of faith, when freedom happens to be the freedom to believe? Judgment concerns in this case the other world only. What is in question belongs exclusively to the individual and depends only upon himself. Each individual alone is able to care for his own soul and to work for his eternal salvation. In that domain, no one can stand for any other.

Of course, there exist churches, that is to say, religious societies in which God is served and adored. But they are 'free and voluntary societies', *societates spontaneae*, of which anyone can become or cease to be a member if he so desires. The churches have no right to use temporal means to force their rules to be respected.[1] In religious societies all temporal sanctions, all temporal restraints, are illegitimate and have to be excluded.[2] Tolerance is the name of freedom in religious societies and the main criterion of a 'true church', *praecipuum verae ecclesiae criterium*.[3] To guarantee the actual practice of religious freedom, Locke proposes to distinguish and separate radically, according to their very nature, the functions of the Church and State and to enclose political societies and religious societies in their exclusive domains.

However, private individuals searching for their salvation are essentially and actually social beings incorporated in political communities; even religious freedom, even the freedom of the mind, cannot be tolerated as an 'absolute freedom'. Freedom has to be compatible with the common goal and the laws of the state.[4]

The first application Locke makes of this principle has not been criticized even by the most tolerant interpreters of Locke. He claims indeed that the political rulers have the right to regulate the religious manners and rites which constitute the external manifestations of a religious belief, in order to make them conform to the laws and order of the state (and which, as they are external, are in fact indifferent to the creed itself).

On the contrary, two other conclusions drawn by Locke from the same principle were often considered as scandalously anti-liberal. On one hand, Locke affirms that the citizens of a certain commonwealth cannot obey two sovereigns at the same time and concludes that the Catholic religion, as far as it implies the temporal subordination of the believers to a temporal sovereign, the pope, cannot be tolerated, except in the papal State itself, without endangering the conservation of any commonwealth, since it creates a permanent factor of disobedience and disorder.[5]

---

[1] *Epistola*, p. 18.   [2] *Epistola*, p. 22.   [3] *Epistola*, p. 2.
[4] *Epistola*, p. 78.   [5] *Epistola*, p. 80.

Locke's conception of freedom

On the other hand, atheism is to be forbidden in a well-ordered commonwealth since, according to Locke's philosophy, moral and political obligations, moral and political virtues, are essentially linked and subordinated to the belief in an all-powerful and perfectly wise God. According to these principles, how indeed could the atheists ever be virtuous men and good citizens?

Are we in the presence of a double incoherence in Locke's doctrine of freedom? Not at all. We have tried to show that, for him, freedom is fundamentally a moral freedom, man a moral man, and we must certainly admit that, within the frame of his system, those who do not believe in God can neither think nor act in conformity with the law of human nature, which is a moral law. Moreover, concerning the principle of the unicity of sovereignty in a commonwealth, it is a self-evident principle, even independently of Locke's doctrine: the permanent conflicts of the Catholic monarchies with the papacy and, also, the original situation of England since the middle of the sixteenth century could easily uphold Locke's idea. If his conclusions are surprising enough for us, it is because we are accustomed to a Catholicism and to a papacy which has by degrees more or less abandoned its temporal ambitions and has completely abandoned its temporal power. In the perspective of his time, these two Lockean conclusions take nothing away from his concept of liberty. We must not forget that his liberalism is a reasonable one and that for him a true freedom is a limited, obliged and meaningful freedom.

With the affirmation of the freedom to believe, we come back to the freedom of judgment, to the freedom of the mind, which was our initial experience and our starting point. As we have proceeded along this circle of thoughts, we have not found any discontinuity. Is this not the best proof, not only of the coherence but also of the real unity of Locke's theory of freedom?

A theory of 'absolute freedom' (a formula wrongly attributed to him and which belongs in fact to Popple, the translator of his *Epistola de Tolerantia* into English) has often been opposed, on his behalf, to the many limits Locke does assign to the moral and political practice of freedom. Such an attempt dangerously confuses in fact liberalism and anarchism. We have tried to show, on the contrary, that freedom for him is nothing but the means given by God to human creatures capable of intelligence, reason and society to incorporate themselves into the order of this world, when they grow mature enough to discover and understand its meaning. Freedom as such is always to be understood as correlative with order. The human being, Locke discovers, as a being capable of freedom and reason, is bound to the divine order of the world through an obligation, the obligation to make himself actually free and reasonable, either in the order of the relations he establishes with other men, or in his relations with the reasonable order of the world. For Locke, freedom exists and is meaningful only if it is bound to the obligation to achieve a reasonable order and a moral one. This principle lies at the bottom of any true and efficient liberalism.

Until now has there been, even for us, a more precious teaching that political philosophy could offer than this one?

Locke, liberalism and nationalism

by M. SELIGER

I

The ideological importance of the idea of the nation and nationalism as a political force have made themselves felt in the wake of the French Revolution. A kindred offspring was the reshuffle of emphases in the evaluation of history. Historicism which stressed the uniqueness of historical periods and phenomena became dominant. The methodological and philosophical concern with distinctiveness went well with the growing national consciousness and aspirations, but collided with the justification of these aspirations on the grounds of historical continuities and tradition. Moreover, the emphasis on distinctiveness provides occasion for controversy or ambiguity over the question to what extent the idea of the nation and nationalism are something new and hence distinguishable from that of the state.[1]

In the history of political philosophy and theory the word 'state' is relatively new, but its connotations are not. The word 'nationalism' is newer still but not the word 'nation' and its use in the sense of a politically self-conscious action unit.[2] Also the justification of the struggle for independence, the epitome of nationalism, precedes the French Revolution, as does the awareness of important components of group cohesion associated in later ages particularly with the nation. In choosing Locke to demonstrate this we find that, to the extent that liberalism provides foundations of modern democracy, it does so also with regard to modern nationalism.[3] But Locke's liberalism is not identical with democracy. The

---

[1] The interdependence between the defining properties of both ideas underlies H. Kohn's classic, *The Idea of Nationalism: A Study in its Origins and Background* (New York, 1946). A. Cobban, *National Self-Determination* (London, 1945), pp. 48 f., stresses the relatively late confluence of 'the hitherto distinguishable, if not entirely separate, ideas of the cultural nation and the political state...' In stressing the novelty, Cobban admits nevertheless the impact of the idea of the state on that of the nation. 'The logical consequence of the democratization of the idea of the state by the [French] revolutionaries was the theory of national self-determination' (p. 51). For a recent analytical treatment see B. Akzin's lucid *State and Nation* (London, 1964), pp. 32, 44 f., 78.

[2] See Kohn, *The Idea of Nationalism*, pp. 15, 19 and *passim*.

[3] *Ibid.* pp. 180-3 points to Locke's emphasis on individual liberty mainly in connexion with toleration and with the formula of government by consent. Kohn does so exclusively in terms of English and—by derivation—American nationalism.

2-2

existence in his theory of such elements which have become attributed to the idea of the nation and nationalism indicates, therefore, that these elements need not be considered as necessarily tied to democracy and opposed to liberalism, as Lord Acton thought,[1] nor as opposed to both, as Treitschke and the fascists did. What Locke's example demonstrates is simply that essential characteristics of nation and nationalism are mainly those which had been all along associated with the body politic whether called *politeia, res publica*, civil society or state.

II

A common language counts heavily among the factors which make for political amalgamation into a national state.[2] The connexion between language, nation and political society was plain to Locke. In the *Essays on the Law of Nature* of the young Locke, language is 'the great instrument and common tie of society' and remains for the mature Locke the pre-requisite for a man to be what he is destined to be, 'a social creature'.[3] This view he repeated in the *Two Treatises of Government*,[4] where he moreover quite clearly assumed the coincidence of language, nationhood and finally full statehood.

The Scriptures recount 'how mankind came to be divided into distinct languages and *nations*'.[5] When mankind 'were all yet of one language', they were 'but *one people*, dwelt altogether,...and were upon building a city together'.[6] A common language, then, is the hall-mark of a nation, even if the whole of mankind forms it. And mankind is a political entity because its unity rests on what characterizes all political societies: the unification of wills through consent. 'They built it [the city of Babel] for themselves as freemen... This was the consultation and design of a people,

[1] Lord Acton, 'Nationality', in *Essays on Freedom and Power*, Selected and with a new Introduction by G. Himmelfarb (Meridian Books, New York, 1955), pp. 144, 158 f. Acton's vein is forcefully enlarged upon by E. Kedourie, *Nationalism* (London, 1961), who adopts (pp. 78 f., 133) Cobban's critical attitude towards the principle of national self-determination (*National Self-Determination*, pp. 44 f., 77 f.). Kedourie's view of nationalism appears almost interchangeable with what Talmon defines as 'totalitarian democracy'. Indeed, Talmon himself in his second study uses 'political messianism' to include also nationalism in the fundamental pattern of 'totalitarian–democratic expectation', J. L. Talmon, *Political Messianism: The Romantic Phase* (London, 1960).
[2] K. W. Deutsch, *Nationalism and Social Communication* (New York, 1955).
[3] *Essays on the Law of Nature*, ed. with an Introduction by W. von Leyden (Oxford, 1954), pp. 156–7 and *An Essay concerning Human Understanding*, ed. with an Introduction by J. W. Yolton (Everyman's Library, London–New York, 1961), III, I, §1.
[4] *John Locke: Two Treatises of Government*, ed. P. Laslett (Cambridge, 1960), II, §77. In using Laslett's edition, I have rendered the quotations into modern English. The italics are throughout mine.
[5] *Two Treatises*, I, §145 in reference to Gen. x. 31.
[6] *Two Treatises*, I, §146.

Locke, liberalism and nationalism

that were at liberty to part asunder, but desired to keep in one body.' If, as long-established opinion has it, popular sovereignty is the prerequisite without which a doctrine like nationalism is inconceivable, there seems to be no reason why Locke should not have adumbrated the doctrine. As the quotations show, he used people or nation synonymously in translation of the Hebrew *goy* of the Bible and considered them by reference to the principle of consent as political societies. If he did not equate primitive societies with fully fledged political societies, it was because these '*nations*...have no *certain* kings',[1] not because he denied them the properties of an independent nation. 'In many parts of America, every little tribe was a distinct people, with a different language... they were divided into little independent societies, speaking different languages.'[2]

The use of the word *nation* in this context and meaning is not restricted to Locke's commenting on the Bible or on primitive peoples. For one thing, Locke commented on the Bible for the purpose of establishing the doctrine of government by consent. While the division of mankind, 'this great and natural community...into smaller and divided associations' is due to men's failings,[3] their 'withdrawing themselves, and their obedience, from the jurisdiction they were born under...from whence sprang all that number of petty commonwealths' exemplifies men's right to live under a government they consent to.[4] Next, Locke discussed not only contemporary primitive peoples in America but also European settlements there with reference to the terms of biblical evidence. He said that 'in peopling of Carolina, the English, French, Scotch, and Welch that are there, plant themselves together, and by them the country is divided *in their lands after their tongues, after their families, after their nations*'.[5] He used nation and people interchangeably also when he spoke of England. 'The power of calling parliaments in England' is a prerogative to be used only 'for the good of the *nation*...'[6] When, in the Preface to the *Two Treatises*, he states his intention 'to justify to the world, the people of England', he says that the 'love of their just and natural rights...saved the *nation* when it was on the very brink of slavery and ruin'. The missing part of the *Two Treatises* is irrelevant in so far as events have disproved Filmer, 'the king, and body of the *nation*', having 'since so throughly confuted his hypothesis', that everybody can find out for himself that 'there was never so much glib nonsense put together in well-sounding English' as in Sir Robert's discourses. The opening sentence of the *First Treatise*, there-

[1] *Two Treatises*, ii, §102.
[2] *Two Treatises*, i, §144.
[3] *Two Treatises*, ii, §128.
[4] *Two Treatises*, ii, §115.
[5] *Two Treatises*, i, §144. The italics are in the text as quoted by Locke from Genesis.
[6] *Two Treatises*, ii, §167.

fore, states: 'Slavery is so vile and miserable an estate of man, and so directly opposite to the generous temper and courage of our *nation*; that it is hardly to be conceived, that an Englishman, much less a gentleman [*sic*], should plead for it.'

According to Locke, a common language is the prerequisite for men to live together as a nation in a self-sustaining political system which has its form and government and its governors determined by consent. But the nation is not merely a contractual action-unit with a common language as its irreplaceable means of communication. It is not only natural in the sense of being the inevitable form of existence. Locke's political society presupposes the coexistence of contractual with such natural ties as the modern conception of a nation associates with it.

III

Locke's historical and otherwise empirical demonstration of incorporation by compact shows the compact effected by tacit consent and as an outgrowth of family life.[1] The father's rule becomes formally political when his sons come of age and go on living in the family. Nothing but their tacit and scarcely avoidable consent turns their father into their monarch. The same form of consent obtains where some families unite by accepting one of the fathers as their leader. The assumption is that 'government is hardly to be avoided amongst men that live together'[2]—and on Locke's showing men do so without notable exception. No gradual appearance of people's inclination to live together is observed. The passage from a less to a more pronounced form of political organization is as insensible as it is inevitable. Common descent is joined to common language in the explanation of the emergence of political society. Its emergence is by way of a process, not through an act. Societies in their beginning are conceived by Locke in terms analogous to those which especially since Tönnies have been reserved for 'community' and 'nation'.[3]

Since political society is legitimated only by consent, consent is in fact the intermediary which turns family into political ties. Biological ties cease to be a discernible factor of cohesion in expanding and differentiating groups. Locke reckoned, therefore, from the outset with emotional togetherness and affection beyond the family circle. As if analysing 'national-

---

[1] See my *The Liberal Politics of John Locke*, chapter VII, 2. I shall refer to my book for detailed proof also for the interpretation of some other tenets of Locke's political philosophy and theory which are drawn together in this essay inasmuch as they bear on nationhood and nationalism.

[2] *Two Treatises*, II, §105.

[3] F. Tönnies, *Community and Society*, ed. and translated by Charles P. Loomis (East Lansing, 1957).

Locke, liberalism and nationalism

ist' attitudes, Locke coupled neighbourly attachment with apprehensions of outsiders. The propensity for natural cohesion enabled, and danger from the outside necessitated, political society. 'Since then those, who liked one another so well as to join into society, cannot but be supposed to have some acquaintance and friendship together, and some trust one in another; they could not but have greater apprehensions of others, than of one another: And therefore their first care and thought cannot but be supposed to be, how to secure themselves against foreign force.'[1]

Voluntariness and naturalness are to varying degrees part of the basic human associations. In this they are different from 'voluntary societies for the time', as for instance 'a band made up' by 'a man in the West-Indies', the crew of a ship and the like.[2] Although compact is 'no natural tie or engagement, but a voluntary submission',[3] Locke grafted it upon the natural proclivities that draw men towards each other. In fact, his recognition of the power of instinctive over and above reflective responses led him so far as to maintain that, while government rested on consent, no other form of pristine government could have evolved than patriarchal monarchy. Natural rights, in the sense of rights grounded on the law of nature and of reason, do not replace historical rights embodied in precedent or custom, but serve as their yardstick.[4]

The information about distant societies caused the young Locke to fasten upon their differences rather than their similarities.[5] For the mature theorist, however, ' . . . in the beginning all the world was America'.[6] He referred to the American Indians and other primitive peoples to validate empirically the general applicability of the fundamental tenets of his theory. In his maturity as in his youth he was aware of the partiality of different peoples to their customs and critical of their foundation in rationality, especially in view of the political utilization of people's reverence for customs. In the *Two Treatises* he enlarged on the unnatural character of some of the customs of the ancient Israelites, the Romans and the Peruvians,[7] although otherwise he referred to them, or their like, as examples of the golden age of early government. He strongly denounced what 'folly or craft began' and 'custom makes. . .sacred',[8] as part of his

[1] *Two Treatises*, II, §107.   [2] *Two Treatises*, I, §131.   [3] *Two Treatises*, II, 73.
[4] Seliger, *The Liberal Politics of John Locke*, chapter VII, 3.
[5] *John Locke: Two Tracts on Government*, ed. with an Introduction, Notes and Translation, by P. Abrams (Cambridge, 1967), pp. 63, 93.
[6] *Two Treatises*, II, §49.   [7] *Two Treatises*, I, §§56-8.
[8] *Two Treatises*, I, §58. Similarly in the early *Essays on the Law of Nature*, pp. 164-5, 166-7. In *Essay* II, XXVIII, §10 *passim*, where the negative overtones are missing, the essential sameness of the moral judgments embodied in 'the law of opinion or reputation' is stressed, together with 'a great measure everywhere' of correspondence 'with the unchangeable rule of right and wrong, which the law of God has established' (§11).

onslaught on the Filmerian theory of absolute paternal monarchy. In this context he invited his readers to survey impartially 'the *nations* of the world' to find 'so much of their governments, religions, and manners brought in and continued amongst them by these means', i.e. by fashion established by craft and folly. History with its customs and precedents is not so much dismissed, as the right vindicated to do that which 'will be thought impudence or madness', namely, 'to contradict or question... governments, religions, and manners' with 'but little reverence for the practices which are in use and credit amongst men...'[1] True, Locke declared that 'at best an argument from what has been, to what should of right be, has no great force', and that, therefore, 'one might, without any great danger, yield them [the absolutists and paternalists] the cause'.[2] Yet the same Locke went out of his way to prove his case by historical evidence. Liberal rationalism reveals itself not as the uncompromising enemy of history and tradition. Reason is the judge of history and precedent but it gains also weight through historical and other empirical evidence. Locke proclaimed victory over the absolutists on the two fronts of reason and history, 'reason being plain on our side, that men are naturally free, and the examples of history showing, that the governments of the world, that were begun in peace... were made by the consent of the people'.[3]

Broadly speaking, Locke's combination of rational and historical criteria situates his conception of political society-nation not so far removed as one would think at first sight from the common denominator, say, of the views of a Burke and a Renan. This is the more evident, if we recognize that Locke's individualism ungrudgingly allows for superior rights of the collectivity.

'The first and fundamental natural law, which is to govern even the legislative itself, is the preservation of the society, and (*as far as will consist with the public good*) of every person in it.'[4] Locke fought against the principles and political arrangements which, he thought, entrenched individual rights more than the security of political society demanded. He did not steer towards a distinction between the whole as the sum total of individuals and the whole as the embodiment of a 'general will'. He could derive from the individualist presuppositions of contractualism such maxims as nationalist thought was to appropriate with particular fervour from traditionalist political thought.

Much as he believed in the ultimate compatibility of the private and the public interest, *salus populi suprema lex est* remained for him an un-

[1] *Two Treatises*, I, §58.   [2] *Two Treatises*, II, §103.   [3] *Two Treatises*, II, §104.
[4] *Two Treatises*, II, §134. See also II, §§16, 123, 128, 129, 149, 159, 168, 220.

assailable rule of political life. While the infringement of the right of 'one or a few oppressed men'[1] was as good a cause for revolt as the infringement of the rights of the majority, it was 'safer for the body [politic], that some few private men should be sometimes in danger to suffer, than that the head of the republic should be easily, and upon slight occasions exposed'.[2] He judged it a civic virtue that the majority 'are more disposed to suffer, than right themselves by resistance'.[3] The patience of the masses with misgovernment was a factor of stability. While Locke was guided in these evaluations by the plea of *raison d'état*, the underlying assumption was that of the involvement of the whole community in the safeguarding of its proper existence against dangers from within and from without. As in modern nationalism, the fundamental given of the state is the nation. This is even more pronounced in Lockean liberalism than in most modes of nationalist thought, inasmuch as in his political society government is the nation's agent, dependent on its consent.

IV

Although Locke allowed the majority the realization of consent only through the right of engaging in active dissent, the notion of consent served him to distinguish between the community or people and the government. Both form the commonwealth, mostly called political but also civil society. The community is the immediate recipient and perpetual repository of the rights which the individuals surrender for the sake of living in civil society. In entering it a man 'has thereby quitted his power to punish offences against the law of nature...' and 'given a right to the *commonwealth* to employ his force, for the execution of the judgments of the commonwealth...'[4] To maintain these judgments in internal and external affairs 'men having authority *from the community*',[5] that is, 'the legislative and executive power of civil society', are entitled 'to employ all the force of all the members when there shall be need'.[6] Civil society is so conceived as to permit the community to take its stand against its *de facto* rulers if they turn tyrants as well as to preserve its identity when it falls under foreign rule. The designation as 'conquest' of the two cases which legitimize the resistance of the community expresses that moral equation by which the most incisive conclusion of liberal contractualism supports the most pervasive element of the nationalist creed.

No community can subsist without a government. But the existence of

---

[1] *Two Treatises*, II, §208.   [2] *Two Treatises*, II, §205.
[3] *Two Treatises*, II, §230.   [4] *Two Treatises*, II, §88.
[5] *Two Treatises*, II, §87.   [6] *Two Treatises*, II, §88.

the community is not irrevocably tied to a particular form of government or rulers. When the people have recourse in revolution to 'a right to resume their original liberty' with the result that 'all former ties are cancelled, all other rights cease...',[1] the oppressive government is dissolved but not society.[2] The nation's right, whenever it can, to resist tyranny and foreign conquest is founded on the right of the individuals to punish a criminal when 'there is no judge on earth' and 'wherever violence is used, and injury done, though by hands appointed to administer justice...'[3] Individual consent remains the foundation of the confluence of the individuals in the collective will. Collective is derived from individual self-determination. There is a right of personal withdrawal by emigration and a collective right of deposing native governors and of rejecting a conqueror. In contradistinction to some modern national ideologies, the attachment to the community is terminable according to Locke. But on the basis of individual commitment he enunciated the irredentist stance of modern nationalism.

Because consent is the only lawful basis of political obligation, lawful conquest is no conquest at all but warding off aggression. The lawful conqueror has a right to temporary occupation to secure military objectives and indemnities for the costs and damages of war.[4] While those who have participated in or abetted aggression forfeit their lives, their land like that of all the rest ought not to be sequestrated by the victor. Hence, besides those who have not participated in the war, 'the posterity even of those that did...are free from any subjection to him [the conqueror], and if their former government be dissolved, they are at liberty to begin and erect another to themselves'.[5] Even if all the male members of the country have joined in an unjust war or have condoned it, this may cause only the temporary loss of the community's independence. Whether as aggressors or defenders, Locke assumed the possibility of the active involvement of the whole community in matters of national prestige and existence. But according to Locke's theory of conquest, what we could call the historical right of the nation can never be voided by others. 'The people who are the descendants of, or claim under those, who were forced to submit to the yoke of a government by constraint, have always a right to shake it off.'[6]

---

[1] *Two Treatises*, II, §§222, 232.
[2] Seliger, *Liberal Politics of John Locke*, chapter IV, 3. C. E. Vaughan, *Studies in the History of Political Philosophy Before and After Rousseau*, 2 vols. (new ed., Manchester, 1939), II, 156, has already considered this distinction to reflect the rationale of nationalism, as has R. H. Cox, *Locke on War and Peace* (Oxford, 1960), pp. 125–6, in respect of the involvement of the whole community in the issues concerning the external prestige and power of the commonwealth.
[3] *Two Treatises*, II, §§21, 20.   [4] Seliger, *Liberal Politics of John Locke*, chapter IV, 2, A.
[5] *Two Treatises*, II, §185.   [6] *Two Treatises*, II, §192.

Locke, liberalism and nationalism

Locke did not only envisage this way of solving the problems posed by modern national consciousness in a multi-ethnical state. He thought that incorporation of the conquered and the conquerors 'into one people, under the same laws and freedom' was the most frequent occurrence.[1] He accepted as normal what later liberals preferred, namely multi-national coexistence on the basis of equality in the same state. But failing this, he insisted certainly no less than his successors, that independence remained the legitimate goal, however long it might take to realize it. 'Who doubts but the Grecian Christians descendants of the ancient possessors of that country may justly cast off the Turkish yoke which they have so long groaned under whenever they have a power to do it? For no government can have a right to obedience from a people who have not freely consented to it.'[2] Not religious diversity by itself carries with it the historical rights of a nation but all that goes into the maintenance of the secular will to resuscitate political independence. The advocacy of irredentism is one facet of nationalism. Yet conquest which gives rise to irredentism is also part of nationalist politics; it is a contradictory part of Lockean politics too.

Although he laid out the principles for doing so, it would be wrong to ascribe to Locke any intention of countenancing a general redrawing of the map of Europe on the basis of the principle of national self-determination. This is explicitly ruled out by his arbitrary restriction of the validity of the interdict of territorial annexation to Europe alone. He justified in this way the illogical but far from rare outgrowth of nationalism: the denial of the right of self-determination to other peoples. In Locke's case the denial appears in its sharpest form, precisely by being confined to colonial peoples.

V

Locke's distinction between lawful and unlawful conquest, or lawful and unlawful war, amounts to the truism that just war is defensive and unjust war is offensive. The distinction is operationally as useless as it is self-defeating. On the one hand, Locke evades the application to external war of the maxim of internal relations, the admission of 'resistance when tyranny is but in design'.[3] He does not trouble himself with the question whether what is technically aggression is not in effect forestalling the intention of the real aggressor. On the other hand, if only the consent of the inhabitants of a territory renders its annexation or separation legiti-

[1] *Two Treatises*, II, §178.   [2] *Two Treatises*, II, §192.
[3] *Two Treatises*, II, 239. Cf. II, §220.

27

mate, inter-state relations must become highly unstable. While according to Locke, abstention from active resistance is evidence of the people's tacit consent, only resistance shows that preceding acquiescence might not have been identical with tacit consent. Locke also never fully reconciled his theory of national self-determination with his view that in Europe 'states and kingdoms' have bound themselves either expressly or tacitly to respect their boundaries. The apparent reason is that this view served him to justify colonial conquest.

In the same breath in which he rejected the lawfulness of annexing territories by conquest, Locke complained 'that where there... [is] more land, than the inhabitants possess, and make use of..., there conquerors take little care to possess themselves of the lands of the vanquished'.[1] Since 'anyone has liberty to make use of the waste', but waste land is not simply unoccupied land, or land which is appropriated but not used, but also land which is improperly used—an additional criterion is needed for determining the right of annexing land belonging to another nation. This is whether or not the nation has consented to the use of common money. Such nations are supposed to have no waste land and to be parties to 'the leagues that have been made between several states and kingdoms, either expressly or tacitly disowning all claim and right to the land in the other's possession'.[2] From these conventions Locke excluded the owners of great tracts of flexibly defined waste lands, 'the inhabitants thereof not having joined with the rest of mankind, in the consent of the use of their *common* money...' Meaning not simply money but common money, which is to say, 'the silver money of Europe',[3] he granted the developed states the right to determine what was more land than the inhabitants of underdeveloped areas could make use of. The unavoidable implication of the whole inane argument[4] is that the natives' resistance to the conquest of their waste land turns them into aggressors and the Europeans, who appropriate the 'waste', into the party which wards aggression off. Since on his terms captives in a just war become slaves, Locke, the administrator of slave-owning colonies, who considered the slave raids of the Royal Africa Company as just wars,[5] and spoke in the *Fundamental Constitutions of Carolina* of the freeman's 'absolute power over his negro slaves',[6] was not disowned by Locke, the mature liberal theorist.

He spoke of slavery in universally applicable terms, i.e. he abstained from any distinction between nations concerning the issue of slavery,

[1] *Two Treatises*, II, §184. [2] *Two Treatises*, II, §45. [3] *Two Treatises*, II, §184.
[4] Seliger, *Liberal Politics of John Locke*, chapter IV, 2, B.
[5] Laslett in *Two Treatises*, pp. 302–3, and L. Stephen, *English Thought in the Eighteenth Century*, 2 vols. (London, 1902), II, 139.
[6] *The Works of John Locke*, 10 vols. (London, 1823), X, 175 f., article CX.

Locke, liberalism and nationalism

although in accordance with the opinions and practices of his time, the justification of slavery made sense only in connexion with colonial conquest. He likewise made no attempt to link the justification of colonial conquest with the question of the universal applicability of natural law. Both abstentions reflect Locke's reluctance frankly to admit that in its entirety natural law is not equally applicable to the whole species of men.

There remains, then, an unresolved tension in Locke's liberal theory between the right of the community to retain or regain its independence and the guarantee of existing boundaries in virtue not only of express but also of tacit conventions to this effect, and between each of the aforementioned principles and the justification of colonial conquest. Such dichotomies have shown themselves to be endemic to nationalist thought of almost all shades. The regard for the independence of one's nation is not necessarily coupled with that for the liberty of other nations. It has only lately been extended to colonial peoples. The ideal of a 'universalist revolutionary nationalism' of a Mickiewicz and a Mazzini[1] is beset at least potentially with a national–supranational antinomy on account of the Messianic leadership of one nation or its apostle. The antinomy is present also where nationalism professes to be self-centred as well as other-regarding. In view of the facts attesting almost universal controversy about national frontiers and mutual accusations of expansionism, and of nation-states shouldering 'the white man's burden'— not necessarily a misleading metaphor—it is well to remember the perplexities attendant upon the determination of the territorial boundaries of the nation-state. When the German romantic Arndt referred to both language and natural boundaries, he suggested criteria which more often contradict than supplement each other. The most ruthless product of modern nationalism, German National-Socialism, exhibited, besides the drive for *Lebensraum* at the cost of 'inferior' nations, a dichotomy between its national and international commitments, between abiding by the universality of its biological law of nature—the perversion of the traditional human law of nature—and limiting its applicability according to the expediency of power politics.[2]

VI

We find, then, firmly embedded in Locke's liberal political philosophy, presuppositions and conclusions that have become part and parcel of the rationale of modern nationalism. The rationale is neither completely developed nor explicitly envisioned as such. But the extent to which its

[1] Talmon, *Political Messianism*, p. 268.
[2] E. Nolte, *Der Faschismus in seiner Epoche* (München, 1963), pp. 50, 501 and 405 f., 496 f.

29

components are visibly present not only foreshadows the later alliances between liberalism and nationalism but indicates that presuppositions and conclusions of nationalism are perforce included in political philosophy and ideology. The reason is that the idea of the nation is as inclusive as the idea of the state, the age-old subject of political philosophy. In both instances a totality of social relationships, a self-subsistent social system, is under discussion. In one case political organization occupies the forefront, yet it is by no means absent in the other.

Consider a recent definition which adequately broadens the concept of the nation to render it applicable to the peoples of the new states in Asia and Africa: 'a nation is any cohesive group possessing "independence" within the confines of the international order as provided by the United Nations, which provides a constituency for a government effectively ruling such a group and receiving from that group the acclamation which legitimizes the government as part of the world order'.[1] Out of the five characteristics Karl Deutsch enlarges upon—independent, cohesive, politically organized, autonomous, internally legitimate[2]—only one, cohesive, is not immediately related to the nature and function of political organization. Friedrich's definition and Deutsch's amplification could, like the older definitions, without difficulty have the 'state' as their subject. For the nationalism of the decolonized states attests the old truth in a new setting that 'the creation of the nation-state strengthens nationalism',[3] if, as we may add, it does not create nationalism to achieve durability. Hence, nationalism may also precede the crystallization of a nation.[4]

Since in political philosophy and theory, as in ideology, the nation is the substance which requires political organization, the differences between conceptions of the state are naturally the same as those between the conceptions of the nation. The kind of 'ism'—étatism, liberalism, conservatism, socialism, etc.—involved in particular systems of political thought defines in most cases also a particular brand of nationalism. This is not to say that the relationship between political ideologies and nationalism is always straightforward. Especially in our times nationalism has shown itself adaptable to all ideologies, even to such as, like communism, were originally opposed to it and made no more than tactical concessions.[5] Yet even where, as in Soviet Russia, official ideology speaks another language than the facts, the étatism of the system as it works goes together with suppressive nationalism. Likewise, although Hegel's rational conception of the state was different from the nationalist preoccupations

---

[1] C. J. Friedrich in *Nation-Building*, ed. K. W. Deutsch and W. J. Foltz (New York, 1963), p. 31.
[2] *Ibid.* pp. 11–12.
[3] Kohn, *The Idea of Nationalism*, p. 19.
[4] Akzin, *State and Nation*, pp. 171–81.
[5] *Ibid.* p. 22.

Locke, liberalism and nationalism

of his time,[1] his étatism invites its association with them in virtue of his anti-democratic and illiberal conception of both *Volk* and *Staat*. By the same token, the liberal institutionalization of the right of self-determination and political participation leaves also the conception of the nation rooted in individualism and contractualism. The conviction of their universal applicability is revealed in the American realization of the tenets of Lockean civil society. As has been said about America, 'it is the paradoxical nature of its nationalism, its universalism, which has created the nation', a 'state-nation or citizen nation'.[2]

The romantic sentiment of diversity may well attach itself to liberal principles, as for instance in Augustin Thierry, without the principle of self-determination becoming shrouded in mystification; Thierry rather carried the principle to the extreme. Conceiving history in terms of the hereditary animosity created by conquest between national groups, and disclaiming the lawfulness of conquest as radically as Locke, Thierry declared that 'the most disastrous epoch in the history of the inhabitants of southern France was when they became French'.[3] The universal application of self-determination does, however, not demand re-fragmentation. Diversity and universality can coexist. While the independence of small national units had to give way to the progress of European civilization, the preservation of their cultural identity was henceforth safeguarded by the universal ideal of liberty upheld by the American and French Revolutions.[4]

John Stuart Mill succinctly expressed these terms of the alliance between liberalism and nationality. 'Where the sentiment of nationality exists in any force, there is a *prima facie* case for uniting all the members of the nationality under the same government, and a government to themselves apart. This is merely saying that the question of government ought to be decided by the governed.'[5] Hobhouse made the inseparability of the principles that underlie the conception of state and nation still more explicit by asking: 'What is a nation as distinct from a state?'[6]

[1] S. Avineri, 'Hegel and Nationalism', *The Review of Politics*, xxiv, no. 4 (October 1962), 461–84.
[2] Y. Arieli, 'Individualism and National Consciousness in the United States', *Scripta Hierosolymitana*, vii (1961), 297. See also by the same author, *Individualism and Nationalism in American Ideology* (Cambridge, Mass., 1964).
[3] A. Thierry, *Histoire de la Conquête de l'Angleterre par les Normands*, 3 vols. (Paris, 1825), iii, 325. See my 'Race-Thinking during the Restoration', *Journal of the History of Ideas*, xix, 2 (April 1958), 273–82 and also 'The Idea of Conquest and Race-Thinking during the Restoration', *The Review of Politics*, xxii, 4 (October 1960), 544–67.
[4] Thierry, *Histoire de la Conquête*, iii, 382 f.
[5] J. S. Mill, *Utilitarianism, Liberty and Representative Government* (Everyman's Library, London, 1910), p. 486.
[6] L. T. Hobhouse, *Liberalism*, Reprinted with an Introduction by A. P. Grimes (a Galaxy Book, New York, 1964), p. 26.

M. Seliger

By way of an answer he reaffirmed the liberal position from Locke to Mill: Either the coexistence of two—or more—nations on the basis of 'ordinary laws applicable to both parties...and fulfilling all the ordinary principles of liberty...'—or independence. For otherwise, 'the most liberally minded democracy is maintaining a system which must undermine its own principles'. Hobhouse could quote Spencer in support of this conclusion. Lord Acton did thus not represent the predominant liberal attitude, but fastened upon one of the alternatives it affirmed. He actually took issue with Mill in appraising the ability to accommodate, like the British and Austrian Empires, different races and nationalities as the test of a civilized state.[1] One might agree with Lord Acton that liberty as the rational end and fulfilment of man owed little, if anything, to nationality.[2] Yet we must add that the opposite is still more true.

Obviously, the indebtedness of nationality to the idea of freedom does not detach it from the political thought centring around the state; it does not obviate the distinction between liberal and illiberal standpoints either but ties both—to vastly varying degrees though—to the notion of consent. There is, indeed, an empirical aspect to Locke's normative stipulation that civil society rests on consent. Consent is the instrumentality of political freedom and the presupposition for ascribing a will and hence self-consciousness to a group. The rulers hardly ever claim to represent only themselves. Whatever else they purport to represent, somehow the will of the people—or of its 'spirit'—enters the picture as at least one of the constituent elements of the polity. No system of political thought that affirms group cohesion and any kind of communication except that between oppressors and oppressed can do without some concession to the principle of consent. Not the absence or presence, but the form of consent distinguishes between liberal and illiberal conceptions of state and nation. Even Plato did not base cohesion merely on assuring belief in the myth of the children of the earth—a metaphor anticipating the more crude semantics of nationalism. The myth must ensue in the consent to the political order of the best state on the part of those, too, who were denied any share in its management or influence upon it.[3] From the genuine concessions to democratic consent by Aristotle the way led again back to the political application of *consensus exterquetur* of scholasticism and forth again to Marsilio, and so on in a perpetual to and fro until the formal expression of the will of the people became part of nearly all regimes and all conceptions of state and nation. In this way differences between regimes

[1] See Acton, 'Nationality', in *Essays on Freedom and Power*, p. 158 and G. Himmelfarb, *Lord Acton: A Study in Conscience and Politics* (London, 1952), pp. 85–6.
[2] Himmelfarb, *Lord Acton*, p. 183.
[3] *Republic*, IV, 431; cf. also *Statesman*, 276 E.

and conceptions are reduced. But those that remain in respect of the indebtedness to the idea of freedom and the forms of its institutionalization are still the most important ones.

It is, then, not surprising to find in Locke's liberal theory of civil society the more prominent features of the rationale of nationality and nationalism. What ought to astonish us is that the relationship between liberalism and nationalism should ever have been considered as anything but natural.

Locke and English liberalism:
the *Second Treatise of Government* in its
contemporary setting[1]

by ESMOND S. DE BEER

I wish to discuss Locke's *Second Treatise of Government* in its immediate historical context: not as political philosophy in the abstract, but as an event in the establishment of the English limited monarchy. I shall be concerned with Locke's purpose in writing it, and consequently with the dates and circumstances of its inception, composition, and publication; and with its contents in relation to the general views of the English constitution prevailing in its time. Further, as it seems to me, the *Second Treatise* exhibits, as much as any other of his works, one of Locke's most deep-seated intellectual habits; I shall therefore leave my central argument for a digression on this characteristic.

The first of Locke's *Two Treatises of Government* is a refutation of Sir Robert Filmer's *Patriarcha*; the *Second Treatise* is closely connected with Filmer's other writings. Before his death in 1653 Filmer published some of his smaller pieces, and there was some circulation of *Patriarcha* in manuscript, but the important dates are those of the publication of the collected smaller pieces (called, from the first piece, *The Free-holders Grand Inquest*), 1679, with a new edition in 1680, and of *Patriarcha*, 1680. There was another edition of *Patriarcha* in 1680, and another, called the second, in 1685; and a new edition of the smaller pieces in 1684.[2]

The documented dates for *Two Treatises* are few. It was licensed on 23 August 1689 for publication. At that time Locke had lost the latter part of the *First Treatise*, the refutation of *Patriarcha* (he never tried to replace it). The first edition is dated 1690, but was published about the beginning of December 1689; antedating of the kind was habitual in

[1] This paper was read at the Third Anglo-Netherlands Conference of Historians, London, 19–24 September 1966. I have included some passages that were omitted in reading it, but have not tried to recast it.

[2] There appears to have been another collection of the smaller pieces in 1680. There were further editions of one or other of the collections in 1695 and 1696. The 'concise bibliography' in *Patriarcha and Other Political Works of Sir Robert Filmer*, ed. Peter Laslett (Oxford, 1949), pp. 47–8, is rough and hard to follow.

Locke and English liberalism

England in the later seventeenth century. The second edition appeared in 1694, and the third in 1698; the fourth not until some years after Locke's death. Jean Le Clerc published a summary in his *Bibliotheque universelle* for December 1690. A French translation of the *Second Treatise* was published at Amsterdam in 1691.

The book was published anonymously, and Locke did not acknowledge his authorship until he made his will in 1704. He not only evaded his friends' inquiries; the extant correspondence relating to the second edition suggests that he was at pains to conceal his authorship from the publisher, Awnsham Churchill. A friend of Locke's, Edward Clarke, was the intermediary; Locke could not prevent Churchill from guessing; but for this edition he was not to see a scrap of writing in Locke's hand, and probably also nothing in the hand of Locke's amanuensis Sylvester Brounower.

There is nothing relating to the dates of inception and composition in Locke's extant correspondence and journals, and only one statement that can be considered relevant: Locke paid for copies of *The Free-holders Grand Inquest* and *Patriarcha* on 22 January 1680. Copies of both books are preserved in the part of Locke's library now belonging to Dr Paul Mellon, and it is likely that they are those that he acquired in 1680; the former is the edition of 1680, not that of 1679. The composition of Locke's *First Treatise* has long since been associated with the publication of *Patriarcha* and, allowing for one interpolation or alteration,[1] is reasonably attributed to the period between 1680 and Locke's departure from England in 1683. Until recently it was generally believed that the *Second Treatise* was written about the time of the revolution in 1688; either in the succeeding months, to justify what had taken place, or in the months preceding William's expedition. In the last few years Peter Laslett has proposed a new date. Arguing from various passages in both *Treatises* he suggests that the *Second* was commenced at some time in 1679, in response to the first publication of Filmer's collected minor writings, and thus preceded the inception of the *First Treatise*. He further suggests that Locke left his manuscript behind when he left England in 1683; recovering it on his return in 1689, he interpolated or added a number of passages, and so made it relevant to the revolution.[2]

None of Mr Laslett's arguments seem to me to necessitate the earlier date, and some of them are weak. On the other hand the later date is also only a surmise. Of the two the earlier, Mr Laslett's, seems to me preferable. The *Second Treatise* in part refutes Filmer's views, which were more dan-

[1] Judge Jeffreys, §129; *John Locke: Two Treatises of Government*, ed. P. Laslett (Cambridge, 1960), pp. 46 and n., 48; he may have been substituted for a Cromwellian judge.
[2] Mr Laslett's views are set out in the introduction to his splendid edition of *Two Treatises*.

gerous in 1680 than in 1688; it fits with the political issues of 1680, and does not touch some topics that might have seemed important in 1689; and it shows no traces of Locke's sojourn in the United Provinces from 1683 to 1689. I propose then in what follows to treat it as a composition of about 1680, revised and expanded in 1689. I do not however accept Mr Laslett's further view that Locke wrote it as propaganda for a projected rising by the first Earl of Shaftesbury. It is a speculative treatise written in answer to a speculative treatise; its immediate purpose was to vindicate the traditional English constitution against an absolutist attack.

To digress now to Locke's habits of mind. He was the most unspeculative of philosophers. Not for him to 'let loose' his 'thoughts into the vast ocean of *Being*';[1] for him the safe shores of observation and experience. This characteristic is frequently visible in his principal writings, and I believe that it is basic in the *Second Treatise*. Much of *Some Thoughts concerning Education* was gleaned from young Franz van Limborch and Pierot Guenellon, and the other children in the homes where Locke was welcomed. It perhaps contributed greatly to the development of his views on religious liberty. In 1660 and about a year later he had written against toleration; in 1667 he advocated it. We have no documents for the process of change, but it seems to me that it may have been due principally to Locke's visit to Cleves in 1665–6. He went as secretary to an abortive diplomatic mission to the Elector of Brandenburg, who was then at Cleves, and spent about two months there. He found there almost complete religious liberty: freedom of worship for Catholics, Calvinists, and Lutherans, and connivance for Mennonites and Jews. Locke visited the various churches, and was kindly received by the Franciscans; while he wrote satirical letters to one friend, he expressed his appreciation in a letter to another:

This distance in their churches gets not into their houses. They quietly permit one another to choose their way to heaven; for I cannot observe any quarrels or animosities amongst them upon the account of religion. This good correspondence is owing partly to the power of the magistrate, and partly to the prudence and good nature of the people, who (as I find by enquiry) entertain different opinions without any secret hatred or rancour.[2]

After that experience toleration was practical politics.

In the *Second Treatise* the state of nature was probably affected by Locke's reading of books of travel. It was a traditional starting point for political philosophers, but the American Indians provided him with illustrations,

---

[1] *An Essay concerning Human Understanding*, ed. J. W. Yolton (London–New York, 1961), I, i, §7.

[2] Locke to Robert Boyle, Cleves, 12/22 December 1665, in *The Works of Robert Boyle*, ed. Birch, 5 vols. (London, 1744), I, 565–7.

and the positive element in his conception of the state of nature, the individual's possession of rights, may derive in part from some traveller's account of a primitive society. Locke read such books avidly, and probably with too little questioning of their authors' powers and opportunities of observation.[1]

The Restoration in 1660 was in appearance a return to the traditional constitution. The enemies of the constitution, whether Republicans or Absolute Monarchists, could find few adherents; there was no occasion for an appeal to basic principles, and no book of any importance was published. The general view was probably rough and ready, something like that stated by Clarendon in his refutation of *Leviathan* (this was written between 1667 and April 1670, when Clarendon was in exile, and was published posthumously in 1676).[2] According to Clarendon, God made Adam 'the sole Monarch of the World',[3] and this passed to his right heirs, who had absolute power over their children and kin. This continued until the time of Noah. Then, as the number of men increased, kings perceived that paternal power had become a source of weakness: men who ceased to feel the bonds of kinship would not exert themselves for their private ends unless they had security of tenure, and would have neither the will nor the means to contribute to the king's power. The kings therefore make grants and concessions to their subjects,[4] and those grants are irrevocable:[5] if the kings infringe them the subjects will resist in practice. Where mutual obligations are best observed 'Soveraignty flourishes with the most lustre, and security'.[6]

The people do not possess a co-ordinate power with the sovereign;[7] laws are made by the king with the 'counsel and advice' of his subjects (here Clarendon is thinking of parliament); but the kings are bound by law and cannot alter laws except in the same course as that of their enactment.[8]

---

[1] The third Earl of Shaftesbury notes Locke's credulity in this respect in 1709, *The Life, Unpublished Letters and Philosophical Regimen of Anthony Earl of Shaftesbury*, ed. B. Rand (London, 1900), pp. 403–4.

[2] *A Brief View and Survey of the Dangerous and Pernicious Errors to Church and State, in Mr. Hobbes's Book, Entitled* Leviathan (Oxford, 1676; I have used the second 'impression', also Oxford, 1676). Clarendon gives the period of composition: pp. 4, 5. He does not set out his views explicitly or systematically; they emerge only as required to controvert Hobbes's statements, and are apt to be expressed as negations. Locke possessed a copy of the book.

[3] *Ibid.* p. 67.   [4] *Ibid.* pp. 69, 71.

[5] Clarendon does not use the word in this connexion, and might have fought shy of it; but he reprobates Hobbes's view that 'he who is Soveraign tomorrow, may cancel, and dissolve all that was don by the Soveraign who was yesterday, or by himself as often as he changes his mind': *ibid.* p. 124; similar objections on pp. 75, 122, 125.

[6] *Ibid.* p. 89.   [7] *Ibid.* p. 96.   [8] *Ibid.* pp. 121–2.

Esmond S. de Beer

Clarendon regards propriety, security of tenure and inheritance in private property, as indispensable for human welfare,[1] and writes freely about 'Covenants and Promises',[2] and the 'paction' between kings and their subjects.[3] He does not develop his thought adequately; he was a statesman, a lawyer, an historian, and not a philosopher; he perceives no clash between Divine Right and Constitutionalism, or at least produces a superficial concord:

> Kings themselves can never be punished or reprehended publicly (that being a reproch not consistent with the reverence due to Majesty) for their casual or wilful errors and mistakes, let the ill consequence of them be what they will; but if they who maliciously lead, or advise, or obey them in unjust resolutions and commands, were to have the same indemnity, there must be a dissolution of all Kingdoms and Governments. But as Kings must be left to God, whose Vice-gerents they are, to judg of their breach of Trust; so they who offend against the Law, must be left to the punishment the Law hath provided for them...[4]

and kings have only a limited power of pardon. Clarendon does not say who is to accuse or what tribunal shall decide, but evidently thinks in terms of the English parliament and the English legal system.

The existing constitution is described in a political year-book of the time, Edward Chamberlayne's *Angliæ Notitia*. The author was a doctor of laws and in good standing with the king; the little-altered repetition of his statements about the constitution from his first edition in 1669 until the sixteenth in 1687, shows that they were acceptable to Charles II. The passage is mainly a high-flying assertion of the splendours and rights of the English kingship, but includes a few sentences that indicate the limitation of its powers.[5] Thus:

> England is such a Monarchy, as that, by the necessary subordinate concurrence of the Lords and Commons in the making and repealing all Statutes and Acts of Parliament, it hath the main advantages of an *Aristocracy*, and of a *Democracy*, and yet free from the disadvantages and evils of either.[6]

> It is such a Monarchy, as by most admirable temperament affords very much to the *Industry*, *Liberty*, and *Happiness* of the Subject, and reserves enough for the Majesty and Prerogative of any King that will own his people as Subjects, not as Slaves.[7]

---

[1] *A Brief View*, p. 111.   [2] *Ibid.* p. 98.

[3] *Ibid.* pp. 111–12. Clarendon may have derived the word from James I: see the passage in James's speech in 1609 quoted by Locke (*Two Treatises*, II, §200). He may have based the expression 'tacitly covenant' (p. 122) on the same passage.

[4] *Ibid.* pp. 135–6.

[5] My citations are from the ninth edition of part 1, 1676.

[6] *Angliæ Notitia*, p. 63.   [7] *Ibid.* p. 63.

Locke and English liberalism

The king holds 'some' of his Prerogatives 'by the Law of Nations, others by Common Law, (excellent above all Laws, in upholding a free Monarchy, and exalting the Kings Prerogative) and some by Statute-Law'.[1] When at the Restoration the hereditary revenue was found to be insufficient for the king's expenditure, duties and taxes were imposed 'with the Kings consent, at the humble request of the Lords and Commons'.[2] There are certain limits to the king's power. For Chamberlayne notably he cannot diminish the royal prerogative. Like all Christian kings, 'by an Oath at his Coronation, and indeed without any Oath, by the Law of *Nature*, *Nations*, and of *Christianity*, he holds himself bound' to allow his people 'their just Rights and Liberties', and so on.[3] 'Two things especially, the King of England doth not usually do without the consent of his Subjects, viz, make *New Laws*, and raise *New Taxes*.'[4] The ground for this is prudential and not moral, much less contractual. Chamberlayne is far nearer than Clarendon to absolutism, but does not I think say anywhere that the king can enact or repeal laws or levy taxes without the consent of parliament.

A view of the constitution as held by opponents of the court is provided by Henry Care in *English Liberties: or, The Free-Born Subject's Inheritance*, 1682. This is principally an assertion of the liberties of the subject, reciting various grants and statutes from Magna Carta onwards. There is little about the royal prerogative, but the king has much the same powers and limitations as in Clarendon and Chamberlayne; Care implies a different moral balance, not a different constitutional relationship. Where he diverges from them is in his views on the succession to the crown.

By 1679 the inadequacy of the constitution was evident. Charles II was pursuing a policy detested by a stable majority in the House of Commons; all that it could do was to frustrate him. He was believed to favour the advancement of Roman Catholicism. An opportunity of breaking the deadlock appeared to have come with the Popish Plot, the fraudulent revelation of an imaginary Catholic conspiracy to assassinate Charles, who would be succeeded by his brother, James, Duke of York, who was a Catholic. There may have been a few sceptics for the Plot, but there were some circumstances that apparently confirmed it, and for a few months nothing occurred to shake the evidence of the principal witness for it; belief in it was widespread and sincere. To meet the danger Charles offered to impose by act of parliament certain limitations on the powers of any Catholic successor to the throne; his opponents considered that these limitations

[1] *Ibid.* p. 79.　　　　　[2] *Ibid.* p. 71.
[3] *Ibid.* p. 94.　　　　　[4] *Ibid.*

would prove ineffectual and introduced the first Exclusion Bill in May 1679. It provided that James should be excluded from the succession to the crown; it did not name any successor; it was assumed that on the death of Charles the crown would pass to the next person in the succession. Although there was a large majority for the bill in the commons, it was unlikely to be passed by the lords; in the country at large Exclusion would not do. Constitutionally and legally it might be in the power of the king in parliament to interrupt the hereditary succession to the crown, but such an act was forbidden by all the sentiments that could be invoked as divine and natural law.

Charles dissolved parliament and summoned a new one, and at the same time did what he could to improve his position and to postpone the next clash. It was in these circumstances that someone thought of Filmer; as I have noted, collections of his miscellaneous pieces and *Patriarcha* were published in 1679 and 1680.

In *Patriarcha* Filmer demonstrates that kings derive their powers from the sovereignty over all his progeny granted by God to Adam. Elsewhere he asserts the absolute power of kings. It is the combination of absolutism and hereditary right that made Filmer's works important. Absolutism is as strong in him as in *Leviathan*. But he associates it with hereditary right. In 1680 *Leviathan* was completely discredited; the right of sovereignty belongs to whoever can seize power; the book was an atheistic vindication of Cromwell. Hereditary right was almost universally accepted; it was in the nature of things. The question raised by the publication of Filmer's writings in 1679 and 1680 was the nature of the heritage.

The only answer to be published at the time is *Patriarcha non Monarcha*, the work of a friend of Locke's, James Tyrrell. The book was published in 1681. Tyrrell demonstrates that Filmer misused his authorities, reading into them more than they contained, and selecting from them only such passages as supported his views; when he comes to Filmer's attack on Philip Hunton's *Treatise of Monarchy* he finds in English constitutional history the rights of king and parliament. Filmer had already used history, both sacred and profane, as illustrations, if not as arguments, to support his assertion of hereditary absolutism and its divine origin; Tyrrell is moving the discussion from the moral to the legal plane.

For Locke this was insufficient as an answer to Filmer. In 1697 he wrote, in a letter to Lady Peterborough, 'True Politicks I looke on as a Part of Moral Philosophie', and in a later piece, which he dictated in 1703 or 1704 to Samuel Bold, he divides politics into two 'very different' parts, 'The one, containing the Original of Societies, and the rise and extent of political power: the other, the Art of Governing Men in Society.'

Locke and English liberalism

The latter part is 'best to be learn'd by Experience and History, especially that of a man's own country'. For the study of the former part he recommends Hooker's *Ecclesiastical Polity*, Algernon Sidney's *Discourses concerning Government*, his own *Two Treatises*, Peter Paxton's *Civil Polity*, and the works of Pufendorff.[1] Though Locke regarded Filmer's views as false, Filmer's books belong to the same class as Hooker's and the rest; they can be controverted only by writings in the same class. Even supposing that Tyrrell's history is sound (and the similar historical findings of his friend William Pettyt were shortly to be attacked as a falsification of history),[2] institutions and legal rights that have arisen in the course of time are no match for divine right; they are a matter of convenience, and have no claim to exist except that of utility. Locke believed in the need for government at least as much as Filmer did; he had to find a foundation for it and for its claim to the obedience of its subjects at least as good as Filmer's.

Locke finds it in man's moral nature. Man is endowed with rights by the law of nature, but so long as he is in the state of nature his enjoyment of them is precarious; for his well-being therefore God has put him 'under strong Obligations of Necessity, Convenience, and Inclination to drive him into *Society*, as well as fitted him with Understanding and Language to continue and enjoy it'.[3] He unites with his fellows by means of a contract, relinquishing some of his rights to secure the certain enjoyment of the rest; and to this end the society or, in Locke's language, the commonwealth, creates suitable institutions. The principal are the legislative and the executive powers (a third, the federative, is closely associated with the executive); and they are nearly a generalized version of the English parliament and king; how closely Locke has the English constitution in mind emerges in passages such as that on the electorate in which he denounces the decayed parliamentary boroughs, where 'there remains...scarce so much housing as a Sheep-coat'.[4] Locke states his position frequently and explicitly: the legislative exists for '*the preservation of the Society*, and (as far as will consist with the publick good) of every person in it';[5] the executive is entrusted with certain powers of government by the legislative, and is responsible to the legislative for its use of them; the powers which the legislative retains 'ought to be designed *for* no other end ultimately but *the good of the People*'.[6]

Although Locke differs from Clarendon in his premises and in his

[1] *A Collection of Several Pieces of Mr John Locke* [published by Mr Desmaizeaux under the direction of Mr Anthony Collins], (London, 1720), pp. 236–7.
[2] J. G. A. Pocock, *The Ancient Constitution and the Feudal Law* (Cambridge, 1957), pp. 193 ff.
[3] *Two Treatises*, II, §77.
[4] *Two Treatises*, II, §157. [5] *Ibid.* II, §134. [6] *Ibid.* II, §142.

forms of expression, in his view of the constitution he comes close to him. Clarendon looks backward. The constitution is a precious heritage; its existence is justified by the fact that it is the law of the land. Tyrrell takes a similar view. In the conduct of politics, and especially on the immediate issue, the proposed exclusion of the next of kin from the succession to the crown, Clarendon and Locke would have been opposed to one another: Clarendon would have held that the principle of hereditary right, based on municipal, natural, and divine law, could not be set aside by any human enactment; Locke would have maintained that James was disqualified for the office of king; he ought not to be entrusted with the executive power because, in Locke's view, as a Catholic he could not, and in practice would not, be bound by the oaths that would be required of him. On the general question, the relations of king and parliament, Clarendon and Locke converge. In the circumstances of their time, when on the one hand the king held his office of supreme governor by inheritance, and chose his ministers as he pleased, on the other the intervals between parliaments and sessions of parliament were long and irregular, and depended on the king's pleasure, it was natural to regard the king and his ministers as an independent body, potentially hostile to parliament, and so to the community; both Clarendon and Locke therefore, though in different degrees, assert the responsibility of the executive to the legislative; Clarendon does what he can to spare the king. On the intellectual issue their positions would have been almost identical. Clarendon would have repudiated the more important parts of *Patriarcha* just as he repudiated *Leviathan*. The limits of his thought appear in his ignoring the question, whether a divinely appointed absolute monarch can divest his successors of any of the hereditary powers which God has conferred on them in succession. Filmer would have shown him that the divine institution of monarchy made it impossible; Louis XIV's treatment of his Protestant subjects exemplified for Locke the refusal of absolute monarchs to be bound by their predecessors. Locke's religion compelled him to state that 'the Supreme Civil Power...is in every Commonwealth derived from God', but he saves himself when he continues that it 'is absolute and unlimited by any thing but the End for which God gave it, *viz.* the Good of the People sincerely pursued, according to the best of the Skill of those who share that Power'.[1] Locke will not allow the claim to obedience of properly conducted lawful power to be tainted by even the slightest association with divine hereditary right.

The question arises, how far Locke was sincere in his course of argu-

[1] *A Paraphrase and Notes on the Epistles of St. Paul*, introduction to Romans xiii. 1–7. This was written towards the end of Locke's life.

ment. He had been a member of Shaftesbury's household, and had served him as secretary and as physician; it might be suggested that in the *Second Treatise* he was constructing arguments in Shaftesbury's favour, creating premisses to give a seeming moral foundation to a desired constitution, a wizard invoking the state of nature and other phantasms to his own questionable ends. I think that that will not do. In 1663 and earlier Locke had been concerned with the law of nature, and it underlies the whole of the *Second Treatise*. I have not studied the law of nature, but for Locke it appears to be a blend of moral and religious principles, and of the municipal laws of civilized states, and especially those of England. It fulfilled his moral and religious requirements; on one occasion he writes of 'the Law of God and Nature';[1] he perhaps never examined its composition, or the psychological necessity for a theory of the kind. Accepting it, he could accept the traditional English constitution as a particular embodiment of it.

If the date and purpose that I have proposed for the *Second Treatise* are accepted, some of its apparent deficiencies are accounted for. Locke does not have to concern himself much with the common assumptions or accepted principles of his time; he is concerned rather with the general rights of existence of institutions, than with the details of their characters; and his views are limited by the circumstances of his own time. In 1680 the continued existence of the English parliament was in jeopardy; for Locke the traditional constitution was infinitely preferable to any form of absolutism; he had learnt that from his travels in France. He mentioned the desirability of the reform of the electoral districts; it was in the public interest that towns such as Leeds and Sheffield should replace Old Sarum and Bramber. He did not discuss the reform of the franchise: in the social and economic circumstances of his century it was almost impracticable, and for his particular purpose it was irrelevant. He mentions 'the people' frequently without defining the term. It is regrettable that he was not compelled to discuss the matter. There can be little doubt that, at any time when parliamentary reform was in agitation, he would have supported its extension up to the reasonable limit.

When Locke left England in 1683 he probably left the manuscript of *Two Treatises* behind; when he returned in 1689 he revised it for publication, at the same time adding to, and adapting, it to justify the revolution. The conception of the legislative as a trustee must always have implied the right of the people to impose sanctions in case of breach of trust. In Charles II's time Locke could not have published the right of rebellion with impunity; now he had to justify a rebellion. This has probably

---

[1] *Two Treatises*, II, §142.

thrown the *Second Treatise* out of balance; it is easy to see it as a plea for absolute liberty, rather than as a foundation for the institutions that, by restricting liberty, make it practical and desirable.

In this essay I have touched on only one element in the *Second Treatise*. Its diffusion and the frequency of new editions are proof of its abiding interest. Its failings and limitations raise the question of the competence of political philosophy: forms of political organization can be analysed, and their problems discussed, but humanity is too diverse, and the individual's experiences too limited, for it to be possible for anyone to educe principles that will be valid universally, or at any rate principles that are much more than aspirations. Political philosophy, as we know it, like politics in practice, ranges between thought and sentiment. It is here that Locke comes into his own. To meet a particular challenge he enunciated the principle that governments exist for the welfare of the individuals who have established them, and that the individuals must give, with complete freedom to give or to withhold, their approval of the governments' actions; he stated what has become a fundamental of the English polity and one of the commonplaces of the Western world.

The politics of Locke in England and America in the eighteenth century[1]

by JOHN DUNN

The Boston Gazette, 1 March 1773 (advertisement of first American edition of *Second Treatise*):

This Essay alone, well studied and attended to, will give to every intelligent Reader a better View of the Rights of Men and of Englishmen, and a clearer Insight into the Principles of the British Constitution, than all the Discourses on Government—The Essays in Politicks and Books of Law in our Language.— It should be early and carefully explained by every Father to his Son, by every Preceptor in our public and private Schools to his Pupils, and by every Mother to her Daughter.

Rev. William Jones, in *A Letter to the Church of England*, 1798 (cited in W. Stevens, *Life of The Author, The Theological, Philosophical and Miscellaneous Works of the Rev. William Jones...*, London, 1801, I, l):

while the age abounds with affected declamations against human authority, there never was a time when men so meanly submitted their understandings to be led away by one another. It is an honour to submit our faculties to God who gave them, but it is base and servile to submit to the usurpations of man in things pertaining to God. And he asks, whether the doctrines of Mr. Locke, whom the world is gone after, will prepare any young man for preaching the gospel of Jesus Christ, when he was the oracle to those who began and conducted the American Rebellion, which led to the French Revolution; which will lead (unless God in his mercy interfere) to the total overthrow of Religion and Government in this kingdom, perhaps in the whole Christian World; the prime favourite and grand instrument with that mischievous infidel Voltaire, who knew what he was about when he came forward to destroy Christianity as he had threatened, with Mr. Locke in his hand.

[1] I should like to acknowledge the generosity of the Commonwealth Fund in supporting the research reported in this article and the kindness of many American scholars in assisting me, most especially Professor Bernard Bailyn who read it for me before it was first given as a talk to the Colonial Society of Massachusetts in December 1964 and who supervised my researches while I was in America, Professor Daniel Boorstin who gave me much help and encouragement when I was beginning the work, and Professor Lyman Butterfield. I should also like to thank Mr Quentin Skinner for giving the article a close and sympathetic reading and suggesting many very necessary improvements.

John Dunn

Leigh Hunt, *The Examiner*, 10 June 1810 (*Leigh Hunt's Political and Occasional Essays*, ed. L. H. and C. W. Houtchens, New York, 1962, p. 108):

it was Locke, and such men as himself, who, in teaching us to give up our mental liberty to no man, taught us to give up our personal liberty to no man; but to prefer even the consciousness of independence to a slavery however worshipful—To such a man as Locke, therefore, every Englishman owes love and reverence, and not even Nelson himself, though he died on the waves bequeathing triumph to his countrymen, deserves a more glorious acknowledgement of their gratitude, than he who, dying in solitude and in silence, with no glories about him but the anticipation of heaven and the meek sublimity of departing virtue, bequeathed to his countrymen the love of what is rational.

It is one of the enduring clichés of American historiography that much of the political theory of the founding fathers of the United States can be identified in a work by an English philosopher of the seventeenth century, 'the Great Mr. Locke'.[1] This particular cliché, like so many others in American historiography, has been subjected to some damaging criticism in recent years. It is widely regarded today as deriving from a somewhat naïve view of the history of ideas[2] and a more than somewhat pernicious view of the nature of the American Revolution.[3] It is not here intended to pass judgment on the conceptual or empirical issue of how far it makes sense to say that Locke's *Two Treatises of Government* were a cause of the American revolution. This diffidence is a product of rational decision as well as simple ignorance. It is not at all clear what the dispute between Professor Boorstin and his critics is about, or precisely what it means to question whether men's political and social ideas derive from their reading or their social experience. In literate communities they necessarily derive in different senses from both, and the language which we have for discussing such an issue at the moment and the psychological theories we

---

[1] See classically Carl L. Becker, *The Declaration of Independence: A Study in the History of Political Ideas* (paperback, New York, 1959), p. 27: 'Most Americans had absorbed Locke's works as a kind of political gospel;...', etc. See also Merle Curti, 'The Great Mr. Locke, America's Philosopher, 1783–1861', *Huntington Library Bulletin* (1937), pp. 107–51, esp. pp. 107–8; Clinton Rossiter, *Seedtime of the Republic* (New York, 1953), p. 141 (see esp. n. 111, p. 491); *Pamphlets of the American Revolution 1750–1776*, ed. Bernard Bailyn (Cambridge, Mass., 1965), I, 25–7.

[2] See Rossiter, *Seedtime of the Republic*, pp. 139–47; Bernard Bailyn, *The Ideological Origins of the American Revolution* (Cambridge, Mass., 1967), esp. pp. 22–54 for a particularly well-articulated documentation. And see in general for the growing assurance of this reading the works noted below (p. 79, n. 1). The problem of relating intellectual history to political and social development is faced boldly by Gordon S. Wood, 'Rhetoric and Reality in the American Revolution', *William and Mary Quarterly*, 3rd series, XXIII, 4 (October 1966), 3–32.

[3] See esp. Daniel J. Boorstin, *The Genius of American Politics* (paperback ed. Chicago, 1959), pp. 66–98 and, for his blisteringly effective assault on the methodology of the influence model applied to eighteenth-century America, see Daniel J. Boorstin, *America and the Image of Europe* (New York, 1960), pp. 65–78, 'The Myth of an American Enlightenment'.

have for analysing it are insufficiently sensitive to make the crude anti-thesis at all enlightening. This essay then is not concerned with any topic as central and unmanageable as the causation of the American Revolution. What is attempted is an outline history of the ways in which a single book was sensed to be relevant in England and America in the eighteenth century, a brief sketch of the sort of work that Locke's book is, an account of the types of intellectual response which it evoked in England and America in the eighteenth century, and some degree of explanation of why these responses should have been as they were, of what made it seem trivial or significant, relevant or boring, attractive or insufferable.

To understand the book itself, as much as the ambiguities which its readers managed to elicit from it, it is necessary to recall a little about the political situation to which it was addressed and the persistent intellectual preoccupations of Locke's life from which it emerged. At the time at which the bulk of the *Two Treatises* was written, John Locke was living largely in London as the confidant, friend, political aide and personal physician to one of the most prominent political figures of the day, Anthony Ashley Cooper, Earl of Shaftesbury. During this period Shaftes-bury was directing a campaign to exclude from the throne the prospective heir, the brother of Charles II, the Catholic James, Duke of York. Shaftesbury's power was based upon an impressive political organization, centred on London and backed by the dissenters, a large proportion of the mercantile interests, a formidable group of country gentry, and the London mob.[1] It was a grouping which carried offensive and immediate historical overtones to much of the community and to no one more than the king himself. Few enduring emotional loyalties can be discerned among the fitful and disenchanted manœuvres of Charles's life, but his family retained for him a certain appeal which men like Clarendon who had given their entire lives to his service seldom exerted. For two full years the patronage resources of the crown, the acquiescent judiciary, the full range of prerogative powers and the private financial assistance of the French monarch were manipulated to crush Shaftesbury and to preserve the succession for James. In Parliament and in the corporations of London and the great cities, in the courts of law, in the counties and in the London streets, the struggle was fought out. It was not just a struggle to exert political power which the protagonists already had at their disposal. It did not end with the manipulation of existing resources of patronage and coercion, but branched out into efforts to create and mobilize new types

---

[1] A convenient summary of the politics of the Exclusion controversy with adequate references to past literature is J. R. Jones, *The First Whigs: The Politics of the Exclusion Crisis 1678–1683* (London, 1961); and the events are effectively placed in the development of English politics in J. H. Plumb, *The Growth of Political Stability in England 1675–1725* (London, 1966).

John Dunn

of political power. It was a struggle to win control of men's minds, an exercise in persuasion, and in consequence it was a struggle waged by necessity in books and pamphlets as much as it was within the normal institutions of English political life.[1] In short it was—and to a degree that threatened the stability of the entire political system—an ideological struggle.

Shaftesbury's tactical aim in the struggle was to extend his political control from the cities into the rural areas, among the gentry. Here he met a difficult ideological target. The major emotive focus of his propaganda, the popish scare, exercised as compulsive a fascination over the Anglican gentry as it did over their dissenting neighbours. But in their case, unlike that of the dissenters, there was no convenient intellectual link between this atavistic and xenophobic theological disquiet and their publicly affirmed theory of politics. Anti-popery, both as an ideology and as a latent form of mass hysteria, had a power over the seventeenth- and eighteenth-century English imagination comparable in its destructive potential to that of the *pactes de famine* which with their most profound convulsion sent the lewd peasant mobs howling through the chateaux of France early in 1789 and turned the manœuvrings of a Frondeur nobility into the first great social revolution of modern history. But although, as Defoe said, 'there be many who cry out against popery who know not whether it be a man or a horse', although it formed as central a part of the English political consensus as anti-communism forms in America to-day, it could only provide in this context reasons why political change was desirable. It could not in itself empower men to take political initiatives which would otherwise have been illicit for them. And in the crisis of 1679–81 this was just the dynamic change which Shaftesbury needed to effect. For the official political doctrine of the Anglican church, as enunciated in almost all its weighty theological treatises from 1600 onwards, as expressed in the canons of the convocation of 1606, as taught to children in the catechism books, and above all as preached to the congregations year after year in the parish churches in what were the largest public gatherings many men attended in their entire lives, was chillingly simple. It was that men's political duties were exhaustively determined by their terrestrial superiors, that though under grave conscientious scruples they might rightly decline to carry out those decrees of authority which were in direct breach of divine law, they could under no circumstances have the right to resist such authority.

[1] There is a useful discussion of pamphlet literature produced on Shaftesbury's behalf in O. W. Furley, 'The Whig Exclusionists: Pamphlet literature in the Exclusion Campaign, 1679–81', *Cambridge Historical Journal*, XIII, 1 (1957), 19–36.

The politics of Locke in England and America

Of course, the image of the English political system was by now sufficiently complex in the minds of many men to make for considerable and
convenient ambiguity as to the precise location of this authority. But for
Anglicans after 1660, however large the segment of the political system
within which the authority was held to reside, this ambiguity did not
readily extend to the notion that there could be sufficient external reserves
of authority to overbalance that of the king. And if one fact was unambiguous about the political situation in these years it was that Charles
opposed the exclusion of his brother from the succession to the throne.
Thus any attempt to prevent the succession of a Catholic to the throne of
England meant explicit and self-conscious resistance to the sovereign.
It implied action which within the law of England was hard, if not impossible, to distinguish from high treason. The resulting choice facing the
Anglican gentry was impossible to decide within the incoherent ordering
of their own most elemental social values. It was a choice between a
levelling republican assault, redolent with the acrid overtones of 1649,
upon the entire structure of social authority, and the acceptance of a royal
policy which outraged their deepest religious prejudices and stimulated
their most obscure emotional anxieties. The practical choice which faced
them was naturally very different, and to the cool manipulative vision of
Shaftesbury or Halifax, Sunderland or indeed Locke, it doubtless appeared
very different. But the choice which the country gentry made was primarily
the choice which they felt themselves to make. To exert influence upon
that choice it was above all necessary to present a more coherent ordering
of their values, to show that the political tradition within which the dissenters saw their conduct was not necessarily either empirically absurd or
socially subversive. The gentry had to be persuaded that there could be
reasons for rebellion which could make it neither blasphemous nor
suicidal.

The most elaborate, and perhaps at the relevant social level the most
influential, exposition of their political ideology was to be found in the
writings of an obscure Kentish squire called Robert Filmer. These demonstrated, with a wealth of scriptural reference and a certain amount of
sustained attention to the currently respectable political theory, that men
are by biological and theological necessity born into a state of helpless
physical and legal impotence, that they live their entire lives under the
dominion of a sovereign power and are indeed his property, to be disposed
of, exploited, maimed or murdered as he wished and without even the
right to object, that this authority had been conferred on Adam, the first
father and hence first king, directly by God, and that all subsequent fathers
had enjoyed such an authority over their sons and all kings such an

John Dunn

authority over their subjects.[1] The sole constraint which operated upon the monarch within this theory was the other-worldly sanction of divine reward and punishment. The only fully political actor, the only player with a creative role, was the ruler himself. In the domain of politics men's duties were their place in a hierarchical order, an order directed in its activities by a king in lonely confrontation with his God. His subjects had no responsibility or religious duty to take initiatives. Their duty was simply to respond. They were meshed from their birth into a web of authority in family as in kingdom, and their sole commitment was not to struggle. To reject this interpretation of political duty in favour of the claim that governments derive their legitimacy from the consent of individuals was thus regarded as a rejection of the revealed will of God in his bequest of authority to Adam. It was also a rejection of the authority of the sole reputable source for early human history, the book of Genesis, and the most elementary biological fact about the human condition, that all men are necessarily born in a state of helpless physical dependence within the authoritarian institution of the family. It is thus vicious, blasphemous, and intellectually absurd to deny the universal political duty of passive obedience. To answer these charges Locke needed to rescue the contractarian account of political obligation from the criticisms of impiety and absurdity. Only in this way could he restore to the Anglican gentry a coherent basis for moral autonomy or practical initiative in the field of politics.

The precise ideological purchase and explicit political intent of Locke's work can be adequately understood from this outline, but the conceptual dimensions of the book require further elucidation.[2] He needed, it is clear, a theory which rescued the contractarian account of political obligation from the damaging charges levelled against it by Filmer. He needed a theory which outlined a set of possible limitations on political obligation without thereby impairing the legitimacy of the existing social and political order. In short he needed a charter for political revolution which would be in no way socially subversive. In many circumstances such an aim could have been simply enough realized by a pragmatic argument. But the deep moral inhibitions felt by the Anglican gentry necessitated a more theoretical and complete form of therapy. The resulting theory cannot be taken as an adequate summary of Locke's ideas about politics. But there is no good reason to suppose that it contains any important structural

---

[1] Sir Robert Filmer, *Patriarcha, passim,* in *Patriarcha and Other Political Works of Sir Robert Filmer,* ed. P. Laslett (Oxford, 1949). I have discussed the structure of Filmer's arguments at length in the study referred to in n. 2 below.

[2] I am presenting this interpretation of Locke's work systematically in a forthcoming study, *The Political Thought of John Locke* (Cambridge, 1969).

ideas which Locke would in any sense have wished to repudiate. The doctrine has two very different aspects to it, one naturalistic and the other theological. It is the latter which forms the basis of Locke's argument for the necessary limitations upon political obligation; and it is the fact that the latter, the theology, was readily mistaken for the former, the psychology, which explains most of the criticism the work has received from 1690 to the present day. The core of Locke's intellectual development from the first of his writings which we have, written at Oxford early in the 1660s, to the expositions of St Paul's epistles upon which he was working at his death resides in a tension between religious conviction and insistent epistemological doubt. All through his life, so far as we know, Locke believed that there was a God, that there were determinate moral rules and that men could in principle have true knowledge of these rules. Yet all through his life he worried over the nature of the criteria for having attained true knowledge. And when at the end of his life he had reduced faith in God to a belief that certain historical propositions were true, and moral excellence to the skilled calculation of extra-terrestrial self-interest, this intellectual contrivance was not a sign that he lacked religious affections or deep moral feelings but only that he had understood that psychological certitude and emotional authenticity are no guarantee of true knowledge. The philosophy which embodied these beliefs is nowhere systematically developed in Locke's works. The subjects of his writings were a set of precise discrete issues. There is nothing which remotely resembles a Lockean *Summa* or even a Lockean *Treatise of Human Nature*—just specific works on coinage or epistemology or the limits of political obligation or education or toleration.

It is possible, nevertheless, to discern in these works at least the outlines of an intellectual system. It is a system of radical individualism, an individualism as radical in social terms as that of Hobbes and in its potential social implications considerably more subversive. It was not devised as a description of society or of individual human psychology and hence can scarcely be criticized as an inadequate description of these. Indeed there are many reasons to suppose that Locke's assumed sociology and psychology were considerably more realistic than those of his recently resuscitated patriarchalist opponents,[1] that he accepted the reality and efficacy of social conditioning so effortlessly that he did not even feel the need by 1680 to discuss it in a work about political obligation. The key image of his philosophy was not that of Hobbes, a set of discrete, irreducible, purposive organisms in ceaseless conflict. He believed as implicitly as

---

[1] Cf. Laslett's introductions to *Patriarcha* (Oxford, 1949), pp. 39–42, and *John Locke: Two Treatises of Government* (Cambridge, 1960), p. 69.

4-2

John Dunn

Hobbes and indeed as most of the contemporary orthodox that men are naturally sinners—in the understanding of the day this was no more than an empirical observation. But he had a much profounder grasp than Hobbes of the majority of men's lack of any sort of psychological autonomy. He feared the arbitrary compulsive reflex destructiveness of the hungry peasantry or unemployed artisans. But he understood his society well enough to know that the threat of anarchy came not from their determined and indomitable wilfulness but from the disruption of the elementary securities of their joyless lives.[1] What really threatened the fabric of seventeenth-century English society was not the exuberant self-will of the consciously exploited but the sheer panic of the starving and helpless. To Locke, men in the world were for the most part heteronomous to the last degree. They drew their religious, their moral, even their scientific views of the world from the blind and unthinking imitation of their fellows. His individualism was not an individualism of psychological, of emotional autonomy. It was, rather, an epistemological individualism. The primary category of human experience was cognition. It was in knowing that a man became properly human, even transcended human experience, and it was as knower that he was necessarily an individual. To be saved a man needed to attain not emotional prostration before a hidden God but a knowledge of the truth of religious propositions. Emotions might well be induced by external manipulation, and a belief in the truth of statements could be instilled in the same way; but knowledge could not. For knowledge by definition was active, a performance. No man could know for another man. Even the incidence of divine grace was to be determined not by emotional conviction but by the purely naturalistic process of believing statements to be true. A terrifying burden was to be placed upon the intellects of all men, and the burden was the more terrifying because it was precisely identical for all men. In the critical experiences of their lives men were henceforth equal, and equal in a thoroughly terrestrial way. Gone were the assumptions that religious discriminations and moral consciousness were a privileged attribute of the higher orders, that the equality of man was at worst a fact about the next world, in which the secret and ambivalent motions of a man's heart were to be the criterion of his salvation and about which one could blithely proclaim that to God all hearts were open, precisely because they were impervious to any more immediate inspection. Instead men's moral performance was to be judged in terms of their understanding, their reasoning, an activity in which the criteria for skill and success had an implacable

[1] John Locke, *Some Considerations of the Consequences of the Lowering of Interest...*, *The Works of John Locke*, 7th ed. (London, 1768), II, 46.

tendency towards publicity. The privileged privacy of the royal conscience was desecrated for ever. Soul-searching must concede to argument its status as the primary mode for the elucidation of right governmental action.

All this is cast at a suspiciously abstract level and may well appear somewhat evasive, but it should eventually go some way towards explaining that peculiar ambiguity of Locke's doctrine, which made it at the same time democratic in long-term implication to an extent that no society in human history has ever been and yet for seventy years sufficiently conservative for most of the English aristocracy and intellectuals to accept it with heedless complacency as a satisfactory ideology for the closed caste-society of eighteenth-century England.

Locke argued in the *Two Treatises* that no man was born into a condition in which another man had a right to dispose of him at pleasure. No human being was born with rights over another human being. The legitimacy of the legal order which exists among men is derived solely from their acceptance of it. Most men come to accept more or less unthinkingly their membership in a highly articulated social order, and obligations are thus incurred by a combination of psychological assent and utilitarian benefit. But men do not have the legal right to incur whatever obligations they may feel psychologically compelled to incur—they can only transfer to rulers an extent of authority which they themselves already possess. And they do not, for instance, possess authority over their own lives. They do not have the right to commit suicide and hence they cannot confer upon the ruler the right to take their life at his will. This has some very odd implications. It means that the psychological acceptance of absolute power is morally more or less equivalent to suicide, is indeed a sin of some enormity; and hence that no degree of psychological passivity on the part of his subjects can confer legitimacy upon the power of an absolute monarch. Only fully legal authority exercised for the general good can be binding upon the conscience of the subject, and each single individual in the community had an irreducible right to judge the legitimacy of the act or the authenticity of the intention, if it impinged upon him in a sufficiently threatening fashion. And it was logically necessary that each individual should be left in this position as judge, both because of his persistent duty, as long as he remained a fully moral agent, to preserve his own life and because to judge was an act of the intellect and no human being could be excluded from the possibility of correct intellection by the judgment of another human being.

I have deliberately pointed up all the most anarchistic implications of Locke's political doctrine in this way in order to show its connexion with

John Dunn

his religious and philosophical ideas. The specific political doctrine which emerged from the work in 1679–81 and which made its publication such a natural gesture in 1690 was merely the dignifying of the legal order of the English polity. The right of political initiative was to be restored to the English ruling class by the demonstration that the hierarchy of social authority could be granted moral rationality without it being necessary to believe in the impossibility of just opposition to the crown. They were to be taught indeed that all the good reasons for obeying the king at other times implied that when he acted illegally and against the public interest he ought to be resisted. This was the doctrine which the great Whig lords like Somers embraced so readily, and it was the doctrine which gave the work its pre-eminent place as the official ideological defence of the revolution of 1688 during the succeeding seventy years.

That it was this doctrine which emerged is not surprising. Not only was it the doctrine in which men wished to believe; it was also the doctrine which Locke intended to advocate. The image which he held of the society in which he lived combined a very acerbic moral vision with a considerable degree of acceptance of the conventional social pieties. It is no accident that when he talks of the deepest religious sin, he talks of it as rebellion against God. It is not by accident that in the course of the *Two Treatises* he attempts to demonstrate that if a king acts tyrannically it is the king who is properly guilty of rebellion and not his subjects who resist him. Locke's emotional involvement with the maintenance of social stability was at all times acute and his understanding of the contemporary social order was firmly hierarchical.[1] He clearly felt instinctively a lot of the aristocratic overtones in the contemporary value system and both expected and accepted the continued psychological dependence of the majority of the population upon clergy, gentry and aristocracy. The degree of moral responsibility incurred by the individual who initiated a rebellion was huge and alarming. It was not a responsibility which Locke could have imagined any but the members of the aristocracy carrying with success. The right to destroy the legal order of society because of the threat of unjust power was a right that each man held; but it was a right which by the necessities of social structure few could exercise with responsibility, and its validity as a right depended logically upon the responsibility with which it was used. But there remained for Locke a persistent tension between an acceptance of this conventional fabric of values and the prescriptions implied by his philosophical views. It remained after all true that he *had* justified rebellion, and the terminological quibble over just

[1] I have stressed the importance of this elsewhere, 'Consent in the Political Theory of John Locke', *The Historical Journal*, x, 2 (1967), 153–82.

who was really guilty of rebellion reflected moral outrage at the Filmerian notions as well as embarrassment at the breach of a taboo.

Many of the assumptions about the relative value of different social groups which were made explicit in Filmer's works Locke found deeply revolting. The notion that children were at the disposal of their fathers, were almost created to be at their disposal, that subjects were created for the benefit of monarchs, seemed to him blasphemous. The primary category of his religious thought, the equality of men as liable to sin and as capable of the knowledge of religious truth, disrupted these subliminal convictions of seventeenth-century social values. In such a perspective it was not just irrational, it was emotionally impossible to believe that the majority of mankind were delivered over into the hands of the rich, like the animals, to be enjoyed at their pleasure. Psychological dependence and compulsive acquiescence might justify themselves morally by their utility, but moral paternalism can no longer be prescriptive, a matter of right. Social configurations which serve the happiness of mankind remain morally secure, but the criterion is no longer trifling. The manipulative control of one man over another is no longer necessarily an embodiment of divine providence. Providence is torn up out of the social world which men have created by their actions, and each part of this world is made subject to challenge and scrutiny. Henceforth men confronted each other in a social world created by the intricate patterns of their own compulsions, and they confronted each other alone. No longer were they braced against or enveloped within institutions which embodied the indefeasible provision of their God. Their sufferings in the world were demythologized, ceased to wear the protective vestment of divine punishment, and became natural events to be guarded against to the best of their active abilities. The world was to be given back to men to make what they could of it, free from the inhibitions born of centuries of misunderstood theology. Even that almost automatic psychological acquiescence on which Locke was so justified in relying in the stable society of seventeenth-century England as the formal basis of the state's legitimacy bore its own dialectical implications. If the complex of seventeenth-century social duties is incurred through unthinking acquiescence, there is placed upon every dissentient member of the society, from the beginning of his adult life, the duty of making vocal and active the dissent which he feels. If thoughtless servility brings down upon the individual such a crushing moral burden, there is a moral as well as a psychological incentive to make explicit a dignified but total dissent.

The potential activism contained in this complex of notions can be well understood in a contrast between Locke and Hobbes. It is Locke's superior insight into social psychology, his deeper sense of the empirical cohesiveness of society, which made it possible for him to combine a purely ethical individualism and a broader social basis for permitted political action with an assurance that society would not thus collapse. Hobbes's crushing sense of elemental human hostility combined with his epistemological individualism led him to restrict the possibility of correct and autonomous individual action to the immediate biological drive of avoiding death and to extrude the very possibility of it from the field of politics. In this perspective his political doctrine is simply a secularized version of the prevalent Anglican or Filmerian theory, but without the latter's equivocations. Locke's theory too is based upon the necessity of individual epistemological autonomy. But his epistemological doctrines were much less sceptical than those of Hobbes. They emerged largely out of reflexion upon the notions of ethical and religious knowledge. Hobbes's epistemological individualism was not of this immediate political relevance. It was of no importance that the ignorant and the stupid, who seemed to him just as to Locke to make up the huge mass of the population, necessarily had to garner their knowledge for themselves. The necessary privacy of cognition of the stupid was a matter of no social purchase. But even the stupid have souls and hence cannot escape from their responsibility for the cognition of their elementary duties, both religious and political. 'The candle that is set up in us shines bright enough for all our purposes.'[1] The metaphor is not a careless one. The central truths and duties of human experience are accessible to all through their intellects. In the relationship with God in which, through the mediation of grace, they come to know the truths of religion, all men are equal. It is the possibility of this perception which confers an irreducible autonomy on every human individual. In the field of politics it is this religiously guaranteed autonomy which ensures that men can only incur their political duties through their own actions and that they can never be deprived of the right to claim that these duties had been abrogated. Their claim, when made, was in Locke's words 'an appeal to heaven'.[2] The words were meant literally. It was a fact about the public world and not merely about each man's soul that he had such a right of appeal.

The work which emerged anonymously from the presses in the aftermath of the revolution of 1688 enjoyed no great immediate éclat. Only three Englishmen who were not personal acquaintances or correspondents of Locke are known even to have mentioned it with approval in the

---

[1] John Locke, *An Essay concerning Human Understanding*, ed. J. W. Yolton (London, 1961), I, I, §5.
[2] *Two Treatises*, II, §§20, 21, etc.

fourteen years before its author's death,[1] and at no time do we know him to have made explicit written admission of his authorship. In the various obituaries which appeared in the two years after his death, it nowhere features very prominently.[2] All through the eighteenth century its reputation trailed that of his major philosophical work, *An Essay concerning Human Understanding*. In France, where it was not published under Locke's name until 1749,[3] it was almost unknown as a work of his throughout the first half of the century. In England its status as the outstanding exposition of the principles of 1688 derived more from the enormous esteem in which the *Essay* was held than from any close reading of the book itself. That the greatest of modern European philosophers should have written a work in defence of the revolution was a sufficient recommendation. It was felt to contain principles of the most indubitable and parochial political orthodoxy and its intellectual quality was guaranteed by the identity of its author. It seemed above all to be an unexacting exposition of those features of the English way of conducting politics which made it so clearly superior to that of any other community. It was this slackly ideological reading of the book which represented the characteristic English understanding of it for most of the eighteenth century. Indeed it persisted with considerable tenacity even after a time at which the implications of the book for practical politics had become violently contested.[4] At this

[1] See [William Atwood,] *The Fundamental Constitution of the English Government...* (London, 1690), pp. 97 (= p. 101), 102, appendix, p. 19 (I owe this reference to Professor Gordon Schochet) (p. 97: 'The Author of the best Treatises of Civil Polity which I have met with in the *English* Tongue...'); Walter Moyle, *Essay on the Lacedaemonian Government* (1698), *The Whole Works of Walter Moyle...* (London, 1727), p. 58; [Simon Clement,] *An Answer to Mr. Molyneux, his Case of Ireland's being bound by Acts of Parliament in England...* (London, 1698), p. 30.

[2] Cf. Le Clerc, *The Life and Character of Mr. John Locke...* (London, 1706), pp. 16–17 with the length at which the *Essay concerning Human Understanding* is discussed there. See also Pierre Coste's letter in *Nouvelles de la République des Lettres* (February 1705), pp. 154–77. *A Complete History of Europe: or, A View of the Affairs thereof, Civil and Military, for The Year 1704...* (London, 1705), pp. 589–92, 'Mr Locke's Death'.

[3] The 1691 Amsterdam printing and the 1724 Geneva printing were both anonymous. The Brussels *Du Gouvernement Civil de Mr. Locke* of 1749 was the first French edition to bear Locke's name. The first French editions of other works of Locke to bear his name include *Thoughts on Education* (Amsterdam, 1695), *An Essay concerning Human Understanding* (Amsterdam, 1700), *Œuvres Diverses* (Rotterdam, 1710), *Reasonableness of Christianity* (Amsterdam, 1715). For French editions of *Two Treatises* see conveniently Laslett's list in *Two Treatises*, p. 126. For other works see British Museum and Bibliothèque Nationale holdings and John Hampton, 'Les Traductions françaises de Locke au XVIIIe siècle', *Revue de Littérature Comparée*, XXIX (1955), 240–51.

[4] At times the implications of this conception of theoretical truth were reduced to an inscrutable minimum. Cf. Sir John Hawkins, *The Life of Samuel Johnson, LL.D.* (London, 1787), p. 503, 'Nor has any of those who deny the right of a mother-country to tax its colonies, attempted to prove an exemption, by any other arguments than are to be found in Mr. Locke's Essay on Government, a discourse of general import, and which applies to no existing constitution on earth'.

John Dunn

point what was contested was normally not its theoretical truth but its substantive relevance.

It seems to have retained this tensionless ideological comfort for both radicals and conservatives, for William Molyneux and Walter Moyle, Richard Price, Richard Watson, and James Burgh as much as for the more conventional John Cary and Simon Clement, Chesterfield and Blackstone, Sir John Hawkins and Thomas Elrington.[1] It was a work much recommended to the young and seldom read with any care by the adult.

There are very simple literary reasons for this career, a number of plain facts about the character of the book which although obscured in recent years by the progress of the history of political science make the vagaries of public interest in it and of its reputation easy to explain. It was a work which expounded a single argument and which expounded it in a dogged and less than elegant manner. Locke's intellectual tactics in this as in most of his other works are perhaps best described in the jargon of a very different activity, as a sort of saturation bombing. They owe more than he himself would have cared to admit to the scholastic procedures of the educational institution in which he spent his early maturity, procedures which he afterwards rejected with such scorn. In most of his works these tendencies were to some degree checked by the constructive intellectual urge to expound his own notions in an unambiguous fashion. But in the *Two Treatises* he was in fact released from the need to do this. The intention of the book was twofold, to destroy the current Anglican theory of politics so completely that it ceased to exercise any influence upon the wills of his political audience, and to persuade these latter to take the political initiative and resist the crown. For emotional and conceptual reasons the first was a very difficult assignment, but the alarm generated by anti-

[1] William Molyneux, *The Case of Ireland's Being Bound by Acts of Parliament in England Stated* (Dublin, 1725) (first published Dublin, 1698), pp. 18 (pp. 12–18 are simply a summary of the treatment of conquest in the *Two Treatises*), 101, 104, etc. Walter Moyle, *Works*, p. 58. Richard Price, *Observations on the Nature of Civil Liberty, the Principles of Government and the Justice and Policy of the War with America* (London, 1776), pp. 16, 93, 100; *Additional Observations on the Nature and Value of Civil Liberty*, 2nd ed. (London, 1777), pp. xvi, 25, 45–6. Richard Watson, *Anecdotes of the Life of Richard Watson, Bishop of Llandaff...* (London, 1817), pp. 57, 96. James Burgh, *Political Disquisitions: Or, An Enquiry into public Errors, Defects and Abuses*, 3 vols. (London, 1774–5), I, vii, 72–5, 116, 279. John Cary, *A Vindication of the Parliament of England in Answer to a Book Written by W. Molyneux...* (London, 1698), p. 103. [Clement,] *An Answer to Mr. Molyneux*, p. 30. *The Letters of Philip Dormer Stanhope* ([London], 1932), ed. B. Dobrée, IV, 1307. For the appearance of Locke as a paradigm of intellectual virtue see *ibid.* III, 784, 1130; IV, 1260, 1269, 1358, 1717, etc. Sir William Blackstone, *Commentaries on the Laws of England*, 21st ed. (London, 1844), I, 51, 126, 178, 243, 251 (but for distinct reservations on several points see I, 161, 213; II, 8–9). Hawkins, *Life of Samuel Johnson*, p. 503. Thomas Elrington (ed.), *An Essay concerning the True Original Extent and End of Civil Government*, by John Locke (Dublin, 1798), notes *passim*. (For the circumstances surrounding the preparation of this edition see R. B. McDowell, *Irish Public Opinion 1750–1800*, London, 1944, chapter VIII, esp. p. 164.)

popery made the second a matter of no difficulty whatsoever once theoretical inhibitions of patriarchal passive obedience had been shattered. Hence the almost perfunctory fashion in which Locke treats the question of the justification of specific revolutionary action and the endless length at which Filmer's ideas are savaged from one end of the book to the other. What the Tory gentry in the full tide of their xenophobia needed was not to be persuaded that this if ever was the time to resist the monarch, but rather to be persuaded that it could ever under any circumstances be legitimate for them to resist the monarch. What they needed was to be persuaded that their existing political inclinations were legitimate, to be told the reasons why what they wanted to do but feared that they should not do was the *right* thing to do.

It was this very specific role, the justification of political resistance by the ruling class to the logically and psychologically linked threat of idolatry and arbitrary power, which created the vulgar meaning of the book. Whether their taste was for conservative or for radical action, provided it was within the currently permitted dimensions of the English political system men could devise a painless historical and political sanction for their political intentions. It was at most a symbol for an entire tradition in the conduct of politics, an ambiguous tradition as all such traditions are, and of those who did read the book most read it as men read the Declaration of Independence today, as an affirmation of faith in the viability of the tradition, not as an exercise in the critical assessment of contemporary political achievement. It remained in all the pejorative overtones of the phrase a theoretical work, pre-eminently a work which one would recommend to one's nephew to read at university as Chatham[1] did, or to one's pupil as Richard Watson did.[2]

The circumstances in which it was likely to be read carefully were restricted. Philosophers and academic writers on political theory, worried reactionary clerics or political revolutionaries, might have reason to take it seriously, and at different times members of all of these categories did do so. But for the most part it was no more than a name in a litany, even if intellectually the most distinguished name. For those of radical proclivities the litany would contain many names, Sydney, Milton, and Somers, later Hoadly, Trenchard and Gordon, and it would portray the events of 1688 as a less lurid re-enactment of 1649. For those of a more

---

[1] *Letters Written by the Late Earl of Chatham to his Nephew Thomas Pitt, Esq. (Afterwards Lord Camelford) Then at Cambridge*, 3rd ed. (London, 1804), pp. 15, 42–3, 50.
[2] Richard Watson, *Anecdotes of the Life of Richard Watson, Bishop of Llandaff*... (London, 1817), pp. 49 (Lord Granby to Watson, 'I can never thank you too much for making me study Locke; while I exist, those tenets, which are so attentive to the natural rights of mankind, shall ever be the guide and direction of my actions'), 51–2.

John Dunn

conservative disposition it would probably refer to fewer names, frequently only to Locke and the immortal Hooker, and 1688 would appear as a re-enactment of 1558, not of 1649. In neither case would the ritual incantation exert any more discernible operational impact on their political conduct than would, say, that of Abraham Lincoln in the politics of contemporary America. It was not that Locke meant nothing to those who favoured the different litanies; merely that there is no reason to suppose that anything Locke ever wrote caused the least deflection of their political behaviour from the paths it would otherwise have followed. The use of his name was more a feature of their affective life than a guarantee of any energetic conceptual exploration. It belonged to the rhetoric not to the analysis of politics. It may seem surprising that the name and the book it stood for should have exerted such a persistent and effortless appeal, but societies frequently exhibit over long periods of time a level of incoherence in their ideology which outrages the *a priori* certainties of many sociologists. It was only a recurrence of the circumstances for which the work had first been written, the need for justifying revolution in the future in conditions of extreme danger instead of the flaccid rationalization of a past *coup d'état*, which brought the two interpretations into dramatic confrontation.

Yet the dispute for the soul of Locke which split the airy Whig consensus over the last thirty-five years of the eighteenth century did not exhaust the range of critical responses which the book evoked. There are two separate traditions of its rejection which go back to the early years of the century, a self-consciously philosophical, and a more uninhibitedly conservative one. The philosophical can be traced through the writings of Shaftesbury and Bolingbroke, Hume, Paley and Bentham to its incarceration in the flatter platitudes of nineteenth-century political science.[1]

[1] Anthony Ashley Cooper, Third Earl of Shaftesbury, *Characteristicks of Men, Manners, Opinions, Times,* 5th ed. (Birmingham, 1773). For the details of what Shaftesbury saw as the implications of Locke's philosophy see I, 97–8, 107–8, 109–11, 116–17, 125, 127; II, 67–9, 308–9, 312, 319–20; III, 143–6. The evidence for taking these attacks as attacks applying to Locke's philosophy as well as to that of Hobbes is to be found in two letters in *The Life, Unpublished Letters, and Philosophical Regimen of Anthony, Earl of Shaftesbury,* ed. B. Rand (London, 1900), pp. 403–4, 414–16. There is a discussion of Shaftesbury's critique of Locke by Jason Aaronson, 'Shaftesbury on Locke', *American Political Science Review,* LIII, 4 (December 1959), 1101–4, but it does not bring out the central theme of Shaftesbury's hostility to Locke, their disagreement over the existence of innate ideas. See esp. Shaftesbury, *Second Characters or The Language of Forms,* ed. B. Rand (Cambridge, 1914), pp. 173–8. Bolingbroke, *The Works of Lord Bolingbroke...* (Philadelphia, 1841), IV, *Fragments or Minutes of Essays,* pp. 194–9. The main thrust of Bolingbroke's arguments is directed against Hobbes (*ibid.* 145–51, 156–60, 168, 183, 188), though Filmer comes in for passing abuse (*ibid.* 183, 187, 193–4, 199). It is not Locke's substantive political doctrine (with which in fact Bolingbroke agreed) but his philosophical exposition of it which is criticized (on Bolingbroke, see Isaac Kramnick's important forthcoming study). David Hume, 'Of the Original Contract' (1748), *Essays*

The politics of Locke in England and America

The more conservative, which remained throughout the century the dominant teaching of the Anglican church and by far the most widely believed theory of political obligation in the population at large, was first outlined at length as an explicit attack on Locke's political thought by the non-juror Charles Leslie in 1703.[1] It can be traced in this form by explicit acknowledgment through the writings of George Horne, Bishop of Norwich, and William Jones, Jonathan Boucher and John Whitaker of Manchester.[2] But in a slightly less full-blooded but equally conservative persuasion it represented throughout the eighteenth century the official Anglican theory of 1688 as embodied in the writings of William Sherlock and Offspring Blackall, Bishop Berkeley, Samuel Johnson and Dean Tucker.[3] As they stand these categories are somewhat misleading—

Moral, Political and Literary (London, 1903), pp. 452–73 and see p. 62, n. 3, below. William Paley, *The Principles of Moral and Political Philosophy* (London, 1785), pp. xviii–xix, cf. pp. 99–105, 414–24. Jeremy Bentham in Elie Halévy, *La Formation du Radicalisme Philosophique* (Paris, 1901), I, appendix, pp. 416–23. Cf. e.g. Bertrand de Jouvenel, *The Pure Theory of Politics* (Cambridge, 1963), p. 45: "'Social contract' theories are the views of childless men who must have forgotten their childhood'; and for evidence that de Jouvenel would see this as applying to Locke see B. de Jouvenel, *Sovereignty* (Cambridge, 1957), p. 232.

[1] Charles Leslie, *The New Association of Those Called Moderate-Church-Men with the Modern Whigs and Fanatics to Undermine and Blow Up the Present Church and Government* (London, 1703), part II, appendix, 'A Short account of the Original of Government'.

[2] George Horne, *Discourses of the Right Reverend George Horne, D.D., Late Lord Bishop of Norwich* (London, 1812), II, 18–33; III, 121–34, 'Submission to Government'. Cf. William Jones, *The Life and Writings of Dr. Horne etc.*, *Works of the Rev. William Jones* (London, 1801), XII, 73–5. William Jones, *A Letter to the Church of England Pointing Out Some Popular Errors of Bad Consequence*, *Works*, XII, cf. pp. 315 and 325–6. Jonathan Boucher, 'On Civil Liberty, Passive Obedience, and Non-resistance', in *A View of the Causes and Consequences of the American Revolution* (London, 1797), pp. 495–560, esp. 516–19 (against Locke), 522, 527–33, 551–2 (pro-Filmer v. Locke), 525 (Overall), 548 (Sherlock), 551 (Berkeley) and 332, 361, 543 (Hobbes); 257–9, 408 (Locke); and see also Jonathan Boucher, *Reminiscences of an American Loyalist* (Boston, 1925). [Sir James Allan Park,] *Memoirs of William Stevens, Esq., Treasurer of Queen Anne's Bounty*, 2nd ed. (London, 1814), pp. 169–78. John Whitaker, *The Real Origin of Government* (London, 1795), esp. pp. 17–20, 22–4, and cf. (anon.), *Divine Institutes of True Religion and Civil Government* (London, 1788), esp. pp. 27–30 for acknowledgments to Horne.

[3] William Sherlock, *The Case of the Allegiance due to Soveraign Powers, Stated and Resolved According to Scripture and Reason...* (London, 1691). For Sherlock and other Anglican passive obedience theorists contemporary with him see conveniently Gerald M. Straka, *Anglican Reaction to the Revolution of 1688* (Madison, Wisconsin, 1962). Offspring Blackall, *The Subject's Duty. A Sermon...* (London, 1705); *The Divine Institution of Magistracy, and the Gracious Design of its Institution...a Sermon...* (London, 1708). George Berkeley, *Passive Obedience* (1712), in *The Works of George Berkeley, Bishop of Cloyne*, ed. A. A. Luce and T. E. Jessop (London, 1953), VI, 15–46 (esp. p. 15). And for the important disjunction between the measure of the subject's obedience and the bounds of the ruler's power noted in his letter to Percival on 21 October 1709, see *Works*, VIII, *Letters* (1956), p. 23. Stock appears to claim that it was the *Two Treatises* which directed Berkeley's attention to the subject in 1712 (J. Stock, *An Account of the Life of George Berkeley, D.D.*, London, 1776, pp. 3–4). But this is hard to reconcile with the evidence of the 1709 letter. Josiah Tucker, *A Letter to Edmund Burke, Esq....* (Glocester, 1775), Advertisement, pp. 11–13; *Tract V. The Respective Pleas and Arguments of the Mother Country and of the Colonies, distinctly set forth;...* (Glocester, 1775), see esp. p. v (the key question posed by the American Revolution: 'Permit me therefore to ask, Why are not the

John Dunn

Tucker for instance and even Berkeley give lengthy philosophical reasons for their dissent, and Hume, among the unambiguously philosophical critics, is clearly motivated by a conservative political intention. The conceptual core of their criticisms of Locke is for the most part simply a rejection of the historical plausibility and analytic relevance of the notion of the state of nature. The great bulk of this criticism is totally irrelevant to anything Locke said but since it shares this irrelevance with much contemporary academic comment on the text this is hardly surprising. What is interesting about the various objections is not their more or less sophisticated presentation of a limited number of arguments but the structures of feeling within which the unacceptable features of the Lockean doctrine are located. In the purely academic tradition of discussing political obligation, the work is seldom even noticed in the first half of the century in Britain, and only once, in an annotated Latin edition of 1724 by a Scottish professor called Carmichael of Pufendorf's standard text, the *De Officio Hominis et Civis*, was the Lockean doctrine adopted in its entirety and the *Two Treatises* recognized as the relevant academic authority.[1] Elsewhere, as in Hutcheson, a similar doctrine is adopted directly from Locke's continental sources or as with Hume, Paley or Bentham the theories appear only for perfunctory dismissal.[2] It was only in the second half of the century when Locke's vast philosophical eminence conferred an intellectual stature on the work despite its previous low reputation, and when its practical implications became so hotly contested, that there was any great pressure to treat it with full intellectual seriousness. With the possible exception of Hume's initial attack in the *Treatise of Human Nature*,[3] the only politically disinterested philosophical attack on Locke's

poor Negroes, and the poor Indians entitled to the like Rights and Benefits?') and pp. 12, 13, 13 n.; *The Notions of Mr Locke and his Followers*... ([Glocester], 1778), *passim*; *A Treatise concerning Civil Government in Three Parts* (London, 1781), parts I and II *passim*; *A Series of Answers to Certain Popular Objections against Separating from the Rebellious Colonies*... (Glocester, 1776), pp. 102–6 (further attack on Locke's treatment of slavery in *Two Treatises* and *Fundamental Constitutions of Carolina*); *Four Letters on Important National Subjects. Addressed to the Right Honourable the Earl of Shelburne*... (Glocester, 1783), pp. 20, 50–1, 53–4, 55–8, 67, 89–113.

[1] S. Puffendorfii, *De Officio Hominis et Civis*... ed. Gerschomus Carmichael (Edinburgh, 1724), pp. 12 n., 122–4 n., 216 (but cf. 224), 316, 327–8, 330–1, 338, 357, 366, 379, 386–7, 405, 409, 423, 453, 482, 497.
[2] Francis Hutcheson, *Philosophiae Moralis Institutio Compendiaria* (Glasgow, 1742), pp. i–ii and *passim* (cf. English translation, *A Short Introduction to Moral Philosophy*, 2nd ed., Glasgow, 1753, p. viii). For Hume, Paley and Bentham see p. 60, n. 1 above.
[3] David Hume, *A Treatise of Human Nature*, 2 vols. (London, 1911), II, book III, 191–202, 233–55. For an indication that this criticism should be taken as bearing upon Locke's work see Hume's letter to Francis Hutcheson of 10 January 1743, 'P. 266. L. 18. & quae seq: You imply a Condemnation of Locke's Opinion, which being the receiv'd one, I cou'd have wisht the Condemnation had been more express', *The Letters of David Hume*, ed. J. Y. T. Greig (Oxford, 1932), I, 48. (Cf. in Hutcheson's *Philosophiae Moralis Institutio Compendiaria*,

political doctrines before the 1760s was that of his pupil and friend the Third Earl of Shaftesbury, and Shaftesbury's careless and ill-conceived rejection was directed more by his violent hostility towards Locke's epistemological rejection of ethical naturalism than by any understanding of the meaning of the *Two Treatises*.[1] Except for their shared and not very relevant conviction that the state of nature was empirically a dubious notion and a certain dim sense that it might have subversive implications, there is little of interest in the self-consciously philosophical critiques.

It is with the more uninhibited attacks of the Tory divines from Leslie to Boucher, Whitaker and the author of the *Divine Institutes*, that more interesting responses can be found. There were many facets to their rejection of Locke and there were shifts of emphasis over the century— scriptural history for instance tended to play a diminishing role in the argument—but the main structure of their ideas remained stable. Since it represents in many ways a less hysterical and better-judged response to the political theory of the Enlightenment than the lurid and much praised bludgeonings of De Maistre, it is worth a brief and sympathetic treatment. In the hands of its first protagonist, the non-juror Charles Leslie, the criticism achieved its most invigorating and perhaps its most thorough exposition. The destructive criticisms levelled against the book may have owed a heavy debt to Filmer; but in Leslie's writings the patriarchalist hypothesis had found, as even Hoadly grudgingly admitted, its ablest exponent to that date.[2] The attacks on the historical plausibility of the contract theory, while not for the most part criticisms of the precise theory which Locke had enunciated, undoubtedly devastated the entire conventional Whig political theory of the succeeding century. And the image of the social order which they advanced to refute Locke was undoubtedly the image held as an item of religious faith and moral belief by the majority of their contemporaries. For them the texture of the social world which confronted men was at all points homogeneous.

p. 266, l. 18.) For the continuity of Hume's impatience see his 'Of the Original Contract', *Essays*, pp. 452–73; the letter to Lord Elibank of 8 January 1748 in E. C. Mossner, 'New Hume Letters to Lord Elibank', *Texas Studies in Language and Literature*, IV, 3 (1962), 437 (Professor J. H. Plumb kindly called these letters to my attention); and the splendid footnote identifying the authors of 'Compositions the most despicable both for style and matter' which Hume added to later editions of the *History* (cf. *The History of Great Britain*... 2nd ed. London, 1759, II, 443 with a posthumous edition). All the direct attacks subsequent to the *Treatise* imply that Hume thought Locke's political theory practically dangerous as well as theoretically incoherent.

[1] See works cited in p. 60, n. 1 above, and esp. Shaftesbury, *Life, Letters*, p. 415: 'Locke, whose *State of Nature* he supposes to be chimerical, and less serviceable to Mr Locke's own system than to Mr Hobbes's that is more of a piece as I believe.'

[2] Benjamin Hoadly, *An Humble Reply to the Right Reverend the Lord Bishop of Exeter's Answer in which the Considerations Lately Offered to his Lordship are Vindicated*... (London, 1709), p. 48: 'the ablest Hand that ever yet managed "the Patriarchal Scheme"'.

John Dunn

From the womb to the grave men were at every moment powerless. The vast articulated order of social authority protected them throughout their lives, taught them all their duties and repressed all their anarchic impulses. It confronted them at every point as a visible embodiment of the providence of God. Its ethical legitimacy was no more defeasible by the will of an individual than was the law of gravity. That this was a matter of literal truth, not of metaphor, in Leslie's eyes can be seen from a very surprising claim which he makes in an attack on Hoadly.

> The Sum of the Matter betwixt Mr. *Hoadly* and Me is this, I think it most Natural that *Authority* shou'd *Descend*, that is, be *Derived* from a *Superiour* to an *Inferiour*, from *God* to *Fathers* and *Kings*, and from *Kings* and *Fathers* to *Sons* and *Servants*: But Mr. *Hoadly* wou'd have it *Ascend*, from *Sons* to *Fathers*, and from *Subjects* to *Sovereigns*; Nay to *God* Himself, whose *Kingship* the Men of the *Rights* say, is *Derived* to *Him* from the *People*! And the *Argument* does Naturally Carry it all that Way. For if *Authority* does *Ascend*, it must *Ascend* to the *Height*.[1]

For men to claim credit for the creation of the miraculous edifice of eighteenth-century English society was an act of almost unbelievable presumption. If men could confront the work of God in this way and blandly appropriate responsibility for it, there was no knowing where their pride would end—why stop at society? Why not claim the further embodiment of God's handiwork? Why not claim, as indeed parts of the Lockean epistemology almost seemed to, in this paranoid vision, to have created God, or at least to have conferred on him by their recognition the attributes which made him worshipful? The whole way of thought logically implied blasphemy. The order of nature was ruptured; the great chain of being was torn apart. It was not an accident that the most insipid eighteenth-century attack on Locke's theory of government came in the writings of the flattest of eighteenth-century optimists, in a work in which Soame Jenyns sets out a peculiarly ill-considered exposition of this well-worn cosmic image.[2] He recorded the vision with still greater metaphorical assurance elsewhere.

> The Universe resembles a large and well-regulated Family, in which all the officers and servants, and even the domestic animals, are subservient to each

---

[1] Charles Leslie, *The Finishing Stroke. Being a Vindication of the Patriarchal Scheme of Government...* (London, 1711), p. 87.

[2] Soame Jenyns, *Disquisitions on Several Subjects* (London, 1782); Disquisition I, 'On the Chain of Universal Being'; Disquisition VII, 'On Government and Civil Liberty' (cf. the tactics used earlier in his *The Objections to the Taxation of our American Colonies by the Legislative of Great Britain Briefly Consider'd*, London, 1765, pp. 7–8). The latter disquisition was taken as an attack on Locke (B. N. Turner, *Candid Suggestions in Eight Letters to Soame Jenyns, Esq...*. London, 1782, pp. 126–7, 130–3, 135–8, 141–4 and [?R. Watson,] *An Answer to the Disquisition on Government and Civil Liberty...* London, 1782, pp. 22, 27–30, 35).

other in a proper subordination; each enjoys the privileges and perquisites peculiar to his place, and at the same time contributes by that just subordination, to the magnificence and happiness of the whole.[1]

Such a level of blandness was altogether beyond Leslie—he felt no need to rely on such tepid metaphysical certainties. The strained horror which he felt at the Lockean image of a social order whose continuing legitimacy was maintained only by the individual assents of its members is shown in the wild charge of blasphemy. But his response goes beyond this deep emotional revulsion. His criticisms both personal and intellectual are exceedingly enlightening. Even though he felt the Lockean argument to be almost blasphemous, he still could not quite believe that Locke meant it seriously. With graphic scorn he sketched a picture of how a household would be run, if the Lockean notions were to be applied to it. There was no need to discuss the matter further—the picture was emotionally in-conceivable.[2] All the seventeenth-century notions of family authority were quite incompatible with it. And as for the broader social implications— what if the common people were suddenly to cease consenting—the entire civilized world would crumble into ruins.[3] And how, in any case, could it be truthfully said that consent was manifested in the existing political order? 'Would they send Men about to poll the whole nation?' he sneered, with finality.[4] Leslie's successors in this line of reasoning were on the whole men of less intellectual vigour, though not of less prolixity. But as the social threats envisaged in Leslie's most nightmarish imaginings became actual in America, in France, even in England itself, the reasoning acquired fresh emotional force and by the end of the eighteenth century Locke had become again in some men's eyes, not a slightly misguided philosopher but a social incendiary.

There were two very different contexts in the eighteenth century in which this insurrectionary threat was given social immediacy and which showed very clearly that the transposition of Locke's doctrine into a very different structure of society did indeed have subversive implications. The first of these was the relationship between England and its subject territories. The second was the development of an English working-class political movement. The response to both showed that the majority of English writers, however glibly they might cite Locke's authority, accepted his doctrine only in a very parochial fashion, as at best the intellectual exposition of the theodicy of 1688. The Irish situation is in many ways the most interesting, for here Locke's work was used and acknowledged

---

[1] Soame Jenyns, *A Free Inquiry into the Nature and Origin of Evil* (London, 1757), p. 40.
[2] Charles Leslie, *The New Association*... (London, 1703), part II, appendix, pp. 6–7.
[3] *Ibid*. pp. 4–5, 10, 14. [4] *Ibid*. p. 10.

John Dunn

publicly by a friend, William Molyneux, in a political controversy about the rights of the Irish parliament, in which the two had previously co-operated intensively over a period of several years.[1] Molyneux used the book and named Locke as its author at a time when Locke refused to acknowledge it even in private, and without asking his permission.[2] The reception of Molyneux's book in England was unenthusiastic. The House of Commons ordered the book to be investigated on suspicion of treason, and the investigation was still in progress at the time when Molyneux arrived to stay with Locke for the first time in his life.[3] A critic pointed out graphically that Molyneux's arguments, if taken seriously, were not a justification for the legislative independence of the Irish parliament, constituted as this was exclusively of Protestant English gentry, but rather a charter for rebellion on the part of the Catholic Irish peasantry.[4] Since the threat of precisely such a rebellion was an ever-present anxiety of the English ascendancy, Molyneux's work enjoyed a queasy reception even among those on whose behalf it had been written.[5] What Locke thought of its use of his ideas we do not know; but he can hardly have felt much enthusiasm. The policies towards Ireland which he had favoured on the Board of Trade were altogether more conciliatory and pragmatic. After the ferocious reception of Molyneux's book, his friendship for the Irishman did not lessen discernibly,[6] but he seems to have felt neither capacity nor inclination to set out any theoretical clarification of the issues at stake. The reputation of Molyneux's work survived to be taken up with each burst of Irish national sentiment throughout the century, by Swift and Charles Lucas, by Grattan and Pollock, even eventually by Wolfe Tone.[7]

[1] The political background is described helpfully in H. F. Kearney, 'The Political Background to English Mercantilism: 1695–1700', *Economic History Review*, 2nd series, xi, 3 (April, 1959), 484–96. The personal relationship can be investigated in *Some Familiar Letters between Mr. Locke and his Friends*, *Works of John Locke*, 7th ed. (London, 1768), iv, 267–391. There is one important piece of additional information in what remains of the original file of these letters in the Carl H. Pforzheimer Library, New York. (Information by courtesy oi Dr E. S. De Beer.)

[2] See Molyneux, *The Case of Ireland*, p. 18 and cf. *Some Familiar Letters, Works of John Locke*, iv, 269, 306–9, 377 ('How justly they can bind us without our consent and representatives, I leave the author of the *Two Treatises of Government* to consider'), and Locke's reply, pp. 378-9.

[3] *Journals of the House of Commons* (London, 1742), xii, 281, 321, 324, 331. Kearney's account of this episode, *loc. cit.* n. 1 above, should be compared with these texts.

[4] [Clement,] *An Answer to Mr. Molyneux* (London, 1698), Epistle Dedicatory (not numbered, = pp. 5–7, 10–12).

[5] See the responses of Bishop William King (Kearney, 'Political Background', *Economic History Review*, xi, 491), to whom Molyneux had presented a specially bound copy of the work (C. S. King, *A Great Archbishop of Dublin*, London, 1906, p. 175 n.), and of Sir Richard Cox, *Historical Manuscripts Commission, Manuscripts of the Duke of Portland*, iii, 609–10.

[6] See the letters in *Some Familiar Letters, Works of John Locke*, subsequent to Molyneux's admission of his authorship of *The Case of Ireland*, iv, 380.

[7] Jonathan Swift, *The Drapier's Letters and other Works 1724–1725* (Oxford, 1941), pp. 62, 86. Charles Lucas, *The Political Constitutions of Great Britain and Ireland Asserted and Vindicated...*

The politics of Locke in England and America

But the precise application of Locke's political doctrine as such to the colonial relationship remained unexamined for the most part until the 1760s, and no particular incongruity was perceived between the idea of the legislative sovereignty of the English parliament and the conventional Whig theory of politics. The opponents of Molyneux in 1698 indeed based their argument that emigration removed the right of direct representation on the plain fact of the dependency of the American colonies upon the English parliament.[1] It simply did not occur to them that this interpretation of the constitution could be challenged in the case of America.

In 1794 Thomas Hardy, a London artisan and leader of the London Corresponding Society, the first large working-class English political organization, was prosecuted along with several other leading radicals for high treason. The charge was based upon two allegations; the first, that the society had plotted military insurrection, and the second, that it had planned to cow parliament by nationwide petitioning into granting a wide measure of parliamentary reform.[2] The first was impossible to bring home against Hardy, and most of the evidence was probably generated exclusively by *agents-provocateurs* of the government. But the second was unquestionably true and the defence plea turned upon the issue of whether private citizens had the right to attempt to coerce parliament in this way. It turned in fact upon the meaning of the idea of representation in the British constitution, on whether the ordinary citizen had a political per-

2 vols. (London, 1751), I, xxviii, xxxiii, 113. There is a valuable recent discussion of Lucas's role in the development of a radical press in Dublin in Robert Munter, *The History of the Irish Newspaper 1685–1760* (Cambridge, 1967), esp. pp. 170–85. Speeches of the *Rt. Hon. Henry Grattan* in *The Irish Parliament in 1780 and 1782...* (London, 1821), p. 45 ('Spirit of Swift! Spirit of Molyneux! Your genius has prevailed!'); see also pp. 36, 53, 54, etc.; but cf. *Hibernian Magazine* (May 1782), pp. 277–9 and (July 1783), pp. 380–2. For the problems of authenticity in the texts of Grattan's speeches see Richard Koebner, 'The Early Speeches of Henry Grattan', *Bulletin of the Institute for Historical Research*, xxx (1957), 102–14. [J. Pollock,] *The Letters of Owen Roe O'Niall* (printed with Molyneux's *Case of Ireland*) (Dublin, 1782), p. 73. *Memoirs of Theobald Wolfe Tone. Written by himself...*, 2 vols. (London, 1827), I, 34, 263.

[1] John Cary, *A Vindication of the Parliament of England...* (London, 1698), p. 96: 'If this be allowed to the Gentlemen of Ireland, why should it be denied to those who are settled in our Plantations in America...?' Molyneux himself was eager to repudiate the aspersion that Ireland was a colony, *Case of Ireland*, pp. 100–1.

[2] See *The Trial of Thomas Hardy for High Treason...taken down in shorthand...*, 4 vols. (London, 1794–5). For the presentment and prosecution case see vols. I–III, 381. For Richmond's appearance in court see IV, 3–21. For Erskine's references to Pitt, Burke and Richmond's sympathy for ideas ostensibly espoused by Hardy see III, 228–33, 235–40. And for references to Richmond in the second defence speech see IV, 144–54. See also Erskine's emphasis that one of the most 'incendiary' documents in question, Henry Yorke's speech in Sheffield, derived entirely from Locke, III, 241: 'It is proved that Mr Yorke held in his hand Mr. Locke upon Government, when he delivered his speech on the Castle Hill at Sheffield.' Cf. *The Spirit of John Locke Revived...* (Sheffield, 1794).

sonality and a right as an individual to make his views felt in the conduct of politics, or whether the political rights of the populace at large were exhaustively comprised in the simple act of voting on the part of those few who were fortunate enough actually to possess the suffrage. The leading counsel for the defence, Thomas Erskine, was a lawyer of considerable skill, and the tactics he pursued were crushingly successful. The Duke of Richmond, by this date a suitably conservative peer,[1] was hauled into court to acknowledge the authorship of the bill for parliamentary reform which he had been so injudicious as to advocate in 1780 and which the society had been formed to implement in the 1790s. The past support for parliamentary reform of the prime minister himself was cited by the defence. Time after time Erskine hammered away at the same point. Mr Burke could use the language of natural rights to advocate parliamentary reform; the Duke of Richmond could use it; Mr Pitt could use it, without anyone querying their impeccable constitutionality. But if the ordinary citizen, the London artisan, were to use it, it was high treason. What possible legal justification, he demanded, could there be for such an interpretation? All that the London Corresponding Society had done was to demand parliamentary reform, and for such a demand there was unimpeachable authority. 'One of the greatest men that this country ever saw', he said, 'considered universal representation to be such an inherent part of the constitution that the King himself might grant it by his prerogative even without the Lords and Commons.' This 'maxim...stands upon the authority of Mr. Locke, the man, next to Sir Isaac Newton of the greatest strength of understanding which England perhaps ever had; high too in the favour of King William, and enjoying one of the most exalted offices in the state'.[2] The authority of Locke thus stood between the first leader of an English working-class political movement and the gallows on which William Pitt and his ministers were attempting to hang him. It was not perhaps a role which Locke would have relished. And when yet more radical agitators like Thomas Spence invoked Locke's theories of property to justify the end of the existing property structure, the role might have seemed still less appealing.[3] But it was not until

[1] On Richmond's career see Alison Gilbert Olson, *The Radical Duke: Career and Correspondence of Charles Lennox, third Duke of Richmond* (Oxford, 1961).

[2] *Trial of Thomas Hardy*, III, 243–5.

[3] Thomas Spence, *The Rights of Man as Exhibited in a Lecture...to which is now added, An Interesting Conversation...* 4th ed. (London, 1793), p. 23 (after quoting Leviticus xxv): 'Well, we have heard what God has said on the subject, let us next hear what man says. Locke in his Treatise of Government writes thus: "Whether we consider natural reason [cf. *Two Treatises*, II, §25, ll. 1–8]..."' See also p. 24: 'Here we find this great man concurring in these same fundamental principles as we shall likewise.' *The Case of Thomas Spence, Bookseller...* (London, 1792), p. 5: '...two runners, at the instance of a Mr. Reeves, came to T. Spence's stall, and bought by mistake, Spence's Rights of Man, instead of Paine's Rights of Man.

The politics of Locke in England and America

Thomas Hodgskin set out to assert the immediacy of Locke's natural right to property against the abstract legislative scheme of the Benthamites[1] and until Karl Marx fused these doctrines with the dialectic of Hegel that the fullest potential threat of Locke's work became apparent. In this form it is a threat which we have yet to meet today.

Apart from an isolated copy to be found in the library of the planter Ralph Wormely in Virginia in 1701,[2] we do not even know that copies of the *Two Treatises* reached the American colonies before 1724.[3] Even when it does become possible to trace its availability at all widely in the northern colonies, it is in a form which can have done little to encourage the casual reader. The form in which it entered the library of Harvard College between 1723 and 1725,[4] in which as a part of George Berkeley's

Immediately on which they took him, . . . before the civil magistrate. . . Mr Spence told him in his defence, that he might as well commit every one who sold Gulliver's Travels, More's Eutropia, Lock on Government, Puffendorff on the Law of Nature, &c, &c. all of which treated the subject of Government in a manner vastly opposite to the British system.' *Ibid.* p. 6. *The Important Trial of Thomas Spence* . . . (London, 1803), pp. 59–60: 'Locke's Essay on Government and many other eminent works as well as the Bible have contributed to strengthen my confidence in this my Millennial Form of Government, and therefore such Books ought in Justice to stand or fall with mine' [quotes *Two Treatises*, II, §25, ll. 1–8]. 'This Gentlemen is the Rights of Man! And upon this Rock of Nature have I built my Commonwealth, and the Gates of Hell shall not prevail against it.'

[1] Thomas Hodgskin, *The Natural and Artificial Right of Property Contrasted*. . . (London, 1832), esp. pp. 25–6 (esp. 26 n.: 'It is not a little extraordinary that every writer of any authority, since the days of Mr Locke, has theoretically adopted this view of the origin of the right of property, and has, at the same time, in defending the present right of property in practice, continually denied it') and pp. 12, 16–17, 21, 22, 24, 28, 34–6, 41–2, 53, 55, 61–2, 68, 106, 115.

[2] 'Inventory of Ralph Wormeley, II', *William and Mary College Quarterly*, 1st series, II, 3 (January 1894), 172.

[3] This does not, of course, mean that *no* other copies did reach the colonies, a most improbable state of affairs. The claims about evidence are based on the results of the following types of investigation: an examination of holdings of Locke works which can be traced back to a definite colonial provenance in some fifty of the major American libraries; an investigation of listings of libraries, published and unpublished, from the colonial period (Mr Edwin Wolf II and Professor Theodore Hornberger were extremely generous in helping me with this); an investigation of booksellers' lists in the colonies up to 1780, both those printed separately and those published in the newspapers (up to the end of 1775); an inspection of the entire file of the colonial press up to the end of 1775, of all magazines published in the colonies before 1776, and of a large proportion of the Evans microcard series. These were supplemented by further manuscript research, wherever secondary authorities suggested that this was likely to be fruitful. The results of this investigation certainly do not *demonstrate* that few Americans read the *Two Treatises* before the revolutionary period but they certainly call into severe question the evidential status of the received opinions about the *scale* of the book's distribution and consequent availability. For an early example of the way in which the reputation and the meaning of the book were absorbed by the colonial élite see the letter of the Quaker Isaac Norris I, of 1707 from England, noted by Frederick B. Tolles, *Meeting House and Counting House* (paperback ed. New York, 1963), pp. 171–2. The 1728 edition of the *Two Treatises* is the earliest of which I could trace copies with a definite colonial provenance.

[4] Cf. Harvard Catalogue, *Catalogus Librorum Bibliothecae Collegii Harvardini*. . . (Boston, 1723), containing over 2,800 titles including, e.g., Pufendorf, Grotius, Machiavelli, *Vindiciae contra*

gift it entered that of Yale College in 1733,[1] and in which as part of Governor Belcher's gift it entered the library of the college of New Jersey in 1755[2] was in the *Collected Works of Locke,* three clumsy and faintly forbidding folio volumes. The men whom we can show to have read it with any care before 1745 were few. Unlike the *Essay,* no Jonathan Edwards came upon it with the enthusiasm of a miser clutching at fine gold,[3] and no Franklin recorded his early study of it.[4] As in England, the reputation of the political writing derived from the prior reputation of the philosophy. There is no evidence that the *Two Treatises* figured in the set curriculum of any American college before the revolution,[5] though it was on the recommended list of reading at the College of Philadelphia in 1756, and William Smith was defended by his students against charges of partisanship with the claim that he never advanced any other political principles than what were warranted by their standard authors, Grotius, Pufendorf, Locke and Hutcheson.[6] This list is a decent enough indicator of the type of academic continuum in which the book was seen, a moderately unenticing academic treatise on government, a work whose relevance to political life was likely to be adventitious and occasional, but an acceptable embodiment of the current political pieties.

But this is not perhaps surprising. Its academic standing had never been all that high: it never held the unimpeachable eminence of the works of Grotius or Pufendorf. Its subject matter was too limited and it was, as a student at William and Mary College complained in 1801, so exceptionally diffuse that it almost exhausts the patience of the reader.[7] It was in its

Tyrannos, Lawson on Hobbes, Harrington, Clarendon, Bodin, etc., with the Catalogue supplement of 1725 in which the arrival of the *Complete Works* is recorded in the 3-volume London 1722 edition.

[1] Louis Shores, *Origins of the American College Library* (New York, 1935), p. 261.
[2] *Ibid.* p. 263.
[3] Sereno E. Dwight, *The Life of President Edwards,* in *Works of Jonathan Edwards* (New York, 1829–30), I, 30. Jonathan Edwards manuscript Catalogue of Books which he proposed to read, 1723–57, is in the Beinecke Library at Yale, MS. Vault. Sect. 4, Dr. 4, Folder IX. It lists as independent items Locke on *Human Understanding,* Locke on *Education,* Locke on *Toleration,* and Locke on the *Reasonableness of Christianity,* then the *Complete Works* in 3 vols. This hardly argues a consuming interest in the *Two Treatises.*
[4] *The Autobiography of Benjamin Franklin,* ed. L. W. Labaree *et al.* (New Haven, 1964), p. 64 and n.
[5] There is a convenient summary of information on this point in Anna Haddow, *Political Science in American Colleges and Universities, 1636–1900* (New York, 1939). I have confirmed this by comparing it with the standard histories of all the colonial colleges and with surviving manuscript materials from the pre-revolutionary period which remain in their libraries.
[6] T. H. Montgomery, *A History of the University of Pennsylvania. From its Foundation to AD 1770* (Philadelphia, 1900), pp. 239, 273.
[7] 'Letters from William and Mary College 1798–1801', *The Virginia Magazine of History and Biography,* XXIX, 2 (April 1921), 160: 'Another great fault in Locke is, that he is so exceptionally diffuse, and beats the same track continually over again, that he almost exhausts the patience of the reader.'

potential political utility rather than its didactic value that its enticements lay. And it was direct and focused conflict between the colonies and England which made this potential actual.

The first occasion that the work appears on the New England political scene was superbly ironic. John Checkley, a dissident and pugnacious proponent of Anglican ideas, had long been a thorn in the flesh of the Massachusetts clergy. When in 1724 he published an inoffensive and apologetic work by the English non-juror Charles Leslie and added to it a somewhat rewritten treatise on the merits of episcopacy, their patience gave way completely.[1] He was dragged into court and accused of publishing an offensive libel and of impugning the legitimacy of the king. What Checkley in fact impugned was the Whig theory of political obligation. In a parallel which gave him evident delight he demonstrated to his own satisfaction that Congregational theories of church polity rested on as absurd an historical basis as what he called republican theories of government. When some of the more incautious phrases about usurpation which he used in this demonstration were produced at his trial as evidence of his seditious attitude, he defended the criticisms of Whig political theory at greater length. Even Mr Locke, he pointed out, had been unable to make sense out of the theory—for he insisted that the vote of each individual was necessary to constitute the populace and this was plainly an impossible requirement.[2] Checkley was convicted of publishing the libel, though the jury made efforts to shelve the responsibility for the decision. But on the charge of insulting the king they made no similar attempt at evasion. In 1724 to impugn Locke's account of political obligation and argue for the tenets of patriarchalism was certainly not enough to constitute sedition and no jury was prepared to tolerate such an equation.[3] Somewhat later in the same year the Rev. John Bulkley, completing his preface to Roger Wolcott's *Poetical Meditations*, put Locke's work to a

[1] Edmund F. Slafter, *John Checkley: or the Evolution of Religious Tolerance in Massachusetts Bay...*, 2 vols. (for the Prince Society, Boston, 1897), prints most of the surviving documentation for the Checkley affair. The publication which led to his prosecution was *A Discourse Concerning Episcopacy* (added to Charles Leslie, *A Short and Easie Method with the Deists...*) (London, 1723). See esp. pp. 107–8 and 45, 53, 62–3, 98, 105, 118–19. There is a fine presentation of the significance of the episode in New England history in Perry Miller, *The New England Mind: From Colony to Province* (paperback ed., Boston, 1961), pp. 466–74.

[2] *The Speech of Mr. John Checkley upon his Tryal at Boston in New-England...* (London, 1730), pp. 11–18, esp. p. 15: 'That great Man Mr. Locke expressly says, that the free Vote of every individual is absolutely necessary to the erecting of Government, and, at the same time, says *that it is impossible to be had*. And nothing is more certain than this, that no Country or Nation can be produced, where *every one of the People* hath a free Vote in the choice of their Rulers.'

[3] Miller, *The New England Mind*, p. 473. For the legal history of Checkley's battle, see C. A. Duniway, *The Development of the Freedom of the Press in Massachusetts* (New York, 1906), pp. 84–6, 107–10.

John Dunn

more approving use.[1] Uniquely among the colonial applications of the doctrine, it claimed a relevance which Locke himself might well have considered and even accepted. The argument which he developed, an attempt to deny the legal or moral necessity of holding lands in New England by title from the Indians, was presumably of local and practical intent. But the discussion which draws at great length from Locke's chapter on property is remarkable for its intellectual poise. It refuses determinedly to transfer categories elaborated for a developed legal system to the more irregular social practice of the Indians. The subsistence pattern of the Indians was not in itself depreciated but, in an application which Locke would have approved, the lack of possible motive for the Indians to appropriate land and to labour upon it in the pre-monetary economy was used to destroy the idea that they could have appropriated any great area.[2] The traditional natural-law basis of property right, the right of occupation, was more remarkable when contrasted with the claims of labour for its legal convenience and precision than for its moral force. The Indian type of territorial occupation might well be held to meet the traditional criterion, but in the more morally exigent analysis which Bulkley drew from Locke its moral claim was deeply unimpressive. In what was probably the only sustained application of Locke's theory of property to American circumstances, the moral dignity of labour was deployed to give powerful moral embellishment to the expropriation of the Indians by the laborious and God-fearing people of New England.[3]

[1] John Bulkley, in Roger Wolcott, *Poetical Meditations, Being the Improvement of some Vacant Hours*... (New London, 1725), pp. xii–lvi, *passim*. For the background to Bulkley's concern over the basis of land titles see Richard L. Bushman, *From Puritan to Yankee: Character and the Social Order in Connecticut, 1690–1765* (Cambridge, Mass., 1967), chapter 3, esp. pp. 50, 52–3, 84–9, 93–5, 97, 99, 102. And for the continuity of Wolcott's attitudes in these disputes see *ibid*. p. 102.

[2] Bulkley, *Poetical Meditations*, pp. xxiv–xxix, xxxvi–xli, esp. p. xxxviii: '...Living almost entirely on what *Nature* prepared to their Hands, and so disproportioned in number to the quantity of their Provisions that after their Consumption of what was needful for them, there remained enough for perhaps *Ten Times the Number*, and at the same time nothing in the *Island* either because of its *Commonness* or *Perishableness* fit to supply the place of *Money*; what Inducement could such Societies have by *any Compact* either with one another, or among themselves respectively, to fix a *Property in Lands*, beyond what was done in the way before mentioned by *the Law of Nature*, for my own part I can't Excogitate any.'

[3] There was nothing original in the substance of this claim. It stretches back at least as far as Thomas More. See *Utopia, Complete Works of St. Thomas More*, ed. Edward Surtz, S. J., and J. H. Hexter (New Haven, 1965), IV, 136, ll. 14–17: 'nam eam justissimam belli causam ducunt, quum populus quispiam ejus soli quo ipse non utitur, sed velut inane ac vacuum possidet, aliis tamen qui ex naturae praescripto inde nutriri debeant, usum ac possessionem interdicat', etc. It justified the Puritans in their early confrontations with the Indians (see Alden T. Vaughan, *New England Frontier. Puritans and Indians 1620–1675* (Boston, 1965), esp. pp. 104–21 (but cf. Chester E. Eisinger, 'The Puritans' Justification for taking the Land', *Essex Institute Historical Collections*, LXXXIV (1948), 131–43); Wilcomb E. Washburn, 'The Moral and Legal Justifications for Dispossessing the Indians', in *Seventeenth-Century America*, ed. James

The politics of Locke in England and America

In the years that followed the book was distributed more widely—the first separate edition which is frequently to be found in American libraries is that of 1728. It attained a degree of casual acceptance which made it easy for Jared Eliot to refer to it in his election sermon of 1738 at one point for a single particularly dubious historical argument, without it having any noticeable impact on the doctrine expounded. Eliot's theological views were of course a trifle spineless, and it is not surprising that he should have assumed a rather Anglican assurance about the implications of the book. The doctrine of the sermon was less than incisive, a banal reiteration of the need for legality in just government.[1] A sharper insight into the radical implications of the work came with Elisha Williams's anonymous pamphlet of 1744. In the emotional context of the Great Awakening, Locke's dignified intellectual insistence on autonomy of judgment becomes sharply radical. The theory of government which Eliot had expounded in 1738 was no more secular than that contained in John Wise's work of 1717[2] and it was considerably less radical. The religious structure of New England might have become a trifle etiolated by 1738 in comparison with the great days of Winthrop, but the solid fabric of social order did not seem to have been noticeably impaired. Yet six years later in Williams's dazzling assault all the lineaments of authority were wrenched aside. Locke's notions of toleration were fused with a brilliant presentation of his theory of government, and a doctrine of startling originality appeared. Williams was not in any sense a secluded scholar without understanding of the lives of men in the world. He had seen the Great Awakening tear apart the staid order of New England society and he meant just what he said when he insisted that no act was a religious act without the understanding and choice of the agent, that it was every man's duty to concern himself actively with public affairs, that for the civil power to attempt to exert any influence whatever upon the religious practice of individuals

Morton Smith (Chapel Hill, 1959), pp. 15–32), and it remained a major strain of apologetic throughout much of subsequent Indian–white relations, see e.g. William T. Hagan, *American Indians* (Chicago, 1961), pp. 39, 43, 68–9, 140. For its significance in the interpretation of American history see esp. Louis Hartz, *The Founding of New Societies* (New York, 1964), pp. 94–9. My point here is that this example does not show Locke imposing a new language or a new vision on the bemused Connecticut minister but rather that it records his delighted recognition that 'that Great Man Mr. Lock' was speaking in the most reassuringly familiar of accents.

[1] Jared Eliot, *Give Cesar his Due. Or, The Obligation that Subjects are under to their Civil Rulers...* (New London, 1738). Cf. the work as a whole with the statement on p. 27.

[2] John Wise, *A Vindication of the Government of the New England Churches* (Boston, 1717). There was a time when scholars detected 'the influence of Locke' in this work (but then there was a time when one of the most distinguished of American historians detected the possible influence of Locke's *Essay* on the Harvard curriculum before the book had been printed in any form). For an astute placing of the work see Miller, *The New England Mind*, pp. 289–302.

was blasphemy.[1] When the cool epistemological individualism of the scholar's closet was fused with the insistent Puritan demand for emotional autonomy, the two became transmuted into a doctrine which in the radicalism of its immediate and self-conscious social vision could not have been conceived anywhere else in the eighteenth-century world. It is possible that Williams's practical political intentions were little more radical than those of Wise, but the explicit implication of his work was more radical than any society in the early eighteenth century could have accepted.

Locke's writings on toleration played a minor role in the controversies of the Great Awakening as they did later in the controversy over the taxing of the Baptists to maintain the Congregational clergy.[2] They emerged, for instance, in the course of a fracas between President Clap and a New Light student at Yale.[3] But the *Two Treatises* evoked on the whole less interest. By the time that they appear prominently in colonial controversies with England, early in the 1760s, they had become an uncontentious and somewhat unexciting work. The role they played in the ensuing controversies in the instructions which the committee of the Massachusetts General Court, including incidentally Thomas Hutchinson, drew up in June 1762 to send to their new agent Jasper Mauduit[4] and the work of Otis later in that year,[5] through the full run of the revolutionary pamphlets, to the Declaration of Independence itself, was not conceptually a very interesting one. Over the preceding century the colonies had elaborated a tradition of political behaviour in which the

---

[1] [Elisha Williams,] *The essential Rights and Liberties of Protestants. A seasonable Plea for the Liberty of Conscience and the Right of private Judgement...* (Boston, 1744), pp. 2–8, 12, and esp. p. 6: '...I cannot forbear taking notice of *one Point of Liberty* which all Members of a free State and particularly *Englishmen* think belonging to them, and are fond of; and that is the *Right* that *everyone* has *to speak his Sentiments openly* concerning *such Matters as affect the good of the whole*. Every Member of a Community ought to be concerned for the *whole*...' On Williams see the biography by Clifford K. Shipton in *Sibley's Harvard Graduates*, v, 588–97, and Francis Parsons, 'Elisha Williams: Minister, Soldier, President of Yale', *Papers of the New Haven Colony Historical Society*, VII (1908), 188–217. For the impact of the Great Awakening on Connecticut see Edwin S. Gaustad, *The Great Awakening in New England* (New York, 1957), and Bushman, *From Puritan to Yankee*, esp. pp. 195, 230.

[2] For Backus's use of Locke see esp. his *Seasonable Plea for Liberty of Conscience...* (Boston, 1770) and *A Letter to a Gentleman in the Massachusetts General Assembly...* (n.p., 1771). His major interest in Locke was always as an exponent of the right of toleration, and he does not seem to have acquired a copy of Locke on *Government* until the appearance of the Boston 1773 printing (see T. B. Maston, *Isaac Backus: Pioneer of Religious Liberty*, London, 1962, p. 75 n.). He seems to have developed his main ideas before there is any reason to suppose that he had read Locke (see Maston, *op. cit.* pp. 105–6). The major biographical source is Alvah Hovey, *A Memoir of the Life and Times of the Rev. Isaac Backus, A.M.* (Boston, 1858).

[3] Louis L. Tucker, *Puritan Protagonist: President Thomas Clap of Yale College* (Chapel Hill, N.C., 1962), p. 146.

[4] *Jasper Mauduit, Agent in London for the province of Massachusetts-Bay, 1762–65*, *Massachusetts Historical Society Collections*, LXXIV (1918), 39–40. 12 June 1762.

[5] James Otis, *A Vindication of the Conduct of the House of Representatives of the Province of the Massachusetts-Bay...* (Boston, 1762), pp. 17–20.

actual structure of social authority had become increasingly divorced from the formal structure of political authority, in which the operational control was no longer seriously dependent upon a hierarchical legal order under the crown of England. As Professor Greene has shown with great cogency,[1] the political tradition which the colonists had thus evolved was perceived by them firmly in terms of English precedent and within English legal forms, but it no longer bore any clear relationship to the English view of their constitutional status. The legal order which they saw as existing in America was superbly unLockean, almost wholly the creation of prescription as opposed to formal legality. But by the 1760s there were few in the colonies who did not see it as the legal order. Within the very general prescriptions of the Navigation Laws the lords of trade and the plantations and their local emissaries, the governors, were, on the occasions when they attempted to intrude, closer to being a diplomatic problem than an effective political superior. The cant of the disputes between governors and assemblies was belligerently constitutional in character, but the feeling behind it was seldom brought to any inter-colonial focus. Moderate English conservatives like Hawkins claimed that the only argument that was ever used to justify the American revolution was Locke's doctrine of the illegitimacy of taxation without consent.[2] But this was certainly not the only portion of Locke's work that was brought to bear in the course of the struggle. Not only was the fundamental basis of the rights of Massachusetts in 1762, or the illegality of every fresh substantive attack by the British parliament, proclaimed with the phrases of Locke; but even Hutchinson's summoning of the General Court to meet in Cambridge instead of Boston was subjected to the same assault.[3] The precise application of the book varied enormously, but the form remained identical. There existed a legal order, and the political moves of the English government or the governor of Massachusetts were in breach of this order. Endlessly the work of Locke was summoned to expound the tautology that illegality was not legal. Gradually their notion of the legal order changed and grew more coherent. At one point in this transition, over the specific issue of taxation, Locke's text was of some precise assistance, but for the most part it could only

[1] Jack P. Greene, *The Quest for Power; The Lower Houses of Assembly in the Southern Royal Colonies 1689–1776* (Chapel Hill, N.C., 1963). See also more extendedly J. R. Pole, *Political Representation in England and the Origins of the American Republic* (London, 1966).
[2] Sir John Hawkins, *The Life of Samuel Johnson, LL.D.* (London, 1787), p. 503.
[3] *The Writings of Samuel Adams*, ed. H. A. Cushing (New York, 1906), II, 22 (House of Representatives to Lieutenant-Governor Hutchinson, 3 August 1770): 'We beg Leave to recite to your Honor what the Great Mr. Locke has advanced in his Treatise of civil Government, upon the like Prerogative of the Crown.' See also p. 23: 'We would however, by no means be understood to suggest that this People have Occasion at present to proceed to such Extremity.'

form a passage in a circular argument. And at times the phrasing was less than happy. 'I know', complained Thomas Hutchinson, after being read a particularly severe lecture by Sam Adams, 'of no conspiracy to destroy you.'[1] It was often difficult to see the relevance of the citations from Locke at such a point. Hutchinson's irritable incomprehension was a little reminiscent of John Cary's answer to Molyneux—whatever Locke had been talking about he had clearly not been talking about the propriety of holding the General Court in Cambridge.[2]

Those who read Locke differently, and on the whole more accurately, were in many cases men with closer ties to England, and with more of a feel for the political or social world of which the intruding governors were the emissaries. Only the redoubtable near auto-didact Boucher, product of the archaic northern counties of England, felt called upon to challenge frontally the whole conceptual system within which the colonists were operating. Many of the other Tories, particularly the Anglican clergy, probably held a very similar basic view of politics to that of Boucher. But it took a man of considerable intelligence who had both fought his own way up in a hierarchical society and then attempted to transfer the rigid attitudes thus acquired to a very different society, to feel the emotional need to call in question the entire structure of American political argument with such stubborn insistence. That there was little or nothing original in his presentation of the High Anglican position he himself acknowledged and is scarcely the point.[3] What is significant is the practical realism, emotional subservience or theoretical paralysis

[1] Thomas Hutchinson, *History of the Colony and Province of Massachusetts-Bay*, ed. Lawrence Shaw Mayo, 3 vols. (Cambridge, Mass., 1936), III, 395: 'Your quotation from Mr. Locke, detached as it is from the rest of the treatise, cannot be applied to your case. I know of no attempt to enslave or destroy you, and as you, very prudently, would not be understood to suggest that this people have occasion at present to proceed to such extremity as to appeal to heaven, I am at a loss to conceive for what good purpose you adduce it.'

[2] Cf. *ibid.* with [John Cary,] *A Vindication of the Parliament of England...* (London, 1698), p. 103: 'Pray what means all the Clamour you have made against our late Kings and the Parliaments of England, for infringing your Liberties and breaking through the very design of settling Communities, and putting you in a worse Condition than you were in the state of Nature. You are very much beholding to the ingenious Mr Lock for the fineness of your Argument about the State of Conquest Etc in the former part of your Book, which I do not at all blame you for, because I think no Man can handle a Subject smoothly, whereon he hath treated, that doth not follow his Copy; but I blame you for not applying those excellent Arguments more fitly.' Hutchinson himself extended his exposition of the very different implications of Locke's political theory in his unpublished writings, see e.g. *Massachusetts Archives*, xxv, 121–35 etc. (My attention was called to these by Professor R. Calhoon of the University of North Carolina, Greensboro.)

[3] Boucher, *Causes and Consequences of the American Revolution*, see esp. pp. 486–7, on continuity of the Church of England's doctrine of non-resistance, and pp. 495–560 *passim*. It is not certain that the text of the sermon as published in 1797 was the same as that of 1775. The heavy footnote documentation seems to assimilate the polemic against Locke to the more systematic critique of Locke developed by the group of High Anglicans to which Boucher belonged in the early 1790s. See p. 61, n. 2 above.

which made the other Anglican clergy incapable of all but the most superficial and tactical of reactionary polemics.

If Boucher was almost the only authentic Tory to take the Lockean argument seriously, there was at least one other man, as near to being a neutral in the struggle as an American could well be, who took it equally seriously. Peter Van Schaack, a prominent New York lawyer, had been an enthusiastic supporter of the earlier stages of the colonial resistance, but by 1776 he had begun to develop qualms of conscience.[1] Eventually he retired to his country farm and settled down to read the standard authorities on political theory. After deep consideration and a peculiarly close perusal of the works of Locke, he decided that the provocations of the British government were not in fact adequate to justify revolution, that they had indeed acted with persistent injustice, but that it was not clear that their motives were in any sense malicious, or threatening enough to free a subject from his duty of obedience.[2] Van Schaack did not approach the text of the book with a mind made up—he continued to feel emotionally close to the colonists throughout the war and he remained a close friend of several of the revolutionary leaders. The Adamses and Jefferson, Dickinson and Franklin, Otis and Madison, had come to read the *Two Treatises* with gradually consolidated political intentions and they had come to it to gather moral support for these intentions. Van Schaack came to it in conscientious indecision and what he found in it—to hazard a wild historical conjecture—was probably closer than any other man in America to the prescriptions which Locke himself saw in it. To most men in America by 1774 the affective force which attached to the duty to obey social norms, the internalized structure of social control, had become irrevocably detached from the legal order of the English polity. The authority which they felt and responded to was an authority operative in their own society. It was not a formal symbol across the ocean. Only a man with a somewhat abstract sense of social obligation or a man with a

[1] Henry C. Van Schaack, *The Life of Peter Van Schaack, LL.D.* . . . (New York, 1842), pp. 16–47 (leading role in early resistance of New York), pp. 54–8 (conscientious doubts and casuistry of the right of resistance, January 1776).

[2] *Ibid.* pp. 56–7: 'In short, I think these acts may have been passed without a preconcerted plan of enslaving us, and it appears to me that the more favourable interpretation ought ever to be put on the conduct of our rulers. I cannot therefore think the government *dissolved*; and as long as the society lasts, the power that every individual gave the society when he entered into it, can never revert to the individuals again, but will always remain in the community (Locke).' See also p. 57: 'I am fully convinced, that men of the greatest abilities, and the soundest integrity, have taken parts in this war with America, and their measures should have a fair trial. But this is too serious a matter, implicitly to yield to the authority of any characters, however respectable. Every man must exercise his own reason, and judge for himself; "for he that appeals to Heaven, must be sure that he has right on his side", according to Mr. Locke.' And see p. 58, for his systematic consultation of authorities in the effort to 'enlighten his mind'.

John Dunn

great capacity to infuse emotional seriousness into an oath taken to a shadowy entity in a distant country could feel the duty of political obedience with any immediacy. Only such a man could feel any emotional pressure to stand on his own for conscience' sake against the mass emotional certitude of his countrymen.

Once the climactic point, the outbreak of revolution, was past, the book was never again to be such an intellectual cynosure or to display such an apparent relevance. John Adams's remark that the constitution of Massachusetts embodied the doctrines of Locke and Sydney was a piece of rhetoric rather than an analytical point.[1] The analytical position was better stated by Benjamin Rush in his dismissal of the book's relevance to the formation of the constitution of Pennsylvania. It was a work of pure theory.[2] Even Jefferson, while he recommended it as being perfect as far as it went, promptly observed that if one descended from theory to practice *The Federalist* was an excellent work.[3] For the most part Americans found no need in the ensuing years to ascend to a level more theoretical than that of *The Federalist*, and by the time that they did need to do so Locke's work had become a historical curiosity. A man as sophisticated as Francis Lieber could mourn that political theory had ended with Locke,[4] and George Fitzhugh could still at times identify the philosophy of *laissez-faire* individualism which he was engaged in excoriating as the theory of Locke,[5] but the book was never again to

[1] *The Works of John Adams...*, ed. Charles Francis Adams, 10 vols. (Boston, 1850–6), IV, 216: 'There never was an example of such precautions as are taken by this wise and jealous people in the formation of their government. None was ever made so perfectly upon the principle of the people's rights and equality. It is Locke, Sidney, and Rousseau and De Mably reduced to practice, in the first instance.' For the relative interest manifested by Adams in Locke as a philosopher and Locke as a political writer before the heights of the revolutionary struggle cf. *Diary & Autobiography of John Adams*, ed. L. H. Butterfield *et al.* (paperback ed. New York, 1964), I, 177, III, 272, etc. with III, 358–9: 'I had read Harrington, Sydney, Hobbs, Nedham and Lock, but with very little Application to any particular Views: till these Debates in Congress...' (November–December 1775).

[2] Benjamin Rush, *Observations on the Government of Pennsylvania*, in *Selected Writings of Benjamin Rush* (New York, 1947), p. 78: 'It is one thing to understand the *principles*, and another thing to understand the *forms* of government. The former are simple; the latter are difficult and complicated...Who understood the principles of mechanics and optics better than Sir Isaac Newton? and yet Sir Isaac could not for his life have made a watch or a microscope. Mr. Locke is an oracle as to the *principles*, Harrington and Montesquieu are oracles as to the *forms* of government.'

[3] Jefferson to Thomas Mann Randolph, Jr., 30 May 1790, *The Papers of Thomas Jefferson*, ed. J. P. Boyd (Princeton, 1961), XVI, 449: 'Locke's little book on Government is perfect as far as it goes. Descending from theory to practice there is no better book than the Federalist.'

[4] Francis Lieber, *Manual of Political Ethics...* (Boston, 1838), p. 356. MS. note in Lieber's own copy, now in library of Johns Hopkins University: 'All this I will present clearer. and mention how the English mind left the theory of politics and turned to political economy entirely. Pol. theory ended with Locke, and pol. econ. began with Adam Smith.'

[5] George Fitzhugh, *Cannibals All...*, ed. C. Vann Woodward (Cambridge, Mass., 1960), pp. 12–13; p. 71: 'Modern social reformers, except Mr. Carlyle, proceeding upon the theory

be an emotional or conceptual focus in the discussion of the politics of the nation.

Whether the book had ever exercised causal impact upon the way men thought, whether it had ever been more than the most distinguished name that could be appended to men's prior political convictions, whether it gave to the American revolution more than a few specific phrases, remains hard to tell. But some points can now be made clearer. The claim that Locke's book exercised a great influence in America can be put in a stronger and a weaker form. The stronger form is simple—that most educated Americans derived their view of politics directly from it. This is not persuasive. The book was of no great popularity before 1750 and the tradition of political behaviour[1] within which the colonists conceived their relationship with England was already highly articulated by this date in its most general values, though not of course in its specific understanding of the constitutional relationship. It cannot have been Locke's *Two Treatises* which taught them this tradition of behaviour because there is no reason to suppose that many people had read it with care in the colonies by 1750. The weaker form seems more appealing—that the ideas were absorbed by a sort of intellectual osmosis, so that Americans could be of Locke's party without knowing it, rather as men earlier in the century could be Newtonians without having read a word of the *Principia*. The analogy seems tempting but is entirely spurious. The *Principia* achieved an immediate European pre-eminence. It was recognized as being a distinctively new achievement, a watershed in both science and philosophy. The *Two Treatises* never enjoyed such an unchallenged European reputation. It was not even particularly widely known outside the English-speaking world for eighty years after its composition and it became well

of Locke, which is the opposite of Aristotle, propose to dissolve and disintegrate society, falsely supposing that they thereby follow nature. There is not a human tie that binds man to man that they do not propose to cut "sheer asunder".' See also George Fitzhugh, *Sociology for the South . . .* (Richmond, Virginia, 1854), pp. 187, 209. See also the letter of Fitzhugh to George Frederick Holmes, quoted in Harvey Wish, *George Fitzhugh, Propagandist of the Old South* (Baton Rouge, 1943), pp. 118–19. For Fitzhugh's championship of Filmer against Locke see esp. Vann Woodward's introduction to *Cannibals All* and cf., for Holmes's views of Locke, the MS. notes on *Two Treatises* in his edition of the *Collected Works* in the Alderman Library, University of Virginia.

[1] Caroline Robbins, *The Eighteenth Century Commonwealthman* (Cambridge, Mass., 1959), presents exhaustive documentation of the more radical exponents of this theme, and J. G. A. Pocock, 'Machiavelli, Harrington, and English Political Ideologies in the Eighteenth Century', *William and Mary Quarterly*, 3rd series, XXII, 4 (October 1965), 549–83 provides a brilliant interpretation of the character of its development. The history of its reception in America has been illuminated by many American scholars, notably Professor Douglass Adair. The most effective recent treatments at length are H. Trevor Colbourn, *The Lamp of Experience. Whig History and the Intellectual Origins of the American Revolution* (Chapel Hill, N.C., 1965) (on historical writing), and Bailyn, *Ideological Origins of the American Revolution* (on the whole range of ideas).

known then only because of the huge influence of Locke's epistemology. It was never recognized as being peculiarly original, and in those points in which it was considered to be so, it was frequently regarded as being mistaken. Above all it was only one work among a large group of other works which expounded the Whig theory of the revolution, and its prominence within this group is not noticeable until well after the general outlines of the interpretation had become consolidated. The readiness with which many scholars have detected the influence of the *Two Treatises* in England and America is at least in part a product of the fact that they have read so little else of the English political writing contemporary with it.

The intellectual stature of the book's author can hardly have been without some slight influence in making respectable sundry of the doctrines which it contained. But the work's prominence in controversy in America was largely confined to the post-1760 constitutional writings of the highly educated, and if we wish to understand the literary influences upon the rhetoric in which the dispute was conducted at all levels but the most legalistic, and the sentiments to which this rhetoric gave expression, we need to look at works which were a good deal less demanding on the intellect and exhausting to the patience. For the American population at large the revolution may have been about many things, but in very few cases can it possibly have been thought to have been in any sense about the *Two Treatises of Government* of John Locke.[1]

[1] The most memorable expression of this point of view is perhaps Judge Mellen Chamberlain's interview in 1842 with a ninety-one-year-old veteran of Concord: 'Then I suppose you had been reading Harington or Sidney and Locke about the eternal principles of liberty?' 'Never heard of 'em. We read only the Bible, the Catechism, Watts' Psalms and Hymns, and the Almanac.' Quoted from Samuel Eliot Morison, *The Oxford History of the American People* (London, 1965), p. 212.

The family and the origins of the state in Locke's political philosophy[1]

by GORDON J. SCHOCHET

It has been the genius of recent scholarship to question seriously—if not to dispel altogether—one of the standard myths associated with the political philosophy of John Locke—that the target of Locke's *Two Treatises* was the contractual absolutism of Thomas Hobbes. Peter Laslett has presented compelling reasons for believing, on the contrary, that Locke was criticizing the divine-right patriarchalism of Sir Robert Filmer.[2] So bold a reassessment of Locke's purpose is an invitation to reinterpret the substance of his teaching as well, for it calls attention to questions that were not previously recognized as important. Among them is the relationship that Locke saw between political and paternal authority; this essay is devoted to an analysis of that relationship.

There is no question that Locke's *First Treatise* was a direct and in some cases a virtual page-by-page criticism of Filmer's political writings. Locke himself described the *First Treatise* as an essay in which '*The False Principles and Foundation* of Sir *Robert Filmer*, And His Followers, Are Detected and Overthrown'.[3] However, it is no longer sufficient to say that Locke's critique of patriarchalism consisted of a detailed exegesis of biblical passages, a refutation of Sir Robert's view that Adam had been an absolute patriarchal sovereign, and a demonstration that paternal political power (even if it had once existed) had not descended through Adam's heirs to the English House of Stuart.[4] What must be equally understood

[1] This article was presented, in somewhat different form, to a conference on the Thought of John Locke at York University in Toronto, Canada, on 2 December 1966. I wish to thank Benjamin Lippincott, Gerald Pomper, and Neal Wood for reading and commenting upon earlier versions. Publication has been assisted by the Research Council of Rutgers, The State University.

[2] See *John Locke: Two Treatises of Government*, ed. Peter Laslett (Cambridge, 1960), Introduction, esp. pp. 45–78.

[3] Title-page of the 1698 printing of the *Two Treatises* as reproduced in Laslett's edition, p. 153.

[4] See, for instance, Richard I. Aaron, *John Locke*, 2nd ed. (Oxford, 1955), pp. 274–5; Maurice Cranston, *John Locke: A Biography* (London, 1957), p. 209; Harold J. Laski, *Political Thought in England: Locke to Bentham*, reset ed. (London, 1949), p. 29; Sir Frederick Pollock, 'Locke's Theory of the State', *Proceedings of the British Academy 1903–1904*, reprinted in *Political Thought in Perspective*, ed. William Ebenstein (New York, 1957), pp. 292–3; and to a lesser extent

is that the very logic and structure of the whole of the *Two Treatises* were responses to Filmer, for only through such a realization is it possible both to appreciate why Locke was interested in certain problems and to grasp the implications of some of the very fine distinctions that he drew.[1]

Locke specifically and emphatically distinguished between the powers of political superiors and fathers throughout his *Two Treatises*, attributing 'the great mistakes of late about Government' to the 'confounding [of] these distinct Powers one with another'.[2] This difference lay at the heart of his political philosophy, and as early as section two of the *Second Treatise* he wrote:

...I think it may not be amiss, to set down what I take to be Political Power. That the Power of a *Magistrate* over a Subject may be distinguished from that of a *Father* over his children, a *Master* over his Servant, a *Husband* over his Wife, and a *Lord* over his Slave. All which distinct Powers happening sometimes together in the same Man, if he be considered under these different Relations, it may help us to distinguish these Powers one from another, and shew the difference betwixt a Ruler of a Common-wealth, a Father of a Family, and a Captain of a Galley.[3]

The distinctions between patriarchal and political authority were evident from their varying origins and ends, Locke contended. '*Nature gives* the first of these, *viz. Paternal Power to Parents* for the Benefit of their Children ...*Voluntary Agreement gives* the second, *viz. Political Power to Governours* for the Benefit of their Subjects...'[4]

Locke had not been eager to separate paternal from political authority throughout his life. In 1672, in a topical sketch of knowledge under the general heading 'Sapientia', he accepted 'Jus Paternum' along with 'Consensus populi' as the 'Fundamenta' of politics.[5] Locke added 'Arma' in his own hand to a later version of this outline prepared by his copyist

George H. Sabine, *A History of Political Theory*, 2nd ed. (New York, 1950), p. 524. For a striking reversal, based on Laslett, compare Sabine's comments on the same page of the third (1961) edition of his text. Despite its age, John Neville Figgis, *The Divine Right of Kings*, 2nd ed. (1914) (paperback ed., New York, 1965), pp. 156–60, is somewhat more relevant than the works cited above.

[1] See Sterling P. Lamprecht, *The Moral and Political Philosophy of John Locke* (New York, 1918), pp. 126–30 (Locke's state of nature viewed as a response to Filmer); Richard Schlatter, *Private Property: The History of an Idea* (London, 1951), p. 157 (Locke's theory of property and Filmer); and David G. Ritchie, *Natural Rights: A Criticism of Some Political and Ethical Conceptions* (London, 1894), p. 91 (Locke's discussion of marriage as an answer to Filmer). J. P. Plamenatz, *Man and Society*, 2 vols. (London, 1963), I, 214, suggests that Locke's methodology is not very important.

[2] *Two Treatises*, II, § 169.
[3] *Ibid.* II, § 2. See also II, § 71.   [4] *Ibid.* II, § 173.
[5] Bodleian Library, MS. Locke c. 28, fo. 41. An earlier version of this same division—taken from a 1661 manuscript—has now been published. See *John Locke: Two Tracts on Government*, ed. Philip Abrams (Cambridge, 1967), p. 245.

The family and origins of the state

Sylvester Brounower.[1] Similarly, in his early essays on things indifferent—recently published as *Two Tracts on Government*—Locke observed:

Now I find that there are, among the authors who discuss this question [the sources of civil authority], commonly two such foundations...[S]ome suppose men to be born in servitude, others, to liberty. The latter assert an equality between men founded on the law of nature, while the former maintain a paternal right over children and claim that government originates thence...

To these a third way of constituting civil power may perhaps be added: One in which all authority is held to come from God but the nomination and appointment of the person bearing that power is thought to be made by the people. Otherwise a right to govern will not easily be derived from the paternal right nor a right of life and death from the popular.

However, I offer no conclusion about these theories, nor do I consider it of any relevance to our present controversy whether one or other of them be true.[2]

The young Locke does not appear to have been nearly so interested in the origin of political organization as he was to become by the time he wrote the *Two Treatises*.[3] Then, of course, 'Jus Paternum' and 'Consensus populi' were no longer regarded as equally valid bases for the state.

Locke's description of familial power—its source, nature, and extent—is fundamental to his analysis of the relation between patriarchalism and politics. He held that procreation alone is not the source of paternal authority. God, not man, is the maker of children; the rights of fathers cannot spring from generation when the parents are merely God's unwitting agents. 'They who say the *Father* gives life to his Children, are so dazled with the thoughts of Monarchy, that they do not, as they ought, remember God, who is *the Author and Giver of Life: 'Tis in him alone we live, move, and have our Being'*, Locke wrote. God 'is *King* because he is indeed Maker of us all, which no Parents can pretend to be of their Children'.[4] The parents' role in procreation was succinctly described:

What Father of a Thousand, when he begets a Child, thinks farther than the satisfying his present Appetite? God in his infinite Wisdom has put strong desires of Copulation into the Constitution of Men, thereby to continue the race of Mankind, which he doth most commonly without the intention, and often against the Consent and Will of the Begetter. And indeed those who desire and design Children, are but the occasions of their being, and when they design and wish to beget them, do little more towards their making, than *Ducalion* and his Wife in the Fable did towards the making of Mankind, by throwing Pebbles over their Heads.[5]

[1] Bodleian Library, MS. Locke c. 28, fo. 157^v.
[2] Locke, *Two Tracts*, ed. Abrams, pp. 230 and 231.
[3] See *Two Treatises*, Introduction, pp. 19–21 and nn.
[4] *Two Treatises*, I, §§52 and 53. See also II, §65 (especially ll. 7–9).
[5] *Ibid.* I, §54.

Thus, men are 'all the Workmanship of one Omnipotent, and infinitely wise Maker;...[and] they are his Property, whose Workmanship they are'.[1] Similarly, Locke wrote in his *Journal* for 1678 that if a man

comprehend the relation between father & son & finde it reasonable that his son whom he hath begot (only in persuance of his pleasure without thinking of his son), & nourished should obey law & reverence him & be grateful to him, he can not but finde it much more reasonable, that he & every other man should obey & rever law & thank the author of their being to whom they owe all that they are.[2]

The authority to discipline children was not, according to Locke, a necessary attribute of fatherhood, and since it was exercised over God's creatures, it could be held and executed only through some degree of divine dispensation. Beginning with Adam and Eve, all parents were placed 'by the Law of Nature, *under an obligation to preserve, nourish, and educate the Children*, they had begotten, not as their own Workmanship, but as the Workmanship of their own Maker, the Almighty, to whom they were to be accountable for them'.[3] On this ground, Locke said, 'The *Power*, then, *that Parents have* over their Children, arises from that Duty which is incumbent on them, to take care of their Off-spring, during the imperfect state of Childhood'.[4] Thus, in the *First Treatise*, Locke implied that the child was bound to obey whoever nourished and cared for him, whether that person was his natural father or not;[5] and in the *Second Treatise* he specifically said:

Nay, this *power* so little belongs to the *Father* by any peculiar right of Nature, but only as he is Guardian of his Children, that when he quits his Care of them, he loses his power over them, which goes along with their Nourishment and Education, to which it is inseparably annexed, and it belongs as much to the *Foster-Father* of an exposed Child, as to the Natural Father of another...It is but a help to the weakness and imperfection of their Nonage, a Discipline necessary to their Education.[6]

Locke assumed that familial authority belonged to the mother as much as to the father, and he never seemed to tire of pointing out to Filmer's

---

[1] *Two Treatises*, ii, §6. Both of these notions—that men are the workmanship and property of God—are repeated throughout the *Two Treatises*. For references, see Laslett's note to ll. 10–14 of this section.

[2] Locke, *Journal*, 1678, Bodleian Library, MS. Locke f. 3, fo. 202; entry dated 15 July and titled 'Lex Na[tur]ae'.

[3] *Two Treatises*, ii, §56. See also ii, §60 (ll. 17–20).

[4] *Ibid.* ii, §58.   [5] *Ibid.* i, §100.

[6] *Ibid.* ii, §65. See also ii, §69 (ll. 4–8). In March, 1679, Locke made the following entry concerning the children of the Canadian Indians in his reading notes: 'Education not generation gives the obligation & the affection, for the children taken prisoners when men made wars against their parents & country [lived] as heartily as any...' Bodleian Library, MS. Locke c. 33, fo. 10.

apologists that the fifth commandment[1] ordered children to obey both parents, not just the father as Sir Robert implied.[2] Even if the power to control children came from generation, Locke asserted, 'This would give the *Father* but a joynt Dominion with the Mother over them. For no body can deny but that the Woman hath an equal share, if not the greater, as nourishing the Child a long time in her own Body out of her own Substance'.[3] Thus, Locke contended that paternal power might 'more properly [be] called *Parental Power*. For whatever obligation Nature and the right of Generation lays on Children, it must certainly bind them equal to both concurrent Causes of it'.[4] However, Locke soon forgot his own injunction and reverted to the phrase '*Paternal* Power',[5] subsequently suggesting that the terms were interchangeable.[6]

In most matters Locke treated the husband as the superior mate, since 'the Rule, should be placed somewhere [when there are differences between husband and wife], it naturally falls to the Man's share, as the abler and stronger'. Marriage, according to Locke, is a contractual relationship that 'leaves the Wife in the full and free possession of what...is her peculiar Right, and gives the Husband no more power over her Life, than she has over his'. Man's superiority extends only 'to the things of their common Interest and Property',[7] and the conjugal power does not provide the basis of government. If the subjugation of Eve by divine *fiat* gave Adam a monarchical power over her as Filmer had claimed, 'there will be as many Monarchs as there are Husbands', for what was bestowed upon Adam was 'the Power that every Husband hath to order the things of private Concernment in his Family'.[8] It can certainly be inferred from these remarks, however, that final authority over children, which would undoubtedly be among 'the things of their common Interest and Property', belonged to the husband, for Locke does not seem to have questioned this aspect of the traditional patriarchal family.

Parental power is necessary, Locke reasoned, because of the inability of infants to take their places in the world of men, a justification that

---

[1] Exod. xx. 12: 'Honour thy father and thy mother: that thy days may be long upon the land which the LORD thy God giveth thee.'
[2] *Two Treatises*, I, §§6, 11, and 60–6. Cf. II, §§52–3. For Filmer's use of the fifth commandment see *Patriarcha and Other Political Works of Sir Robert Filmer*, ed. Peter Laslett (Oxford, 1949), pp. 62 and 283.
[3] *Two Treatises*, I, §55.   [4] *Ibid.* II, §52.
[5] *Ibid.* II, §69. See Laslett's note to l. 1.
[6] '...*Paternal* or *Parental Power* is nothing but that, which Parents have over their Children...' (*Ibid.* II, §170.) At one point, he said, '*Nature gives...Paternal Power to Parents...*' (*Ibid.* II, §173.)
[7] *Ibid.* II, §82. See also II, §78: '*Conjugal Society* is made by a voluntary Compact between Man and Woman.'
[8] *Ibid.* I, §48. The biblical allusion is to Gen. iii. 16. For Filmer's statement see *Patriarcha*, ed. Laslett, p. 283.

Gordon J. Schochet

Sir Leslie Stephen described as 'simple utilitarianism'.[1] Discipline exists 'for the Benefit of Children during their Minority, to supply their want of Ability, and understanding how to manage their Property'.[2] The parent–child relationship is, therefore, more properly regarded as 'the Priviledge of Children, and Duty of Parents, than any Prerogative of Paternal Power'.[3] Children are born 'ignorant and without the use of *Reason*'[4] and therefore do not enjoy 'that *equal Right* that every Man hath, *to his Natural Freedom*, without being subjected to the Will or Authority of any other Man'.[5] Thus, familial authority as understood by Locke was not in conflict with the principle of natural equality, a criticism that Filmer had made of the anti-patriarchalists of his own day.[6]

In addition, subjection to parents—however legitimate—is only temporary, Locke reasoned, for its bonds 'are like the Swadling Cloths they [infants] are wrapt up in, and supported by, in the weakness of their Infancy. Age and Reason, as they grow up, loosen them till at length they drop quite off, and leave a Man at his own free Disposal.'[7] Parental control serves the double functions of educating and preparing the child for the time when he will be the master of his own actions and simultaneously directing his life by taking the place of the private will and understanding that have not yet developed. But once the child reaches the age of discretion and reason, according to Locke, he achieves the equality of which his infancy had deprived him. The father's 'power of Commanding ends with Nonage',[8] for 'when he comes to that Estate that made his *Father a Freeman*, the *Son is a Freeman* too'.[9]

By far the most significant limit on patriarchal authority was presented in Locke's argument that because '*every Man's Children*...[are] by Nature as *free* as himself, or any of his Ancestors ever were, [they] may, whilst they are in that Freedom, choose what Society they will join themselves to, what Common-wealth they will put themselves under'.[10] That is, as Locke expressed it in another context, a man '*cannot* by any *Compact* whatsoever, bind *his Children* or Posterity. For this Son, when a Man, being altogether as free as the Father, any *act of the Father can no more give away the liberty of the Son*, than it can of any body else.'[11] Filmer had insisted that allowing children to be bound by the acts of their ancestors was a denial of the principles of natural equality and original freedom.[12] Locke

[1] Sir Leslie Stephen, *History of English Thought in the Eighteenth Century*, 2 vols. (paperback ed. New York, 1962), II, 116.
[2] *Two Treatises*, II, §173.   [3] *Ibid.* II, §67.
[4] *Ibid.* II, §57.   [5] *Ibid.* II, §54.
[6] *Patriarcha*, ed. Laslett, pp. 57, 247, 284 and 287.
[7] *Two Treatises*, II, §55.   [8] *Ibid.* II, §69.
[9] *Ibid.* II, §58.   [10] *Ibid.* II, §73.
[11] *Ibid.* II, §116.   [12] *Patriarcha*, ed. Laslett, pp. 65 and 287.

met this challenge head on and carried these principles and the consent basis of government to their necessary conclusions by acknowledging the right of each man to be the author of his own political obligation. Subjugation to parents did not encroach upon political freedom, and Locke properly asserted in one of his most important and effective statements against the Filmerian thesis:

Thus we are *born Free*, as we are born Rational; not that we have actually the Exercise of either: Age that brings one, brings with it the other too. And thus we see how *natural Freedom and Subjection to Parents* may consist together, and are both founded on the same Principle... The *Freedom of a Man at years of discretion*, and the *Subjection* of a Child *to* his *Parents*, whilst yet short of that Age, are so consistent, and so distinguishable, that the most blinded Contenders for Monarchy, *by Right of Fatherhood*, cannot miss this *difference*, the most obstinate cannot but allow their consistency.[1]

Despite this insistence upon the differences between the subordination of children to their parents—and especially to their fathers—during their nonage and man's subjugation to political authority, Locke employed the familial unit as an important element in his explanations of the origins of the state and man's emergence from the state of nature. Next to self-preservation, Locke felt, the strongest drive 'God Planted in Men' was that 'of propagating their Kind, and continuing themselves in their Posterity'.[2] This urge to procreate was presumably one of the 'strong Obligations of Necessity, Convenience, and Inclination' that man had been placed under by God 'to drive him into *Society*', for man had been so created that 'in his own Judgment, it was not good for him to be alone'. Locke accordingly observed, 'The *first Society* was between Man and Wife, which gave beginning to that between Parents and Children; to which, in time, that between Master and Servant came to be added.' None the less, Locke contended that even the complex household 'came short of *Political Society*'.[3] But he went on to say that the familial society could be *transformed* into a state. What must be determined, then, are the reasons why the household was not political and the manner in which civil society was established on the foundation of this non-political association. Only then

---

[1] *Two Treatises*, II, §61.

[2] *Ibid.* I, §88. Locke did not attempt to reconcile this conscious drive to propagate with the argument based on involuntary parenthood that he had previously used against the derivation of paternal power from generation. Note also that Locke has shifted his grounds somewhat, for in I, §54 (quoted above on p. 83) this drive was reduced to a desire to copulate, but here procreation has become a conscious act.

[3] *Ibid.* II, §77. In II, §79, Locke said that the purpose of the '*conjunction between Male and Female*' is 'not barely Procreation, but the continuation of the Species'. Therefore conjugal society ought to endure 'so long as is necessary to the nourishment and support of the young Ones, who are to be sustained by those that got them, till they are able to shift and provide for themselves'.

can the relationship between state and family in the *Two Treatises* be properly ascertained.

It should be clear that the familial association under consideration existed in the state of nature and was therefore a 'pre-political' society; the state of nature emerges at least from *this* context as an historically real condition.[1] It is equally apparent that Locke distinguished between society and political society, a differentiation that has the very important consequence of making social (albeit non-political) institutions perfectly compatible with the historical state of nature.[2] Admittedly, this distinction was not uniformly maintained throughout the *Two Treatises*, but any attempt to extract a rigorous consistency from Locke on this matter would obscure an important feature of his political philosophy. By not always making clear the apparent differences between political and non-political societies[3] while simultaneously contending that non-civil societies existed in the state of nature, Locke developed a conception of politics

[1] The question of whether Locke's state of nature was a logical construct or an historical reality has been much debated. Pollock (in *Political Thought*, ed. Ebenstein, p. 294) and Sabine (*History of Political Theory*, p. 526) regard it as a logical fiction. Lamprecht (*Moral and Political Philosophy*, p. 131) sees it as an 'actual period which preceded in time...civil society'. Richard Cox (*Locke on War and Peace*, Oxford, 1960, pp. 94–104) seems to concur with Lamprecht. Locke appears to have accepted both an historical and a logical view of the state of nature, his use varying with his context. On this interpretation see *Two Treatises*, Introduction, p. 99 and II, § 109n.; C. B. Macpherson, *The Political Theory of Possessive Individualism: Hobbes to Locke* (Oxford, 1962); and Sheldon S. Wolin, *Politics and Vision: Continuity and Innovation in Western Political Thought* (Boston, 1960), pp. 305–9. Also relevant is the very brief discussion in Howard Becker and Harry E. Barnes, *Social Thought from Lore to Science*, 3 vols. (paperback ed. New York, 1960), II, 444.

[2] *Two Treatises*, II, §§ 28 and 211; J. W. Gough, *John Locke's Political Philosophy: Eight Studies*, corrected ed. (Oxford, 1956), p. 92 (Additional Note); and the references cited in the preceding note.

[3] Both Richard Cox and Leo Strauss insist that there are no distinctions for Locke. See Cox, *Locke on War and Peace*, pp. 93, 97, 99, 115 and 116, and Strauss, *Natural Right and History* (Chicago, 1953), p. 225. Cf. John W. Yolton, 'Locke on the Law of Nature', *Philosophical Review*, LXVII (1958), 493, n. 23. Unless this important differentiation is acknowledged, it is impossible to explain why Locke discussed familial authority and the transformation of the pre-political family into a civil society in such detail.

A similar difficulty is found in M. Seliger, 'Locke's Theory of Natural Law and the Foundation of Politics', *Journal of the History of Ideas*, XXIV (1963), 352–3, where it is maintained that 'Locke's distinction between the state of nature and political society is not meant [presumably by Locke] to be complete'. Seliger too fails to appreciate the implications of Locke's claim that the conjugal association 'came short' of being a political society.

Also relevant is the discussion in J. J. Jenkins, 'Locke and Natural Rights', *Philosophy*, XLII (1967), 149–54. Jenkins holds that Locke's state of nature is not consistently social, and persuasively argues that the ambiguities between the social and non-social states of nature cannot be overcome. The difficulty is that Jenkins does not clearly define 'social' and 'non-social'. They appear to relate to the respective presence and absence of co-operation and association, but Jenkins talks of 'the formation of society' (p. 153) without always recognizing Locke's attempts to distinguish between political and non-political societies. Also, Jenkins does not show that familial society is incompatible with what he regards as the non-social version of the state-of-nature thesis, something his own presentation of Locke's theory would seem to require.

The family and origins of the state

in which the transition from the state of nature to government was virtually effortless; it was, in addition, barely perceptible.

A non-political condition does not appear to have lasted very long after people began to live in societies and to recognize their mutual social relations, for Locke said '. . . Government is hardly to be avoided amongst Men that live together'.[1] There was also a certain element of necessity behind the transformation of pre-political society into government; in explaining why '*History* gives us but a very little account of Men, *that lived together in the State of Nature*', Locke wrote, 'The inconveniences of that condition, and the love, and want of Society no sooner brought any number of them together, but they presently united and incorporated, if they designed to continue together'.[2] In other words, the provision by government of 'an *establish'd*, settled, known *Law*',[3] '*a known and indifferent Judge*',[4] and '*Power* to back and support the Sentence [of the judge] when right, and to *give* it due *Execution*'[5]—the three things that were so conspicuously absent from the state of nature—were essential to preserve not only the society into which men were driven by their natures but the resultant advantages and values as well. Thus, an important and persistent acceptance of what is at base Aristotelianism can be extracted from Locke's conceptions of society and government, and the moral aspects of his notion of political origins can be seen to have had much in common with the later theory of Rousseau's *Social Contract*. For it was only by uniting into societies and then setting up governments that the men of the *Two Treatises* were able to develop their personalities and to enjoy fully and permanently the benefits that were potentially theirs by the gift of God and nature.[6] This is true whether the state emerged from the family or from some other pre-political association, but our interest here is in the transformation of paternal power.

'In the first Ages of the World,' Locke wrote, 'and in places still, where the thinness of People gives Families leave to separate into unpossessed Quarters,' it was very easy 'for the *Father of the Family* to become the Prince of it'. Since men living together will always need a formal government and because the children had grown accustomed to the patriarchal authority that had been exercised over them, it was most

---

[1] *Two Treatises*, II, § 105. See also II, § 127: '. . . we seldom find any number of Men live any time together in this State [of nature]'.
[2] *Ibid.* II, § 101. [3] *Ibid.* II, § 124.
[4] *Ibid.* II, § 125. [5] *Ibid.* II, § 126.
[6] Geraint Parry ingeniously argues that according to Locke each person has an obligation as a human being to cultivate his rationality and that this cultivation will lead him to the realization that the state is necessary. However, Parry does not carry his analysis to a teleological conclusion. See his 'Individuality, Politics and the Critique of Paternalism in John Locke', *Political Studies*, XII (1964), 165–6.

likely that political power should, 'by the express or tacit Consent of the Children, when they were grown up, be in the Father, where it seemed without any change barely to continue'. In this manner a father might be endowed with a monarchical power, and Locke hastily added '. . . this was not by any *Paternal Right*, but only by the Consent of his Children'.[1] However, this 'express or tacit Consent' successively deteriorated. 'Thus 'twas easie, and almost natural for Children by a tacit, and scarce avoidable consent to make way for the *Father's Authority and Government*', Locke wrote,[2] and then asserted that 'the natural *Fathers of Families*, by an insensible change, became the *politick Monarchs* of them too'.[3]

The meaning of 'insensible change' is not apparent, but the words seem to qualify Locke's political history *vis-à-vis* his state-of-nature assumptions. In the first place, it is now clear that the presumed gulf between patriarchal and political authority that is so important to the argument of the *Two Treatises* could in practice be bridged—and with very little difficulty—by the transformation of the father into a political ruler. Moreover, government need not have been established in the first instance by the agreement of men who consciously recognized the inconveniences of the state of nature. Instead, mankind may well have casually drifted into political society with the help of acquired social habits. Locke described and justified the process:

the Father having, by the Law of Nature, the same Power with every Man else to punish, as he thought fit, any Offences against that Law, might thereby punish his transgressing Children even when they were Men, and out of their Pupilage; and they were very likely to submit to his punishment, and all joyn with him against the Offender, in their turns, giving him thereby power to Execute his Sentence against any transgression, and so in effect make him the Law-maker, and Governour over all, that remained in Conjunction with his Family. He was fittest to be trusted; Paternal affection secured their Property, and Interest under his Care, and *the Custom of obeying him, in their Childhood, made it easier to submit to him, rather than to any other*.[4]

Locke admitted that monarchy was probably the first form of government in the world because of its compatibility with the unitary rule of

---

[1] *Two Treatises*, II, §74. On the need for government, see in addition II, §105, ll. 19–21.

[2] *Ibid.* II, §75. In the first three printings of the *Two Treatises* the key phrase was 'tacit, and almost natural consent'. (See Collation of the *Second Treatise, ibid.* p. 480.)

[3] *Ibid.* II, §76. In II, §99, Locke similarly wrote that governance was begun 'by barely agreeing to *unite into one Political Society*...' These passages should all be read in conjunction with Locke's insistence that consent is the only source of political authority, discussed below at p. 93, n. 1.

[4] *Ibid.* II, §105. My italics. See also II, §75, ll. 5–10, where Locke emphasized the gentleness of the father. Again, note the contrast between the earlier insistence upon apparently overt consent and the assertion here that sons '*in effect* make him [their father] the Law-maker' (my italics).

the family by the father. His tone was almost apologetic as he defended the claim of monarchy to historical priority:

First then, in the beginning of things, the Father's Government of the Childhood of those sprung from him, having accustomed them to the *Rule of one Man*, and taught them that where it was exercised with Care and Skill, with Affection and Love to those under it, it was sufficient to procure and preserve to Men all the Political Happiness they sought for in Society. It was no wonder, that they should pitch upon, and naturally run into that Form of Government, which from their Infancy they had been all accustomed to; and which, by experience they had found both easie and safe. To which, if we add, that *Monarchy* being simple, and most obvious to Men, whom neither experience had instructed in Forms of Government, nor the Ambition or Insolence of Empire had taught to beware of the Encroachments of Prerogative, or the Inconveniences of Absolute Power, which Monarchy, in Succession, was apt to lay claim to, and bring upon them, it was not at all strange, that they should not much trouble themselves to think of Methods of restraining any Exorbitances of those, to whom they had given the Authority over them, and of ballancing the Power of Government, by placing several parts of it in different hands...'tis no wonder they put themselves into such a *Frame of Government*, as was not only as I said, most obvious and simple, but also best suited to their present State and Condition; which stood more in need of defence against foreign Invasions and Injuries, than of multiplicity of Laws.[1]

Locke's reconstruction of the historical origins of the state was not vastly different from the position of Sir Robert Filmer, for Locke acknowledged both that government had, in all probability, begun in the family and that the first ruler was a patriarchal monarch. But the similarity stopped at these points of superficial agreement. Sir Robert rested his patriarchalism upon a genetic theory of political justification; he believed that it was necessary only to determine the origins of political authority in order to understand what the nature and essence of government ought to be. Filmer saw no logical gap between the presumed beginnings of the state and his own ethico-political doctrine, and he treated the latter as a valid inference from the historical fact.[2] Locke, on the other hand, held that origins have almost nothing to do with subsequent duty. 'An Argument from what has been, to what should of right be, has no great force', he wrote.[3] Similarly, he said,

---

[1] *Ibid.* II, §107. (In the early part of this passage Locke does not seem to have maintained the distinction between society and government.) For an altogether different interpretation see Martin Seliger, 'Locke's Theory of Revolutionary Action', *Western Political Quarterly*, XVI (1963), 553.

[2] In a larger study that I am now completing—provisionally titled *Patriarchalism in Stuart Political Thought*—this interpretation of Filmer is set forth in detail, and it is argued that this genetic method of justification was characteristic of political theory in seventeenth-century England. [3] *Two Treatises*, II, §103.

Gordon J. Schochet

if Princes have their Titles in the Fathers Right, and it be a sufficient proof of the natural *Right of Fathers* to Political Authority,...[this argument] will prove that all Princes, nay Princes only, ought to be Priests, since 'tis as certain, that in the Beginning, *The Father of the Family was Priest, as that he was Ruler in his own Household.*[1]

In other words, Locke separated the two components of Sir Robert's argument; he made the history into a descriptive and morally neutral anthropology and then inserted his own theory of consent and a doctrine of governmental trust in place of the political patriarchalism that Filmer had improperly derived from history. Yet Locke was obviously not willing to explain the nature of politics without inquiring into the past at all. Had he ignored the problem of origins, his accounts of the state of nature and the natural right to property, for instance, would have been super-fluous. But the framework within which he wrote forced Locke to examine these and other questions in order to compose a full answer to Filmer's patriarchalism.[2]

The analysis of origins in the *Two Treatises* was due as much to the very nature of the philosophic task that Locke set for himself, a task that was in many ways similar to Rousseau's proclaimed goal of reconciling man's free birth with the chains of society.

To understand Political Power right, and derive it from its Original, [Locke said,] we must consider what State all Men are naturally in, and that is, a *State of perfect Freedom* to order their Actions, and dispose of their Possessions, and Persons as they think fit, within the bounds of the Law of Nature, without asking leave, or depending upon the Will of any other Man.[3]

Further analysis revealed, as has already been seen, that man was somewhat sociable by nature and needed the help of others to enjoy and retain the benefits of nature. By looking at man in his original, pre-political condition, Locke was able to determine what kind of government would be most consistent with human nature. Origins thus led to government in Locke's writings in a prudential rather than necessary sense. The existence of political authority was justified by an appeal to something more functional and tangible than divine mystery or the nature of things. It was the purpose of government, in general, to protect the life, liberty, and property of the citizens. So long as these protections were afforded by an agency that drew its authority from the consent of the people and did

---

[1] *Two Treatises*, II, §76. See also Sanford A. Lakoff, *Equality in Political Philosophy* (Cambridge, Mass., 1964), p. 69.

[2] See Thomas I. Cook, Introduction to *John Locke, Two Treatises of Government* (Hafner Library of Classics, New York, 1947), pp. xii and xv.

[3] *Two Treatises*, II, §4.

The family and origins of the state

not degenerate into absolutism, political obligation appears to have been complete. However, when the natural rights of the citizens were flouted or when a government became absolutist, the duty to obey the state ceased to be binding.

The insistence upon consent provided a further basis for Locke's claim that the patriarchal and kingly origins of government were irrelevant to contemporary obligation. He asserted that it is '*the Consent of Free-men, born under Government*, which only *makes them Members of it*...'[1] Even the transformation of a family into a state could only be accomplished through the consent of the children. To Locke there was no question 'That the *beginning of Politick Society* depends upon the consent of the Individuals, to joyn into and make one Society',[2] and he believed that reason and history clearly showed that 'the *Governments* of the World, that were begun in Peace,...were *made by the Consents of the People*'.[3] Locke's doctrine of consent is excessively vague and of limited use as an explanation of political obligation in the *Two Treatises*.[4] Still, his commitment to what he called 'consent' is unassailable. What Locke presumably sought was a means of basing political authority on the voluntary actions of free individuals;[5] that he might not have succeeded in no way detracts from his intentions. What is singularly important about the consent thesis in relation to the patriarchal origins of government is that Locke used it to show that however unnoticed the change might have been, the state and the family rested on altogether different moral bases.

It is now possible to appreciate the full significance for Locke of Filmer's remarks about the inconsistency of allowing children to be bound by the

[1] *Ibid.* II, §117. See also II, §§95, 112, 119–21, 192, 197, and 198.
[2] *Ibid.* II, §106. [3] *Ibid.* II, §104.
[4] See E. F. Carritt, *Morals and Politics* (Oxford, 1936), pp. 77–8; Gough, *Locke's Political Philosophy*, chapter III; *Two Treatises*, Introduction, pp. 110–12; J. P. Plamenatz, *Consent, Freedom, and Political Obligation* (Oxford, 1938), chapter 1; and Theodore Waldman, 'A Note on John Locke's Concept of Consent', *Ethics*, LXVIII (1957–8), 45–50. The most recent discussion of the problem is in many ways the most interesting, for it is the only one that attempts to place the question entirely in the context of Locke's own doctrine. See John Dunn, 'Consent in the Political Theory of John Locke', *Historical Journal*, X (1967), 153–82. It is usually argued that consent is both the *source and justification* of political obligation for Locke in much the same way that the obligation to keep a specific promise is derived from one's having made that promise. Dunn's position, very briefly, is that consent is merely the way in which one joins a civil society and falls under (or becomes liable to the fulfilment of) a pre-existing political obligation that has its source in and can be justified as a part of man's more general obligation to obey God. This interpretation, it should be noted, accords with my discussion of the parental obligation to care for their children as a commandment of God. See above, at p. 84, nn. 1–4.
[5] See Joseph Tussman, *Obligation and the Body Politic* (New York, 1961), pp. 32–9; S. I. Benn and R. S. Peters, *The Principles of Political Thought: Social Foundations of the Democratic State* (paperback ed. New York, 1965), pp. 376–82; and Hanna Pitkin, 'Obligation and Consent— I', *American Political Science Review*, LIX (1965), 994–7.

acts of their ancestors while simultaneously proclaiming a doctrine of natural freedom and equality. Filmer's argument is worth examining in detail, for it throws important light on Locke's answer. After asserting that there never would have been any time when all people might have assembled and agreed to a contract of government, and further complaining that those who did not participate—especially children—'ought not to lose their liberty without their own consent', Sir Robert said:

But in part to salve this, it will be said that infants and children may be concluded by the votes of their parents. This remedy may cure some part of the mischief, but it destroys the whole cause, and at last stumbles upon the true original of government. For if it be allowed, that the acts of parents bind the children, then farewell the doctrine of the natural freedom of mankind; where subjection of children to parents is natural, there can be no natural freedom. If any reply, that not all children shall be bound by their parents' consent, but only those that are under age; it must be considered, that in nature there is no *nonage*; if a man be not born free, she doth not assign him any other time when he shall attain his freedom: or if she did, then children attaining that age, should be discharged of their parents' contract. So that in conclusion, if it be imagined that the people were ever but once free from subjection by nature, it will prove a mere impossibility ever lawfully to introduce any kind of government whatsoever, without apparent wrong to a multitude of people.[1]

The context clearly indicates that Filmer was attacking the historical inadequacies of the *original contract* of government. But his arguments were valid on logical grounds as well, for he was ultimately claiming that no man could *legitimately* give away or limit what belonged to some one else by nature. Locke accepted this principle and incorporated it into his own position, essentially, by ignoring the contract and its inevitable dependence upon the acts of ancestors; he emphasized instead individual *consent*. The distinction between contract and consent that is here suggested is not often drawn. Consequently, the reliance of the contract theory upon genetic justification—and its closeness to the patriarchal theory in this respect—has seldom been appreciated. Locke apparently did recognize this aspect of the contract doctrine and was driven by this awareness to formulate his theory of consent as a direct response to Filmer's historicist argument. Consent represented the personal and contemporary manner in which individuals could claim the same freedom that had belonged to their fathers before them.[2]

[1] *Patriarcha*, ed. Laslett, p. 287. It is worth noting that Locke did not refer to this passage in the *Two Treatises*; he introduced the concept of nonage as if Filmer had never criticized it. Still, his treatment of the problem was clearly an answer to Filmer.
[2] From this perspective, it becomes misleading to regard Locke as a 'social contract' theorist and to ask such questions as whether there are one or two contracts in his doctrine. See, for

The family and origins of the state

A further escape from genetic reasoning was provided for Locke by his belief that governmental power—despite its patriarchal origins—exists only for the benefit of the governed. Political authority could therefore be regarded as part of an on-going process; it is held as a sacred trust for the 'publick Good and Safety'.

Thus, whether *a Family* by degrees *grew up into a Commonwealth*, and the Fatherly Authority being continued on to the elder Son, every one in his turn growing up under it, tacitly submitted to it, and the easiness and equality of it not offending any one, every one acquiesced, till time seemed to have confirmed it, and settled a right of Succession by Prescription: or whether several Families, or the Descendants of several Families, whom Chance, Neighbourhood, or Business brought together, uniting into Society, the need of a General, whose Conduct might defend them against their Enemies in War, and the great confidence the Innocence and Sincerity of that poor but vertuous Age (such as are almost all those which begin Governments, that ever come to last in the World) gave Men one of another, made the first Beginners of Common-wealths generally put the Rule into one Man's hand, without any other express Limitation or Restraint, but what the Nature of the thing, and the End of Government required: which ever of these it was, that at first put the rule into the hands of a single person, certain it is that no body was ever intrusted with it but for the publick Good and Safety, and to those Ends in the Infancies of Commonwealths those who had it, commonly used it: And unless they had done so, young Societies could not have subsisted: without such nursing Fathers tender and carefull of the publick weale, all Governments would have sunk under the Weakness and Infirmities of their Infancy; and the Prince and the People had soon perished together.[1]

Basic to this important doctrine of trust is a set of moral and psychological assumptions that Locke made about human nature. The men of the *Two Treatises* were potentially good—that is, they were capable of recognizing their obligations and, in general, could be counted on to act

instance, Sir Ernest Barker, 'The Theory of the Social Contract in Locke, Rousseau, and Hume', reprinted in his *Essays on Government*, 2nd ed. (Oxford, 1951), p. 98. In this very influential essay, the late Sir Ernest continually incorporated Locke's language of consent into a theory of the contract. The same is true of J. W. Gough, *The Social Contract: A Critical Study of Its Development*, 2nd ed. (Oxford, 1957), pp. 127–46, esp. p. 145. None the less, both of these authors recognize the importance of personal consent and governmental trust in Locke's conception of political obligation. Their positions should be contrasted with Laslett's almost total emphasis upon trust: *Two Treatises*, Introduction, pp. 112–15.

[1] *Ibid.* II, §110 (quoted *in toto*). Locke's reference to 'nursing Fathers' suggests Isaiah xlix. 23, *q.v.* Also noteworthy is the use of 'young *Societies*' (my italics) where the context clearly called for a more specifically political concept. This, of course, is another instance in which the society–government distinction of the *Two Treatises* was not consistently maintained.

On Locke's doctrine of trust, which is central to my argument at this point, see Gough, *Locke's Political Philosophy*, chapter VII, and *Two Treatises*, Introduction, pp. 112–15.

upon them[1]—and were other-regarding rather than hedonistic.[2] Such men would have little reluctance about placing great powers in the hands of others, for they would not feel the need to guard continually against potential abuses of authority. Therefore, Locke said, men 'chuse to be under the Conduct of a *single Person*, without so much as by express Conditions limiting or regulating his Power, which they thought safe enough in his Honesty and Prudence'. And when this '*single Person*' was a father whose authority had been allowed to become political, the people did not subsequently believe that 'Paternal Power [ought] to have a right to Dominion, or to be the Foundation of all Government'.[3] Beyond this, it cannot be emphasized too strongly that it was the gentleness of the father that made him a suitable political ruler. Because of 'Paternal affection',[4] the 'tenderness' a father had for his offspring,[5] and his consequently 'easie and safe' rule of the family,[6] children were content to pass out of nonage into maturity without changing the external ordering of their lives. In short, they believed that their fathers would not become tyrants.

Therefore, in the early days when fathers were governors and watched over the people 'for their good, the Government was almost all *Prerogative*. A few establish'd Laws served the turn, and the discretion and care of the Ruler supply'd the rest.'[7] This was as it should be. 'For *Prerogative is nothing but the Power of doing publick good without a Rule*.'[8] Locke had said the same thing of political authority in general in section three of the *Second Treatise*:

Political Power then I take to be *a Right* of making Laws with Penalties of Death, and consequently all less Penalties, for the Regulating and Preserving of Property, and of employing the force of the Community, in the Execution of such Laws, and in the defence of the Common-wealth from Foreign Injury, and all this only for the Publick Good.[9]

---

[1] See *Two Treatises*, e.g. II, §11 (l. 31); II, §14 (ll. 17–19); II, §124 (ll. 8–9); and II, §136 (ll. 5–6).

[2] See *ibid.*, e.g. II, §6 (ll. 19–25); and II, §33 (ll. 1–3). As E. F. Carritt has observed (*Morals and Politics*, p. 72), Locke 'believes in what he calls Laws of Nature or of Reason not dependent upon convention or upon states and governments. They are, in fact, mutual obligations really binding upon men, recognized by them as binding, and able to influence their behaviour.'

This interpretation has been challenged by Richard Cox (*Locke on War and Peace*, p. 72, *et passim*), who argues that when all the accounts of man's behaviour and all the state-of-nature assumptions in the *Two Treatises* are considered together, Locke's view of human nature emerges as very similar to that of Hobbes. However, it is impossible for Cox's reading to account for Locke's doctrine of trust and to explain how the habit of obedience could have prepared men for the transformation of patriarchal into political rule.

[3] *Two Treatises*, II, §112.   [4] *Ibid.* II, §105.

[5] *Ibid.* II, §75. On both affection and tenderness, see II, §170 (ll. 8–12).

[6] *Ibid.* II, §107.   [7] *Ibid.* II, §162.

[8] *Ibid.* II, §166.   [9] *Ibid.* II, §3 (*in toto*).

The family and origins of the state

When rulers failed to act 'for the Publick Good', the bonds of political obligation were dissolved, and power potentially reverted to the people.[1] Historically, it was the abuse of the prerogative and violation of the trust of government by rulers that led to the establishment of specific laws. 'And thus declared *limitations of Prerogative* were by the People found necessary in Cases, which they and their Ancestors had left, in the utmost latitude, to the Wisdom of those Princes, who made no other but a right use of it, that is, for the good of their People.'[2]

Another of Locke's important departures from the patriarchal tradition was his denial of the natural origins of hereditary succession. Even in the early days of paternal rule, the succession of the son to his father's title was generally dependent upon his merit. But when 'the Father died, and left his next Heir for want of Age, Wisdom, Courage, or any other Qualities, less fit for Rule:...There, 'tis not to be doubted, but they [the people] used their natural freedom, to set him up, whom they judged the ablest, and most likely, to Rule well over them.'[3] 'Almost all *Monarchies*,' Locke wrote, 'near their Original, have been commonly, at least upon occasion, *Elective*.'[4] As these patriarchal kings 'chanced to live long, and leave able, and worthy Heirs, for several Successions, or otherwise; So they laid the Foundations of Hereditary, or Elective Kingdoms...'[5] This description was not merely an account of life in the hypothesized state of nature; it seems to have been based upon the actual government of the Canadian Indians. As Locke wrote in his *Common-Place Book*, presumably in March 1679:

The Kings of Canada are elective but the sons never faile to succeed their fathers when they are equal to their virtues, otherwise not; & their Kings are rather obeyed by consent & persuasion, then by force and compulsion, the publique good being the measure of their authority. Sagard, p. 418. And this seems to have been the state of regall authority in its Original at least in all this part of the world. JL[6]

Thus, the state of nature, the probable beginnings of political commonwealths, and the primitive structure of American society and government were assimilated and used to reinforce the proposition that the end of

---

[1] See *ibid.* II, §§221, 222, and 240; Introduction, p. 113 and n.
[2] *Ibid.* II, §162.   [3] *Ibid.* II, §105.
[4] *Ibid.* II, §106.   [5] *Ibid.* II, §76.
[6] Locke, *Common-Place Book*, Bodleian Library, MS. Locke c. 42, pt. B, fo. 6. Passage slightly modernized. The probable dating is derived from Locke's having made a very similar entry in his reading notes on 25 March 1679 (Bodleian Library, MS. Locke c. 33, fo. 10). This entry was lightly crossed out by Locke, indicating that it was re-copied somewhere else, presumably in the *Common-Place Book*. The reference is to Gabriel Sagard's *Canada*, published in 1636, and used extensively by Locke in 1679. (See *Two Treatises*, Introduction, appendix B, no. 72, p. 143, and notes to II, §§58 and 106.)

governance could be nothing but the public good. As understood by Locke, civil authority was always held in trust and never by right.[1]

In terms of the patriarchal explanation of political obligation, the doctrine of trust was one of the most important components of the theory of the *Two Treatises*. It enabled Locke to say, in effect, that the familial origins of government were of no value in understanding the nature of man's subsequent political commitments. And it was precisely Locke's polemic purpose to show how irrelevant the Filmerian analysis of politics was! Locke appears to have believed that allegiance was due to the state because of the trust that it held and only so long as that trust was not violated. Thus, each generation and, in fact, each individual person theoretically retained the right to determine whether or not a government was properly performing its functions. If the answer was no, the base of political authority was liable to be withdrawn. On this reading, the state was conventional, a contrivance that was the creature of those whom it was to serve. At the same time, Locke certainly believed that the state was essential to human existence, but its necessity was functional rather than moral. The political order as he described it did not endow men with additional rights or more personality and individuality, but by providing positive and sure protections, it did make it possible for them to enjoy what was already naturally theirs.

[1] See *Two Treatises*, 1, §93.

The state of nature and the nature
of man in Locke[1]

by HANS AARSLEFF

In recent years Locke's conception of the state of nature has been the subject of much debate and interpretation. The problem is serious and fundamental: since the state of nature clearly occupies a central position in Locke's political philosophy, our entire understanding of that philosophy is at stake. Unfortunately, the debate has not tended to move toward a common core of agreement. On the contrary opinions are now more diverse and incompatible than they ever were. Must we then conclude that the present confusion has its origin in Locke, that he did not really make sense, and that the interpretations that have been offered have their source in difficulties which Locke himself found no way to solve? I do not believe so. Locke is a difficult writer, and our work is constantly frustrated by the absence of a good edition; but I do not believe that he is confused. It is the aim of the present essay to offer a discussion which I hope will move both the debate and the problem on to firmer ground. In the course of my discussion I shall try to show that the perplexities that have evolved, often almost to the point of dogmatic assertions of fact, have no basis in Locke's thought, but are the products of misunderstanding, misreading, or inadequate attention to Locke's writings. It was the aim of the *Second Treatise* to give an account of the 'true, original, and extent of civil government', but it was not its aim to spell out the grounds and reasons of the assumptions that necessarily had to be employed in that account, most prominently concerning the nature of man, his capacities and potential attainments. I think the current confusion has its primary source in two common mistakes: the belief that the state of nature—or the two states of nature—must describe an actual, historical condition, and inadequate attention to Locke's conception of the nature of man and his capacity to gain understanding of the law of nature. I shall briefly

---

[1] Throughout this essay 'Draft *A*' refers to *An Early Draft of Locke's Essay together with Excerpts from his Journals*, ed. R. I. Aaron and Jocelyn Gibb (Oxford, 1936), pp. 1–74. 'Aaron and Gibb' refers to the same work, pp. 75 ff. (the excerpts from the journals). 'Draft *B*' refers to *John Locke, An Essay concerning the Understanding, Knowledge, Opinion, and Assent*, ed. Benjamin Rand (Cambridge, Mass., 1931).

deal with the former in order to give direction to my argument regarding the nature of man, which will occupy the greater part of my essay. I shall especially try to show that Locke already by the time he was writing the *Two Treatises* had worked out a consistent and well-founded conception of the nature of man and the law of reason, fully sufficient to satisfy the demands of the argument in the *Two Treatises*. I shall then debate a few of the more important objections that have been raised against some points which I shall accept as inherent in Locke's argument. Finally, I shall close with some observations on recent Locke scholarship.[1]

Whatever else the state of nature may be, I think there has always been universal agreement that it is a concept that expresses Locke's view of the nature of man and his capacities. Civil society is a collection of individual men for whose welfare, happiness, security, and preservation it was instituted. Its principles must therefore conform to the quality of the raw material. Locke never believed that basic man was a product of society, however much men may now actually differ in various parts of the world, from Ancient Greece to modern England or from Saldanha Bay to London. Unlike Hobbes's Leviathan, Locke's civil society was made according to the nature of man in order to preserve that nature to the highest possible degree and to retain the freedom which his rationality alone makes possible. The problem of the state of nature is essentially a question about the nature of man. The condition of man in nature before government is only a secondary problem, easily solved once the former has been taken care of, and it is not my present concern. It is the defining characteristic of the state of nature that in it '*every one has the Executive Power* of the Law of Nature',[2] and whether he exercises this power rightly, according to reason or not, depends entirely on those qualities that lie in his basic nature, which must therefore in any attempt at interpretation be our first concern. Failure clearly to see the priority of this matter has, I think, been the chief source of confusion.

It is Locke's fundamental belief, stated again and again and indispensable to his entire philosophy, that man is 'by nature rational' and hence capable of knowledge, gained by the play of reason on the materials provided by sense-experience and reflexion, and gained to varying degrees by different men in proportion to their own native endowments, their efforts, and their opportunities. As with the knowledge of things and nature, so also the knowledge of moral rules does not spring invariably from reason and the other faculties of man. Locke's firm rejection of

---

[1] See below, p. 262.
[2] *John Locke: Two Treatises of Government*, ed. Peter Laslett (Cambridge, 1960), II, §13. Cf. *ibid.* II, §19: '*Want of a common Judge with Authority, puts all Men in a State of Nature.*'

innate notions is enough to remind us that all knowledge is achieved by learning and instruction. To be rational by nature does not automatically entail the full, let alone perfect, exercise of reason, and there is of course nothing whatever paradoxical in this conception. Locke could confidently say that he doubted not 'but without being written on their hearts, many men may, by the same way that they come to the knowledge of other things, come to assent to several moral rules and be convinced of their obligation'.[1] The chief obstacle to the exercise of reason, both privately and publicly, is 'our feeble passionate nature',[2] which derives from those 'principles of actions' that are 'lodged in men's appetites', which 'if they were left to their full swing...would carry men to the over-turning of all morality'. Moral rules are subsumed under the general term of the law of nature, and they 'are set as a curb and restraint to these exorbitant desires'.[3] Reason pulls one way and passion the other, but Locke never assumes that mankind at large is wholly dominated either by one or the other. Locke's conception of the state of nature is fitted to this conception of man.

The term 'state of nature' has two separate but not conflicting meanings, and each of these may in turn refer to relations between two men only or to relations among many men at large as a group. The condition of two men may be a state of peace, harmony, and reason, their conduct and opinions being wholly guided by reason, such as was the case between Locke and his good friend William Molyneux. Or it may be a state of unreason and war, characterized by force, violence and purely brutish behaviour in at least one of the two individuals. Both of these states may occur in fact and do so constantly in the ordinary affairs of men, but neither is directly relevant to the establishment of civil society, one giving no cause for an impartial judge and the other no possibility of supplying one. Two men alone will always face each other in the state of nature and must exercise their own choices between reason and unreason. Civil society concerns diverse groups of men at large. In this context the state of nature may refer to a timeless, abstract state that has no existence in fact and can never have had any in this world. It may also be called the state of reason. It is this purely abstract state that has given rise to the opinion that Locke talked about an 'idyllic' or 'pleasant' state of nature which, by also being assumed historically factual or possible, has caused so much confusion. It has a necessary place in Locke's political philosophy as a guide and model for the construction of the basic principles of civil

[1] *An Essay concerning Human Understanding*, ed. J. W. Yolton (Everyman's Library, London–New York, 1961), i, iii, §8.
[2] *Ibid.* ii, xxi, §67.   [3] *Ibid.* i, iii, §13.

society. The antonym of this state of peace and reason is the state of war and unreason, characterized—as in the case of two men alone—by 'a perpetual and deadly hatred among men'.[1] Referring to groups of many men, both of these states are equally abstract, as abstract as the pure exercise of reason and the unrelenting, immediate domination by the appetites in all actions by all men at all times.

The other meaning of 'state of nature' regarding men in groups is not abstract. It is based on experience and on the observation of the actual behaviour of men in their dealings with one another. Taken together they are never, to a man, always wholly peaceful and reasonable or wholly violent, brutish, and unreasonable. They show a mixture of desires guided more or less perfectly by reason toward the attainment of the degrees of happiness for which they are striving. All men invariably seek their own happiness, and the measure of happiness they are capable of envisioning is directly proportional to their exercise of reason, whether self-taught or learnt from others. The law of reason and nature is not innate. Locke's view of the actual behaviour of men firmly ruled out the opinion that this state of nature was 'a mere war of all against all'. There will always be some—and a few are enough—who can show the way of reason to the rest and thus supply the remedy for the presence of 'the corruption and vitiousness of degenerate Men',[2] in whose absence the state of nature would have remained the undisturbed peace and harmony of the pure state of reason. The very phrase 'degenerate men' shows that Locke did not take degeneracy to be the normal and universal state of man, and hence—in line with his general optimism and tolerance—he was bound to use the term 'state of nature' both for the abstract and for the actual condition of human groups, and he could do so without contradiction since they operate on different planes. He does not first set up one state of nature and then proceed to demolish it as the argument advances. If Locke had meant to base his political philosophy on the doctrine that men are hostile rather than friendly to one another, that '(as is maintained by some) there is in the state of nature a general war and a perpetual and deadly hatred among men', then the term 'state of nature' should have been applied to this state of war, both in the abstract to the state of unreason and to an actual state that involves at least one man setting himself up against others by abandoning reason for the use of force and violence. This latter condition is indeed equivalent to the actual state of human groups in the state of nature; if it was not, if unreason and violence

---

[1] *John Locke, Essays on the Law of Nature*, ed. Wolfgang von Leyden (Oxford, 1954), p. 163. Cf. H. R. Fox Bourne, *The Life of John Locke*, 2 vols. (London, 1876), I, 185.
[2] *Two Treatises*, II, §128.

never struck, there would have been no need to leave the state of nature, no need for a political philosophy. But in this sense Locke's state of war is altogether different from the Hobbesian one and from what some recent commentators have imputed to Locke. And the difference is not merely a terminological one, employed by Locke for the sake of caution and concealment of his true opinions. To Locke the proper conduct of life is the conduct of reason; war is an aberration from the normal state of peace and reason. The most fundamental axiom in his entire philosophy, both the political and the rest, is that man has reason, which is the indispensable instrument of knowledge. To equate Locke's state of nature with both the abstract and the actual state of war is nonsense.

It is important to understand that Locke's argument does not depend on demonstration or proof that the state of nature—or the state of men as we may call it—has ever in fact existed. It is in the nature of the case that such proof and demonstration cannot be had. It is sufficient to grant that it might or could have existed according to his conception of man's nature and of men living together at some time prior to civil society and government. Only in this limited sense can it be called historical. Owing to a particular habit of mind, common in his day and a universal mode in the eighteenth century, Locke could not separate principles from sources. He agreed with the sense of Hooker's rhetorical question: 'Is there any thing which can either be thoroughly understood or soundly judged of, till the very first causes and principles from which originally it springeth be made manifest?'[1] His political theory had to be presented as an account of the progress of man from a non-political state to civil society and government by consent. The early state, the original, therefore had to be constructed as an illustration of man's basic faculties and their exercise in conduct, firmly based on the observation of ourselves and others. Hence Locke's evidence from history and travel accounts is not designed to demonstrate anything about the state of nature directly, but about the varieties of human behaviour and the uniformity of human nature underneath the variety. This axiom of uniformity is again fundamental to his entire philosophy, and Locke often stated his belief in it. 'Men, I think, have been much the same for natural endowments, in all times', which in turn guarantees that 'truth is always the same; time alters it not, nor is it the better, or worse, for being of ancient or modern tradition'.[2] And of course, not the least important consequence of this doctrine of uniformity is that the observation of self can reveal what is true of

---

[1] Richard Hooker, *Of the Laws of Ecclesiastical Polity*, 2 vols. (Everyman's Library, London, 1907), I, xvi, § 1.
[2] *The Works of John Locke*, 9 vols. (London, 1794), II, 361–2 (*Conduct*).

Hans Aarsleff

all.[1] Locke's state of men is in fact an example of what Dugald Stewart called 'conjectural or theoretical history', and it can be shown that Stewart took Locke's *Second Treatise* and its state of nature to be the source of that powerful tradition. Further, if the state of nature is conjectural in this sense, it follows of course that the compact is likewise a conjectural construction. Locke felt bound to illustrate his principles as a set of forces that produced a series of events in history that progressed toward civil society. His historical and conjectural model was designed to place government by consent in the nature of creation, in the nature of man.

This interpretation of the state of nature is based on what I take to be Locke's conception of the nature and capabilities of man. Now, since the structure of the argument in the *Second Treatise* is designed to demonstrate that men will both encounter the need and also find the requisite principles for the establishment of civil society, it must be shown that man is in fact capable of making this significant move, that he can, in other words, find sufficient remedies for his 'feeble passionate nature' and 'come to assent to several moral rules and be convinced of their obligation'. Neither innateness nor consent can be their ultimate source.[2] Where are they to be found, how can they be learned, and how can they be known to be binding? Now, to Locke privately a single answer sufficed:

There are fundamental truths that lie at the bottom, the basis upon which a great many others rest, and in which they have their consistency. These are teeming truths, rich in store, with which they furnish the mind, and, like the lights of heaven, are not only beautiful and entertaining in themselves, but give light and evidence to other things, that without them could not be seen or known. Such is that admirable discovery of Mr. Newton, that all bodies gravitate to one another, which may be counted as the basis of natural philosophy...Our Saviour's great rule, that 'we should love our neighbour as ourselves', is such a fundamental truth for the regulating human society, that, I think, by that alone, one might without difficulty determine all the cases and doubts in social morality.[3]

---

[1] Cf. *Works*, III, 139 (to Stillingfleet): 'All therefore that I can say of my book is, that it is a copy of my own mind, in its several ways of operation. And all that I can say for the publishing of it, is that I think the intellectual faculties are made, and operate alike in most men; and that some, that I showed it to before I published it, liked it so well that I was confirmed in that opinion.' *Essay*, IV, XII, § 11: '...the ancient savage *Americans*, whose natural endowments and provisions come no way short of those of the most flourishing and polite nations'. *Essay*, IV, XVII, § 4: 'He that will look into many parts of *Asia* and *America* will find men reason there perhaps as acutely as himself, who yet never heard of a syllogism.' *Two Treatises*, II, § 172: '...Reason...the common bond whereby humane kind is united into one fellowship and societie.' Cf. also *Works*, II, 325, 327–32, 361 (*Conduct*).

[2] See the *Third* and *Fifth Essays on the Law of Nature*, ed. von Leyden.

[3] *Works*, II, 394 (*Conduct*). Cf. Locke to Molyneux, 30 March 1696, Molyneux having encouraged Locke to write a 'treatise of morals': 'Did the world want a rule, I confess there could be no work so necessary, nor so commendable. But the gospel contains so perfect a body of ethics,

104

The state of nature and the nature of man

But Locke had at least two strong reasons for not wishing to found his social and political philosophy on special revelation. To do so would have confined its validity to those parts and periods of the world that had received the word. Locke was nothing if not universal in his intentions. And like many of his most distinguished contemporaries, notably Boyle, he feared that sectarian argument and dissension might be the consequence as so often before in his troubled century. It was an awesome fact that Scriptures had not proved a safe foundation for the maintenance of peace among men:

Nor is it to be wondered that the will of God, when clothed in words, should be liable to that doubt and uncertainty which unavoidably attends that sort of conveyance, when even his Son, whilst clothed in flesh, was subject to all the frailties and inconveniences of human nature, sin excepted.

Fortunately for man, there is another avenue to truth and knowledge:

We ought to magnify his goodness, that he hath spread before all the world such legible characters of his works and providence, and given all mankind so sufficient a light of reason that they, to whom this written word never came, could not (whenever they set themselves to search) either doubt of the being of a God or of the obedience due to him.[1]

This belief in the two kinds of revelation, special and manifest, and in their complete harmony, is fundamental in Locke's thought; he expresses it again and again throughout his works from the first to the last, and hence no reading of Locke, no attempt to understand him, can ignore it. With Bacon, Boyle, and Newton he was fully committed to what is best known as natural theology or the argument from design. No part of nature, man included, failed to exhibit the wisdom and plan of the all-wise

that reason may be excused from that inquiry, since she may find man's duty clearer and easier in revelation, than in herself' (*Works*, VIII, 377). Romans xiii. 9 is also cited, for the same purpose, in Draft *B*, §160, though not in the otherwise corresponding passage in Draft *A*, §26. Likewise in 'Of Ethics in General', §11 (see Peter King, *The Life of John Locke, with Extracts from his Correspondence, Journals and Common-Place Books*, Bohn's Standard Library, London, 1858, p. 312). Cf. Journal, 8 February 1677: '...that one unquestionable morall rule doe as you would be don to' (Aaron & Gibb, p. 87; also in *John Locke: Two Tracts on Government*, ed. Philip Abrams, Cambridge, 1967, p. 137). This is an echo of Matthew vii. 12, 'Therefore all things whatsoever ye would that men should do to you, do ye even so to them'. Hobbes uses it in *Leviathan*, II, xxvi. Locke's introduction to his paraphrase of Romans xiii opens: 'This section contains the duty of christians to the civil magistrate.' His paraphrase of xiii. 9 concludes: '...and whatever other command there be, concerning social duties, it in short is comprehended in this, "Thou shalt love thy neighbour as thyself"' (*Works*, VII, 369).

[1] *Essay*, III, IX, §23. The passage continues: 'Since then the precepts of natural religion are plain and very intelligible to all mankind and seldom come to be controverted, and other revealed truths, which are conveyed to us by books and languages, are liable to the common and natural obscurities and difficulties incident to words, methinks it would become us to be more careful and diligent in observing the former, and less magisterial, positive, and imperious in imposing our own sense and interpretations of the latter.'

Hans Aarsleff

Creator. The divine law was promulgated to man by the light of nature, or reason, as well as by the voice of revelation.[1] Our knowledge, it is true, will always fall short of perfection, but this is no cause for discouragement:

The infinite wise Contriver of us and all things about us hath fitted our senses, faculties, and organs to the conveniences of life, and the business we have to do here... We are furnished with faculties (dull and weak as they are) to discover enough in the creatures to lead us to the knowledge of the Creator and the knowledge of our duty, and we are fitted well enough with abilities to provide for the conveniences of living: these are our business in this world.[2]

We can attain knowledge sufficient to all our needs, both moral and natural. Locke clearly assumed that man in his conjectural state of nature has the means to gain an adequate knowledge of the law of nature, even though 'human reason unassisted... never from unquestionable principles, by clear deductions, made out an entire body of the "law of nature"',[3] for this would be to reach that perfection that lies beyond his capacities. As we shall see, Locke often insists that probable knowledge offers sufficient grounds for right conduct. Even the most highly skilled and most disinterested mind can never reach absolute certainty in its reasonings, except perhaps in the most trivial. We may be misled because 'the principles from which we conclude, the grounds upon which we bottom our reasoning, are but a part, something is left out, which should go into the reckoning, to make it just and exact'. We are not like the angels who, 'having perfect and exact views of all finite beings, that come under their consideration, can, as it were, in the twinkling of an eye, collect together all their scattered and almost boundless relations. A mind so furnished, what reason has it to acquiesce in the certainty of its conclusions!'[4] To Locke privately, special revelation gave certainty by joining religion and morality,[5] which in turn gave the conviction he needed that man's faculties were indeed, even in 'this imperfect state', adequate to the job of gaining moral knowledge. He could confidently found social morality on manifest revelation. Just as natural knowledge ministers to our material 'ease, safety, and delight', so 'an other use of his knowledg is to live in peace with his fellow men and this also he is capeable of'.[6]

Early in the *Second Treatise*, Locke stated the conviction that is fundamental to his conception of man and hence to his political philosophy:

[1] *Essay*, II, xxVIII, § 8. Cf. *ibid*. IV, xVIII, § 4. At the end of *ibid*. IV, x, § 7, Locke makes reference to Romans i. 19–20: 'For the invisible things of him from the creation of the world are clearly seen, being understood by the things that are made.' This is of course the traditional authority for natural religion; it is fully read in this sense in Locke's own paraphrase of these verses (in *Works*, VII, 258).
[2] *Essay*, II, xXIII, § 12.   [3] *Works*, VI, 140 (*Reasonableness*).
[4] *Works*, II, 327 (*Conduct*). Cf. *Essay*, II, x, § 9 and IV, xVII, § 14.
[5] King, *Life of John Locke*, p. 287.   [6] Aaron and Gibb, p. 87.

The state of nature and the nature of man

'Men [are] all the Workmanship of one Omnipotent, and infinitely wise Maker; All the Servants of one Sovereign Master, sent into the World by his order and about his business.'[1] This origin ensures that man shares in the order and contrivance of creation or nature which, rightly understood and used, gives him the opportunity to establish order and find happiness in his own world, 'for, God having, by an inseparable connexion joined *virtue* and *public happiness* together, and made the practice thereof necessary to the preservation of society, and visibly *beneficial* to all with whom the virtuous man has to do, it is no wonder that everyone should not only allow, but recommend and magnify those rules to others, from whose observance of them he is sure to reap advantage to himself'.[2] The universal and immutable, basic principles of civil society can be found in God's dispensation if only man will assiduously apply himself to the search for this knowledge. Civil society itself, however, is secular only, 'all the power of civil government relates only to men's civil interest, is confined to the care of the things of this world, and hath nothing to do with the world to come'.[3] No man or sect has any special claim to infallibility or truth; the ultimate grounds of authority and obligation are public and can be shared by all. This common and public source of moral knowledge is reason, which 'is natural *revelation*, whereby the eternal Father of light and fountain of all knowledge communicates to mankind that portion of truth which he has laid within the reach of their natural faculties'.[4] It goes for the truths found out by reason as for the truths of revelation that every man will consent to them, though each individual does not need to find them by his own effort, for 'as soon as they are heard and considered, they are found to be agreeable to reason; and such as can by no means be contradicted'.[5] To this extent at least all men are rational, while some in addition have sufficiently superior faculties and opportunities to find out as much of the law of nature as is necessary for the guidance of the rest, for 'who will say that entire nations are born blind'. The bonds of the law of nature 'are perpetual and coeval with the human race',[6] and hence all '*Mankind are one Community*, make up one Society distinct from

---

[1] *Two Treatises*, II, §6. Cf. *Essay*, IV, III, §18 and often elsewhere in Locke.
[2] *Essay*, I, III, §6.
[3] *Works*, V, 13 (*Toleration*): cf. *ibid.* pp. 42–3 and King, *Life of John Locke*, p. 300. For misunderstanding on this point see Richard H. Cox, *Locke on War and Peace* (Oxford, 1960), pp. 61–2.
[4] *Essay*, IV, XIX, §4. Cf. *ibid.* I, III, §20 (with irony): 'We and those of our mind are men of reason', and IV, XIX, §2: 'The assuming an authority of dictating to others and a forwardness to prescribe to their opinions is a constant concomitant of this bias and corruption of our judgments.'
[5] *Works*, VI, 140 (*Reasonableness*).
[6] *Essays on the Law of Nature*, ed. von Leyden, pp. 191, 193. Cf. p. 117.

all other Creatures'.[1] Without the guidance of reason, men may be violent, brutal, and unsociable, but men can be instructed to see that such conduct is not in their own best interest. Men are 'urged to enter into society by a certain propensity of nature', they are sociable to the degree that they follow reason, 'according to the law of nature men alike are friends of one another and are bound together by common interests'.[2]

We are thus left with Locke's firm conviction that 'God hath certainly appointed Government to restrain the partiality and violence of Men'.[3] God 'commands what reason does',[4] and 'the *Freedom* then of Man and Liberty of acting according to his own Will, is *grounded on* his having *Reason*, which is able to instruct him in that Law he is to govern himself by, and make him know how far he is left to the freedom of his own will'.[5] This is the question of the determination of the will and of morality, which '*is the proper science and business of mankind in general*'.[6] How does Locke explain that man can attain sufficient knowledge of morality to guide his conduct and secure his happiness? Two things are required: Man must be able to see that there is a law of nature, and he must be capable of understanding that it places a binding obligation upon him, both without recourse to special revelation.

The former point need not long detain us. It is based on the argument from design, is most fully explained in the *Fourth Essay of the Law of Nature*, and crops up again and again throughout Locke's writings. The light of nature is our only avenue of knowledge, and it draws its illumination from the inborn faculties of reason and sense-experience, 'for only these two faculties appear to teach and educate the minds of men and to provide what is characteristic of the light of nature, namely that things

[1] *Two Treatises*, II, §128.
[2] *Essays on the Law of Nature*, ed. von Leyden, pp. 157, 163. Locke frequently insists on the naturally social nature of man, e.g. in the opening words of book III of the *Essay*: 'God, having designed man for a sociable creature, made him not only with an inclination and under a necessity to have fellowship with those of his own kind, but furnished him also with language, which was to be the great instrument and common tie of society.' There is of course not the slightest foundation for the opinion that Locke by the phrase 'drive him into *Society*' (*Two Treatises*, II, §77) really meant to say that man is not a social creature. His sociability is natural, the forces opposed to it are unreasonable. Cf. quotation at p. 113, n. 3, below and Cox, *Locke on War and Peace*, pp. 106, 113–15.
[3] *Two Treatises*, II, §13.   [4] *Works*, VI, 11 (*Reasonableness*).
[5] *Two Treatises*, II, §63. Cf. Hooker, *Of the Laws of Ecclesiastical Polity*, I, VII, §2: 'Goodness is seen with the eye of the understanding. And the light of that eye, is reason.' *Ibid.* I, VII, §3: 'The object of Appetite is whatsoever sensible good may be wished for; the object of Will is that good which Reason doth lead us to seek.' 'Neither is any other desire properly Will, but that where Reason and Understanding, or the show of Reason, prescribeth the thing desired.' *Ibid.* I, VII, §4: 'Where understanding therefore needeth, in those things Reason is the director of man's will by discovering in action what is good. For the Laws of well-doing are the dictates of right Reason.'
[6] *Essay*, IV, XII, §11.

otherwise wholly unknown and hidden in the darkness should be able to come before the mind and be known and as it were looked into'.[1] Sense-experience shows us that 'this visible world is constructed with wonderful art and regularity, and of this world we, the human race, are also a part'.[2] Since this structure could not have come about by chance, it follows 'that there must be a powerful and wise creator of all these things', who must have made both the creatures and man, for neither the creatures nor man could have created man himself.[3] This Creator is not only powerful but must also be wise, consequently 'he has not created this world for nothing and without a purpose'. Man is required to do something, he is subject to 'the will on the part of a superior power with respect to the things to be done by us'.[4] There are then both a law and a law-maker, and 'all men everywhere are sufficiently prepared'[5] to make this discovery or at least assent to it, for it requires effort and application actually to make it: 'God has made the intellectual world harmonious and beautiful without us; but it will never come into our heads all at once; we must bring it home piece-meal, and there set it up by our own industry, or else we shall have nothing but darkness and a chaos within.'[6] A very rational being, perhaps more rational than any mere man ever was, may now be able to deduce man's obligations and duties from these considerations alone. But man being 'in the present state', the important question remains: how will man be able to see what the law of nature actually means, its ultimate import? It is the foundation of all moral rules, but since they cannot be derived *ex nihilo*, man must somehow have occasion to learn what they are. We do not all belong to 'the more rational part of men, in whom there was some sense of a common humanity, some concern for fellowship'.[7]

It is true that 'God commands what reason does', but how can reason 'know' what God commands? We must of course understand that nothing is achieved by reason itself 'unless there is first something posited and taken for granted'.[8] It cannot do anything without being first supplied with the material to work on, that is ideas derived from sensation, whether sense-experience or reflexion. Reason is always to be understood as a short way of saying 'the discursive faculty of the mind, which advances from things known to things unknown and argues from one thing to another in a definite and fixed order of propositions'. Natural law is

---

[1] *Essays on the Law of Nature*, ed. von Leyden, p. 147.
[2] *Ibid.* p. 151.   [3] *Ibid.* p. 153.
[4] *Ibid.* p. 157.
[5] *Ibid.* p. 155. The entire argument of the *Fourth Essay* is closely paralleled by Nicole's essay 'On the Existence of God', which Locke translated some years later.
[6] *Works*, II, 385 (*Conduct*).
[7] *Essays on the Law of Nature*, ed. von Leyden, p. 205.
[8] *Ibid.* p. 125.

Hans Aarsleff

'only the object of reason, not reason itself; that is to say, it is such truths as reason seeks and pursues as necessary for the direction of life and the formation of character'.[1] The law of nature is a kind of knowledge, and it conforms to revelation. It 'can be described as being the decree of the divine will discernible by the light of nature and indicating what is and what is not in conformity with rational nature, and for this very reason commanding and prohibiting'.[2] The materials that reason works on must then supply the guidance that is necessary to arrive at the immutable law of nature. These materials must somehow contain those rewards and punishments that are required before we can call it a law. We here come to the problem that has undoubtedly been the chief obstacle to the interpretation of Locke's doctrine of natural law. Without known rewards and punishments it would, as Locke himself often insists, be nothing. His conception of the state of nature would be reduced to verbal fiddling, and his political philosophy would turn into a rope of sand. Clearly, natural law can be derived neither from the civil law nor from the law of opinion or reputation. Generally, these laws will express the law of nature, but its truth cannot depend on them. It must have its foundation in the divine law as promulgated to man by the light of nature.[3] It must in other words have its origin in man's own nature, which agrees with my contention that the conjectural state of nature is built on Locke's conception of the nature of man.

A successful argument must demonstrate that man will find it to be in his own best and ultimate interest to follow the guidance of reason rather than the promptings of the passions.[4] Briefly, the argument is this: All men invariably pursue happiness, which is gained in terms of the avoidance of pain and the achievement of pleasure, and in higher degrees of pleasure rather than lower degrees. Pain raises uneasiness and longing for its alleviation in a relative pleasure; thus pleasure and pain, in short, cause desire which in turn affects the will to engage in a particular choice of

[1] *Essays on the Law of Nature*, p. 149.
[2] *Ibid.* p. 111. The attributes of the Creator ensure that his work has order, the order that conforms to reason. The decrees of the divine will cannot be arbitrary. It should be remembered that Locke did say that God cannot choose what is not good: 'I think we might say that God himself cannot choose what is not good: the freedom of the Almighty hinders not his being determined by what is best' (*Essay*, ii, xxi, §49). That Locke did not pursue Leibniz's stringent argument on this point surely does not invalidate or raise difficulties about the role he assigns to reason. Locke's requirement that revelation conforms to reason shows how close he was to Leibniz. God and his works are rational.
[3] *Essay*, ii, xxviii, §§7–8.
[4] Only after I had finished my exposition of the role of pleasure, pain, and design did I become aware of Professor Polin's *La politique morale de John Locke* (Paris, 1960). My argument was developed without any knowledge of his. Though I regret my ignorance, I am gratified by the agreement.

action that will avoid the pain and gain pleasure, thus removing the immediate sense of uneasiness. At this point reason can intervene in the determination of the choice of action; man has the power to suspend the immediate prosecution of desire in order to ensure that the first satisfaction does not lead to greater pain later. By this process man will, almost by a sort of evolution or natural selection, arrive at those moral rules which, found out by reason, constitute the law of nature. He will ultimately direct and control his conduct according to the mere probability that there is a future state that will depend on his conduct 'in this time of our probationership here'.[1] The conclusion is that

morally good and evil, then, is only the conformity or disagreement of our voluntary actions to some law, whereby good or evil is drawn on us from the will and power of the law-maker; which good and evil, pleasure or pain, attending our observance or breach of the law by the decree of the law-maker, is that we call *reward* and *punishment*.[2]

If this is called a utilitarian ethic, based on hedonism, the almost certain result will be needless confusion. Locke's so-called hedonism does not conflict with his natural-law teaching; on the contrary they belong together as the two halves of a sphere. The reason is obvious: pleasure and pain also come under the wise dispensation of the Creator and law-maker, whose rewards and punishments they are.

The most complete version of this argument first appeared in the second edition (1694) of the *Essay* as a revision and expansion of the original chapter xxi in book ii, 'Of Power'. The reworking of the chapter was undertaken in response to objections that had been raised to the earlier formulation in the shorter—though still very long—chapter in the first edition, chiefly by Locke's respected friend William Molyneux.[3] But rather

---

[1] Aaron and Gibb, p. 87. Cf. Locke's paraphrase of Romans xiii. 11: 'And all this do, considering that it is now high time that we rouse ourselves up, shake off sleep, and betake ourselves, with vigilancy and vigour, to the duties of a christian life. For the time of your removal, out of this place of exercise and probationership, is nearer than when you first entered into the profession of christianity' (*Works*, vii, 369).

[2] *Essay*, ii, xxviii, § 5. This is also in the first edition, though there of course in chapter xxvii. The references to ii, xx, § 2 and ii, xxi, § 42 at the beginning of the paragraph were first introduced in the fourth edition (1700).

[3] Tyrrell and James Lowde had raised objections to the closely related matter in the sections on 'moral relations' in ii, xxviii. The true import of the revision of the chapter 'Of Power' for the second edition has been obscured by A. C. Fraser's very misleading information in his edition of the *Essay* (2 vols. Oxford, 1894), which seems to have gained general acceptance. In a note to that chapter, he says that the sections after section 27 'were in great part omitted in the Second Edition, and in place of them thirty-five others (sections 28–60) were introduced'. He then prints the original sections 28–38, immediately followed by this contradictory statement: 'In the first edition chapter xxi consists of 47 sections only. Those reproduced above were omitted in the second and succeeding editions.' This is false. Section 28 is the only one which does not appear in the second edition. Sections 29–38 are included (some almost verbatim, others with some omissions) in the following sections in

clear intimations of the argument go back at least as far as the Journal of 1676, and it is also apparent in the first edition, both in the original chapter 'Of Power' and elsewhere. In all editions, the general subject of the chapter is quite different (or at least more specific) than what appears to be indicated by the title. It is an inquiry into human liberty and seeks to explain what makes men act the way they do. It is about the determination of the will. In the first twenty-seven sections, which are virtually identical in all editions, Locke raises the old question whether the will be free, and he shows that this is an improper way of putting the question because man cannot forbear to will or not to will once an immediate need for action has suggested itself. Freedom does not pertain to the will but to agents, 'in our being able to act or not to act according as we shall choose or *will*'.[1] The key question then is what determines the will. In the first edition Locke quickly—within two sections—arrived at the answer that 'Good, then, the greater Good is that alone which determines the Will', man invariably seeking happiness, that is pleasure rather than pain, and pleasure being associated with good.[2] This solution caused serious difficulties for several reasons: most men are not most of the time guided by 'the greater Good', and even if and when they are they may be misled by false appearances and wrong judgments. True, Locke had briefly mentioned that 'our understanding and reason was given us'[3] to overcome our 'feeble passionate nature', but he had quite failed to show how reason could play a decisive role all along the way in guiding man toward 'real happiness' and 'true felicity'. The revision of the chapter 'Of Power' was designed to achieve that.

The fundamental principle of all human action and conduct is the attainment of happiness. From this goal man cannot be deflected, he will invariably seek it though he may for several reasons be mistaken and misguided in his conception of that goal. It comprehends all men's actions, including the urge toward self-preservation, the continuation of the species, the gaining of food, shelter, and raiments, life with other men, the pursuit of knowledge, etc. No activity falls outside the realm of this

the second edition: 41, 42, 48–50, 54–5, 56, 58–60. The new sections in the second edition are: 28–40 (from which the revised argument can be understood by reading the section summaries), 43–7, 51–3, 57, 68–9, 71–2 (summary of the chapter, different of course from the original 46). Fraser's chapter has 75 sections because he, without the authority of any text that I have ever seen, makes a separate section (39) of the second paragraph in 38 and likewise makes two sections of 56 (of which the first paragraph first appeared in the Coste translation and first in English in the fifth edition as part of and preceding the original section 56 in the second, third, and fourth editions).

[1] *Essay*, II, xxi, § 27.
[2] *Essay*, first edition, II, xxi, § 29 at end; this phrase is omitted in later editions, but most of the original § 29 is incorporated in §§ 41 and 42 of the revision.
[3] *Essay*, first edition, II, xxi, § 44, in later editions § 67.

principle, and the pleasures that are sought may pertain to the mind as well as to the body. All voluntary actions have their origin in the will, and the will is determined by the mind. The mind in turn is spurred on to action by some present '*uneasiness*',[1] caused by a present pain and the awareness of an absent good, for instance the immediate alleviation of the pain. This hankering for an absent good, whether immediate or remote, is what is called 'desire', which almost invariably will accompany '*uneasiness*' and therefore will usually appear to be identical with it. An immediate sense of pain invariably raises a desire to be rid of it, but the desire for a remote absent good is strong only in relation to our contemplation of it. And the more distant the absent good is, even though great, the greater the need of contemplation and foresight to conceive sufficient uneasiness for the will to be guided into action toward it, even at the expense of forgoing more immediate pleasures. Desire always precedes the act of willing, and hence desire and will are distinct, which of course gives the mind an opportunity to intervene. Hence the '*good*, the *greater good*, though apprehended and acknowledged to be so, does not determine the *will*, until our desire, raised proportionably to it, makes us *uneasy* in the want of it'.[2] This machinery, as it were, of pain, pleasure, and uneasiness is all part of the great design:

Thus we see our all-wise Maker, suitable to our constitution and frame, and knowing what it is that determines the *will*, has put into man the *uneasiness* of hunger and thirst, and other natural desires, that return at their seasons, to move and determine their *wills* for the preservation of themselves, and the continuation of their species.

If contemplation alone had been enough, pain would have been superfluous:

It is better to marry than to burn, says St. *Paul*, where we may see what it is that chiefly drives men into the enjoyments of a conjugal life. A little burning felt pushes us more powerfully than greater pleasures in prospect draw or allure.[3]

Now, if all the business of man was to remedy the first most pressing uneasiness, he would almost entirely take the guidance of his appetites and passions, and—tastes being different—men might choose different things and yet all choose right. Men would be much 'like a company of poor insects, whereof some are bees, delighted with flowers and their sweetness; others beetles, delighted with other kinds of viands, which, having enjoyed for a season, they should cease to be and exist no more

---

[1] *Essay*, II, XXI, §29.
[2] *Ibid.* II, XXI, §35. This was the error that had especially weakened the argument of the original version of the chapter 'Of Power'.
[3] *Ibid.* II, XXI, §34.

for ever'.[1] But man can save himself from this state of the insect because he has reason and memory, can learn by experience, and can come to act in accord with the fruits of contemplation and knowledge, even if that knowledge only constitutes a probability. Man will begin to compare the consequences of his satisfactions in order to avoid a future pain greater than a particular pleasure he might gain.[2] The constant aim is happiness, and no one will knowingly engage in a pleasurable sequence of actions if he is convinced and fully aware that the final result will be even greater pain. To prevent this sort of error, he will not act before 'due *examination*', which is possible because 'we have a power to *suspend* prosecution of this or that desire, as everyone daily may experiment in himself'.[3] Thus reason is offered the opportunity to determine the will to the best line of action with a view to securing the greatest possible good that may be attainable. Pain and pleasure push men along and prompt them to make use of their reason in their own best interest. And this interest is indeed great, for the possibility of a future life that will depend on our conduct in this one cannot be denied; therefore

he that will allow exquisite and endless happiness to be but the possible consequence of a good life here, and the contrary state, the possible reward of a bad one, must own himself to judge very much amiss if he does not conclude that a virtuous life, with the certain expectation of everlasting bliss which may come, is to be preferred to a vicious one with the fear of that dreadful state of misery which, it is very possible, may overtake the guilty, or at best the terrible uncertain hope of annihilation.[4]

Even if this is so, it may be objected that man cannot without special revelation know what conduct is likely to be rewarded in a possible future life. The answer is obvious: It is clearly Locke's conception that the total wisdom of creation is such that the steady pursuit of happiness under the guidance of reason, disengaged from any immediate and contrary passions, will in fact constitute virtuous conduct. It is in this sense that all men are by nature rational, and if they exercise their rationality they will frame moral rules that secure their happiness; these moral rules are comprehended under the law of nature, which is the law of reason. The law of nature is not the product of every man's own interest except in this sense of constantly looking toward the distant aim of true felicity: 'The rightness of an action does not depend on its utility; on the contrary, its

---

[1] *Essay*, II, XXI, §55, and with somewhat different wording in original §35.
[2] Here as throughout, it goes without saying that Locke did not imagine that each individual had to go through the entire process from the very beginning. Most of the knowledge he needs will already be available from custom and tradition. Cf. *ibid.* II, XXVIII, §11 and Locke's answer to Lowde there.
[4] *Ibid.* II, XXI, §47.   [4] *Ibid.* II, XXI, §70.

The state of nature and the nature of man

utility is a result of its rightness.'[1] This power to suspend any particular desire is given so that 'we short-sighted creatures might not mistake true felicity', 'in this lies the liberty man has',[2] it is the 'hinge on which turns the *liberty* of intellectual beings...that they can *suspend* this prosecution in particular cases, till they have looked before them and informed themselves whether that particular thing which is then proposed or desired lies in the way to their main end, and makes a real part of that which is their greatest good'.[3]

Now it is clear that without this power of suspension, all men would invariably, like automatons, be immediately absorbed in the nearest pleasure, there would be no distinction between will and desire—indeed willing would become a meaningless and empty concept—and men would follow satisfactions as varied and contrary as their tastes. Passion, disorder, and chaos would reign universally. The greatest happiness would willy-nilly consist 'in the having those things which produce the greatest pleasure' rather than in pursuing those actions whose final consequence will be the greatest happiness.[4] Suspension ensures 'that our understandings may be *free* to examine, and reason unbiased give its judgment, being that whereon a right direction of our conduct to true happiness depends: it is in this we should employ our chief care and endeavours'.[5] Why? Because 'the rewards and punishments of another life, which the Almighty has established as the enforcements of his law, are of weight enough to determine the choice against whatever pleasure or pain this life can show, when the eternal state is considered but in its bare possibility, which nobody can make any doubt of'.[6] Men's 'wills carry them so contrarily' because they make wrong judgments about future consequences. Present pleasure, like objects near our view that 'are apt to be thought greater than those of a larger size that are more remote', will hold greater sway than a 'remote and future good'.[7] Men's actions will often terminate in misery rather than in the happiness they hoped to gain, and the cause is wrong judgment owing to '*the weak and narrow constitution of our minds*',[8]

[1] *Essays on the Law of Nature*, ed. von Leyden, p. 215. It is the concluding sentence of the eighth essay, entitled 'Is every man's own interest the basis of the law of nature? No.'
[2] *Essay*, II, XXI, §§ 50, 47.   [3] *Ibid.* II, XXI, § 52.
[4] Cf. Leo Strauss, *Natural Right and History* (Chicago, 1953), p. 249. The distinction between 'having those things' and 'pursuing those actions' is fundamental and obvious when read in context in II, XXI, § 55. Locke's statement is made 'by supposing them [men] only like a company of poor insects', which of course is not the way Locke in fact considers men, as the mention of the insects is designed to make clear. Strauss cites the words as if they state Locke's confirmed belief, i.e. the words are made to do the trick while the argument is totally disregarded. This 'method' alone makes Professor Strauss's argument possible. The examples are legion in his text, and it is unnecessary to show the falseness of every single one of them.
[5] *Essay*, II, XXI, § 53.   [6] *Ibid.* II, XXI, § 70.
[7] *Ibid.* II, XXI, §§ 63 and 57.   [8] *Ibid.* II, XXI, § 64.

Hans Aarsleff

which tend to be dominated by a present pain rather than the prospect of a distant pleasure and happiness. Absolute proof of the non-existence of a future state is not to be had, consequently the knowledge of the mere probability of a future state with rewards and punishments is that which must direct our search for happiness. This search must take reason for its guide since it is evident that the mere satisfaction of the passions produces only temporary and even at best very uncertain happiness owing to the lack of a fixed goal of the greatest possible happiness toward which the exertions of foresight may be firmly directed. Thus it is the wise design of man and creation that he who is 'by nature rational' will take the guidance of reason and knowledge in making such a reckoning of pleasure and pain, reward and punishment, that he may in the end hope to achieve the greatest happiness. Men cannot be diverted from their happiness except by mistake; they will follow the law of nature or reason toward order, peace, and harmony, whether they learn the rules by their own private efforts or from others. Reason will in fact do what God commands. Unsuspended desire acts in the instant, reason puts foresight into operation. The marginal summary to section 53 states the entire issue succinctly: 'Government of our passions, the right improvement of liberty.'[1]

In the revision of 'The Epistle to the Reader' in the second and subsequent editions of the *Essay*, Locke told the reader that he had 'found reason somewhat to alter the thoughts I formerly had concerning that which gives the last determination to the *Will* in all voluntary actions'. Upon second thoughts, he had decided that it is not, 'as is generally supposed, the greater good in view, but some (and for the most part the most pressing) *uneasiness* a man is at present under'.[2] As already mentioned, pleasure and pain, happiness and misery, figured prominently both in the original and in the revised version, but the latter tightened the argument and gave it a firmer base by introducing 'uneasiness', by making the distinction between desire and will, by giving importance to the power to suspend the prosecution of any particular desire, and by providing a fuller discussion of 'wrong judgment'. The result was a greater role for reason and the enlargement of man's liberty. It might then appear as if this argument first occurred to Locke when he wrote his revision of the long chapter 'Of Power', but this is not the case. In fact the original version in the first edition appears anachronistic when compared both with other passages in the same edition and with what he had earlier

---

[1] The marginal summaries were Locke's own addition to the second edition, at Molyneux's request (*Works*, VIII, 309, 313).
[2] *Essay*, II, XXI, §31. Other references to this change of mind occur in II, XXI, §§35, 71, 72.

written on the subject.¹ The original introduction of pleasure and pain in chapter VII of book II had used the word 'uneasiness' in passing, and Locke had strongly insisted that pleasure and pain were divinely instituted for our guidance by 'the wisdom and goodness of the Sovereign Disposer of all things'.² He had returned to the subject in chapter xx—'*pleasure and pain and that which causes them, good and evil, are the hinges on which our passions turn*'—and he had here equated uneasiness with desire, 'which is greater or less, as that uneasiness is more or less vehement'.³ Furthermore, in the chapter 'Of other Relations', he had devoted thirteen important sections to 'moral relations', and here for the first time in the *Essay* firmly identified pleasure and pain with the reward and punishment of the law-maker, who thus set bounds to '*morally good and evil*', a doctrine that was the natural consequence of what he had already said when first introducing the simple ideas of pleasure and pain in chapter VII.⁴ He had also shown that the rules for man's conduct contained in the 'civil law' and in the 'law of opinion or reputation' could not be known to have more than local validity, whereas 'the *divine* law...whether promulgated to them by the light of nature or the voice of revelation' had universal validity as 'the only true touchstone of *moral rectitude*'. This law will, however, tend to find expression in the law of opinion, for 'it is no wonder that esteem and discredit, virtue and vice, should in a great measure every-where correspond with the unchangeable rule of right and wrong, which the law of God hath established'.⁵ Finally, in the first edition Locke had

---

¹ In a letter to Molyneux of 20 January 1692/3, Locke admitted his own reservations about 'my discourse about Liberty'. He had not at first planned it to be part of the treatment of power, and would have left it out if some friends had not persuaded him to the contrary (*Works*, VIII, 304). The revision was written during the summer of 1693. On 15 July 1693, Locke sent Molyneux a list of summaries of the new sections, but this list does not correspond to the final version, though the sense and direction of the changes are clear (*Works*, VIII, 317). On 23 August, he wrote 'my essay is now very near ready for another edition; and upon review of my alterations, concerning what determines the will, in my cool thoughts, I am apt to think them to be right, as far as my thoughts can reach in so nice a point'. He then gave the summary of the argument which is found verbatim in the first part of section 71, from 'Liberty is a power to act' to 'guided by his own judgment' (*Works*, VIII, 325–6). It is also noteworthy that the account of this chapter given in the 'Abstract of the Essay', written for the *Bibliothèque Universelle*, is very short and inadequate (King, *Life of John Locke*, pp. 373–4).
² *Essay*, II, VII, §6. Cf. II, xx, §§3–6.
³ *Ibid.* II, xx, §§3 and 6. It was in the latter section that Leibniz first encountered 'uneasiness', of which he highly approved: 'Cette considération de l'inquiétude est un point capital, où cet Auteur a monstré particulièrement son esprit pénétrant et profond.' Coste's French translation had a clarifying note on this concept. The latter part of section 6 was added in the second edition. It looks forward to the central point in the argument of the revision of chapter xxi, summed up in this succinct statement: 'Where, by the by, it may perhaps be of some use to remark that the chief, if not only, spur to human industry and action is uneasiness.'
⁴ Moral relations are the subject of *Essay*, II, xxviii, §§4–16. See II, xxviii, §5.
⁵ *Ibid.* II, xxviii, §§8 and 11. At the end of this section Locke cites Philippians iv. 8: 'Whatsoever is lovely, whatsoever is of good report, if there be any virtue, if there be any praise, think on

repeatedly, both in the chapter 'Of Power' and elsewhere, insisted that the mere possibility of a future state with rewards and punishments for our conduct 'in this time of our probationership here'[1] is sufficient to guide us to the law of nature and to accepting it as binding, as an obligation, 'for the state we are at present in not being that of vision, we must, in many things, content ourselves with faith and probability'.[2]

It has now been demonstrated that the argument concerning moral rules and the law of nature, which I have derived chiefly from the revised version of the chapter 'Of Power', can also be found in the first edition at large; the original version of that chapter is therefore an anachronism even in 1690. My intent is of course to reject the imputation that my account of how Locke conceived man to gain knowledge of natural law pertains only to arguments which Locke did not develop until after the time of the composition of the *Two Treatises*. We know little about the chronology of the composition of the *Essay*, but even the scanty information we have indicates that its composition in a version much like that of the first edition was contemporaneous with the writing of the *Two Treatises*, and this would seem especially true of Book II.[3] On the basis of writings that have been published within the last generation, it can, however, be demonstrated that Locke even earlier was intensely preoccupied

these things.' On this point Locke was misrepresented by James Lowde, and Locke answered him in a manner that modern interpreters might well profit from: 'It is plain that I brought that passage of St. *Paul* not to prove that the general measure of what men call *virtue* and *vice* throughout the world was the reputation and fashion of each particular society within itself, but to show that, though it were so, yet, for reasons I there give, men, in that way of denominating their actions, did not for the most part much vary from the law of nature, which is that standing and unalterable rule by which they ought to judge of the moral rectitude and pravity of their actions and accordingly denominate them *virtues* and *vices*.' Until the fourth edition, Locke's answer to Lowde was added to the 'Epistle to the Reader', but thereafter moved to its proper place as a note to II, XXVIII, §11. Fraser gives the misleading information that these paragraphs 'are omitted in the posthumous editions'.

[1] Aaron and Gibb, p. 87.

[2] *Essay*, IV, III, §6. 'Faith' does not mean religious belief as commonly understood, but faith in the order, design, and wisdom of all things in creation (cf. also Draft *A*, pp. 55–6, King, *Life of John Locke*, pp. 106, 113). Cf. *Essay*, IV, XIV, especially §§2–3: 'Therefore, as God has set some things in broad daylight, as he has given us some certain knowledge, though limited to a few things in comparison...so, in the greatest part of our concernment, he has afforded us only the twilight, as I may so say, of *probability*, suitable, I resume, to that state of mediocrity and probationership he has been pleased to place us in here...a constant admonition to us to spend the days of this our pilgrimage with industry and care in the search and following of that way which might lead us to a state of greater perfection. It being highly rational to think, even were revelation silent in the case, that as men employ those talents God has given them here, they shall accordingly receive their rewards at the close of the day, when their sun shall set and night shall put an end to their labours. 3. The faculty which God has given man to supply the want of clear and certain knowledge, in cases where that cannot be had, is *judgment*.' Cf. also IV, XI, §10 and, already quoted, II, XXI, §70.

[3] See *Essays on the Law of Nature*, ed. von Leyden, p. 271 n.

with the same problems, with happiness, pleasure, pain, moral rectitude and its rules, and with the determination of the will, in the years prior to the period we have now reached, just as they continued to engage him for the rest of his life. In fact, they are his chief 'concernment', to use the word he himself, though he uses it sparingly, always introduces in the context of these important matters.[1]

In 1681 Locke made an entry in his *Common-Place Book* that looks forward to his formulation of the law of 'opinion or reputation' in the *Essay*. In this entry he observed that virtue and vice are functions of society, whose esteem and reputation give moral strength in the performance of virtuous actions. 'This, if well considered,' he continued, 'will give us better boundaries of virtue and vice, than curious questions stated with the nicest distinctions.'[2] Near the end of the decade, Locke returned to the same problem in 'Of Ethics in General', which as we shall see occupies a central position in his development toward the final position on the sources of our knowledge of natural law in the *Essay*, toward the position that pain and pleasure and the search for the greatest happiness ultimately determine the will and thus behind it the mind in finding out invariable moral rules. For these questions were already clearly debated in Draft *A* and Draft *B* in 1671 as well as in a number of important entries in his journals for 1676 and 1677. Passages from both drafts reappear verbatim in 'Of Ethics in General', and passages from all three in turn in the *Essay*, chiefly already in the original chapter 'Of Relations', but also in the revision of the chapter 'Of Power'. The theme of all these is the same, and their contents steadily move toward the finding of 'the true touchstone of *moral rectitude*'.[3] This position Locke had already essentially worked out in the journal entries of 1676 and 1677. This true touchstone, as already observed, must be found in each man individually; it can neither be a function of society, nor be found by verbal fiddling.

'Of Ethics in General' opens with Locke's ruling principle, 'Happiness and misery are the two great springs of human actions'.[4] In the opening six sections he deals with the observation that 'some kind of morality is to be found everywhere received'. He takes heart in the consideration

---

[1] See, for example, H. R. Fox Bourne, *The Life of John Locke*, 2 vols. (London, 1876), I, 181, 182; *An Early Draft*, p. 20; Aaron and Gibb, pp. 81, 85, 87, 88; King, *Life of John Locke*, pp. 308, 372.

[2] King, *Life of John Locke*, pp. 292–3. King misdates the entry to 1661, corrected by Abrams (*Two Tracts*, p. 9) to 1681. The example of taking away the sword of a man about to harm himself is also in *Essay*, II, XXVIII, §16, i.e. at the end of the sections on 'moral relations', which are also the subject of the entry. [3] *Ibid.* II, XXVIII, 8.

[4] 'Of Ethics in General' is printed in King, *Life of John Locke*, pp. 308–13. The number of sections should be 12, as indicated by von Leyden (*Essays on the Law of Nature*), p. 70 n.: i.e. what King gives as section 10 should be divided into sections 10, 11, 12. Section 11 begins 'but because we cannot', section 12 'To establish morality, therefore'.

Hans Aarsleff

that morality has always been the business of philosophy rather than of religion or the law, 'a plain argument to me of some discovery still amongst men, of the law of nature, and a secret apprehension of another rule of action which rational creatures had a concernment to conform to, besides what either the priest pretended was the immediate command of their God...or the lawyer told them was the command of the Government'. So far, however, the philosophers have failed by not 'deriving these rules up to their original', so that 'the utmost enforcements they could add to them were reputation and disgrace by those names virtue and vice, which they endeavoured by their authority to make names of weight to their scholars and the rest of the people'.[1] The firmest of these rules are those that pertain to the preservation of society, but even those rules with all the rest would still come about even if there were 'no obligation or superior law at all, besides that of society'. What are virtues in one country may be vices in another, 'and in others indifferent, according as the authority of some esteemed wise men in some places, or as inclination or fashion of people in other places, have happened to establish them virtues or vices; so that the ideas of virtues taken up this way teach us no more than to speak properly according to the fashion of the country we are in, without any very great improvement of our knowledge, more than what men meant by such words; and this is the knowledge contained in the common ethics of the schools'.[2] This of course will not satisfy Locke, for the superior law and its obligation are still lacking, for 'whilst they discourse ever so acutely of temperance or justice, but show no law of a superior that prescribes temperance, to the observation or breach of which law there are rewards and punishments annexed, the force of morality is lost, and evaporates only into words, disputes, and niceties'.[3]

[1] 'Of Ethics', §§1–4; so far, though not verbatim, these sections correspond to *Essay*, II, XXVIII, §§10–12, and for §3 especially IV, XII, §11.

[2] 'Of Ethics', §5. Most of §§4–5 are taken almost verbatim from Draft *B*, §157, which in turn corresponds verbatim to Draft *A* from beginning of last paragraph on p. 37 to p. 38, l. 12. Draft *B*, §156 (with the addition of a five-line insert) corresponds verbatim to Draft *A*, first paragraph of §25 on p. 37 (and also *ibid.* pp. 17–18). This reference to the 'ethics of the schools' explains why this law in the first edition of the *Essay* was called, not the law of 'opinion and reputation' as in the second and later editions, but the 'philosophical law, not because philosophers make it, but because they have most busied themselves to inquire after it'. It is significant that Locke's doctrine that 'the ideas of virtues taken up this way teach us no more than to speak properly according to the fashion of the country we are in' finds direct statement as a principle in *Essay*, II, XXVIII, §2, which precedes the important sections on 'moral relations': '...mankind have fitted their notions and words to the use of common life and not to the truth and extent of things'. This involves the doctrine of intranslatability among languages, stated in III, v, §8. This is the point Locke makes in *Two Treatises*, II, §12, which has been often misinterpreted in ignorance of this point.

[3] 'Of Ethics', §9. This paragraph is an amplification of section 6, whose sense, though not the precise wording, is the same as Draft *B*, §158, which in turn (except for two brief inser-

The state of nature and the nature of man

So far we have been concerned with sections in 'Of Ethics' which have direct counterparts in the early drafts, either taken over verbatim or as amplifications of themes already stated there. This is also true of the first half of section 11 and all of section 10, which are taken over verbatim from Draft B.[1] This passage, going back to 1671, contains the important solution to the problem of finding a firm foundation, something more than local words referring to virtues and vices, 'these notions or standards of our actions not being ideas of our own making, to which we give names, but depend upon something without us, and so not made by us, but for us, and these are the rules set to our actions by the declared will or laws of another, who hath power to punish our aberrations'. What Locke is here referring to are of course pleasure and pain, which he has already explained in two earlier sections—7 and 8—which have no counterpart in the early drafts. These two sections contain in embryo the argument of the revised chapter 'Of Power' in the second edition of the *Essay*. 'Moral actions are only those that depend upon the choice of an understanding and free agent', and 'there is nothing morally good which does not produce pleasure to a man, nor nothing morally evil that does not bring pain to him'. The reason is the grand design of things, as Locke says in the concluding lines of section 8: 'Rewards and punishments are the good and evil whereby superiors enforce the observance of their laws; it being impossible to set any other motive or restraint to the actions of a free understanding agent, but the consideration of good or evil; that is, pleasure or pain that will follow from it.'[2] It is this kind of statement that has given rise to the argument that Locke, as he developed increasing dependence on pleasure and pain (i.e. 'hedonism'), came into conflict with his doctrine of natural law. But it is strikingly evident from these passages that the law of nature is lame and ineffectual without enforcement, without rewards and punishments, without pleasure and pain, which 'depend upon something without us'. Far from conflicting with natural law, the hedonism—by now a misleading term—is the means by which man is guided to the moral rules that pertain to the law of nature. It was precisely in this regard that the early *Essays of the Law of Nature* had remained unsatisfactory: they had shown the design of the law-maker in the creatures, but had failed to show how the rewards and punishments worked in each individual toward observation of that law. On this point

tions in Draft B) corresponds verbatim to Draft A, middle of p. 38. The rest of this page, except for the last two lines, is verbatim the first part of Draft B, §159, the rest of which is an amplification of the final four lines of Draft A, §25.

[1] Section 160, from the beginning to King, *Life of John Locke*, p. 313, l. 3, which in turn is verbatim from Draft A, §25 up to l. 5 from the bottom in King, *Life of John Locke*, p. 312, with a five-line insertion in the middle of Draft B, §160.

[2] This says the same as *Essay*, II, XXVIII, §5, already quoted.

the *Essay*, and especially the revision of the chapter 'Of Power', super-
seded the early *Essays*. We shall now see that the argument of the two
important sections 7 and 8 in 'Of Ethics in General' had already been
worked out in the journal entries for 1676 and 1677, that is before the *Two
Treatises* were written with their heavy dependence on the law of nature.¹

As early as the *Fourth Essay of the Law of Nature* Locke had in fact
introduced pleasure and pain, emphatically linked to the design of the law-
maker, though this mention remained an isolated occurrence in those *Essays*:

Since He has Himself created the soul and constructed the body with wonderful
art, and has thoroughly explored the faculties and powers of each, as well as
their hidden constitution and nature, He can fill and stir the one with sorrow
or delight, the other with pain or pleasure; He also can lift both together to a
condition of the utmost happiness or thrust them down to a state of misery and
torment. Hence it appears clearly that, with sense-experience showing the way,
reason can lead us to the knowledge of a law-maker or of some superior power
to which we are necessarily subject.²

The early drafts did not speak so plainly, but did refer to pain and pleasure
in the context of 'moral relations' as 'another sort of moral Ideas or

---

¹ Professor von Leyden argues, *Essays on the Law of Nature*, pp. 70–3, that Locke's hedonism
was in direct conflict with his natural law and that this difficulty remained unresolved, in
fact stymied Locke in all later attempts to deal with morality. On p. 72, Professor von Leyden
cites a deleted passage from 'Of Ethics', §8, and then remarks that 'the passage, I think,
reveals the inherent difficulty in the issue between Locke's hedonism and his belief in an
absolute system of moral principles'. It is already clear why I find this view unacceptable;
indeed the deleted passage works strongly in favour of my argument. 'Moral rectitude'
and 'turpitude' are merely 'good words', for the former, 'which when considered is
but conformity to the natural law of God, would signify nothing and moral goodness be
no reason to direct my action, were there not really pleasure that would follow from the
doing of it and pain avoided greater than is to be found in the action itself'. Professor von
Leyden believes that this passage was 'afterwards deleted, obviously at the time when he
intended to pursue his discussion on natural law at the end of the paper'. But surely the
passage was deleted to avoid repetition because the concluding part of the section gives
better and more forceful statement to the same principle. And the final section of the
paper on ethics may be read both as a summary and as a looking forward to what was
accomplished in the *Essay*, in the revised chapter 'Of Power' especially. Professor von Leyden
further believes that Locke's scepticism about language grew with time, thus causing increasing difficulty to a treatment of morality in his later works (pp. 73–5). But here again,
already in Draft *A* (pp. 12–13) and Draft *B*, Locke spoke as strongly as ever about the tricki-
ness of words and especially of moral words: 'And therefor in the discourse I have here
made concerning humane Intellect I could not avoid saying a great deale concerning words
because soe apt and usuall to be mistaken for things, and therefor I must here again remember
that in all discourses where specific words—espetialy of substances or relations among which
are moral words...' Cf. Draft *B*, §159: 'These moral words are in discourses amongst
men using the same language often not understood by one another, and at best of very
doubtful and uncertain signification.' The main statement is in *Essay*, III, IX, §§5–7, but also
often elsewhere. Locke's note from 1693, quoted by von Leyden (pp. 72–3), relates directly
to the revision of the chapter 'Of Power', which he was preparing at that time. Though
'Of Ethics in General' dates from 1689, it is clearly a digest of passages and notes written
earlier.   ² *Essays on the Law of Nature*, ed. von Leyden, p. 155.

rules of our actions' that depend 'upon something without us and so not made by us but for us'. Both drafts, however, insisted that the evidence we have of 'pain or pleasure, i.e. happynesse or misery' is especially certain, 'beyond which we have noe concernment either of knowing or being'.[1] Draft *A* had also emphatically introduced Locke's theme concerning the probability of all important knowledge on which the judgment must act.[2] Finally Draft *A* had observed 'that it is the nature of the understanding constantly to close with the more probable side, but yet the will hath a power to suspend and restrain its enquirys and not permitt a full and satisfactory examination as far as the matter in question is capable, and will beare it, to be made'.[3] These themes reach their full development toward the final doctrine in a series of journal entries that were set down during Locke's residence in Southern France—and it seems during the years when he was also translating three of Nicole's *Essais*, which appear to have a very close relevance to his great concernment at this time.

On 16 July 1676, Locke made a long shorthand entry which, as Professor von Leyden has pointed out in his commentary, anticipates the revised version of the chapter 'Of Power', though as I have shown above it also anticipated other passages of the first edition of the *Essay* outside the anachronistic original version of that chapter. This entry again takes up the God-ordained nature of pleasure and pain, very much like the earlier passage in the *Fourth Essay of the Law of Nature*.[4] But the chief importance of the entry consists in the first introduction of the concept of 'uneasiness' as the equivalent of desire and in the observation that goes with it—later to become so significant in the revised chapter 'Of

---

[1] Draft *A*, p. 20 at bottom, and verbatim Draft *B*, §39 at end. Draft *B*, §22, further observes that 'the ideas of those things are most deeply impressed and soonest come to be noticed, which do either most frequently affect the senses, or else do bring with them pleasure or pain (the main business of the senses being to give notice of those things which either hurt or delight the body)'.

[2] Especially in Draft *A*, §§32–7; thus §32 takes up the theme later made the subject of *Essay*, IV, XIV 'Of Judgment', §33 that of IV, XV 'Of Probability', and §§34–5 the theme of IV, XVI 'Of the degrees of Assent'. Section 35 went into the *Essay* almost verbatim as IV, XVI, §7. Section 34 contains perhaps the most succinct statement in Locke to the effect that he shared Hume's analysis of cause and effect.

[3] Draft *A*, p. 65. This theme is again taken up in a journal entry for 13 July 1676 (Aaron and Gibb, p. 80): 'Willing *Voluntas*, i.e. wherein the minde doth after consideration or at least some thought begin continue change or stop some action which it findes in its power soe to doe', and 'we have a power to begin continue vary stop or suspend as we thinke fit, when any variation in any of these is made upon thinking we ascribe it to the will'. This corresponds to the matter of the opening sections of *Essay*, II, XXI, especially §5. On 29 July 1676 Locke returned to the subject of probability and the existence of a deity, again using the phrase 'reason, which always follows the more probable side' (Aaron and Gibb, p. 81).

[4] This entry is printed in *Essays on the Law of Nature*, ed. von Leyden, pp. 265–72. Page 265: 'God has so framed the constitutions of our minds and bodies that several things are apt to produce in both of them pleasure and pain, delight and trouble, by ways that we know not, but for ends suitable to His goodness and wisdom.'

Power'—that 'the pleasure and pain I spoke so much of here is principally that of the mind, for impressions made on the body, if they reach not the mind, produce neither pain nor pleasure'.[1] The result is the first emphatic statement 'that happiness and misery seem to me wholly to consist in this pleasure and pain of the mind, of which every little trouble or satisfaction is a degree; and the completion of either is when the mind to the highest degree and utmost capacity is filled and possessed by the ideas of either kind'.[2]

The final development of the thoughts that must have occupied Locke so intensely during his residence in France comes in the journal entry for 8 February 1677.[3] It has the superscription 'how far and by what means the will works upon the understanding and assent', a question that directly links it to the entries we have just been considering. It is the central question about the determination of the will. It may therefore at first appear surprising that the entry does not address itself directly to that question, but deals with the problem whether the extent of the knowledge available to man is sufficient to secure his happiness, both in regard to his material needs and to the moral rules that must guide his conduct. But there is of course no discrepancy at all: to inquire into the determination of the will, which as we have seen is guided by the mind, is to inquire into the knowledge man can gain toward securing his happiness. Thus this entry first presents the synthesis that later gained statement in the *Essay* in the chapters 'Of Power' and 'relations' in Book II, and in Book IV in the chapters devoted to knowledge (both of the existence of God and 'of other things') and its improvement, and to judgment, probability, and the degrees of assent. And just as Locke later in the fourth edition added chapters to both books on the association of ideas and on enthusiasm, so he had also in the early 1680s been much concerned with the sort of pretended knowledge that did not submit to the public test of reason, but laid claim to truth by private inspiration, i.e. enthusiasm, as he already called it then.[4]

[1] *Essays on the Law of Nature*, p. 267.
[2] *Ibid.* p. 268. Locke had in fact introduced 'uneasiness' three days earlier in an entry printed in Aaron and Gibb, pp. 80–1. In addition to the simple ideas of perception and willing, 'there seeme to me to be two others which joyn themselves upon occasion and are produced by allmost all the Ideas both of body and minde and these are those of pleasure or delight on one hand and pain or disturbance on the other. In our English language we call that which is an uneasinesse in the minde trouble or greife...' The example of a man's sitting still or deciding to walk, *ibid.* p. 271, is also in *Essay*, II, XXI, §24.
[3] Aaron and Gibb, pp. 84–90.
[4] These entries are printed in Aaron and Gibb, pp. 114–16 (3 April 1681), pp. 119–21 (19 February 1682), and pp. 123–5 (21 February 1682). On 10 April 1697, Locke wrote to Molyneux that he had begun a chapter, intended for inclusion in the *Essay*, under the title 'The Conduct of the Understanding' (*Works*, VIII, 407).

The state of nature and the nature of man

Naturally, the question whether man's knowledge is sufficient to his happiness receives a strong affirmative answer, which is in no way endangered by the probability of all that man can usefully know. Though it is brief, this entry may well be considered the best, most comprehensive and succinct statement of the ideas that are most fundamental to Locke's entire philosophy and to the motives and aspirations that inspired him in his search for the means to happiness, that is for the guidance of all man's thoughts and actions from the most trivial to the final and firm vision of a probable future state, to the belief that gives a certain and uniform, eternal and unalterable, measure to moral rectitude. Even the structure of this brief discourse reveals a clarity and symmetry that convey conviction and authority. Man has 'facultys and organs well adapted' to discover 'new and beneficiall productions whereby our stock of riches (i.e. things usefull for the conveniencys of our life) may be increased or better preservd', and 'we have noe reason to complain' if 'perhaps the essence of things their first originall, their secret way of workeing and the whole extent of corporeall beings be as far beyond our capacity as it is besides our use'. This is one use of knowledge, and it corresponds of course to the programme of the Royal Society. In addition, 'an other use of his knowledg is to live in peace with his fellow men and this also he is capeable of'. Here Locke reaches the epitome of his conviction:

It being then possible and at least probable that there is another life where in we shall give an account for our past actions in this to the great god of heaven and earth, here comes in another and that the main concernment of mankinde and that is to know what those actions are that he is to doe what those are he is to avoid what the law is he is to live by here and shall be jugd by hereafter, and in this part too he is not left soe in the darke but that he is furnishd with principles of knowledg and facultys able to discover light enough to guid him, his understanding seldome failes him in this part unlesse where his will would have it soe.

Such a perverse turn of the will can occur only if the passions rather than reason are allowed to rule. Man therefore has the means to discharge his business 'to be happy in this world by the enjoyment of the things of nature subservient to life health ease and pleasure and by the comfortable hopes of an other life when this is ended'. What does not relate 'to our happynesse any way [is] noe part of our businesse and therefor tis not to be wonderd if we have not abilitys given us to deale with things that are not to our purpose, nor conformeable to our state or end'. The law man 'is to live by here and shall be jugd by hereafter' is of course the law of nature, i.e. reason working on sense-experience in the search for the one and ultimate happiness that must be the fixed goal. The great passionate

Hans Aarsleff

thought that informed Locke in all his endeavours and writings was his concernment for our conduct, or as he said in the opening chapter of the *Essay*: 'Our business here is not to know all things, but those which concern our conduct.' This was the grand theme that occupied the most universal and cosmopolitan spirits of the seventeenth century, and the only contender that rivals Locke is his great admirer Leibniz. By comparison, Berkeley and Hume in the next century are insular spirits, and it has been the misfortune of Locke's reputation that he has been judged not by his context but on matters which formed a small part of his great endeavour.[1]

Thus I have come to the end of my argument that it is a consequence of Locke's conception of the nature of man that man could also come to the knowledge of the law of nature, and that Locke had worked out this conception by the time he began the *Two Treatises*. Those powerful simple ideas of pain and pleasure, put into man's being by his maker for a purpose, steer him toward happiness and show him that reason (which is short for the light of nature which embraces reason and sense-experience) is indispensable to the attainment of the higher and the highest degrees of happiness.[2] Man will learn that it is in his interest to follow the law of reason, which 'is not so much the Limitation as *the direction of a free and intelligent Agent* to his proper Interest, and prescribes no farther than is for the general Good of those under that Law. Could they be happier without it, the *Law*, as an useless thing would of it self vanish.'[3] The immediate pursuit of momentary pleasures without foresight will lead to disorder, violence, and war. Happiness and violence are incompatible, and 'were there no fear of violence, there would be no government in the

[1] I know of no work that gives a better introduction to the context in question than R. W. Meyer's *Leibnitz and the Seventeenth-Century Revolution* (Cambridge, 1952). It was first published at Hamburg in 1948 as *Leibniz und die europäische Ordnungskrise*. It seems to have received much less attention than it deserves in the English-speaking world.

[2] In a journal entry for 1 October 1678 on happiness, Locke linked happiness to pain and pleasure, and referred not only to 'the experience of all mankind', but also 'to the best rule of this—the Scripture, which tells us that at the right-hand of God, the place of bliss, are pleasures for evermore; and that which men are condemned for, is not for seeking pleasure, but for preferring the momentary pleasures of this life to those joys which shall have no end'. The reference is to Psalm xvi. 11: 'Thou wilt shew me the path of life: in thy presence is fulness of joy; at thy right hand there are pleasures for evermore.' (This entry is printed in King, *Life of John Locke*, p. 116; for precise date, see *Locke's Travels in France 1675-9*, ed. John Lough, Cambridge, 1953, p. 287.) Locke cited the same verse in *Essay*, II, VII, §5, on 'why God hath scattered up and down *several degrees of pleasure and pain in all the things that environ and affect us*'. He repeated it, again in the context of pleasure and pain, happiness and misery, in *Essay*, II, XXI, §41 (in the first edition §29), where he added part of a verse from 1 Cor. ii. 9: '*Happiness* and *misery* are the names of two extremes, the utmost bounds whereof we know not: 'tis what *Eye hath not seen, Ear hath not heard, nor hath it entered into the Heart of Man to conceive*.'

[3] *Two Treatises*, II, §57. The 'direction of a free and intelligent Agent' is the question of the determination of the will.

world, nor any need of it'.[1] The doctrine of natural law adumbrated in the early *Essays* on that subject was incomplete because they failed to show how each individual, by the contrivance of his maker, could come to the knowledge of that law. Obviously, this also means that the publication of these early *Essays* would not, in spite of the expectations of Tyrrell and others, have made any contribution to solving the problem of natural law raised by the *Two Treatises*, in fact their publication would merely have created further confusion. There is no conflict between the early *Essays* and the *Essay*, but the development of an argument that provides a firm basis for man's knowledge of moral rules; the so-called hedonism is the indispensable means to that knowledge. Furthermore, there is no conflict between the *Two Treatises* and the *Essay*, nor between the natural law that is assumed in the former and the account of it that is given in the latter. In addition, the important journal entry for 8 February 1677 reminds us that both works deal with our conduct. The relationship between these two works may, however, occupy us a little further since certain objections have been raised which, if true, would tend to show their essential incompatibility.

One objection says that 'the *Essay* has no room for natural law', and the other suggests that Locke in the *Two Treatises* was inclined to postulate the innateness of natural law.[2] As to the former objection, I think it can now hardly require any demonstration that the only truly fundamental one of the three laws 'that men generally refer their actions to', the 'divine law', comprehends the law of nature. This identification Locke makes so often throughout his works that it cannot be missed. One passage, written to satisfy Tyrrell, recalls all the rest, of which I have already quoted many that antedate both the *Two Treatises* and this addition to the second edition of the *Essay* in 1694: 'The *divine* law, whereby I mean that law which God has set to the actions of men, whether promulgated to them by the light of nature or the voice of revelation.'[3] As has now been pointed out re-

---

[1] Fox Bourne, *Life of John Locke*, I, 185 ('Essay concerning Toleration' from 1667).
[2] See *Two Treatises*, p. 81 and surrounding pages. These arguments are also found in other interpreters.
[3] II, xxviii, §8. This conviction goes back as early as the first tract on the civil magistrate: 'Wherever God hath made known his will either by the discoveries of reason, usually called the law of nature, or the revelations of his word, there nothing is left man but submission and obedience, and all things within the compass of this law are necessarily and indispensably good or evil' (Abrams, *Two Tracts*, p. 124). The acts pursuant to the will of God, that is creation, are conformable to reason, and the will of God is, of course, altogether different from the arbitrary will of a human potentate, whose pronouncements may be directed by self-interest, passion, and other motives that are contrary to reason. It is therefore, in the context of Locke, without foundation to see any conflict between a divine 'voluntaristic' law and the law of reason. Cf. also Locke's frequent use of phrases linking God and nature or the law of God and nature (obviously meaning that they coincide), e.g. *Two Treatises*, I, §§ 111, 116, 119; II, §142; Draft *A*, p. 39; Draft *B*, pp. 46, 303; King, *Life of John Locke*, p. 316.

peatedly by reference to a number of passages, Locke believed that man was by nature provided with faculties that were adequate to his discovery of the law-maker's design and man's place in it; he could not mistake the final happiness that might be his if he aimed for it. In this context Locke's answer to Tyrrell in the letter of 4 August 1690 has often been cited.[1] Tyrrell and his friends had apparently raised the same question about the knowability of natural law that modern commentators have also raised, a problem he had somewhat better reason to raise since he presumably did not have our advantage of knowing what Locke had written in his journals and did not as yet have the revision of the chapter 'Of Power', though it must be admitted that Tyrrell still had the means of understanding Locke better than he did. The problem was whether the law of nature was part of the divine law. Tyrrell and his friends thought not, and consequently they did not understand what the law of nature was. Locke answered that he had already in Book 1, 'where it was proper for me to speak my opinion of the law of nature [affirmed] in as direct words as can ordinarily be made use of to express one's thoughts, that there is a law of nature knowable by the light of nature'. Tyrrell had especially referred to the sections on moral relations in the *Essay*,[2] and had come to doubt that it was possible to demonstrate the rewards and punishments that Locke there talks about. Locke answered, in line with what had been perfectly explicit in his thought for at least thirteen years, that the mere probability of a future state that would depend on our conduct 'here', would be sufficient, and he quite rightly pointed out that it was not in that chapter his business to deal with the foundation of those rewards and punishments, but merely with the fact that men are observed generally to refer their conduct to certain rules, whether true or not. He did not, as he said, 'design to treat of the grounds of true morality, which is necessary to true and perfect happiness'. The central point, however, is Tyrrell's misunderstanding that Locke should have said that the 'only enforcement' of the divine law was the rewards and punishments of another life. In the passage Tyrrell misunderstood, Locke had said that God 'has goodness and wisdom to direct our actions to that which is best; and he has power to enforce it by rewards and punishments of infinite weight and duration in another life...This is the only true touchstone of *moral rectitude*.'[3] Locke quite rightly and fairly answered that '*only* is of your putting in, and not mine'. Thus I do not find that this is an 'icy' letter in which

---

[1] The letter is printed in King, *Life of John Locke*, pp. 198–201.
[2] II, XXVIII, often referred to; in the first edition this was chapter XXVII.
[3] This is in *Essay*, II, XXVIII, §8, which is by now familiar. Strauss, *Natural Right and History*, p. 203, makes the same mistakes as Tyrrell, apparently ignorant of Locke's answer on that point.

The state of nature and the nature of man

Locke 'lost his temper', and least of all, as someone else has said, an 'evasive' one. In addition, Locke might quite reasonably have felt some irritation that Tyrrell appeared to go errands for his old and captious detractors in Oxford. The only surprise in fact is that Locke, perhaps tactfully, abstained from citing an earlier passage in the same chapter which should have been answer enough, namely that 'good and evil, pleasure or pain, attending our observance or breach of the law by the decree of the law-maker, is that we call *reward* and *punishment*'.[1] That Locke did not make reference to the original chapter 'Of Power' is understandable, for he was not at all satisfied with that version and had not at first meant to include it. If the later revision owes something to Tyrrell, in addition to Molyneux, he may be forgiven his misunderstanding. The *Essay* has ample room for moral rules and the determination of the will, i.e. for natural law.

The other objection has it that the natural law of the *Two Treatises* appears to be innate. Quite apart from Locke's express statement that the law of nature is not innate, I think I have sufficiently shown that man comes by it as he comes by all other knowledge, and as with all knowledge more or less adequately in different men. A passage in the *Second Treatise* has, however, been used to support this error, though only by over-refined interpretation of a few words—a procedure that is never safe with Locke. In fact Locke seems deliberately to have used a variety of words or expressions for the same notion in order to divorce the sense of his discourse and argument from any dependence on particular terms, especially when he had a chance, as in this case, to subvert the sanctioned usage of a particular term whose meaning he found empty.[2] In one of the early sections of the *Second Treatise*, Locke observes that Cain after the murder of Abel cried out: '*Every one that findeth me, shall slay me*; so plain was it

---

[1] It occurs two sections earlier in II, xxviii, §5; it has already been cited above.
[2] This aspect of Locke's discourse was often made the subject of commentary by his contemporaries, and could cause such amusingly absurd opinions as that the *Essay* was a metaphysical treatise in the Cartesian manner. It was Henry Lee in *Anti-Scepticism* (London, 1702), p. 48, who observed that he had not always been able to follow the *Essay* because it was 'writ in a kind of new language'. In *Essay*, II, xii, §4, Locke remarked that, 'if in this I use the word *mode* in somewhat a different sense from its ordinary signification, I beg pardon...' A striking example is Locke's defiant term 'nominal essence', which Leibniz immediately seized upon in his commentary on *Essay*, III, III, §15. He had heard of nominal definitions but never of essences so called 'à moins que par Essences nominales on n'ait entendu des Essences fausses et impossibles qui paroissent estre des essences, mais n'en sont point'—which of course was precisely Locke's point. Locke himself commented on this aspect of the *Essay* in a prefatory notice to the French edition, just as Coste remarked on it at the end of his translation of the précis of the *Essay*. Locke's procedure was advocated both by Robert Hooke and by Robert Boyle as a way of overcoming the cheat of words; see e.g. Boyle in the *Origin of Forms and Qualities* (1666) in *Works*, ed. Thomas Birch (1772), III, 6.

writ in the Hearts of all Mankind.'[1] The phrase 'writ in their hearts' is itself biblical, hence fitting in the context. It comes from Romans ii. 14–15, and Locke takes it to mean the same as 'known by the light of nature', which of course rules out innateness. The law was so fundamental that it was known even to Cain, the first killer of another man. Locke's own paraphrase of these verses says:

> For, when the gentiles, who have no positive law given them by God, do, by the direction of the light of nature, observe, or keep to the moral rectitude, contained in the positive law, given by God to the Israelites, they being without any positive law given them, have nevertheless a law within themselves; and show the rule of the law written in their hearts, their consciences also bearing witness to that law, they amongst themselves, in the reasoning of their own minds, accusing or excusing one another.[2]

Furthermore, in the introduction to Romans i. 16–ii. 29, Locke says with reference to this passage that men 'might come to the knowledge of the true God, by the visible works of the creation', and he again refers to 'the light of nature' by which 'they know what was right'.[3] Thus, even though Locke elsewhere uses the phrase 'writ in their hearts' as equivalent to innateness, there is no reason to believe that he does so here—apart from the overwhelming evidence for the obvious fact that the law of nature has the same status as all other knowledge; it must be acquired by means of those faculties with which man has been equipped for that purpose.[4]

The odd belief that Locke in the *Two Treatises* could have meant the law of nature to be innate has had very strange consequences. In 1925 Professor C. E. Vaughan wrote: 'Now, if there ever was an innate idea, it is the law of nature, as expounded in the *Civil Government* of Locke. It springs fully armed from the brain of man, at the very dawn of his history.

---

[1] *Two Treatises*, II, §11. Cox, *Locke on War and Peace*, pp. 54–6, takes up this passage to show that Locke deliberately misquoted and subverted the sense of the Bible. It would imply discourtesy to the reader's intelligence and mere ability to read to point out the variety of absurd misunderstandings that are there set forth as 'proof'. There is not the slightest evidence that Locke ever had any such intentions. For Locke the Bible was the revealed word and as such the ultimate authority in all human matters. To believe otherwise is to ignore the plainest evidence in all of Locke's writings.

[2] *Works*, VII, 265–6.

[3] *Ibid*. VII, 256. The same passage from Romans ii. 14–15 is also used in *Reasonableness* (*Ibid.*, VI, 13), where Locke shows that "tis plain, that under the law of works, is comprehended also the law of nature'. The more traditional interpretation of 'written in their hearts' is that it refers to conscience, as indeed it may here. It need hardly be mentioned that Cain lived before the promulgation of the Mosaic law. Luther's commentary, in the *Lectures on Genesis*, on the other two biblical verses used by Locke in the Cain passage (Gen. iv. 14 and ix. 6) is of considerable interest to the entire context.

[4] In *Essay*, I, III, §8, Locke does use the phrase as equivalent to innateness. The phrase also occurs in Jeremiah xxxi. 33.

The state of nature and the nature of man

It is the gift of intuition, pure and simple.'[1] Now if this were really so, then it would, according to the very doctrine of innateness that is here invoked (viz. that of Book I of the *Essay*), follow that all men will invariably fully know that law of nature and as invariably allow it to guide their conduct—otherwise it would not satisfy Locke's criteria of innateness. In that case man would, from the very dawn of his history, be in the full state of reason, and consequently there would never be any occasion for the intervention of an impartial judge and hence no need to leave the state of nature and no need for civil government. Since Locke never assumed that these inferences had the slightest factual validity, not even in the *Two Treatises* where the pretended inconsistency would seem most immediately dramatic, it follows either that the law of nature is not innate or that Locke was up to something very special: perhaps he did not know his own mind or perhaps he was deliberately being a rather contemptible prevaricator in order to conceal his true doctrine. Anyone may of course have his own choice of nonsense or prevarication, but both are so easily to be had that there would seem to be no reason to go to the trouble of seeking those aberrations where they are not to be found and do not exist. The *Essay* makes it clear that the law of nature is not innate, but the same point had been made as early as the *Second Essay of the Law of Nature*. Here Locke met the objection that 'if all men are led to the knowledge of it by the light of nature', 'how does it arise that very many mortals are without knowledge of this law and nearly all think of it differently, a fact that does not seem possible if all men are led to the knowledge of it by the light of nature?'. Locke answered with perfect clarity:

This objection would have some force in it if we asserted that the law of nature is inscribed in our hearts. For, if this were assumed, it would necessarily follow that what is thought about this law would be everywhere the same, since this law would be written down in all men and be disclosed to the understanding as one and the same. Our answer, however, is that, granted that our mental faculties can lead us to the knowledge of this law, nevertheless it does not follow from this that all men necessarily make proper use of these faculties.

Proceeding to his favourite analogy in this context that not all men with the requisite faculties turn out geometers or arithmeticians, Locke concludes that 'careful reflection, thought, and attention by the mind is

---

[1] *Studies in the History of Political Philosophy before and after Rousseau*, 2 vols. (Manchester, 1925), I, 163. The surrounding argument takes up, among other things, the pretended conflict between the political philosophy and the *Essay*; it is evident that these pages have had a long, largely anonymous history in the interpretation of Locke. On p. 164, Professor Vaughan shows that he took Locke to mean 'that man comes into the world with a ready-made knowledge of good and evil'.

needed, in order that by argument and reasoning one may find a way from perceptible and obvious things into their hidden nature'.[1]

◆ This relativity of men's knowledge is an important principle in Locke, and it may perhaps be called the doctrine of the differential attainments and capacities of men, which in turn will in large measure depend on the opportunities they have to extend their knowledge. It is closely related to what has rightly been called Locke's interest in comparative anthropology, in Locke's case chiefly satisfied by travel accounts as well as by personal observation on his own travels. It is complementary to the basic uniformity of human nature, whose chief trait is that all mankind is capable of being rational; individuals who cannot themselves trace the arguments of reason to their consequences will consent once they are pointed out or accept them on authority just as most of us accept Kepler's laws of planetary motion or Newton's law of gravity though we could not have found them on our own or even understand the arguments behind them when made acquainted with them. The assent of reason does not mean that an individual will also automatically act in accordance with it, but it is the beginning of enlightenment and order though narrow self-interest, passion, and men's appetites may carry them in the opposite direction. In the *Conduct of the Understanding* Locke devotes a long passage to this principle of the differential attainments of men, and he often restates the conclusion that 'we are born with faculties and powers capable almost of any thing, such at least as would carry us farther than can easily be imagined: but it is only the exercise of those powers, which gives us ability and skill in any thing, and leads us towards perfection'.[2] 'What then should be done in the case? I answer, we should always remember what I said above, that the faculties of our souls are improved and made useful to us, just after the same manner as our bodies are.'[3] Indeed,

the greatest part of mankind want leisure or capacity for demonstration; nor can carry a train of proofs, which in that way they must always depend upon for conviction, and cannot be required to assent to, until they see the demonstration...The greatest part cannot know and therefore they must believe... The instruction of the people were best still to be left to the precepts and principles of the gospel.[4]

---

[1] *Essays on the Law of Nature*, ed. von Leyden, pp. 132–5. For the remarkable consistency of this view in Locke, see his marginal notes to Burnet's *Third Remark* (1699), printed in John Yolton's *John Locke and the Way of Ideas* (Oxford, 1956), pp. 56–7, especially the passage 'I never deny'd such a power to be innate, but that which I deny'd was that any Ideas or connection of Ideas was innate'.

[2] On this subject of the attainments of men, see especially *Works*, II, 327 ff. (*Conduct*). This passage is on p. 331.

[3] *Ibid.* II, 337, and again pp. 330 and 338. Cf. also *Essay*, I, IV, §§ 17, 20, 23; *Essays on the Law of Nature*, ed. von Leyden, p. 199; and *Works*, VI, 135, 136, 139 (*Reasonableness*).

[4] *Works*, VI, 146.

But this mode of instruction can of course be used only where Christianity prevails and thus will not do for the universal foundations of political philosophy.

In the *Second Treatise* Locke did not forget this important qualification—'and Reason, which is that Law, teaches all Mankind, who will but consult it'—which in turn means that many men will not come by their moral rules by their own efforts. They will absorb them from the general tenor of society, even in pre-political society (since the law of opinion and reputation will generally express the law of nature); or they will learn them from superior individuals and assent to them once they are pointed out. One great stumbling block to an understanding of natural law in the state of nature as set forth in the *Second Treatise* has been the mistaken assumption that the law of nature must be equivalent to a total code of rules of conduct which all men must know *in toto* before it can make any sense to say that the state of nature is governed by it.[1] Quite the contrary: what Locke means is that each man, in the absence of positive civil laws, is guided exclusively by his reason in so far as he is guided toward order at all, for to Locke it makes no sense to say that man's conduct may be ordered by his passions and appetites precisely because they can assure no final goal and no final stability such as is promoted by the uniform, rational nature of man. But each man will follow reason according to his lights, some more some less. It works even on a very basic level. A man who finds himself on the tenth floor of a building and conceives a desire to be in the street below will not jump out of the nearest window, though that action would certainly carry him faster and with less effort to the goal of his desire; but reason and sense-experience—the light of nature—have informed him that jumping out will cross his happiness, in this case his self-preservation. If instead he found himself on the second floor, he would presumably still take the stairs rather than jump; now his self-preservation might not be in the balance, but the uncertain pain that might result would guide him in his choice of the more conventional means. Similarly, a man may restrain himself from saying hard words to his neighbour or from stealing from his potato patch because he will have rational foresight enough to see that the farther consequence may be less pleasant than the immediate satisfaction. The would-be embezzler in the bank will think twice before he goes into action, either because his ultimate vision of happiness gives private assurance that he should not steal, or because he knows that the positive civil laws will mete out punishment if he is caught. Only corrupt and degenerate men will wholly go against the law of nature; all men will in some measure follow it.

[1] See Cox, *Locke on War and Peace*, pp. 79–81.

Hans Aarsleff

It is in this sense that the law of nature rules Locke's conjectural state of nature, whose perfection in turn is measured by the absolute, abstract state of reason. Even men who already find themselves in civil society will to a large extent let their conduct be guided by reason, and the more capable they are of following reason the less they stand in need of the pronouncements of the civil positive law, which must contain nothing that is contrary to the law of nature. If it does or if the sovereign acts arbitrarily contrary to the law of nature, then the other members of that political society have the right to rebel to secure a return to the order and peace ensured by following reason according to the grand design which the maker imposed on the entire creation for the benefit of its centre, man. God not only 'wished there to be order, society, and government among men'. He also put those faculties into man that could guide him toward it: reason, sense-experience, pain, pleasure, and the inalienable pursuit of happiness. The state of nature is imperfect and undesirable because man may, owing to ignorance or the domination of his appetites, mistake his real happiness and true felicity. The limiting test case is the situation in which a man is called upon to be an impartial, rational judge where his own interest is at stake. This is too great a burden for most men not to be in danger of departing from the law of reason, which for him to be impartial must apply as severely to himself as to the other party. If he errs from reason, his error may go undetected, or, if it is detected, the same problem of the impartial judge will arise once more.

But precisely because a state of ignorance, passion, and degeneracy is not the most fundamental attribute of man, there is also a way of overcoming the 'inconveniences' of the state of nature. When Locke according to his definition rejected the innateness of knowledge, he also rejected the possibility that truth could be private. It must be public, for all to see and assent to, and it is public because reason is the measure. Locke's conjectural state of nature prior to civil society is shaped according to his conception of the nature of man, and it is the nature of man to be rational. Reason alone is universal, public, and the guarantor of peace and order. Naturally therefore, Locke's conjectural state of nature will describe the uncertain and arbitrary workings of ignorance and appetites, but it is not a universal state of war of all against all, for if it were there would on Locke's premises be no way of ever getting out of it. Such a state of universal war would be tantamount to the utter absence of reason in man, even on the most basic level—not jumping out of the tenth-floor window, not stealing from his neighbour's potato patch or sleeping with his wife. Locke may well have thought of the history of man in terms of a passage he translated from Nicole's essay 'On the Existence of God': 'If you observe the constant progress of the world [i.e. history]...it will appear just parallel to the life of a man, growing up from infancy, and passing through his other ages.'[1] Such a view of the analogy between the progress of the individual and the progress of man in history is precisely conformable to what Dugald Stewart called 'conjectural or theoretical history', and in the eighteenth century they often and explicitly go together.

Now, since Locke did not—he had common sense—believe that all men can rise to the higher degrees of rationality by themselves and since his political theory does not rest on any such assumption (though it has widely been assumed that it does), he did make allowance for the appearance and guidance of especially gifted individuals; great contributions to knowledge are not every man's business, whether in the realm of morality or natural philosophy. In the *Second Treatise* he suggested that

perhaps at first...some one good and excellent Man, having got a Preheminency amongst the rest, had this Deference paid to his Goodness and Vertue, as to a kind of Natural Authority, that the chief Rule, with Arbitration of their differences, by a tacit Consent devolved into his hands, without any other caution, but the assurance they had of his Uprightness and Wisdom.

Later, since such 'preheminency' could not be secured in his successors, his attainments would have to be institutionalized for the sake of preservation and continued control in 'collective Bodies of Men, call them Senate, Parliament, or what you please'.[2] But the beginning had been made by the gifted individual. As early as the treatise on the civil magistrate, Locke had observed that 'nature gives no superiority of dominion, but all men seem equal till some one's eminent virtues, or any other advantages hath directed the choice of the people to advance him'.[3] In the *Essay* he made an analogous point with regard to the discovery of iron:

Were the use of iron lost among us, we should in a few ages be unavoidably reduced to the wants and ignorance of the ancient savage *Americans*, whose natural endowments and provisions come no way short of those of the most flourishing and polite nations. So that he who first made known the use of that one contemptible mineral may be truly styled the father of arts and author of plenty.[4]

[1] *John Locke: Discourses translated from Nicole's Essays*, ed. Thomas Hancock (London, 1828), p. 15. The translation seems to have been made in France between September 1676 and July 1678 (see *Locke's Travels in France*, ed. Lough, pp. 111 and 202). Fox Bourne's conjecture of 1672–3 seems to have no good foundation (*Life of John Locke*, 1, 296). Thus Locke's preoccupation with Nicole's *Essays* falls in the same years as he made the important and suggestive entries in his journals between 1676 and 1678, which we have been considering above, and also precedes by a short time his first work on the *Second Treatise*. The relevance of the Nicole *Essays* is strikingly evident, especially the essay 'Concerning the Way of Preserving Peace with Men'. The subject is the same as that of the *Second Treatise*. A number of Laslett's findings (which make no reference whatever to Nicole) are confirmed by this relationship. I shall devote a separate essay to this matter.

[2] *Two Treatises*, II, §94.   [3] Abrams, *Two Tracts*, p. 126.   [4] *Essay*, IV, XII, §11.

Thus Locke's political philosophy does by no means assume that all men in the state of nature must be students of the law of nature. It is enough if a few people by their natural talents reach 'preheminency'.[1] Reason is man's best guide, both publicly and privately, to ensure his happiness both in this time of 'our probationership here' and hereafter. He has the means to gain the natural knowledge he stands in need of— and 'an other use of his knowledg is to live in peace with his fellow men and this also he is capeable of'.

[1] Both Strauss (*Natural Right and History*) and Cox (*Locke on War and Peace*) make much of this as one of the chief inconsistencies in Locke's argument, which they then in turn see as part of his deliberate stratagem of involving his sense for the sake of concealment. There is, as the nature of their arguments and supporting 'evidence' clearly reveals, no basis for that view. Since they make so much of their interpretation of self-preservation in Locke, it is well to remember what Locke wrote in 1677: 'An Hobbist, with his principle of self-preservation, whereof himself is to be judge, will not easily admit a great many plain duties of morality.' ('Of Study during a Journey', King, *Life of John Locke*, p. 103.)

John Locke, the great recoinage, and the origins of the Board of Trade: 1695–1698[1]

by PETER LASLETT

On 26 June 1696 there was held, in a room in the rambling royal palace of Whitehall at Westminster, the first meeting of 'His Majesty's Commissioners for promoting the Trade of this Kingdom, and for inspecting and improving His Plantations in America and elsewhere'. We may imagine ten Stuart noblemen and gentlemen sitting in their silken knee breeches in front of pewter sandboxes and goose-quill pens, listening to their commission being read. No doubt it was an interesting meeting, for the men who mingled in the offices of government in that generation were interesting personalities. Charles Montagu was there, the clever and dissolute chancellor of the exchequer; so was John Somers, lord keeper, ablest of all the great political lawyers—Whiggery in person. Both these men were authors and patrons of authors, and both in their time were presidents of the Royal Society. Further down the table sat Abraham Hill, treasurer of that distinguished and influential body, and John Locke, F.R.S., the Whig philosopher himself. This was the beginning of the old

---

[1] This is a slightly modified reprint of an article with the same title published in 1957 in the *William and Mary Quarterly*, 3rd series, no. xiv. This issue of the *Quarterly* was published in celebration of an important anniversary in the settlement of the North American continent by English-speaking colonists, which accounts for the presence of many statements not perhaps strictly relevant to the subject and certainly not to Locke's part in it. Many of these passages have been deleted but some remain. I have also removed a number of over-emphatic expressions, which I have found after ten years to become a little embarrassing.

The rest of the text is substantially the same as the original, and it even perpetuates some statements which I now know to be a little inaccurate or to give rather a wrong impression. Some of these passages are indicated in the footnotes, which also include references to a proportion, though not a large proportion, of the work which has appeared on subjects relative to this one since 1957. Nearly all of these references, however, which are important to the original, are to a work as yet unpublished and in progress. This is the research of Mr Patrick Kelly of Peterhouse, Cambridge, who has been working with me at Cambridge on Locke's economic writings, on the great recoinage and the Board of Trade. I am most grateful to Mr Kelly for allowing me to make comments on my text in the light of his discoveries, and I have very occasionally changed a point of detail where he has shown the original to be factually inaccurate.

I perhaps ought to mention at this point that the results of Mr Kelly's most recent researches indicate that Mr Kelly and I may finally differ in our general interpretation.

Board of Trade, the architect and instrument of the old Colonial System. It went on sitting year in, year out, until 1766, when catastrophe was about to fall on the first British Empire, and finally expired in the anxious twilight of the year 1782.

Everything which has to do with the United States in the era before the revolution, her Old Testament times, has a certain interest. But when we think of the American colonies, it is not only the settlers themselves we must have in mind, but the families from which they came, and all the other Englishmen who created the enterprise and energy and wealth which made colonization possible. It is not easy to determine who decided that colonies should be settled. Many people had parts to play in this process, most of them no doubt unaware of the implications of what they were doing. But the most important of them, undoubtedly, were the king and his ministers. When we ask who advised the government, who provided the intelligence, the suggestions, or the contacts with people outside politics with the necessary knowledge, we arrive at colonial committees and commissions. Without the men who sat on them, colonial policy would have been impossible.

This was a challenging arena for English kings and English ministers, for English thinkers too—a challenge to intelligence and imagination as well as to administrative organization and skill. We should not be surprised, then, that it took so long to decide the form, the functions, and the membership of a body of colonial advisers, as well as its exact constitutional position. A final solution to these problems did not come before Victoria. Throughout the first century of colonial activity, a century of marked political instability, there was a complicated succession of British committees, commissions, and councils of trade and plantations,[1] in most cases both trade and plantations, since to the men of that day they were almost inseparable. The Board of Trade of 1696, however, was a relatively stable and satisfactory institution, and a permanent one, lasting as it did for three generations. These were the generations when American political society grew to maturity. And here we meet with a striking paradox. For the doctrine of self-government and the doctrine of trust,[2] the informing

---

[1] See Charles McLean Andrews, *British Committees, Commissions, and Councils of Trade and Plantations, 1622–1675,* Johns Hopkins University Studies in Historical and Political Science (Baltimore, 1908), and Louise Fargo Brown, *The First Earl of Shaftesbury* (New York, 1933), chapter IX, 'Theories and Councils of Trade and Plantations'. Andrews insists that the Plantation Office attached to the privy council did have a continuous history, in spite of the vagaries in the advisory council, and that in its professional members, as well as in the clerks to the various councils, everyday policy for the colonies did have a reliable instrument.

[2] On the Trusteeship and Locke's role in its development—for he did not invent it—see J. W. Gough, *John Locke's Political Philosophy* (Oxford, 1950), chapter VII, and John Locke, *Two Treatises of Government,* ed. Laslett (Cambridge, 1960; 2nd ed., 1967), Introduction, § V, and references.

principles of the second British Empire, were given eloquent early expression by John Locke, a founder-member of the body which became a historical symbol of the determination to deny these doctrines in the case of America and everywhere else.

Here is historian's work enough, and the resolution of this paradox is no straightforward matter. It will have to be sought in the personal attitude and situation of Locke himself, as well as in the particular circumstances in which the board was set up, in the relationship of government and administration with intellectual life in general, as well as in Locke's connexions with the politicians. We shall not find the great liberal theorist as an opposition member, or odd man out, arguing against the attitude of a body he did not create. On the contrary: the evidence goes to show that Locke may well have helped to bring it into being and that he played an interesting part in its earlier history. He was one of the working members and was paid £1,000 a year, along with two political noblemen, a permanent civil servant, and four or five others like himself. The great politicians in the big offices, like Somers and Montagu, were not paid for their membership and did not ordinarily attend, though in these early years a member of the cabinet, usually the secretary, would sit at it.[1] Nevertheless the final responsibility remained with the ministers. Like its predecessors, the board advised the Royal Council; it could not execute or administer directly.

Locke was certainly not the first thinker or man of letters to be associated with a colonial advisory committee. A friend of his earlier days, Robert Boyle the chemist, and the poets Denham and Waller assisted there in the early 1660s, and the very successful council of the early 1670s associated with the first Earl of Shaftesbury had John Evelyn as a member, and Locke as its professional secretary after 1673.[2] Nor was this the first occasion when men of information and experience had been paid for their services.[3] But though these and other features of the Board of Trade in 1696 were not entirely new, it is true to say that in England in the 1690s there was available for the first time a really weighty body of expert opinion on political and economic matters. This was the generation when rationality and empiricism dominated philosophy and were beginning to

---

[1] Professor J. H. Plumb tells me that this was set policy at this time, a part of the planned structure of cabinet and related committees. I gratefully acknowledge a general debt to Professor Plumb in the preparation of this paper.

[2] Locke seems never to have received his money as secretary of Shaftesbury's council; he certainly went to some trouble to make sure that he got his £1,000 in the 1690s. This payment for services unspecified obviously invited abuse for the purposes of patronage. See below, p. 164.

[3] Andrews, *British Committees of Trade*, and Brown, *Earl of Shaftesbury*, and information from Mr Kelly, who dates the use of experts in this capacity at a period earlier than that implied.

Peter Laslett

have a more general effect. The names of men remembered for what they did to bring about this development—Newton, Wren, Davenant, Wallis, as well as Locke—also appear in the foundation of the Board of Trade. The subsequent history of the Board is an odd commentary on these distinguished names, and on that of Locke particularly. But though it has always been known that this supremely intellectual man was a founder-member of the Board of Trade, no serious attempt has ever been made to assess the significance of that fact. The historians who have concerned themselves with the Board of Trade do not appear to have consulted Locke's biographers, and so have overlooked some interesting evidence, some of it in print for over a century.[1] It is more understandable that they should have offered no comment on the beginnings of specialized knowledge in administration, for the subject is intricate and difficult; it is unusual that an opportunity to study it as a defined problem should present itself.

Those who attended the first meeting of the Board would all have agreed, politicians and intellectuals, that the presence of a theoretical problem beyond the traditional resources of government was a main reason for their being together. As we shall see, it was the prolonged and still-deepening crisis over the balance of payments and the dangerous state of the coinage that brought the politicians to the necessity of a new Board of Trade. The problems, mostly long-term problems, of the plantations did not present so sharp an issue. Still, colonial matters had entered into another crisis, a constitutional crisis over who should create and control that board—parliament or the king. The words of the Royal Writ under the Great Seal represented a decisive victory for what was to become an important constitutional principle. To understand why this was so we must look at the contemporary state of opinion on the proper constitution of a regulating body for trade in general, trade with the colonies, and colonial relations.

We may content ourselves with a summary glance at these matters, for they have been authoritatively discussed elsewhere.[2] It cannot be said that

[1] Neither Andrews nor R. M. Lees ('Parliament and the Proposal for a Council of Trade, 1695–6', *English Historical Review*, LIV, January 1939) nor a writer such as Gertrude Ann Jacobsen, whose *William Blathwayt* (New Haven, 1932) is a standard source for administrative history in these years, makes any reference to a biography of Locke. Lord Peter King's *The Life of John Locke*... (London, 1829, 1830) printed some outstanding documents, and in the standard biography by H. R. Fox Bourne, 2 vols. (London, 1876), there is a lengthy and remarkably accurate account of Locke and the Board of Trade. This was greatly extended by Maurice Cranston in his *John Locke, A Biography* (London, 1957, new edition in preparation).

[2] See Brown, *Earl of Shaftesbury*, Andrews, *British Committees of Trade*, and more especially Andrews's later work, *The Colonial Period of American History* (New Haven, 1934–8), IV, chapter IX, 'The Origin and Work of the Board of Trade', and Lees, 'Parliament and the Proposal for a Council of Trade'. These two last essays, published so close together, cover much of the same ground and even print some of the same material.

on the high theoretical level there had been much development of doctrine away from the Roman imperial colonizing tradition still enshrined in the dominant doctrine of natural law; there was Francis Bacon's down-to-earth discussion in his essay on plantations, the brief and typical characterization of colonies as the children of a commonwealth in the *Leviathan* of Thomas Hobbes, and, more to our purpose, a provision for 'the annual election of foure Knights out of the third Region of the Senate into the Council of Trade, consisting of twelve Knights, foure in every Region', in Harrington's *Oceana*.[1] But where English writers on 'the politics' had little or nothing to say, interested parties and particularly interested merchants had concrete proposals to make. Between the 1650s and 1670s a variety of forms for a council of trade were proposed, and some were tried out. In the economic stress of the early 1690s the discussion reached its climax. There were four critical questions: Should there be one council for both colonies and trade, or one for each? Should it be a large, representative council, or a small committee? Should its members be merchants themselves, or men with commercial experience, or 'experts', or a mixture, and in what proportion? Should it be appointed by the king or by parliament?

These points may seem trivial, matters of administrative machinery and crude economic pressure rather than of abstract principle and high policy. Much of the discussion was undoubtedly carried on by small-minded men, making *ad hoc* proposals for their particular interests, but they showed signs of political insight. It is remarkable how many of them, although they were merchants themselves and spoke often for their own regions, recognized that a man actually in trade was no fit counsellor for economic policy.[2] One of the issues, moreover, was of first-class importance. Sir William Petty, that eminent intellectual, sketched out two separate schemes for an economic *parliament*, a representative assembly with members from all areas of the British Isles and from the American colonies too, and James Whiston actually published a similar suggestion in 1693.[3] If this had developed, the Houses of Parliament would soon have ceased to be the expression of the economic organization of Britain. But perplexed and infuriated merchants of the 1690s had already decided where to seek a remedy for their alarming losses of ships, for the quickening inflation, and for the ineffective lassitude of the Lords of Trade, the

---

[1] *James Harrington's Oceana*, ed. S. B. Liljegren (Heidelberg, 1924), p. 106. 'Region' here does not mean region of the country.
[2] Andrews, *Colonial Period*, IV, 280. He believed that there was general agreement on this point.
[3] Petty's editor, Lord Lansdowne, supposes that these notes were written in the 1660s: *The Petty Papers* (London, 1927), pp. 4, 11–13, 35. For James Whiston's *A Discourse of the Decay of Trade* (London, 1693) see Lees, 'Parliament and the Proposal for a Council of Trade', *English Historical Review*, LIV, 45, where the idea is described as unique. Locke does not seem ever to have owned, or even to have read, Whiston's book.

committee of the whole Royal Council then officially in charge of plantation and economic policy. They were busy in the House of Commons
amongst the merchant members and business spokesmen. They were
determined to get a Board of Trade appointed by parliament and responsible to it, a committee which knew what it was doing and which would
listen to them.

If they had succeeded, it might have meant 'a change of our Constitution, in a very essential point', as Bishop Burnet recognized.[1] They
proposed to remove a department from the executive to the legislative,
a department which might have brought with it, finally, the control of the
navy and even of the treasury, for so men thought at the time and so
Edmund Burke thought in 1780.[2] King William was warned that this
would reduce him to the position of a Duke of Venice. When we remember how important it has been to both British and American government to preserve 'the vital distinction between government and discussion
of government',[3] giving administrators and advisers the freedom of
anonymity behind the undisturbed executive prerogative, we may recognize in this controversy one of the most interesting constitutional questions
which arose among the aftermath of 1688.

This unprecedented proposal failed, leaving no discernible trace in constitutional and administrative tradition.[4] The ragged alliance which put
it forward—merchants and economic critics, upholders of parliament
against the prerogative, patriots who resented Dutch influence, and interested Tory politicians—nearly brought down Dutch King William and
his Whig ministers in 1695. They may have imperilled the Revolution
Settlement, as some historians have claimed, but they got nowhere with
their parliamentary Board of Trade. The government had taken its advice
and decided its policy before ever the proposal got to the House of
Commons. The functions, the constitution, and even the membership of
the Board of Trade were decided upon some days earlier, but the consultations had been going on for months. The Board was adopted by the

---

[1] Bishop Burnet's *History of His Own Time* (London, 1724–34), II, 163.
[2] 'Speech on...the independence of Parliament, and the economical reformation of the
civil and other establishments', in *Works*, II, in Bohn's 'British Classics' (London, 1855),
III.
[3] Lees, 'Parliament and the Proposal for a Council of Trade', *English Historical Review*, LIV, 41.
He rightly reproaches Macaulay for his neglect of this affair, and it is remarkable how little
it has been noticed. Mark A. Thomson devoted a paragraph to it in *A Constitutional History
of England, 1642 to 1801* (London, 1938), but David Ogg makes the surprising error of
asserting that parliament in fact named the members of the board: *England in the Reigns of
James II and William III* (Oxford, 1955), p. 305.
[4] Though Lees has described an analogous case in 1689, the commissioners for wool, 'Parliament and the Proposal for a Council of Trade', *English Historical Review*, LIV, 40, referring
to his articles in *Economica*, XIII, nos. 40 and 41 (May and Aug. 1933).

king not because of parliamentary action, or perhaps even the threat of action, but because of pressure of a very different kind.

With access to the private papers of John Locke, we can look at the evidence not open to previous historians in a way which shows up the succession of events more fully,[1] and the story is a commentary on all the issues presented above. We can see that the merchants and the economic experts, the men who wanted a separate council for the colonies, and the men who felt that this was a matter for parliament, had had their opinions considered at the apex of executive power, by the confidants of the sovereign. But John Locke's advice was very important too, and his advice seems to have been taken where that of others was registered and laid aside. The part this philosopher and many others had to play is a conspicuous example of the early use of men of expert knowledge in government and administration.

We could begin our account of Locke and the Board of Trade at a much earlier period, when he was Shaftesbury's companion and his 'assistant pen' between 1667 and 1675. He had been secretary of the proprietors at the Carolina colony as well as of the earlier board, and he had collaborated with Shaftesbury or some other member of the Shaftesbury circle in the production of the notorious *Constitutions of Carolina*.[2] But it is enough to say that Locke's extensive experience marked him in the 1690s as one of the most practised as well as the ablest of all qualified people outside the actual administration of colonies and trade. It so happens that we have no record of his personal thoughts on the constitution and function of an advisory body on these matters. However, the Earl of Shaftesbury preserved from the year of the foundation of his council of trade, 1668, a year when Locke was writing out for him theoretical advice on other aspects of his colonial and economic policy, a paper written by a man who had spent many years in this field and who had preceded Locke in Shaftesbury's confidence in economic and colonial affairs. The opinions in this paper become Locke's opinions, though we have no knowledge of how far Locke helped to work them out.[3]

Trade, it insisted, was an affair of policy: members of the council must be able to distinguish and understand the ends that are to be pursued by

---

[1] In the Lovelace Collection, Bodleian Library, Oxford, cited hereafter as MS. Locke.

[2] For Locke's relations with the first Earl of Shaftesbury, incomparably the most important figure in colonial affairs in Restoration times, see Cranston, *John Locke*, and Laslett's *Two Treatises* (1967 ed.), Introduction, §11, with references. The issue of the authorship of *The Constitutions of Carolina* is vexed and difficult. Mr Kelly seems willing to play down Locke's possible part in it rather more than I am prepared to do.

[3] Mr Kelly's researches confirm that the author of this paper was Benjamin Worsley (cf. Brown, *Earl of Shaftesbury*, p. 142), and reveal a very interesting career in economic and colonial matters.

them as different from the intrigues and private designs of merchants, and proceed 'upon unvariable reason to the general good and concern of the nation'. The council was to consist of 'such of the gentry of the nation whose interest it may be to be more concerned in the generality of the trade of the nation' than private merchants. The emphasis on policy and reason are very like Locke, and we can be confident that he had views of his own. He read and owned books on the subject: he knew the men who wrote them, he was there when such things were discussed.[1] No private individual living in England in 1695 was in a better position to advise that a Board of Trade should be set up, even down to the details of its constitution, functions, and membership.

It has never been doubted that Locke's writings on economics played a conspicuous part in the decision to call in the English coinage at this time and to reissue it at its traditional weight and fineness in silver; indeed in our age of welfare economics it is usual to blame him personally for this 'social crime':[2] a sudden, forced deflation, made when the nation's economy was least capable of standing it and paid for in the last resort by the poorer people. It has been supposed also that it was because the chief figure in the government of the day, Sir John Somers, was under the influence of Locke's opinions that his policy was adopted, and that this influence was not new, but went back to the year 1691.[3] It can now be added that Locke's economic theories were formed very much earlier, earlier even than 1680, and that his influence with Somers had also had a long history by the year 1695. We cannot linger here on the first of these points, interesting as it is in another context,[4] but it does have a bearing

[1] Locke must have known Child and Davenant quite well: he certainly knew Petty, and he corresponded with Cary (see below). He had in his library some, though not all, of the relevant works of those writers, and 127 titles in all which can be classed as 'economic', very many of them concerned with trade and currency. For these facts see John Harrison and Peter Laslett, *The Library of John Locke*, The Oxford Bibliographical Society, n.s. XIII (Oxford, 1965). Nevertheless there are reasons for doubting whether Locke was as well informed on these subjects as on the others he professed. See the prefatory essay, *ibid.* p. 25.

[2] This phrase is used of the great recoinage by Sir John Craig, *Newton at the Mint* (Cambridge, 1946), p. 10. The words used by W. A. Shaw are even more significant: 'In this conspicuous instance in 1696, when the advice of a philosopher prevailed in its counsels, the English Government went astray and committed a blunder' (*Select Tracts...of English Monetary History*, London, 1896). See also A. E. Feavearyear, *The Pound Sterling* (Oxford, 1931), chapter VI, and *Two Manuscripts by Charles Davenant*, ed. Abbott Payson Usher (Baltimore, 1942), Introduction. It has to be said that Mr Kelly has found evidence which suggests a very different interpretation of Locke's aims and of his success in achieving them. When published this evidence will modify the view presented here.

[3] Locke's first publication on economics, *Some Considerations of Lowering of Interest and Raising the Value of Money* (London, 1692), was in the form of 'A letter to a member of Parliament', i.e. Somers, dated 7 November 1691.

[4] See *Two Treatises*, Introduction. The development of Locke's economic opinions requires separate treatment, which is being undertaken by Mr Kelly. In MS. Locke, c. 8, is to be found a complete draft of Locke's views on interest, dated 1668 and belonging, as do his

on the second. Locke had met Somers in the early 1680s, at the outset of that young lawyer's rise to fame and political importance; in the revolutionary year 1689, even after Somers's appointment to be solicitor general to the new monarchs, he had written to Locke asking a surprising question—should he go on circuit or attend at parliament? And in the following year they had exchanged papers on a subject of the first concern to both of them, the value of money and the evils of depreciation. A paper setting out views very similar to Locke's own convictions is to be found amongst Locke's papers, and the hand is remarkably like that of Somers.[1]

What are we to think then of the relationship between the two men in 1695, when we find Somers the leading figure in the government, in the cabinet council when William III was in England, and amongst the Lords Justices who governed in the king's name when he was out of the country? What are we to think, for example, when we find that a copy of a report by the Lords Commissioners of the Treasury, dated 3 July 1695, and signed by Montagu, was sent by the Secretary of State to Locke, requesting comment? This paper hinted at the advisability of legalizing a reduction in the silver content of the coin, and in his reply Locke opposed such a course.[2] Other men, other 'experts', were asked their advice later, and some, perhaps most of them, advised on the coinage in a contrary way; there was clearly a conflict within the ministerial circle itself. But there can be no doubt of Locke's access to Somers on the question of the currency and so on the question of the Board of Trade.

We are not at the end of Locke's influence and control, or even of the area they covered, for they penetrated into the Houses of Parliament. Thomas Herbert, Earl of Pembroke, Lord Privy Seal, cabinet counsellor, Lord Justice, one of the Lords of Trade, and an *ex officio* member of the 1696 board, was quite literally a pupil of Locke's. They had become close friends after the years of tutelage, and Pembroke had been a constant

political, his educational, and even his epistemological positions, to the years of his association with Shaftesbury. This writing is printed in William Letwin, *The Origins of Scientific Economics* (Oxford, 1963), and discussed in chapter 6 of that book. Compare Brown, *Earl of Shaftesbury*, p. 144 and note—a contemporary copy of this draft marked by Coventry 'Writ by Mr. Lock directed by Lord Ashley [Shaftesbury]'. When he referred to his views on interest 'having been put into writing a great deal above' twelve years, as he does in the dedication to Somers of 1691, it is this period he had in mind. His point of departure in the various notes he made between then and the 1690s was Thomas Manley's *Usury at Six Per Cent* (London, 1669), a book not in his final library.

[1] MS. Locke, b.3, folios 18–21, undated but closely connected with the previous document, endorsed by Locke, '*Moneta 90 Of raising our Money*'.

[2] MS. Locke, b.3, folios 39–44 and Locke's reply, folios 48–9, endorsed 'A paper written at Sr. Wm Trumbulls request…upon occasions of a paper of the Lds. Cmrs. of the Treasury submitted to the Lds. Justices 30 July 95', dated August 1695.

patron of the philosopher in his most difficult years: it was to him that the *Essay concerning Human Understanding* was dedicated.[1] The volatile Charles Mordaunt, then Earl of Monmouth and later Earl of Peterborough, was at this time far less settled in his influence on royal policy than he had been before and was to be again, but late in 1695 he was temporarily in favour and to some degree in confidence. He was also a correspondent of Locke's and open to his advice, a constant guardian of his interest.[2] It was owing to Monmouth, it would seem, that Locke was already possessed of a government post or sinecure as a 'Commissioner of Appeals'.

Both Somers and Pembroke exercised control by patronage over seats in the House of Commons, as indeed they had to do if the political system at that time was to work at all.[3] But the most interesting feature of Locke's political influence, an intellectual influence on beliefs, is that it transcended political 'connexion' as it is now beginning to be understood: it was not quite independent, for the usual links by family and locality can be traced, but it relied nevertheless on a different, a superior motive. It could be claimed that in the Lockean group in the parliaments after the revolution we have an association of politicians with something like a set of rationally conceived policies, a programme based not only on a common sentiment, but on superior information.

In the House of Commons it was at most four or five members strong: Edward Clarke, member for Taunton, Sir Walter Yonge, member for Honiton, Sir Francis Masham, member for Essex, and more vaguely Lord Ashley (the future third Earl of Shaftesbury), member for Poole, and Maurice Ashley his brother, member for Weymouth. The secret of success was the link with the great ministers we have listed and through them with the House of Lords. The institution which held them all together was a typical Lockean foundation, typical in its name and in its methods, the 'College'.[4] It had three members and a patron: Edward Clarke, M.P., John Freke, lawyer and political man about town, John Locke, and Somers. When all were in London together, the College met as a club, but for most of the year its function was correspondence to and from Locke in the country. In this way during the years 1694 and 1695 Locke

[1] See *Two Treatises*, Introduction, and Cranston, *John Locke*, for Locke and Pembroke. The year of their greatest intimacy seems to have been 1689.

[2] See *Two Treatises*, Introduction, for their relationship in 1688-9. Monmouth was also a Lord of Trade.

[3] Robert Walcott allots six seats to Somers and three to Pembroke in his *English Politics in the Early Eighteenth Century* (Oxford, 1956). Pembroke, he tells us, was a supporter of Danby, who was certainly no friend to Somers. Locke's connexion, therefore, cuts across Walcott's account of the alignments as he sees them.

[4] The club seems to have been founded only a few months, at most a year or two, before the events discussed here.

carried on a parliamentary and propaganda campaign inside and outside parliament, a campaign largely responsible for the final disappearance of the licensing of the press in England. Then, as later, the College championed recoinage as Locke and Somers wanted it. John Freke would record the opinions and policies of Somers, and correspond with Locke; Edward Clarke would make the speeches in the House; Locke would work out the principles for him, write and publish pamphlets at the effective moment,[1] advise the use of advertisements in the nascent newspapers, do everything possible at that time to publicize and persuade. Meanwhile sympathetic parliamentarians did all they could to see that the House divided on the right side. If we sought proof that an intellectual at a distance could exercise an influence at this time, an influence over policy and administration, it is in the history of Locke's College that we should find it.[2]

Somers and Pembroke retained the king's confidence throughout the period of Locke's membership on the Board of Trade, from 1696 to 1700— years generally accounted a period of increasing 'Whig' supremacy— though Monmouth fell heavily from grace in 1697. From lord keeper and knighthood Somers rose to lord chancellor and the peerage in the same year, and the College maintained its effectiveness. Any judgment of the executive importance of the early Board of Trade, at its time of greatest activity, must take into account this personal connexion with a very senior minister and with a group of parliamentarians. Even legislation might be affected by this instrument of influence. The journal of the board records that on 19 August 1696, 'Mr. Locke was desired to draw up a scheme of some method for determining differences between merchants by Referees'. On 9 November he reported that he had inquired about Dutch methods of doing such things, 'whereupon he had consulted with others experienced in our law, who had drawn up an Act of Parliament for that purpose which he delivered to the Board'. It was reported to His Majesty, and became the law of the realm in 1698.[3]

We have said that the king's ministers had been giving their attention to a new instrument for advice on colonial and economic policy and control months before the Board of Trade became an issue in parliament. This is evident from the privy council minutes and papers of the Earl of

---

[1] It is obvious, for example, from the College correspondence (e.g. Locke to the College, 11 March 1695, *Correspondence of Locke and Clarke*, ed. Rand, p. 409) that his pamphlet *Short Observations on a Printed Paper...Coining Silver Money* (London, 1695) originated in this way, before the government took up the recoinage.

[2] This account of the College will be extended and revised by Mr Kelly's research.

[3] 9° Gul. III, cap. xv. The question of such remedies had agitated economic writers for a long time; see e.g. Sir Josiah Child, *A New Discourse of Trade*, 2nd ed. (London, 1694), chapter VI, 'Concerning a Court Merchant'.

Peter Laslett

Shrewsbury, chief secretary of state.[1] There are three very interesting documents preserved there, one of which was certainly submitted to the cabinet council before the constitution, functions, and membership of the board had been finally decided, and probably the others also. The first is headed 'Considerations of the present Benefit and better Improvement of the English Colonies in America'. It proposed that 'the care of America may be the province of a select number of Lords and gentlemen, be it five, seven or nine...one of the Secretaries of State, an able lawyer and an ingenious merchant, to be authorized under the broad Seal of England, by the style of Lords Commissioners of the English Plantations in America'. This bears a close resemblance to the board as it was finally set up: the document provided salaries of £1,200 a year and the right to recommend governors for colonies. But the differences are more striking: this is not a Board of Trade at all, but a separate advisory authority for the plantations, and only the American plantations are named. And the insistence on the presence of a merchant and on the commercial interest generally raises the whole controversial issue surrounding the birth of the board.[2]

Trade in general is provided for in the other two documents, which may well have been intended to complement the first. But it is provided for at a lower level, for in the 'Scheme for a Council of Trade', the second paper, no salaries were mentioned. The twenty-one councillors, fourteen of them merchants and only seven noblemen and gentlemen, were merely to sit for one year.[3] The last paper is evidently a list of candidates for these merchants' places, and it shows that a representative commercial committee was being proposed, covering thirteen separate trade routes, trade generally, and the Bank of England. The representative of the Bank was to be Michael Godfrey, whose name makes it possible to date this document, for Michael Godfrey was killed on 27 July 1695, in the presence of King William, before the ramparts of Namur.[4]

[1] Unfortunately this evidence cannot be supplemented from the papers of Somers, at least from those which escaped the fire in which most of them perished in the eighteenth century, nor from those of Pembroke, now completely lost, as Lord Herbert tells me. These losses seriously impair our knowledge of Locke's political and administrative influence.

[2] Historical Manuscripts Commission, *The Manuscripts of...the Duke of Buccleuch*... (London, 1897–1903), II, part II, 735–7, author unknown: 'Governors [*sc.* of colonies] should have more of the breeding of merchants than soldiers'; regular reports are insisted on.

[3] *Ibid.* p. 738. The internal, official character of this scheme is indicated by the mention of both Privy and Great Seals and the provision for incidental expenses.

[4] *Ibid.* Baltic, East Indian, Turkish, Virginian, Italian, Spanish, and African trades were among those represented, and Sir John and Sir James Houblon, Gilbert Heathcote, and Charles Chamberlain appear as members; see below, p. 134. This representative scheme resembles Whiston's, though less ambitious; cf. Lees, 'Parliament and the Proposal for a Council of Trade', *English Historical Review*, LIV, 45–7.

148

The great recoinage, and the origins of the Board of Trade

The cabinet council, then, had given its attention to this possible solution to the problems of advice and control and of the ambitions of the merchant interests, perhaps to other schemes as well, at least four months before the commercial men made such a storm in parliament the following December.

We can only guess who was making these proposals. We do not know what advice was sought on the problem by individual ministers or by the cabinet generally. We do know, however, that the cabinet had begun its consideration of what to do about inflation and the coinage before July, and that an opinion had been officially requested from Locke during that month. We know also that this was the period when the secretary to the treasury, William Lowndes, was writing his famous report contradicting Locke's advice and advocating the calling-down of the coin. Somers evidently began to expect that Lowndes's policy would prevail: on 21 September he summoned Locke to him—there had certainly been other meetings throughout the summer. On the twenty-fourth he allowed Locke to read an abstract of Lowndes's recommendations before they were even seen by the cabinet.[1] On the twenty-sixth and twenty-seventh the Lords Justices patiently sat through a complete reading of what Lowndes had written, a monument of accuracy and acumen, one of the finest of all the products of the civil service mind.[2] Then they took the action which joined all the issues together; the recoinage, the proposed board, the ambition of the merchants and parliamentarians, and the appeal to expert opinion. They 'resolved to consult Mr. Locke, Mr. D'Avenant, Sir Christopher Wren, Dr. Wallis, Dr. Newton, Mr. Heathcote, Sir Josiah Child, and Mr. Asgill, a lawyer'.[3]

Here were experts and intellectuals indeed: Davenant, man of letters and economist, one of the ablest of his day; Wren, scientist and savant as well as architect and surveyor of the royal works; Wallis, Savilian Professor at Oxford; Newton, Lucasian Professor at Cambridge; Child and Asgill, also economists, Asgill of the familiar eccentric variety. But there were men of business amongst them also: Child was a merchant as well as an economic writer, Heathcote a merchant only: he was the trader to

---

[1] Somers to Locke, Lovelace MSS. The abstract 'will shew you what he aims at, tho' his reasoning does not appear'. Locke had written another official note at Trumbull's request (cf. p. 145, n. 2 above) in September—MS. Locke, b. 3, folios 62 ff.

[2] William Lowndes, *A Report Containing an Essay for the Amendment of the Silver Coins* (crown imprint, 1695). After all the prejudiced abuse by Macaulay and the Victorians, this is now universally praised by economists. Locke's copy (Harrison and Laslett, no. 1816) has extensive marginal notes in his hand which seem unfortunately not to be of much importance to the issue.

[3] Minutes and Proceedings of the Lords Justices, 27 September 1695, *Calendar of State Papers, Domestic Series, of the Reign of William and Mary*, ed. William John Hardy (London, 1895–1906), v, 71.

Peter Laslett

New York and Jamaica on the list of 'Merchants proposed for the Council of Trade' which we have noticed. On 1 October it was decided to take more opinions, from Abraham Hill, treasurer of the Royal Society, and from three others, two of them amongst the 'merchants proposed'.[1] It has now been possible to recover the replies of nine out of these twelve men who were consulted. Together they make an instructive commentary on the economic and monetary predicament of that moment, and on the themes of this present essay. It is clear for one thing that there was no convinced majority in favour of the policy of an immediate recoinage at current face value. But what interests us particularly is this. Two of the weightiest replies, those of Wren and Davenant, make specific proposals for a Board of Trade as an essential part of the remedy for the economic problem, and a third, Isaac Newton's, suggests something similar but almost modern in its flavour—Newton wanted a price-control authority. Moreover, Davenant's Board of Trade was to have 'those powers which will be needfull for the producing of any good effect, It must be Established by Authority of Parliament'.[2]

Wren and Davenant agreed on a point vital to our discussion. They both argued, logically enough on their premises, that since the value of English money varied with foreign trade, it could only be kept constant if incomings and outgoings were known so that they could be controlled, and this meant an instrument for economic intelligence and advice, in fact a Board of Trade. But whereas Wren wanted it to be 'not Numerous, but Consisting of Persons of good understanding, Publick Spirited, Vers'd in Trade, but not Traders themselves', Davenant said 'It Should cheifly consist of Merchants', though men without present dealings, some or

[1] Sir J. Houblon and Charles Chamberlain; *Cal. State Papers, Domestic*, v, 74. The other name, Sir Joseph Herne, was of a man engaged in remitting money to the English army in Flanders. Sir Josiah Child is repeated from the first list; apparently it had been felt that the advice of businessmen was being neglected.

[2] *Davenant*, ed. Usher, p. 53, printed from Harleian MS. 1223, folios 115–56, British Museum. The title of this treatise is 'A Memorial Concerning the Coyn of England', and it answers four specific questions which from a comparison with the form of seven other replies must have been put to all the consultants. This and the date (November 1695), together with the address to Godolphin, one of the Lords Justices, seem to me to put it beyond doubt that the treatise is the actual text of the reply from Davenant read to the Lords Justices on 12 November 1695, though neither Usher nor Lees ('Parliament and the Proposal for a Council of Trade', p. 43) recognizes this fact. Six of the other replies (Locke's, in two parts; Wren's; Heathcote's; Sir John Houblon's; Wallis's; Newton's) are to be found in official copy in a MS. volume now in the Goldsmiths' Library, University of London (MS. 2 62). Craig, *Newton at the Mint*, p. 8, makes use of these treatises in relation to the events of 1695–6, but he does not seem to realize that they were official replies to official questions. The eighth reply, Child's, is still amongst Shrewsbury's privy council papers, abstract in Hist. MSS. Comm., *Buccleuch MSS.* 11, 721–2. Mr Horsefield has found Hill's reply in the Additional MSS. at the British Museum (no. 2902, papers dated 11 October, 26 November 1695). This leaves Asgill's, Chamberlain's, and Herne's to be recovered.

most elected by the House of Commons.[1] They differed too on their advice about the recoinage: indeed the straightforward Locke–Somers solution to this problem had to be vigorously defended by the lord keeper in the cabinet, by the College in parliament, and by Locke in print—hence his *Further Considerations Concerning Raising the Value of Money, Wherein Mr. Lowndes...Late Report...Examined.* The situation was urgent. The new parliament was to meet on 22 November, and it was already the twelfth when Davenant's paper was read to the ministers. In the intervening ten days someone had to produce a coherent policy on coinage and Board alike, to decide that Davenant's advice was to be rejected, and to reckon with the economic and parliamentary consequences. It seems that Somers was the man who did these things, and the man advising him was Locke.[2]

Locke was back in the country where he belonged at this time of year, safe in the moated Tudor house where Lady Masham took care of his ailing lungs, when the recoinage proposals were debated in parliament. But as midwinter approached, Somers recalled him, and this time we know that they discussed the Board of Trade. What had happened in the meantime has a dramatic quality. The plan for the Board was perhaps adopted by the government later than the recoinage, but it was probably the procrastination of the king which held up its approval by the privy council until 9 December. Somers told Locke some of the details the very next day in a College letter, and warned him to expect a summons.[3] Even then the elusive king had not signed, and it was this delay which brought about the parliamentary crisis. The supporters of a merchants' parliamentary board seem to have got wind of the fact that they were to be disappointed: perhaps there was a leak from the council through Godolphin to Davenant and beyond. Anyway on 12 December a surprise

---

[1] *Davenant*, ed. Usher, p. 53. It must be noted that Lees quotes not this work of Davenant's but a later one in the same Harleian volume, the 'Memoriall concerning a Council of Trade' ('Parliament and the Proposal for a Council of Trade', *English Historical Review*, LIV, 42–3, 62–6).

[2] The succession of events between 1 October and 12 December, the crucial period, is too complex to give in full. Locke's *Further Considerations* was written for Somers in response to a request made through the College as early as 8 October (Freke to Locke, Lovelace MSS.) and dedicated to him. In a letter dated 'Nov. 95' he had told Locke that Lowndes was directly challenging Locke's position. The book can be followed through the press in the College correspondence; it was quite distinct from Locke's official reply to the Lords Justices (Goldsmiths' MSS. and the drafts in Lovelace MS. b. 3, folios 66–74), which was in two parts, the second significantly being answers to extra questions from Somers. When Davenant's paper was read to the ministers on 12 November (Hist. MSS. Comm. *Buccleuch MSS.* 1, 255) it was decided: 'My Lord Keeper to propose the scheme for calling in the money...' Montagu had to be convinced about the necessity for recoinage. Newton was not in favour, nor were Heathcote and Child.

[3] Freke to Locke, 10 December 1695, Lovelace MSS.—the earliest surviving record of the final plan for a board. Locke himself and the five or six other experts paid at £1,000 a year are mentioned.

motion was made in the Commons for a parliamentary Board of Trade. This put the government tacticians into a fine flurry: whilst the speech-makers were on their feet in the Commons, others rushed up to the Lords and a deputation sped out to the king at Kensington Palace to get his signature on the spot. But even the announcement of a royal Board of Trade failed to win the final division, for the opposition gave it out that a trick was being played on the House. They won by a single vote. When Locke came up to see Somers a week later, the Board was stalled, stalled until such time as the parliamentary move could be played out.

This picture of king, ministers, and parliamentary management comes from a letter Monmouth wrote to Locke on the very day of the debate.[1] It contains a phrase significant of Locke's political position with both ministry and parliament: 'What the event will be I know not, but for the little I am able, I shall endeavour Mr. Lock may be the choice of the house as well as the Kings.' There is no indication that this check held up Somers's plan for a moment, but if so it was only for five days.

On 17 December 1695, three letters were dispatched to Locke—from the lord keeper, from the secretary of state, and from the College. Somers asked him to come to town at once, relying on the College for 'having acquainted you with the King's resolution to make you one of the Commission for Trade and the Plantations'. So much did Somers think that Locke would have taken his appointment for granted that his name had been put in without his 'express consent'.[2] The letter from Sir William Trumbull, His Majesty's principal secretary of state for the northern department, deserves fuller quotation:

Sr. I hope the King's nomination of you to be one of the Council of Trade, will not (in the first place) be prejudiciall to your Health in giving sometimes your attendance: if that point be secure I am sure the publick will have the advantage. I am so afraid of saying anything that lookes like a Complement, that I dare hardly be civill, or expresse any things of my owne satisfaction. I beg of you to sacrifice a little of your philosophicall inclinations to the great neces-sities we labour under in this matter of Trade, and now the voice of your Countrie calls for your help, do not refuse it.[3]

From these two letters it would seem that Locke had been character-istically cautious about his own willingness to serve on the Board, what-

[1] MS. Locke, c. 17, fo. 161; it is printed in full by King (*Life of John Locke*, 1830 ed., I, 442–4) and in part by Fox Bourne and Cranston. [2] Somers to Locke, Lovelace MSS.
[3] Trumbull to Locke, 17 November 1695, Lovelace MSS. If this date were correct, it would alter considerably the succession of events as worked out here, but the careful Locke has endorsed it 17 December, and I have assumed that Trumbull's dating was a slip. Mr Kelly has a different interpretation of the reasons why Locke had to be pleaded with by the govern-ment to serve on the board and insists that his relations with Trumbull were more personal than official.

ever advice he may have given on the sort of person who should be selected for it. It was perfectly true that he resented the interference with his work as a philosopher and man of letters which such an appointment brought with it, though Trumbull touched the appropriate chord when he appealed to his sense of public duty and kept off compliments. It was true also that Locke's health would not allow him to sit for longer in each year than the hundred warmest days,[1] and it is noteworthy that the government should have wanted him to serve none the less. But this insistent pleading gives us an opportunity to look at the affair from the other side, from the point of view of the ministry. They clearly wanted Locke's name. This is at once a tribute to his parliamentary leverage, particularly important at that moment, and to the prestige—political prestige, a tangible asset to a government—of the most prominent intellectual of the time.[2]

The third letter, from the College, is also highly instructive. It began by advising Locke to send a copy of his *Further Considerations* to 'every one of your Brother Commissioners', a further confirmation of the link between the recoinage and the establishment of the Board of Trade. It went on thus: 'my Lord Keeper commanded me to write earnestly to you to be here as soon as you possibly could, and said the loss of a day by your absence at this time would be of consequence'. Perhaps Somers wanted to discuss the detailed working of the Board with Locke, now that its establishment was declared ministerial policy. It is obvious that Somers had no intention whatsoever of allowing the heated discussions in parliament, which were to go on until 18 February 1696, to deter him from proceeding with the Board as originally conceived. The rest of the letter bears this out. It recited the membership of the commission, listing first the seven great officials, then the seven paid members; it summarized its purposes as to trade and to colonies in some detail. Although six months were to go by before the Board actually met, the differences between the new writ made out for it in May and the government's plan of December represent no concession to the opposition. As we have said, the whole parliamentary campaign waged by the Tories and the merchants, in which opposition to deflationary recoinage attached itself to a plan, Davenant's plan, for a parliamentary, a businessman's Board of Trade, accomplished exactly nothing. Locke knew this, and he approved.[3]

[1] Locke's consciousness of this and the murmurs of his fellow commissioners made him offer to resign in 1698, but Somers would not hear of it.
[2] I am grateful to Professor Plumb for putting the affair in this light.
[3] For the resemblances, so close as to be quite convincing, between Davenant's advice and the parliamentary board, see Lees, 'Parliament and the Proposal for a Council of Trade', *English Historical Review*, LIV, 62–6. The College letter is in the Locke MSS., Freke to Locke. It

When he came up to see Somers on about 20 December, then, Locke had excellent information about official intentions. It is interesting that the list of intended members which did leak out and which was duly reported home by l'Hermitage, the Dutch envoy, included 'le Sr. Clarke, commissaire de la douane'. Edward Clarke of the College was a commissioner of the excise. It also included 'un autre nommé Poplar',[1] which must be the name of William Popple, who became secretary to the Board of Trade when it finally met. Popple was a friend of Locke's, a theological and literary friend, the translator into English of the letter on *Toleration*. He had never written to Locke on any political or economic subject before, and yet on 2 January 1696, a day or so after Locke's return from his consultations with Somers, Popple wrote a letter describing a debate in the Commons on the Board of Trade. One of the things which Locke and Somers seem to have discussed may have been the job of the secretary. Surely it was Locke who had suggested this very unlikely man, telling him so in conversation. Popple was a great success at the board, and founded a dynasty of Popples who served it in filial succession until the year 1737. In his private poetry book, this nephew of Andrew Marvell wrote in eulogy of his job:[2]

RONDEAU

Busness of Trade
Has been for private Gain
Of my past Life the fruitless Pain
But now kind Heavn, in Recompense, has made
Th' Employment of my Age
For Publick Good, on Publick Stage,
Business of Trade
And may Success attend
Tho mine still fail that Publick End,
For since therein my Country's Weal is laid
I above all things prize
That which all Publick Wants supplies
Busness of Trade

shows differences in detail between the Board as contemplated in December and the Board as constituted in May. The chancellor of the exchequer is omitted from the officials; there are seven paid members (Bridgewater, the Earl of Stamford, Meadows, Blathwayt, Locke, Pollexfen, 'Samuel Clarke vice Ab. Hill') as opposed to eight (Bridgewater, the Earl of Tankerville, Meadows, Blathwayt, Locke, Pollexfen, Abraham Hill, and John Methuen). Whatever significance these changes had, they certainly register no concession to a parliamentary or merchants' Board of Trade.

[1] L'Hermitage on this matter is printed in full by Lees. The 'Samuel Clarke' of the College letter can hardly have been Edward Clarke; such a mistake would be impossible.

[2] Additional MS. 8888, British Museum.

The great recoinage, and the origins of the Board of Trade

Not only did Locke's friend Popple become secretary to the Board of Trade, his own personal servant and amanuensis Sylvester Brounower left him to become a clerk to the Board at ten times the salary. Locke's hand may also be seen in the order that 'some of the printed newspapers, one of each sort, be taken for the use of the board'.[1] Nevertheless, William Blathwayt, the secretary of the permanent officials, cordially hated Locke, his friends, his policies, and his appointees. Secretary to the privy council, responsible there for all colonial business, named as the paid commissioner from inside the civil service on the Board of December and of May, Blathwayt knew everybody and was entitled to know everything. But he was not made privy to the discussions of Somers with Locke over Christmas. He was furious when he finally got to know of Popple's appointment, which was not until July, and then from a minor official. He was told that his own candidate was 'obviated by the Lord Keeper who very early disclosed to the Board that one Mr. Popple was nominated thereto by His Majesty'. 'I should tell you likewise', the letter continued, 'how I have been solicited by him who is a philosopher and by his friends.'[2]

This was not to be the last time that Blathwayt came up against this inconvenient philosopher, nor was he the only professional civil servant whose advice was overset. A much more important defeat was suffered by William Lowndes when the great recoinage was carried through, if not in quite the way Locke wished it, then decidedly not as Lowndes recommended. We can go no further here with the story of how it was done, and of the continued activity of Locke and the College in the matter. We may notice, however, that the Board of Trade was not given direct responsibility for surveillance over the rise and fall of the value of English money. This was not mentioned in the commissions and does not seem to have been discussed to any great extent at the Board, though it did concern itself with coinage in the colonies. The Board's indirect responsibility was understood nevertheless, for a major object of its activities must have been to keep English currency in precisely the condition which Locke had proclaimed to be imperative, a condition in which each piece of money was worth its exact official weight in silver. In September 1698, the Board in fact made a report to the Commons on the overvaluation of gold in England. Though this report was to some extent a confession of the failure of the recoinage policy, it was strongly Lockean in tone.[3]

[1] See Brounower to Locke (Lovelace MSS.) and the MS. journal of the Board of Trade (Colonial Office Papers 391/9, Public Record Office) for the newspapers, supplied no doubt by Churchill, Locke's publisher and stationer to the board.
[2] Jacobsen, *Blathwayt*, pp. 299–300. Mr Kelly has found that there was a personal history to the mutual dislike of Locke and Blathwayt.
[3] *Board of Trade Journal*, XI, 9/9, 14/9, 15/9, 20/9 (1698); the report, dated 22/9, in the *House of Commons Journal*, XII, 511, 14/2 (1698/9). See also *Davenant*, ed. Usher, p. v, where it is not

In fact Locke's advice to Somers about the relation of the Board to the recoinage seems to have been this: put men on it who are in favour of the restoration of the coinage as we see it,[1] but keep all the responsibility within ministerial hands.

It is well known whose were the hands charged with the difficult practical details; on 2 May 1696 Mr Isaac Newton took oath as Warden of the Mint.[2] For the rest of the century, then, these two men were part and parcel of English administration. To Newton it was, perhaps, a job, an escape from Cambridge to the capital, as much as an opportunity for public service. To Locke it was first and foremost a duty, a citizen's responsibility in the strict sense which underlies his political theory, and we may pause a little to look at the qualities which he brought with him as an economic and as a colonial adviser.

We must not be surprised that the Dutch ambassador had obviously never heard of Locke in 1695: 'un Locke' is all he said of this name in the commission. For it was as a philosopher that he was publicly known, not at all as a political theorist. Although his *Two Treatises on Government* were printed in 1689, Locke never admitted in his lifetime that he had written them.[3] 'The most ingenious and learned Author of Human Understanding' who needed 'but once to have an Account of any Affair, though it were never so intricate' was how a hard-pressed colonial governor described him.[4]

But Locke had many identities other than that of the philosopher, and most of them entered easily enough into the atmosphere of the early Board of Trade. There was his reputation as an economist and an expert on currency. There was his prolonged championship of religious toleration, with its obvious implications for colonial settlement, and his belief in a 'general naturalization'.[5] His qualifications as a physician and his work as a theologian have a relevance which is not so obvious at first

recognized that it was the Board of Trade which made the report, and C. R. Fay, 'Newton and the Gold Standard', *Cambridge Historical Journal*, v (1935), 109–17. In his earlier article in the same journal, 'Locke versus Lowndes', iv (1933), 143–55, Fay insists that, in spite of Locke's monetary obtuseness, his policy succeeded in an object of supreme importance to all that the Board of Trade has tried to do since its beginnings, to instil an absolute confidence in English currency all over the world.

[1] Meadows, Pollexfen, and Hill all seem to have supported the Locke–Somers view. There is a paper endorsed 'Sr P Medows 95' on the coin in MS. Locke, b. 3, folios 84 ff.

[2] Craig, *Newton at the Mint*, p. 13. The actual appointment was undoubtedly Montagu's doing, but it must be remembered that Locke, probably through Monmouth, had tried to get a post in the Mint for Newton in 1691.

[3] See *Two Treatises*, Introduction. He also concealed his works on toleration and theology.

[4] Francis Nicholson to Locke, 30 March 1697 and 4 February 1698/9.

[5] See a paper in his hand under this title at the Houghton Library, Harvard University, and *Second Treatise of Government*, §42.

sight. But in his interest in the effects of climate on health, which made him one of the earliest recorders of temperatures and pressures, we may see the beginnings of the attention paid to tropical diseases by so many subsequent colonial administrators. His notorious attempt to reduce Christianity to a single straightforward proposition was finally as important to the African slave and the American Indian as it was to 'the day labourers, the spinsters and dairy maids' of his own country. When he asked James Blair, president of the College of William and Mary, about 'a Baroscope and a Thermoscope', 'the improvement of natural philosophie', and 'all strange and curious plants',[1] his preoccupation with the weather appears in its proper context. Locke was a virtuoso and a savant rather than an applied scientist as we now know them, but it is surely significant that colonial policy should have had such a man as one of its founders.

Locke was not a merchant, he was not a professional administrator, he was not a politician: he was an independent, free-moving intellectual who gave of his time because he was interested in the task of making policy in this particular sphere. The events between December and June brought out his differences from the merchants, even the most enlightened and disinterested of them. An important part in the campaign for a parliamentary Board of Trade was played by the merchants of Bristol and their representatives in the House. They did not stand for themselves alone, for particular trades, but for the merchant interest generally and for the rest of the country as contrasted with London.[2] In November 1695 the economist amongst the merchants of Bristol, John Cary, had published an *Essay on Trade* urging a Board of Trade to be established on the pattern of the Bank of England, with particular care to keep out courtiers.[3] When the membership of Somers's board became known, Cary condemned it: the king's proposed commissioners were 'altogether improper for such an undertaking and we hope the House will be of the same opinion, for they are wholly unskilful in trade'.[4] Although he must have known that Locke was one of the royal nominees, he sent a copy of his book to him on 11 January.

Locke's connexion with Bristol was close; it was the commercial centre of the area from which his support in the Commons came, and his own distant relatives were in business in the city. Here was an open oppor-

[1] Locke to Blair, 16 October 1699, MS. at Colonial Williamsburg, Inc.
[2] See Andrews, *Colonial Period*, IV, 287–8, and Lees, 'Parliament and the Proposal for a Council of Trade', pp. 57–61.
[3] Cary, *An Essay on...Trade* (Bristol, 1695), pp. 140–1.
[4] Andrews, *Colonial Period*, IV, 287, quoting a letter of Cary's to the Bristol M.P.s of 1 January 1695/6 from BM. Add. MS. 5540. Cf. letter of 28 December from Cary and others in Lees, 'Parliament and the Proposal for a Council of Trade', p. 59.

tunity for him to express his opinion on the parliamentary proposal, or even to ensure that he would himself be a parliamentary nominee, as Monmouth had suggested. He thought very highly of Cary's book, and there was an interesting exchange of letters between the two men.[1] 'I see no party or interest you contend for but that of truth and your country', Locke wrote to Cary, and they agreed on a vital point: 'The country gentleman who is most concerned in a right ordering of trade, both in duty and interest, is of all the most remote from any true notions of it, or sense of his stake in it.' But to Locke the country gentlemen meant the House of Commons, the 'squires' as they are called in the College letter, and from this we may deduce that Locke did not trust the Commons with a board of trade. He may even have advised Somers in this sense. He wanted neither parliamentarians nor merchants on the board; he most certainly would not have agreed that the Bank of England was a proper model.[2]

This interchange is, typically, much more significant for what it omitted to mention than for what it actually contained. Nowhere in any of the surviving letters or papers is there any reference whatsoever to the constitutional issue, the separation of powers. Here, then, is Locke, who is often regarded as the initiator of the separation of powers, apparently quite unaffected when his own contemporaries discussed it, even in a context which affected him personally. The College told him about it of course, and we have his comments on the debates in January and February on the question of whether the members of a parliamentary board should have to take an oath. During the period which came between the tailing-off of the parliamentary proposal in February and the revival of the Somers board at the end of March, he seems to have lapsed into indifference about the whole matter.[3] But whatever its cause, Locke's silence should serve as a warning not to be literal about our interpretation of the relation between political theories, political theorists, and the circumstances in which they become important.

If we did turn this into an abstract exercise, and related Locke's evident

---

[1] *Correspondence of Locke and Clarke*, ed. Rand, pp. 433, 460, 463, 472, 477, 491.
[2] Locke was a supporter of the Bank, and he invested £500 in it at the outset, a large sum for him. But there is in his hand a very curious dialogue revealing a profound suspicion of the London capitalists who floated it (MS. Locke, b.3, folios 35 ff.). In the College letters about the recoinage his contempt for the squires in economic matters comes out repeatedly, so also does his overt hostility to the London goldsmiths. Cary evidently did not believe that the 1696 Board of Trade was ever of any value; in the second edition of his *Essay* (1709), p. 86, he came out strongly for a parliamentary committee.
[3] See the letters in *Correspondence of Locke and Clarke*, ed. Rand, for this period. On 30 March Locke wrote to his friend Molyneux: 'I shall not be sorry if I scape a very honourable Employment with a thousand pounds a year annexed to it' (*Works*, London, 1714, III, 545). Mr Kelly uses this and other evidence to suggest that Locke was disappointed with the Board of Trade project, and had a rather different attitude to it generally than is implied here.

unwillingness to allow the legislature to found the Board with his doctrine of the separation of powers, we could reach an interesting result. It will be remembered that his division is between the legislative, the executive, and the 'federative' powers in the commonwealth. The functions of the board, if they were not to be allotted to the legislative, belong rather to the federative than to the executive because they were external functions. Trade and colonial relations fall quite easily under the 'Power of War and Peace, Leagues and Alliances and all the Transactions with all Persons without the Commonwealth',[1] which is the federative power, distinct in itself, though hardly to be placed in different hands from those of the executive.

Now if it is justifiable to suggest that Locke viewed his membership on the Board as helping in the exercise of the federative power of the community of England, these things may be said to follow from the doctrine Locke set out in his *Two Treatises*. He did not assume that the colonies were represented in the legislature at Westminster: they had or should have their own legislatives in the colonial assemblies, but they shared with the community of England a common executive and federative. On this view, the federative in some way not defined was presumably responsible for relations between the constituent communities as well as for their common external relations. It did not, it could not on Locke's political theory, remove from any constituent community the ultimate sovereignty of its people. They could revolt.

Such an abstract construction is interesting in another way because it was a feature of the increasingly rational attitude of political thinkers to regard external relations as an autonomous activity. Locke's 'federative power' is an example of this, though it is not easy to tell quite what he meant by it. We have seen that Locke showed no sign that he contemplated any such extension of his political theory. Indeed during the years of his service at the Board we can watch him struggling with the principles he had announced in *Two Treatises of Government* when faced with the case of Ireland as presented to him by his friend and correspondent, William Molyneux, and by the policy of parliament, government and Board of Trade.[2] What interested all these parties in Ireland, and Locke wrote to

---

[1] *Two Treatises*, II, §146 and notes, see also Introduction. Mr John Dunn takes a different view of the implications of Locke's attitude to the issue over the Board for the doctrine of the separation of powers (*The Political Thought of John Locke*, Cambridge, 1969).

[2] Professor McIlwain and others have insisted that the public history of the movement which ended in the American Declaration of Independence begins in 1698 with the publication in Dublin of Molyneux's *The Case of Ireland's Being Bound by Acts of Parliament in England, Stated*. The view expressed in the original article on Locke's attitude to Ireland over wool and flax has been modified here in view of Mr Dunn's work on the point, and of an article by Hugh Kearney, 'The Political Background to English Mercantilism, 1695–1700', *Economic History Review* (April 1959).

Molyneux about this, was the competition of the Irish wool trade with the English. He drew up a report for the Board, and so for the government and parliament, which can be regarded as an attempt to moderate the determination of English interests to destroy woollen manufacture in Ireland. Locke recommended the gradual substitution of a flax industry, though by fantastically complicated and unpractical methods. Even this is not easy to reconcile with Locke's political principles, however interpreted, nor is the whole regulatory trend of the Board's policy. We have to face the fact that Locke was a profound and earnest believer in government by the consent of the governed, and yet at the same time without doubt a 'mercantilist'. But we are learning to recognize that it is dangerous to assume that believers in the rights of the people were also critics of economic regulation. To make this mistake is to give way to the persistent habit of seeing colonial society not in terms of itself but in terms of the United States that was to come. This is what we call in England the Whig interpretation of history, in its peculiarly American form.[1]

When he sat at the Board of Trade, then, John Locke did not concern himself with the pursuit of abstractions. What interested him was the creation of a policy, and the significance of his presence there is not so much the content of his political thinking, as his insistence that men capable of abstract thought were also the men who could and should create policy. The same point might be made of Lavoisier as a farmer general of the French customs up to the French revolution, or of John Stuart Mill at the India House.[2] But it applies to Locke particularly, not only because he was a conspicuous example of such a man in such a position, but also because it was a matter of fundamental principle to him.

There is an example of John Locke's methods and outlook in colonial matters, in this case the affairs of the colony of Virginia, which is particularly well documented in his literary remains. It must be said at once that these papers have only a very minor political importance. The subject is the replacement of Sir Edmund Andros by Francis Nicholson as governor of Virginia in the summer of 1698, an event usually regarded as one incident in the struggle between the redoubtable Commissary Blair and the Virginians over the status of the Church of England in the colony

---

[1] A more direct example might be Andrews talking of 'Englishmen, thinking, unconsciously, of the British empire that was to come' (*Colonial Period*, IV, 381). It is surely time we recognized that explanations in terms of unconscious anticipations are not explanations at all. Professor Caroline Robbins assures me that more radical thinkers than Locke did condemn 'mercantilism'.

[2] Where, it may be noted, the principles of *Representative Government* were apparently relegated to the same context as those of *Two Treatises* in the case of Locke—information from Dr R. E. Robinson of St John's College, Cambridge.

and the establishment of the College of William and Mary. All that is added to the story is the fact that the source of Blair's great influence over royal policy in 1698 was not simply ecclesiastical, the support of the Archbishop of Canterbury and the Bishop of London, but also the alliance of John Locke. It is of some interest that the course of the struggle to get Andros out brings to light two parties amongst the Commissioners of Trade, the one in favour of leaving him alone, led by Blathwayt the civil servant, the other a reformist party led by Locke.

This was the first piece of business referred by the Lords Justices to the Board of Trade, a week before it actually met. Locke was already in London. His interest in Virginian affairs may well have arisen simply because he took them up as a token issue, an opportunity to demonstrate his conception of the way the commissioners should go about their business.[1] All our sources go to show that he was in close personal contact with the ministry. On 5 July, for example, in time for the second meeting of the Board on the sixth, he took the sacrament along with William Popple 'at our Church of St. Annes' in the company of Trumbull, the secretary of state, and on 26 September he was Trumbull's guest at dinner with Lord Monmouth.[2]

He attended every meeting that year until 16 November, when the acrid air of London forced him back to the country. It was so in all the following years, and the attendance register[3] shows us why the Virginian affair took so long to mature; it was because Locke was absent for so much of the year. If only for this reason, his biographer goes too far in saying of Locke's work on the board: 'Locke devoted himself very heartily to the business; and he was in every way its chief director and controller. All the more important undertakings of the Council were begun when he was present, and continued under his guidance. All its more important decisions were written, dictated or inspired by him.'[4]

Nevertheless he took great pains over Virginia. Locke's file on that colony, all carefully placed in the same little pigeonhole in his enormous desk, consisted finally in a little sheaf of documents, endorsed 'Trade

---

[1] Order of Lords Justices referring the petition of Bowtell and Wenbourne to the Council of Trade and Plantations, 18 June 1696, *Calendar of State Papers, Colonial Series, America and West Indies, 1574–1711*, ed. W. N. Sainsbury and others (London, 1860–1924), 1696–7, no. 46.

[2] Diary of Sir William Trumbull, Downshire MSS. deposited at the Berkshire Record Office, Reading—transcript loaned by Professor Plumb. Locke and Popple were obliged to take the sacrament to hold their offices, but it is of some importance to find this documentary proof that they did so, in view of the unitarian leanings of both men and the frequent assertion that Locke dissented from the Church of England in his later years.

[3] Taken from the Board of Trade Journal.

[4] Fox Bourne, *Life of John Locke*, II, 353. Mr Kelly has evidence which will show little foundation for such a statement.

Virginia 97'.[1] The date was 1697 since the council got no further than the examination of witnesses about the abuses in the government of the colony in 1696, and it was not until James Blair himself arrived in London in July 1697 that Locke got down to the details. But when he did, he went right to the fundamentals, down to the geology, the climate, the vegetation of the area, and all through the intricacies of its government and the personal history and weaknesses of its politicians. In late August or early September 1697, he took Blair up with him to his room in Mr Pawling's house in Little Lincoln's Inn Fields. Armed with a list of the Virginia councillors,[2] he made Blair write out for him a complete treatise entitled 'Some of the Chief Grievances of the present Constitution of Virginia with an Essay towards the Remedies thereof'.[3] Acting on this, he dictated a list of searching queries to an amanuensis in Blair's presence, and this list became an official document, sent out by the Board to its Virginia witnesses on 9 September 1697.[4] On 20 October 1697 these witnesses sent in a report based on Locke's queries. This report has become a classic, although Locke's part in it has never previously been suspected. It is the well-known account of *The Present State of Virginia and the College*, first printed in London in 1727.[5] It has been regarded as an account of the colony written at leisure for any interested reader, but in its origin it was a policy-making document.

But Locke did not stop here, and the struggle with Blathwayt took place in the following year, in July and August 1698, over the instructions to Nicholson as successor to Andros. Blathwayt's fierce opposition is revealed in a letter of 31 May 1698. Talking of the Virginia report of 1697 he says, 'I should think it a sin while I take the king's money to

---

[1] Locke's Virginia papers are now to be found in the volume labelled 'Trade and Colonies', in MS. Locke, c.30. The longest of them is separately bound, ref. e.9. The very summary account printed here is based on these documents, on *Cal. State Papers, AWI*, and the Board of Trade Journal with other colonial papers in the Public Record Office, and on the correspondence of Nicholson (letters of Mar. 30 '97, May 26, '98, Feb. 4 '98/9) and Blair (letters of Jan. 30, '97/8, Feb. 8 '98/9) together with Locke's replies to the last letter of each man preserved in Colonial Williamsburg (both written in October 1699). The story could be told at much greater length, and with a detailed comparison between MS. Locke e. 9 with *The Present State of Virginia* (see below, n. 5) and Nicholson's instructions. From all these sources an exact and exemplary account could be drawn up of the actual handling of a colonial issue by Locke's Board of Trade.

[2] MS. Locke, c.30, 36/7, with 'great rivers' scribbled on it in Locke's hand.

[3] MS. Locke, e.9, first part.

[4] Compare *ibid*. second part and final part, with *Cal. State Papers, AWI, 1696–7*, no. 1314. Another copy of Locke's original is MS. Locke, c.30, 59/60.

[5] Henry Hartwell, James Blair, and Edward Chilton, *The Present State of Virginia and the College*, reprinted in Massachusetts Historical Society, *Collections* (1798), and republished in Williamsburg Restoration Historical Studies, no. 1, ed. Hunter Dickinson Farish (Williamsburg, 1940). Farish did not compare the 1727 printing with the originals in the Public Record Office, and his indications of the parts written by the three authors are unreliable.

agree to it'.[1] But Nicholson's instructions were drawn up in accordance with Locke's recommendations, although the Board were quite well aware that they were breaking precedent.[2] 'The general ground' of the new instructions 'is that in the Administration of the Government of Virginia all things are made so dependent on the Governor's single will and pleasure.' Virginia councillors were to take oaths as judges, they were not to be suspended without good reason, they were not to monopolize all the offices of government. There was to be a new survey of the colony, a new method of granting land, a codification of the laws, a taxation reform. We can find in these provisions, if we wish, signs of Locke's own profound suspicion of arbitrary government with its attendant body of creatures.

He won this victory over Blathwayt by hard and intricate work, and his policy, a down-to-earth, realistic reform of a particular colony's affairs, was incorporated into Nicholson's instructions. He was unpopular for it, not only with the civil servants, but with his own kind, the men of letters. How was it possible, one of the critics of his theories of education and of religion was asking, how was it possible that 'a Man may be a Commissioner of Trade...and yet be a just writer'?[3] The instructions may have had little effect, and the new regime in Virginia was soon disturbed again by the impossible Blair, but there was one adventitious result which Americans looking back on their colonial past can still admire—the governor's mansion in restored Williamsburg. The document which Nicholson took with him to Virginia made elaborate provisions about the building of an official residence, and the stately house which finally grew up still dominates the Middle Plantation, Williamsburg, the splendid capital of Virginia in her golden age.

Such then was the particular individual issue which occupied the greatest single portion of Locke's attention between 1696 and 1700 whilst he was a member of the Board of Trade. Not a question of high policy, though we have seen him taking up his somewhat self-effacing position on matters of great historical consequence. Not a great economic problem, though he did pronounce on economic matters too, and helped to settle the English and the American attitude on the greatest of them all for two succeeding centuries, their attitude, that is to say, to 'sound money'. Not the only matter of detail which he mastered, for several others have left their mark in his papers and letters.[4] Not even an issue which raised

---

[1] Jacobsen, *Blathwayt*, p. 308.
[2] See their representations to the Lords Justices justifying the departures in *Cal. State Papers, AWI, 1697–8*, no. 767.
[3] John Edwards, *A Brief Vindication of...the Christian Faith* (London, 1697), p. 5.
[4] Two other colonial issues might be mentioned—the Darien Scheme and the posting of Locke's friend Bellomont to the governorship of New York.

in a dramatic form the general questions his political and social theory tried to answer. But a detailed, concrete problem of what to do at a particular time in a particular situation, where the large-minded, public-spirited man felt called upon to do better than the interested politician and the professional administrator.

Locke resigned from the Board of Trade in June 1700 and was succeeded by another man of letters in the public service, the poet Matthew Prior. He resigned when Somers ceased to be lord chancellor and Edward Clarke also left his offices. The epitaph on the old Board of Trade has been uttered by the greatest master of English eloquence, Edmund Burke, his words billowing over the House of Commons in its fervour for administrative economy in the year 1780:

This Board, Sir, has had both its original formation, and its regeneration in a job. In a job it was conceived, and in a job its mother brought it forth. It has perfectly answered its purposes. It was intended to quiet the minds of the people, and to compose the ferment that was then too strongly working in parliament. The courtiers were too happy to be able to substitute a board which they knew would be useless, in the face of one which they feared would be dangerous. It is the only instance of a public body which has never degenerated; but to this hour preserves all the health and vigour of its primitive institution. I shall propose to you to *suppress the board of trade and plantations* and to recommit all its business to the council from whence it was very improvidently taken.[1]

Burke seems to have remembered on less heady occasions that Locke was a founder of the Board of Trade. He may have been right when he suspected that patronage was one of the forces at work when Somers set it up, as he was certainly right to believe that it was the stifling dust of patronage which choked all its vitality as the young eighteenth century grew older. The presence of such a man as Forde Grey, Earl of Tankerville, in the commission of 1696 can scarcely have any explanation other than the usefulness of a job at £1,000, with no particular duties, to a great political manager with someone to reward. But we have tried to show that it was not a job to the philosopher John Locke. It was his opportunity to demonstrate to the world what was meant in his day, and for all succeeding generations, by the social and political responsibilities of the intellectual.

[1] Burke, *Works*, II, 110–15, excerpted. The board which Burke thought might be dangerous to the Court was presumably the parliamentary board discussed above.

Locke, Newton and the two cultures

by JAMES L. AXTELL[1]

In 1959 C. P. Snow delivered the Rede Lecture at Cambridge University on 'The Two Cultures', those of the scientist and the literary intellectual, which opened an impassioned dialogue that has recently lapsed into silence. His diagnosis of many of our present cultural ills pointed to the ever-widening communication gap that separates these two groups— 'comparable in intelligence, identical in race, not grossly different in social origin, earning about the same incomes'. Many had been aware of the problem before, but Snow articulated it: 'Persons educated with the greatest intensity we know can no longer communicate with each other on the plane of their major intellectual concern.' In other words, we are firmly ensconced in the Age of the Specialist and have been, according to Snow, since the nineteenth century.

The reasons for the existence of the two cultures are 'many, deep, and complex, some rooted in social histories, some in personal histories, and some in the inner dynamic of the different kinds of mental activity themselves'. Western literary intellectuals—'natural Luddites' all—have 'never tried, wanted, or been able to understand' the industrial and scientific revolutions of the past century and a half.[2] But it was not always so, and I would like to consider an auspicious moment in western history when intellectuals found themselves similarly confronted with an unnerving scientific revolution and tried their best to understand and appreciate it.

Men in the seventeenth century, as do men in any age, felt the psychological need for a satisfying world-view, a cosmology that would give meaning and a point of reference to all their actions, thoughts, and feelings. The majority were content to accept the picture offered by the church in its catechism, prayer book, and sermons; the priest was their cosmologist and the picture he painted was orderly, immutable, and universal. In such

[1] I am grateful to the Social Science Research Council for their generous support in 1965–6, during which time most of the research for this essay was completed under a Postdoctoral Research Fellowship.
[2] C. P. Snow, *The Two Cultures: and A Second Look* (Cambridge, 1963), pp. 2, 60, 22.

a universe the farmer and the servant found comfort and a secure place in God's creation.

But the intellectuals of their society, those men who were not merely content to feel or act or will but were driven to think and reflect about the problems of the world they lived in, needed something more. They were aware of a larger world, a more unbounded physical universe in which a bewildering variety of phenomena—both old and new—demanded explanation. Theorists stepped forward, some confidently, some humbly, with interpretations. First Copernicus and his propagandist Galileo, then Descartes, and finally a whole family of corpuscularian philosophers presented plausible explanations of the taunting phenomena of ancient tomes and modern telescopes. But each was incomplete and never wholly satisfactory; no replacement for the antiquated Aristotelian cosmology that had served for almost two centuries came forward as the new paradigm.[1] Almost a century of experimentation and observation, collection and classification, passed before Isaac Newton offered his theory of gravitation as the most economical explanation of natural phenomena to date. The scientific revolution that had been fought on the printed page over the past century and a half was climaxed by the publication of *Principia mathematica naturalis philosophiae* in 1687. Intellectuals, at least, now had the materials to construct for themselves a new world-view, one that would solve their most compelling intellectual puzzles and give structure to their future explorations of nature and thought. But what they soon found they needed badly were directions; for Newton's was no ordinary book and the materials he presented were, though necessary, far from manageable.

Some time after Newton had published the *Principia* one of a group of Cambridge undergraduates was heard to remark as they passed him, 'There goes the man who has writt a book that neither he nor any one else understands.'[2] Allowing for the exaggeration of youth, this seems a fair characterization of the initial reaction to the tortuous, 500-page Latin treatise that appeared in serious bookshops in July 1687. Newton, terse in conversation and largely humourless, was even more austere in his greatest work. Fontenelle accurately diagnosed the reasons for its slow reception and slower assimilation; it was written, he said, with 'a great deal of learning', the conclusions were often so hastily drawn from the premisses that 'the Reader is frequently left to supply an intermediate chain of Consequences', and its author was 'very sparing of his expres-

---

[1] Thomas S. Kuhn, *The Copernican Revolution* (Cambridge, Mass., 1957) and *The Structure of Scientific Revolutions* (Chicago, 1962).

[2] King's College, Cambridge, MS. Keynes 130.5, no. 2. The source was Martin Folkes, President of the Royal Society, 1741–53.

sions'.[1] Furthermore, the language in which it was written—mathematics —was a special hybrid of Newton's own device. Many intellectuals of the day knew that 'As a Geometrical Problem is handled Arithmetically (by Algebrists) so an Arithmetical Question may be handled Geometrically by protraction & Geometrical reasoning'.[2] The sophistication of algebra in the early decades of the century, its analytical application to geometrical problems by Descartes in the 1630s, and the independent discovery of the calculus by Leibniz and Newton all served to make algebra—or 'Analysis' as Newton called it—the fashionable mode of mathematics in the later years of the century. Tradition has it that Newton favoured this new analytical approach and discovered the propositions of the *Principia* by the use of his own fluxional calculus, only to convert his results into respectable geometrical dress for publication. Although he provided authority for this traditional explanation himself, some of his other statements lend support to Rupert Hall's opinion that 'only occasionally, perhaps in his most intricate investigations', did he rely upon a fluxional analysis.[3] David Gregory, a Scottish mathematician and friend of Newton, once heard him say that 'Algebra is the Analysis of Bunglers in Mathematics'.[4] And in a manuscript draft entitled 'Historia Methodi Infinitesimalis', he parried the 'Modern' approach with the 'ancient' which he so admired.

The ancients had their [mathematical] Analysis, [he conceded,] but admitted nothing into Geometry before it was demonstrated by Composition [i.e. synthesis]. The moderns are intent only upon Analysis, & admit analytical inventions into Geometry before they are demonstrated by Composition. Synthetical Demonstrations are easier to read, render Propositions more certain, & convey them better to posterity. For the symbols used in Analysis are apt to be changed from time to time.

It was for these reasons, he said, that after he had invented his propositions by Analysis, he 'demonstrated them by Composition'.[5]

We may believe his faith in the classical approach, but his concluding statement was intended for posterity—and was false. Newton not only

[1] Bernard de Fontenelle, *The Life of Sir Isaac Newton* (London, 1728), p. 5.
[2] *David Gregory, Isaac Newton and their circle. Extracts from David Gregory's Memoranda, 1677–1708*, ed. W. G. Hiscock (Oxford, 1937), p. 39.
[3] A. R. Hall, *From Galileo to Newton 1630–1720* (London, 1963), p. 101.
[4] *David Gregory*, ed. Hiscock, p. 42. See also Henry Pemberton, *A View of Sir Isaac Newton's Philosophy* (London, 1728), Preface 2v.
[5] Cambridge University Library, Add. MS. 3968B, no. 13, fo. 185. This was one of several drafts that Newton wrote in preparing the anonymous 'Account of a Book entitled, Commercium Epistolicum' for the *Philosophical Transactions* of the Royal Society (of which he was president) which defended his claim to priority over Leibniz in the invention of the calculus. *Philosophical Transactions* (1715), p. 206.

did not solve more than a small handful of problems in fluxional terms, but also did not present his results in traditional Euclidean dress, as his allegation about 'Composition' would have us believe. William Derham, who had known Newton for 'about 30 years', understood that the controversies with Leibniz, Hooke, Linus, and others about the nature of light and colours 'made sr Is[aac] very uneasy; who abhorred all Contests ...And for this reason, mainly to avoid being baited by little Smatterers in Mathematicks, he told me, he designedly made his Principia abstruse; but yet so as to be understood by able Mathematicians, who he imagined, by comprehending his Demonstrations, would concurr with him in his Theory.'[1] It seems that he succeeded beyond his wildest expectations. For by writing in a 'severely compressed form which one can only call Newtonian, one flexible enough to be able to contain traditional Greek geometry and also a rigorous geometrical calculus of limits (which is exactly an infinitesimal calculus...)'[2] he effectively rendered the *Principia* unintelligible not only to the virtuosi and intellectual laymen who wanted and needed an understanding of the new world-view, but to the large majority of professional mathematicians as well. 'Mathematicians of character', Fontenelle testified, 'were oblig'd to study it with care, before they could be masters of it; and those of a lower rank did not dare to venture upon it, till encourag'd by the more learned.'[3]

The interesting question is just how many 'mathematicians of character' could understand the *Principia* fully in the year immediately following its publication. It is probably safe to say that Christiaan Huygens, the second greatest scientist of the day; Leibniz, co-inventor of the calculus; Edmond Halley, the astronomer who guided and financed the *Principia* through the press; David Gregory of Edinburgh, whose 200-page manuscript *Notae* (1694) was the first large-scale review and critique of the *Principia*; John Craig, also of Edinburgh and a student of both Gregory and Newton; and perhaps one or two more could master its geometrical intricacies and comprehend the design and execution of the proofs. But even these giants had their difficulties. Newton admitted—or boasted—that even Halley, though the 'best astronomer' according to Newtonian specifications, 'did not understand that part relating to the fluids' in book II, section VII—understandably enough as Newton considered that 'the hardest part of his book'.[4] John Craig, in attempting to prepare a 'satis-

---

[1] King's College, MS. Keynes 133, fo. 10 (18 July 1733).
[2] Private communication with D. T. Whiteside of Cambridge University, the editor of Newton's mathematical works, 13 April and 12 July 1964. See also R. J. Forbes and E. J. Dijksterhuis, *A History of Science and Technology* (Harmondsworth, 1963), I, 258.
[3] Fontenelle, *The Life of Sir Isaac Newton*, p. 5.
[4] King's College, MS. Keynes 130.5, no. 2, fo. 3; 130.6, folios 12–13; *David Gregory*, ed. Hiscock, p. 36.

Locke, Newton and the two cultures

factory account of Mr Newtons book' for fellow mathematician Colin Campbell, found it to be 'a task of no small trouble' and sent the book instead.[1] But David Gregory, a product of the fine Scottish tradition in mathematics, had a firm grasp of its principles and thanked Newton for his contributions to science on behalf of the 'few' who had profited by them.[2]

And now wee can perceive that the insufficiencie of the physicall theories came not from the want of the know[n] Geometry of the Naturalists, but also from this that the Geometers hade not advanced their science sufficiently, and most especially hade never found out a Methode of determining geometrically what it is which represents and measures physicall qualities. And tho your book is of so transcendent fineness and use that few will understand it, yet this will not I hope hinder you from discovering more hereafter to those few who cannot but be infinitly thankful to you on that account.

Though disciples of Newton, such as Abraham DeMoivre, John Keill, Fatio de Duillier, and John Machin (who Newton in later life felt 'understood his principia best'),[3] eventually advanced to the point of mastery in the decades after 1687, David Gregory's prediction was accurate —few did understand the *Principia*. But it was increasingly important to do so, for upon it was constructed a whole new picture of the universe, one in which natural objects behaved exactly on earth as they did in the heavens and man's reason subdued nature by speaking her passionless mathematical language. All but the very best mathematicians 'did not dare to venture upon it', as we have seen, 'till encourag'd by the more learned; but at last, when the Book came to be sufficiently known, the approbation, which had been so slowly gain'd became so universal, that nothing was to be heard from all quarters but one general cry of Admiration'.[4] If only a mathematical élite could be expected to cope with the technical arguments of the *Principia*, who, then, were some of the 'lower rank' of intellectuals who struggled with it, some successfully, some less so, in an attempt to come to terms with its obvious importance?

Sir William Petty, autodidact, surveyor, founding member of the Royal Society, professor of anatomy at Oxford, author of *Political Arithmetic*, and mechanical philosopher, died in December 1687, but not before seeing the *Principia* in print. 'As for Mr Newton's book, I would give 500£ to have been the author of it,' he wrote, 'and 200£ That Charles [his son] understood it. My bad eyes disable mee to make the most of it,

[1] *The Correspondence of Isaac Newton*, ed. H. W. Turnbull (Cambridge, 1960), II, 501 (29 December 1687).
[2] *Ibid.* II, 484 (2 September 1687).
[3] King's College, MS. Keynes 130.5, no. 2, p. 3.
[4] Fontenelle, *The Life of Sir Isaac Newton*, p. 5.

for diagrams cannot bee read by others.' Though he was half-blind and not far from death, Petty was one of the few laymen to recognize immediately the importance of Newton's work. But he lamented 'poor Isaac Newton', fearing that, like himself, he would not get 'Buter to [his] parsnips or hobnayles for [his] Shoes', for 'I have not met with one Man that puts an extraordinary value upon his Book'.[1]

From his retirement Gilbert Clerke, former fellow of Sidney Sussex College, Cambridge, and a mathematician of some ability, informed Newton in September 1687 of a few places in the *Principia* that confounded him: 'though I confesse I doe not as yet well understand so much as your first three sections [concerning the inverse square law and conic sections], for wch you doe not require yt a man should be *mathematicè doctus*'. But, he continued, 'if I must not tell you, till I understand those sections & your third booke very well; perhaps I must never tell you, your booke comeing to me in ye evening of my declineing age'.[2] A brisk correspondence between Newton and Clerke developed that tried to help the former mathematics tutor over his difficulties.

Still another Cantabrigian capitulated when confronted by the imposing diagrams and calculations of the *Principia*. On 13 February 1692 Richard Bentley, classicist and chaplain to Bishop Stillingfleet, was chosen by the trustees of Robert Boyle's bequest for the establishment of an annual series of lectures 'against Atheists, Deists, Libertins, Jewes &c.' to be their first preacher. Less than a month later this man, of whom it was said that 'had he but the gift of humility, he would be the most extraordinary man in Europe', delivered the first of eight monthly lectures at St Martin's Church.[3] During the ensuing months he battered away at the folly and unreasonableness of the modish but dangerous atheism and deism that was fermenting in taverns and coffee-houses. The first six lectures were devoted to proving the existence of God from the faculties of the human soul and the structure and origin of bodies, but in the last two, on the first Monday in November and December, Bentley unleashed for the first time the powerful new ally of religion—the Newtonian world-view.

Bentley was a classicist, not a mathematician, but he had an impressive

---

[1] *The Petty–Southwell Correspondence 1676–1687*, ed. Marquis of Lansdowne (London, 1928), p. 279 (23 July 1687); p. 282 (16 August 1687).

[2] *The Correspondence of Isaac Newton*, ed. Turnbull, II, 485 (26 September 1687). Clerke refers to Newton's statement in the introduction to book III that 'It is enough if one carefully reads the Definitions, the Laws of Motion, and the first three sections of the first Book. He may then pass on to this Book, and consult such of the remaining Propositions of the first two Books, as the references in this, and his occasions, shall require.' English ed. by Cajori (Berkeley–Los Angeles, 1962), p. 397.

[3] *The Diary of John Evelyn*, ed. E. S. de Beer (Oxford, 1955), pp. 88–9, 94. Evelyn was one of the four trustees.

curiosity and a powerful intellect. Before the Boyle lectures had even been conceived, he had recognized the importance of Newton's new book for all areas of intellectual endeavour and had set out to procure aid in his reading of it. In June 1691 he asked John Craig, the Scottish mathematician, for suggestions of preliminary reading. Impressed by Newton's achievement as he was, Craig sent a required bibliography of at least *forty-five* different works, with recommendations of many others.[1] It is a wonder that Bentley was not one of the 'great many' who had been frightened away from the Newtonian philosophy by 'the Thoughts of being oblig'd to understand Mathematicks'.[2] Obviously overwhelmed by the unexpected wealth of Craig's 'help', he decided Newton himself was the best person to ask. In July Newton sent a more manageable list of eight titles (five of which Bentley thought essential) and the following directions: 'When you have read ye first 60 pages, pass on to ye 3d Book & when you see the design of that you may turn back to such Propositions as you shall have a desire to know, or peruse the whole in order if you think fit.'[3] This was Newton's suggestion for any intellectual who desired to understand the general principles and major results of the *Principia*, but who lacked the extensive mathematical training necessary to master it all. But at least a modicum of mathematical knowledge was required, as several people learned to their dismay.

When the Earl of Halifax asked Newton 'if there was no method to make him master of his discoveries without learning Mathematicks, Sir Isaac said No, it was impossible', but someone 'recommended [John] Machin to his Lordship for that purpose, who gave him 50 Guineas by way of encouragement'. Machin confessed that he tried several schemes but never any that satisfied the Earl, and gave it up in despair.[4] Other intellectuals as well despaired of ever comprehending the book. Humphrey Newton, Newton's unrelated secretary, recalled in 1728 that after the *Principia* was printed 'Sir Isaac was pleas'd to send me with several of them, as Presents, to some of the Heads of Colledges, & others of his Acquaintance, some of which (particularly Dr. Babington of Trinity) said that they might study seven years, before they understood anything of it'.[5]

Thus we have met with three groups of intellectuals: those who had mastered the *Principia* through an understanding of higher mathematics, those who were unable to follow any part of it, and those who, with some

[1] David Brewster, *Memoirs of...Sir Isaac Newton* (Edinburgh, 1855), I, 465–9. William Wotton was Bentley's intermediary in this exchange.
[2] J. T. Desaguliers, *A Course of Experimental Philosophy* (London, 1734), I, preface.
[3] Brewster, *Newton*, I, 469; *The Correspondence of Isaac Newton*, ed. Turnbull (1961), III, 155–6.
[4] King's College, MS. Keynes 130.5, no. 2, p. 4. I have expanded contractions and added punctuation for clarity.
[5] King's College, MS. Keynes 135 (17 January 1727/8).

James L. Axtell

background in mathematics and the help of Newton's own suggestions, were able to grasp the general drift of its message and some of the proofs upon which it was grounded. Numerically it is difficult to say which of the last two groups was the more important, but the last group certainly held the future in its hands. One reason is that the intellectuals with a capacity for at least a partial understanding of Newton's work were eager and ready for the numerous attempts to popularize his discoveries in the early years of the eighteenth century. Another is that this group included John Locke, who was one of the first to appreciate Newton's new world-view and methods, and to assist in many ways in communicating them to the intellectual classes of England and Europe. His scientific biography is also illustrative, I think, of the impact of the Newtonian revolution on 'traditional' intellectuals—non-specialist, polymathic thinkers—at the end of the seventeenth century and of their serious attempts to come to terms with an unfamiliar explanation of the natural world with which they had been long familiar.

Of Locke's scientific biography only the medical chapters have been written.[1] And much that we would like to know has been lost to the past. For example, we know almost nothing about the undergraduate lectures that he attended at Oxford; we know only slightly more about the nature of his college tutorial instruction. Perhaps because we are frailer beings than our Victorian predecessors, we no longer assume that because lecture courses in mathematics and natural philosophy were prescribed by statute every undergraduate of the period faithfully attended them.[2] But what we do know is that Locke's whole Oxford educational experience leaned heavily on the side of the literary humanities, neo-Aristotelian and later Cartesian philosophy, and the medical, non-mathematical aspects of the new philosophy. At that time Robert Boyle, corpuscular chemist and mechanical philosopher, was Locke's scientific mentor and paradigm. Beyond some algebra and Euclidean geometry, Locke was probably not familiar with higher mathematics.[3]

When Locke left Oxford for Shaftesbury's London his scientific environment changed very little. The intellectual atmosphere of Boyle's laboratory on High Street was very nearly duplicated in Gresham College, where the Royal Society had been meeting since the Restoration and where Locke now found himself drawn. He was elected a Fellow on 26 November

[1] Kenneth Dewhurst, *John Locke (1632–1704), Physician and Philosopher: A Medical Biography* (London, 1963).
[2] H. R. Fox Bourne, *The Life of John Locke* (London, 1876), I, 43–9, 55.
[3] This is an impression gained from a reading of Locke's notebooks, memoranda, and library lists, from his subsequent relations with Newton, and from contemporary estimates of his mathematical ability.

172

1668 and remained of that company for half his life. In the early years of his membership he paid his dues faithfully and was elected to various committees and the governing Council, though his irregular attendance at these extraordinary sessions suggests that Shaftesbury was monopolizing his time in governmental affairs. Yet he seems to have taken an interest in the regular meetings of the Society, when he occasionally joined the ranks of the 'free and unconfined'. On 10 March 1670 he was present at a meeting where Sir George Ent, Dr Timothy Clarke, Dr Jonathan Goddard, Dr William Croune and Boyle experimented on the artificial tin arm of one of Dr Goddard's devices 'to find, whether pulsation was made by an intumescence of the artery or not'. When several of the physicians disagreed on the findings,

Dr Goddard moved, that a dog might be opened, in order to observe carefully the pulsations of the heart and artery. It being intimated by him, that the bore of all the ends of the capillary arteries, taken together in bulk, was probably of the same capacity with the single great bore of the artery receiving the blood of the heart; and that therefore the blood might pass out of the arteries as easily as it came in, and therefore needed not to distend them.

Then Locke, another acute student of medicine, 'desired, that it might be considered, that though that were so, yet there was more superficies in the whole bulk of all the ends of the arteries together than in the single great artery'.[1] He was, of course, correct.

The next recorded indication of the bent of his scientific interests is dated 6 November 1672. On that Wednesday Robert Hooke presented to the Society Otto von Guericke's *Experimenta nova Magdeburgica de vacuo spacio* (Amsterdam, 1672), recommending that it be bought for their library. 'He mentioned, that among Mr. Guericke's experiments there was one which he thought deserved to be tried before the Society, viz. that of a sulphur-ball having a considerable attractive power, and representing the properties of the earth.' At which point 'Mr. Locke intimated, that himself had made some experiments with such a ball, and promised, that he would bring it to the Society at the next meeting'. The following week 'Mr. Locke being called upon for his sulphur-ball, which he promised at the last meeting to produce at this, excused himself, that he had forgot it, promising to bring it at the next'. Two weeks later, the absent-minded don had still failed to bring in his sulphur-ball, so 'Mr. Boyle produced a ball of sulphur melted in a glass ball, which, like electrical bodies, attracted several light substances, as also filings of fine copper'.[2] Though his former teacher had to compensate for his forgetfulness, Locke was sufficiently interested in Guericke's experiments to purchase a copy

[1] Thomas Birch, *The History of the Royal Society* (London, 1756), ii, 426–7.
[2] *Ibid.* (1757), iii, 59–63.

of his book some time thereafter. But in general it is safe to say that Locke was more interested in clinical medicine than experimental or mathematical science at this time.[1]

Further indications of the drift of his scientific interests before 1687 come from his reading notes on the scientific–literary periodicals of the day and from his commonplace memoranda of books lent, borrowed, or recommended. Before 1687 there are almost no references to reviews of purely mathematical books, partly because few journals felt the need to review them, but partly because Locke was not interested in the internal developments in that field. Occasionally he listed a series of page numbers under the heading of 'Mathematica', but nothing further was noted, not even the title or author. His real interests, so obvious to even the casual reader of his memoranda, were travel literature, medicine and botany, the non-technical aspects of astronomy and cometography, and the philosophical ramifications of Cartesianism, such as mechanical souls and senseless brutes.[2] Indeed this is the kind of varied reading we would expect of a man who was preparing works on the nature and functions of the human understanding, civil government, toleration, and education. There was simply little time and less need for any detailed attention to the intricacies of higher mathematics.

But when the *Principia* was published such a need did arise. A new world-picture demanded a re-tooling of the mind, for which every available mathematical device had to be taken out of storage and refurbished. In most instances, as in Locke's, they also had to be updated—or at least the attempt made. So in the 1690s we find him noting several books on algebra and geometry, obviously a few intended for Edward Clarke, whom he was advising on the education of his son, but most for his own re-education. Tacquet's *Elementa geometriae planae ac solidae* (1665) and a 1667 edition of *Nouveaux Elémens de Géometrie* for 'ordinary geometry' and the *Elémens des Mathématiques* for 'arithmetic and algebra' was one memorandum. The Earl of Pembroke, the virtuoso in whose salon Locke first met Newton, recommended in 1693 the second edition of Pascal's *Geometry* as the 'best booke to begin with', to be followed by the second edition of Malebranche, 'the best Geometrie'. In 1698 someone told Locke that 'Branchards Algebra published by [John] Pell' was 'the easiest method for Algebra [and] applicable also to plain [*sic*] Geometry'.[3] And as late as the year before he died Locke was still interested in the heart of Newton's achievement. In July 1703 Awnsham Churchill, his publisher, sent him a copy of David Gregory's excellent but demanding *Astronomiae Physicae &*

[1] Dewhurst, *John Locke, Medical Biography*, p. 44.
[2] MS. Locke, c.33, Bodleian Library, Oxford.
[3] MS. Locke, f.29, folios 62, 150, 162.

Locke, Newton and the two cultures

Geometricae Elementa (1702), the first textbook composed on gravitational principles and remodelling astronomy to conform with physical theory.[1]

We might wonder, then, how well Locke was mathematically prepared for the *Principia* when it appeared in 1687. His final library contained less than twenty works on mathematics; the great majority were elementary French treatises. There was none representing the more recent developments in calculus, fluxional analysis, analytical geometry, or trigonometry. Euclid, Pascal ('Triangle Arithmetic'), Gregory, and Tacquet were the most advanced authors.[2] It is not surprising, then, that Locke's near-contemporaries assumed, if they were not certain, that 'he was not a great mathematician' and 'was ignorant of the mathematical method'.[3]

Intellectual determination, however, when it is combined with the fineness and strength of mind such as Locke had, can often move mountains. Recognizing the transcendent importance of Newton's new work, Locke would not be held back by his own technical inadequacies and plunged into the *Principia* with a daring that we can only applaud. When Jean LeClerc, his close friend and editor of the widely read *Bibliothèque Universelle*, asked him to review the book newly arrived from England for the March 1688 issue, he had been through it once already. While staying in Rotterdam with Benjamin Furly in September 1687 he had taken four large folio pages of notes and excerpts from the book, then only two months old. The ironic thing about this first reading of one of the most demanding books in the history of science is that it appears that Locke did it in bed, where he was confined with an illness for the whole month of September and most of the next two months.[4]

The following March he took another set of notes which served as the basis of his review of the same month. In it he took pains to give his European reader, who for the most part was interested in the latest scientific advances of the day but incapable of following the intricate mathematical reasoning and computations upon which they were founded, a thorough taste of the more important results and the general methodology of the *Principia*, through extensive quotations, enumeration of all the rather explanatory chapter headings, and through clear and concise

---

[1] Locke returned it on 19 October. MS. Locke, c.5, fo. 198 (3 July 1703); f.10, fo. 559 (19 October 1703).

[2] John Harrison and Peter Laslett, *The Library of John Locke* (Oxford, 1965), *passim*. I am grateful to John Harrison for a list of the mathematical books which are not analysed separately in his catalogue. Locke also had Isaac Barrow's *Lectiones geometricae* (1670), a gift of the author, but gave it to Maurice Ashley, the brother of his most famous pupil, the third Earl of Shaftesbury, in 1693. MS. Locke, f.10, fo. 188.

[3] Voltaire, *Lettres Ecrites de Londres sur les Anglois et autres sujets* (Frankfort, 1735), p. 69; G. W. Leibniz, *Philosophical Papers and Letters*, ed. L. E. Loemker (Chicago, 1956), II, 1066.

[4] Maurice Cranston, *John Locke, A Biography* (New York, 1957), pp. 288-9.

James L. Axtell

commentary upon some of the more difficult and important aspects of Newton's work, such as his demolition of the Cartesian vortices. The result was that Locke's fourteen-page review, appearing in French and easily accessible to a wide lay audience, assumed the major part of the task of introducing Newton's ideas and results to the growing intellectual class of French-speaking Europe. The only other two continental reviews, both published after Locke's, were either too short and unfavourable, or inaccessible and written for a specialist audience.[1]

Shortly after Locke's return to England in February 1689, his meeting with Newton took place in Pembroke's salon and sparked the close and occasionally rocky friendship that endured until Locke's death.[2] There were three results of this personal friendship that bear upon our story. The first was a simplified 'Demonstration That the Planets by their gravity towards the Sun may move in Ellipses' which Newton prepared for Locke in March 1690.[3] Presumably Locke had asked Newton for an alternative proof of Prop. XIII, Theor. XIII of Book III shortly after they had met, in an effort to consolidate his understanding of the gravitational foundations of the Newtonian world-view. It is one more example of Locke's earnest assault on the *Principia*.

The second outcome was that sometime in 1691 Newton presented his new friend with a corrected copy of the *Principia*. On the first blank page of the book, now in the library of Trinity College, Cambridge, Locke wrote 'Liber Johannes Locke Ex dono Acutissimi Authoris Qui errores propria manu correxit', and drew his secret sign beneath the 'Finis' on the last page. Newton's corrections followed his recommended pattern of reading for laymen: the first sixty pages of Book I were extensively corrected, clarified and augmented; Book II was wholly neglected except in two places where a few numbers were changed; and Book III again was fairly extensively corrected. The majority of his notations were made for the sake of understanding rather than strict accuracy and obviously reflected his estimate of Locke's ability to follow the *Principia*.

But apparently Locke had been underestimated. For in that year, probably through the incentive of Newton's gift, he took up the book for the third time and filled several pages of a notebook called 'Adversaria Physica' with detailed notes, each after the date '[16]91'. He did not, as Newton must have expected, sneak fearfully past the second book. His notes reveal him plunging headlong—or at least dipping unabashedly—into some of its finer points, such as the distances of the pulses of sound

[1] For details, see my 'Locke's Review of the *Principia*', *Notes and Records of the Royal Society of London*, xx, 2 (December, 1965), 152–61.
[2] James L. Axtell, 'Locke, Newton, and The Elements of Natural Philosophy', *Paedagogica Europaea*, I (1965), 235–7.   [3] MS. Locke, c.31, folios 101–104v.

Locke, Newton and the two cultures

propagated in an elastic medium (Prop. L, Prob. XIII) and the very obscure English equivalent (Prop. XL, Prob. X, Schol. Gen.) of a French measurement in Book III to prove that the moon gravitates toward the earth.[1] Unless he took notes that he did not understand (which is highly unlikely), Locke must have been familiar with more than the recommended minimal assignment for novices, and certainly more than most of his non-specialist contemporaries. The clarity and acuteness of his review of the *Principia* in the *Bibliothèque Universelle*, coupled with his determined threefold reading of the book over a period of five years, warrants a more critical handling of the traditional belief that 'the celebrated Locke... was incapable of understanding the Principia from his want of geometrical knowledge'.[2] It is more judicious as well as more accurate to say, as John Desaguliers said and Newton himself verified, that when Locke realized that he could not substantiate the mathematical proofs by himself, he asked Christiaan Huygens whether they were true; and being assured that they were, 'took them for granted...carefully examined the Reasonings and Corollaries drawn from them, [and] became Master of all the Physicks' and the first 'Newtonian Philosopher without the Help of Geometry'.[3] From what we have seen, the emphasis should be placed on the positive aspects of Locke's achievement, the mastering of 'all the Physicks' *in spite of* his mathematical handicap. There is no need, as his contemporaries often felt in apostrophizing the potency of Newton's 'heaven-born mind' and the 'radiance of his...divinity', to inflate the importance of his work with the lowing breaths of 'the herd' below, where presumably even the greatest living philosophers stood.[4]

The third and final result of their friendship arose out of Locke's publication of *Some Thoughts concerning Education* in 1693. In advising gentlemen on an adequate scientific education for their sons he suggested that after a boy had become familiar with the elements of terrestrial and celestial geography,

it may be time to give him some Notions of this our planetary World, and to that purpose it may not be amiss to make him a Draught of the Copernican System, and therein explain to him the Situation of the Planets, their respective Distances from the Sun, the Center of their Revolutions. This will prepare him to understand the Motion and Theory of the Planets, the most easy and natural Way.[5]

At the time of its publication and until the end of his life, Locke was living in the Essex household of Sir Francis and Lady Masham, whose son Francis Cudworth was being educated under his benevolent hand.

---

[1] MS. Locke, d.9, folios 108, 83.   [2] Brewster, *Newton*, I, 339.
[3] Desaguliers, *Experimental Philosophy*, I, Preface.
[4] Newton, *Principia*, ed. Cajori, I, xiii–xv (Ode to Newton by Edmond Halley).
[5] John Locke, *Some Thoughts concerning Education*, 5th ed. (London, 1705), §180.

James L. Axtell

Some time after 1698 Locke composed an elementary treatise entitled 'The Elements of Natural Philosophy' for young Frank, then twelve, along the lines he had mentioned in the *Education*. As its first editor said, 'it is an abstract or summary of whatever is most material in Natural Philosophy; which Mr. Locke did afterwards explain more at large, to that young Gentleman'.[1] In addition to the Copernican system, 'Draught' and all, its fifty pages touched upon a wide variety of subjects: air and atmosphere, vegetables, animals and minerals, springs, rivers and seas, and the five senses. The concluding chapter on 'The Understanding of Man' is a sparkling four-page epitome of his own reflexions contained at large in the *Essay concerning Human Understanding*.

But three things of more importance mark this little treatise. The first is that Locke, the able popularizer of his own epistemology, explained equally well, in a simple, clear, and untechnical manner, the principal elements of the Newtonian synthesis of physical and astronomical universe. Nor was it all child's play; it was said that 'persons of riper years, may improve by it: either by recalling ideas, that had slipt out of their memory; or by informing themselves of several things, which were unknown to them'.[2] Whatever its value to adults, it was the first effort to popularize the Newtonian philosophy for children. That it was felt necessary or even desirable to do so speaks volumes about the new awareness and perceived importance of Newton's discoveries and about Locke's central role in their dissemination.

We can gauge more accurately the role of Locke's treatise in spreading the Newtonian gospel by witnessing an amusing incident of literary piracy in which a precocious child named Tom Telescope (supposed by many to be an alias for an adult Oliver Goldsmith) demonstrated in 1761 the 'Elements of Natural Philosophy' as a *Philosophy of Tops and Balls* while standing on a table before an enraptured audience of children and parents, without, however, the least of his customary bows to Locke's priority. In addition to at least two separate reprintings of the 'Elements' itself, Tom's lilliputian book was published in England and America at least eight times before 1830, reaching a fourth edition as early as 1770. So when Newton cast a giant shadow on the age of Enlightenment, it was partly because he was standing on the shoulders of Locke.[3]

---

[1] *A Collection of Several Pieces of Mr John Locke*, [published by Mr Desmaizeaux under the direction of Anthony Collins] (London, 1720), Preface. For details, see my 'Locke, Newton, and The Elements of Natural Philosophy', *Paedagogica Europaea*, 1, 235-7.　　　[2] *Ibid.*
[3] In addition, Locke's avid praise of Newton's method and *Principia* in the *Education* reached a vast audience of gentle (and other) readers in the eighteenth century when it was reprinting at least 25 times in English, 18 times in French, twice in Dutch, 7 times in German, 6 in Italian, and once in Swedish. See *The Educational Writings of John Locke*, ed. James L. Axtell (Cambridge, 1968), 4 pp. 98-104.

Locke, Newton and the two cultures

Secondly, it appears probable from the available evidence that Newton himself, a frequent visitor to the Masham estate at Oates, contributed an essay on the latest advances (mostly his own) in physics and astronomy which helped Locke to write the first four chapters of his treatise. From two similar unidentified manuscripts in Newton's remains in the Cambridge University Library, it appears that, when asked by Locke for assistance, he made a few drafts as he usually did before sending the final copy to Oates. A textual comparison of these drafts and the 'Elements', and Locke's position as tutor with a particular need and as a particularly well-qualified friend, strongly suggest Newton's direct involvement in popularizing his own discoveries, a task he did not always relish, but one which he was most capable of performing when a specific request was made of him.[1]

Finally, it is important to notice that when Locke came to write a proper work on natural philosophy, the only one he ever attempted though contemporaries thought him capable of 'a complete work', he followed the axiomatic-mathematical method of Newton's *Principia* in his organization.[2] Coupled with what we have seen of his untiring attention to Newton's work and his efforts to popularize it, this must revise the view that he 'did not understand the logic, procedure, and goal of the new mathematical physics'.[3]

As close as they came together in the philosopher's advancing years on the importance of the new mathematical approach to nature, Locke and Newton remained apart on the proper educational approach to science in general, and perhaps exemplified the polar divergence between the empirical physician—with whose procedure, we might add, the literary intellectual is more likely to sympathize—and the mathematical physicist. About 1690 Newton drafted a set of proposed reforms of the college teaching and direction of studies of Cambridge undergraduates. There were to be four lecturers and a tutor in each college, including a Philosophy and a Mathematics Lecturer.[4]

The Philosophy Lecturer [is] to read first of things introductory to natural philosophy, [such as] time, space, body, place, motion & its laws, force [etc.] ...& then to read natural Philosophy beginning with ye general systeme of

[1] Cambridge University Library, Add. MS. 4005, folios 21–2, 23–5. The *Guardian* thought Newton 'easier to understand than [Henry] Pemberton', the highly subscribed author of *A View of...Newton's Philosophy* (1728). King's College, MS. Keynes 130.5, no. 2.
[2] Both Pierre Desmaizeaux and Christiaan Huygens thought him capable. See 'Locke, Newton, and The Elements of Natural Philosophy', *Paedagogica Europaea*, I, 237–8.
[3] David Givner, 'Scientific Preconceptions in Locke's Philosophy of Language', *Journal of the History of Ideas*, XXIII (1962), 340–54.
[4] *Unpublished Scientific Papers of Isaac Newton*, ed. A. R. and M. B. Hall (Cambridge, 1962), pp. 369–73.

the world & thence proceeding to ye particular constitution of this earth & the things therein, [such as] Meteors, elements, minerals, vegetables, animals & ending with Anatomy if he have skill therein.

Furthermore, 'All students who will be admitted to Lectures in naturall Philosophy [are] to learn first Geometry & Mechanicks...For wthout a judgment in these things a man can have none in Philosophy.' For college students, then, Newton would start with a grand synthesis and descend to particulars, leaning most of the way on a solid background of mathematics and physics.

If we look at 'The Elements of Natural Philosophy', where we move from an initial chapter on 'Matter and Motion' through 'the Universe', 'our Solar System', and 'the Earth, consider'd as a Planet' to Newton's 'particular constitution of this earth & the things therein', Locke, though his audience was only twelve years old, seems to agree completely with Newton. Perhaps by that time he did, which would mark another significant shift in his thinking due to their friendship and collaboration. But we should not ignore a lifetime of urging young men to pursue 'a course of Natural philosophie, Chymistry, or, wch I should rather choose to begin with, Anatomie, because that consists only in seeing the figure, texture & situation of the parts & some little matter about their use'. For he had always thought, even as late as 1697 when he wrote this, that 'in all the sciences the easiest should always be begun with wch are those yt lye nearest the senses, & from thence by degrees to proceed to those that are more abstract & lie wholy in thought'.[1] Such an educational philosophy, adumbrated throughout the *Essay*, *The Conduct of the Understanding*, and the *Education*, clashed with the mathematician's newly important axiomatic, conceptual approach, and perhaps we are the legatees of that clash to an extent greater than we realize. For in the eighteenth-century universities, where new philosophies were jockeying the old out of the schools, it was the Newtonian style that carried the day and permanently impressed upon the western world the undeniable importance and correctness of the new world-view and the mathematical procedure by which it was achieved. It was also then that mathematical science began to enter the everyday world of living for the first time and became increasingly relevant to the needs and problems of all classes of men.

In the first half of the seventeenth century the Cambridge that became synonymous with higher mathematics in the nineteenth was not mathematical at all. Mathematics were 'scarce looked upon as *Academical* studies, but rather *Mechanical*' and were 'more cultivated in *London* than

[1] MS. Locke, c.24, fo. 197^v. '*Education* $\left(\dfrac{97}{A}\right)$ To the Countesse of Peterborow' for her son Lord Mordaunt. See also the *Education*, 5th ed. (1705), p. 291.

in the universities'.[1] Oxford was no better. But by 1813 it could be said that although Cambridge supported three classes of subjects—natural philosophy, moral philosophy, and the classics—'it is to the first that the predominant attention is devoted; and, as subsidiary to it, mathematics, in all their branches, are cultivated with uncommon ardour'. In the lectures, the tutorials, and the rigorous Tripos examinations, there was no doubt that 'the genius of the Cambridge system leans decidedly, and some may say exclusively, to the mathematics', the goal of which was admission to the 'vestibule of the Principia of Newton'.[2] Though she offered firmer resistance to both Locke and Newton, even Oxford—or at least her scholars—gradually responded to the intellectual currents of the time. In 1702 Newton's Scottish protégé David Gregory, then Savilian professor of astronomy at Oxford, noticed that only one-fifth as many sons of common folk and clergymen had enrolled at this university as in 1693, from which he concluded that 'its plain that the Church was overstocked, and that the people encline more to Mechanick Arts'[3]. By 1779 it was indeed true, as Doiley exclaimed on the stage in Hannah Crowley's *Who's the Dupe?*, that 'everybody has heard of Sir Isaac'.[4]

In the seventeenth century we can be sure that the intellectual class of England and of most of western Europe was compact, relatively homogeneous, and notoriously able to 'communicate with each other on the plane of their major intellectual concern[s]'. It was the age of the polymath, the virtuoso, the non-specialist, the conversationalist—Locke's age. But after Newton, *le déluge*. When we approach the nineteenth century we have lost our certainty. The universities and schools gave up the pretence of trying to educate all students alike, to give them a common basis of culture, and in Germany the graduate school was born to frighten conservatives with its specialization, weighty dissertations on minute subjects, and applied knowledge. And if Lord Snow is correct, it was then that literary intellectuals and hidebound academics shrank from the new 'culture' that was likewise born of the Industrial and Scientific revolutions.

Their predicament—and ours—was not essentially different from that of Locke and his contemporaries. They too felt an uneasiness, an intellectual tension because of the pressing demands of higher mathematics for a full understanding of the *foundations* of the world-view that they felt com-

---

[1] Christopher Wordsworth, *Scholae Academicae: Some Account of the Studies at the English Universities in the Eighteenth Century* (Cambridge, 1910), p. 65, quoting John Wallis, *c.* 1635.
[2] Rev. M. Russel, *View of the System of Education at present pursued in the Schools and Universities of Scotland* (Edinburgh, 1813), appendix I, pp. i-iii, ix, 'On The Cambridge University, from a correspondent there'.
[3] *David Gregory*, ed. Hiscock, p. 20.   [4] Wordsworth, *Scholae Academicae*, p. 71.

pelled by the force of reason to share. The Newtonian world-view called for a re-orientation of minds long used to other modes of thought and systems of reference, a demand that the traditional educational system was slow in satisfying. Some laymen themselves, paced by Locke's initial efforts, pitched in and filled an impressive shelf of popularizations, encyclopedias, and dictionaries designed to carry the Newtonian philosophy to the non-specialist, for it was believed that 'tho' its Truth is supported by Mathematicks, yet its Physical Discoveries may be communicated without'.[1] The demand was great. Courses of demonstrations and lectures were extremely popular among both men and women throughout England. Sermons once filled with the stuff of scholastic divinity or tedious homilies acceded to the popular penchant for physico- and astro-theology. Henry Pemberton, with Newton's advice and approval, tried to make men masters of his discoveries without mathematics 'with great emolument to himself' by soliciting '3000 subscriptions [to his book] at a Guinea wch shewed the earnest desire of all ranks' to come to terms with them.[2]

Perhaps all this was the pretension to understanding of incompetents, a psychological mechanism that said, 'Yes, we really *do* understand our new world-view, don't we' even if they didn't. Perhaps they were only whistling in the darkness of their ignorance. But it seems that even if this was so the crucial thing is that they cared enough to pretend, to try to come to grips with their world as it had been refashioned by the slightly eccentric Cambridge genius. Once science had entered their homes, had begun to matter, they welcomed it and did their best to understand and accommodate it. The present lull in the controversy over 'The Two Cultures' suggests that maybe we have given up the pretence as well as the concern, and that we are resigned to sink in a sea of specialities when a man like Locke would have chosen to swim.

[1] Desaguliers, *Experimental Philosophy*, 1, Preface.
[2] King's College, MS. Keynes 130.5, no. 2.

The science of nature

by JOHN W. YOLTON

The nature of things 'as they are in themselves, their relations, and their manner of operations' (*Essay concerning Human Understanding*, IV, XXI, §1) is one of three areas that, according to Locke, come within man's understanding. The constitution, properties, natures, and operations of body and spirit are the subject matter of natural philosophy. Speculative truth is the goal of natural philosophy, truth which man must fetch from divers sources: 'God himself, angels, spirits, bodies' (*Essay*, IV, XXI, §2). Contemplation is suggested as the means for attaining this sort of truth. Locke was not concerned in the *Essay* to extend speculative truth. Rather he was interested in 'things as they are in themselves knowable'; this third and last formulation of the first division of the sciences (IV, XXI, §5) reveals Locke's main objective, not to extend our knowledge of things but to show us some of the ways of doing so, even to explain how Boyle, Newton, and Huygens were extending human knowledge. The scope of things knowable is far less than that of things speculated about. Locke's account of the former goes on in the context of the latter, he has a metaphysical theory of nature which falls outside his own account of knowledge but which in many respects provides the causal and explanatory basis for human cognition and what knowledge of nature is possible.

Working in close proximity with science and scientists, Locke knew that a science of nature was possible. His concern was with characterizing that science, with showing what scientific knowledge was entitled to claim, how it is achieved. His analysis of these matters began with the account of the nature of things shared by theologians and corpuscularians, the great chain of being and insensible particles. The appeal of observation and experimentation was strong, the Baconian prescription was popular, especially when innatism was the only alternative. The appeal for Locke of the corpuscular hypothesis was due not only to the eminence of and his respect for Boyle, it supplied him with a more significant content for the concept of body than philosophical tradition offered. There is a conceptual necessity about our concept of body which is more meaningfully filled by 'insensible particles' than by 'substratum'.

John W. Yolton

What we learn through careful attention to nature is the order of co-existing qualities, but since we cannot imagine how those qualities 'can subsist by themselves, we accustom ourselves to suppose some *substratum* wherein they do subsist' (II, XXIII, §1). When we say of a particular body that it is a thing which is extended, figured, capable of motion, or of a spirit that it is a thing capable of thought, the word 'thing' captures what we feel is necessary over and above the observed properties. Such an idea of a subject for the qualities is neither clear nor informative but we cannot conceive how qualities can subsist alone so we find ourselves caught with the unclear notion (§4). Locke retained the formula—'a collection of qualities plus something I know not what'—but used the corpuscular hypothesis to suggest what the unknown and unobserved portion of body is. Theory and hypothesis fill in what thought requires but experience fails to supply.

Most of *Essay*, II, XXIII is concerned to get the reader to realize that the only clear idea of a thing (whether it be material or immaterial) he has is made up of the observable (or reflective) and behavioural properties he finds coexisting in his experience. Locke takes ordinary objects—man, horse, sun, water, iron, bread—and challenges the reader to produce any content for these objects which is not an observable property or a power inferred (e.g. the power of a magnet to attract iron) from observed behaviour. The best answer we can give to the question, what is the subject of these observed qualities and inferred powers, is, 'the solid extended parts', meaning the observable parts (§2). We cannot, without theory, find a subject for the sensible solid, extended parts. Locke does not shy away from theory. He has clearly formulated the corpuscularian hypothesis in II, VIII, he uses it throughout II, XXIII (§§8–14, 23, 26). The discussion of substance in III, VI, makes extensive use of particle talk and asserts unequivocally that (*a*) 'every substance that exists has its peculiar constitution whereon depend those sensible qualities and powers we observe' (§13) and (*b*) 'it is evident the internal constitution, whereon their properties depend, is unknown to us' (§9). The main bent of III, VI is to argue that our classification of objects is not done in terms of the internal constitution but in terms of the observed properties. Whether we are talking of thinghood in general or of particular objects, the internal, causally basic cohering particles are unknown. The corpuscularian hypothesis enables us to articulate a plausible account of that inner constitution; that account nevertheless is hypothesis, not knowledge.

There is a difference between observing and knowing the internal constitution of an object. The latter is knowing in the sense of understanding the workings of that inner configuration of particles. Locke did not think the particles were unobservable in principle. He considered that micro-scopes had made some progress in extending the range of our observation of bodies. He believed that such progress was limited in practice, would be disorienting for man, and would never lead us to an understanding of the *essentia* of any body. Locke raises the possibility of our senses being acute enough 'to discern the minute particles of bodies' and asserts these 'microscopes plainly discover to us' (II, XXIII, §11).[1] Under these condi-tions, the colour of gold disappears, being replaced by 'an admirable texture of parts, of a certain size and figure'. Similarly, the opaqueness and whiteness of sand becomes pellucid, hair loses its colour, blood shows 'only a few globules of red, swimming in a pellucid liquor' (§11). With more powerful lenses, the red globules of blood would very likely appear different still. Magnification of '1000 or 100,000 times more acute than it is now by the best microscope' would enable us to see things 'several millions of times less than the smallest object' of our sight (§12). Under these conditions we would 'come nearer the discovery of the texture and motion of the minute parts of corporeal things, and in many of them probably get *ideas* of their internal constitutions' (§12). If we were to think of ourselves or of angels as having microscopical eyes, we would find ourselves in 'a quite different world from other people', the 'visible *ideas* of everything would be different', the 'appearance and out-ward scheme of things would have quite another face to us' (§12).

Microscopical eyes (and other sense organs similarly intensified) would handicap if not paralyse us for action. Discovery by microscopes is useful only when we can relate those discoveries to our ordinary world, in particular when those discoveries would enable us to understand why bodies have and present the qualities they do. Extension is one of the original qualities of body, a quality caused by the cohesion of particles. Microscopical investigation of the minute particles of body will be helpful only if it reveals 'how the solid parts of body are united and cohere together to make extension' (II, XXIII, §23). Locke was careful to point out that the cause of the cohesion of the parts of body must be internal to those parts: '*the pressure of any ambient fluvia,* how great soever', for example, '*can be no* intelligible *cause of the cohesion of the solid parts of matter*' (§24). His reasoning for rejecting external pressure as sufficient is that this would

[1] The microscopist Henry Power had made this claim in 1664; it was probably a generally held view. See his *Experimental Philosophy...Containing New Experiments, Microscopal, Mer-curial, Magnetical*: 'Herein we can see what the illustrious wits of the Atomical and Corpus-cularian Philosophers durst but imagine, even the very Atoms and their reported Indivisibles and least realities of Matter' (quoted by Marie Boas in 'The Establishment of the Mechanical Philosophy', *Osiris*, x (1952), 434 n.). Locke had in his library a copy of Power's book as well as other works on the microscope, e.g. Robert Hooke's *Micrographia* and the books of Swammerdam.

John W. Yolton

not prevent the separation by a motion in a line parallel to the pressure. Thus, 'if there were no other cause of cohesion, all parts of bodies must be easily separable by such a lateral sliding motion'. To understand the extension of body requires us to understand how the particles are held together. The microscope has not made such a discovery and, Locke suggests, such a discovery is far off, requiring as it does an explanation of the consolidation of 'the least particle of matter that exists' (§ 26).

Locke was close to saying the *understanding* of matter is of a different order from the *observation* of body. He speaks throughout these passages of 'making it intelligible' and of cohesion being incomprehensible.[1] Matter and motion was as far as the corpuscular theory could go. An explanation of the solidity of matter was lacking. Locke may seem to be too cautious in concluding that 'the simple *ideas* we receive from sensation and reflection are the boundaries of our thought' (§ 29), since he made use of theories which went beyond these boundaries, but in point of fact the corpuscular theory did not go beyond the possible boundaries of sense and reflexion. The entities postulated by that theory differ only in size, not in kind, from sensible objects. The qualities they were said to have were the same as macro-objects have. The insensible particles are beyond the reach of our ordinary perception, the microscope had not revealed the particles of every object. Even did we have microscopical eyes, and hence actually saw (or otherwise sensed) the internal constitution of bodies, our sensation and reflexion would still be the boundaries of our thought about body since we would not have penetrated to the cause of consolidation and cohesion of the particles we were then seeing (see IV, VI, § 9). The conclusion is tempting, that this feature of body is not observable in principle. Two conclusions *are* clear: (*a*) we in fact do not observe the inner workings of the bodies we meet with, and (*b*) we do not, even with Boyle's help, understand those workings. It is this double conclusion that Locke has in mind when he says that we do not know the real essence of any body (III, VI), that we have no clear or distinct idea

[1] Although Locke is very close to Boyle on most points covering the nature of matter, he does not follow Boyle on cohesion. Boyle explained cohesion in terms of the mechanical hypothesis: 'as to what is very confidently as well as plausibly pretended, That a substantial form is requisite to keep the parts of a body united, without which it would not be one body; I answer, That the contrivance of conveniently figured parts, and in some cases their juxta position, may, without the assistance of substantial form, be sufficient for this matter' (*The Works of Robert Boyle*, ed. Birch, London, 1772, p. 43). Usually 'it is on the roughness and the irregularity of corpuscles, that their cohesion depends' (*Mechanical Origin of Volatility and Fixedness, Works*, V, 306, quoted by Marie Boas, *Osiris*, p. 474). In *Absolute Rest (Works*, I, 444, quoted by Boas, p. 475) Boyle suggests that 'where the inward motion of the insensible particles is almost infinitely slow', the cohesion of bodies can be explained by that slow motion.

186

of the 'supposed something' to which the observed qualities of body belong (II, XXIII, §37).[1]

That Locke saw that an understanding of the real essence of any object would be different from the observation of the minute particles making up the internal essence of that object, is most strongly suggested by his careful, extensive, and repeated remarks about what we would know had we that understanding. Necessary connexion is the epistemic analogue of the cohesion of particles. If I had an idea of the real essence of any object, the observed properties would be deducible from that idea, thereby disclosing the *necessary* connexion between observed properties and real essence (II, XXXI, §6). The comparison is with the dependence of all the properties of a triangle and their deducibility from 'the complex *idea* of three lines including space'. If our ideas of geometrical figures were acquired by examining particular figures, learning only some of the properties of that kind of figure, we would be in the same position in geometry as we are in physical knowledge, i.e. we would not see any necessary relations. Starting with 'the whole essence' of an ellipse, for example, we can from that discover its properties 'and demonstratively see how they flow and are inseparable from it' (§11). Just as the essence of geometrical figures 'lies in a very little compass', that is, a few ideas (e.g. that of a triangle consists of three lines enclosing space), so Locke conjectures that the real essence of substances lies 'in a little compass, though the properties flowing from that internal constitution are endless' (II, XXXII, §24). A knowledge of the *essentia* of man would show us how 'his faculties of moving, sensation, and reasoning, and other powers flow' from the *essentia* (III, VI, §3). This is the sort of knowledge God has of all objects; it is possible that angels also have a deductive knowledge of things.

The coexisting qualities we discover and in terms of which we classify objects into kinds carry 'no visible necessary connexion or inconsistency' with each other (IV, III, §10). We cannot know which qualities 'have a necessary union or inconsistency one with another; for, not knowing the root they spring from, not knowing what size, figure, and texture of parts

[1] Mandelbaum (in *Philosophy, Science and Sense Perception: Historical and Critical Studies,* Baltimore, 1964) thinks it 'fundamentally mistaken' to ascribe, as I have done in earlier writings, substratum talk to physical objects. The notion of a substratum is, he suggests, 'an indeterminate notion connected with our sensible *ideas* of such qualities' (p. 41 n.). Locke did not find substratum talk informative, especially as it occurred in the tradition of substance theories, but he sought to find a meaningful substitute for it in the talk of particles cohering together. In this scientific translation, it is the cohesion of the particles which is unknown and, probably, unknowable for man. There is nothing fundamentally mistaken in saying the real essence is 'hidden away in the unknowable but necessary substratum', though it is more precise to talk of the unknowability of real essences because of our inability to understand how particles cohere. (See my article, to which Mandelbaum refers, 'Locke's Unpublished Marginal Replies to John Sargent', *Journal of the History of Ideas,* XII, 1951, 555.)

they are, on which depend and from which result those qualities which make our complex *idea* of gold, it is impossible we should know what other qualities result from or are incompatible with the same constitution of the insensible parts of *gold*, and so consequently must always *coexist* with that complex *idea* we have of it, or else are *inconsistent* with it' (§11). It is certain and indubitable rules of connexion between secondary and primary qualities, and between primary qualities and sensations, that a knowledge of the internal constitution would yield (§13). The term 'connexion' means 'necessary connexion', as Locke immediately explains in section 14. There are a few qualities which do have a necessary connexion with other perceived qualities, as 'figure necessarily supposes extension, receiving or communicating motion by impulse supposes solidity' (§14), but those connexions are very few. We do not discover these necessary connexions by observation but rather through intuition or demonstration. The two examples Locke cites here might better be called 'conceptual necessities'. He cites several more such necessities in §15: that each particular extension, figure, number of parts, and motion 'excludes all others of each kind', that 'no one subject can have two smells or two colours at the same time'. In IV, VII, §5, 'that two bodies cannot be in the same place' is cited as self-evident. (I presume Locke would add to these last examples appropriate qualifications—'in the same respects', etc.) A better formulation of this last conceptual necessity is: 'it is as impossible that the very same particle of any body should at the same time differently modify or reflect the rays of light, as that it should have two different figures and textures at the same time' (§15).[1]

Aside from these few rather obvious and uninteresting necessities, our knowledge of bodies (and of spirits) does not reach any further than experience; sense and reflexion are our boundaries. Whatever hypothesis about the nature of body we accept (Locke says the corpuscularian hypothesis is 'thought to go farthest in an intelligible explication of the qualities of bodies', §16), 'our knowledge concerning corporeal substances will be very little advanced by any of them, till we are made to see what qualities and powers of bodies have a *necessary connexion or repugnancy* one with another; which in the present state of philosophy I think we know but to a very small degree' (§16). The rational, non-experimental character of this sort of knowledge is stressed even more later in the same chapter, where Locke remarks that if we knew the mechanical affections of the particles of any object we would 'know without trial several of their operations one upon another' (§25). We would be able, for example, 'to

[1] Some *ideas* 'require others as necessary to their existence or conception'. For example, 'motion can neither be nor be conceived without space', solidity is inseparable from the idea of body (II, XIII, §11).

tell beforehand that *rhubarb* will purge, *hemlock* kill, and *opium* make a man sleep'. With such knowledge, we could understand why silver dissolves in *aqua fortis* and gold in *aqua regia*, and not the other way round. As it is, our reason carries us 'very little beyond particular matter of fact' (§25). Certainty and demonstration do not extend to our knowledge of substance, universal truths of body cannot be had, *experimental* philosophy replaces *scientifical*, this latter term being Locke's word for rational, deductive, certain knowledge. 'The things that, as far as our observation reaches, we constantly find to proceed regularly, we may conclude do act by a law set them, but yet by a law that we know not' (§29).

So important was it for Locke to deny the possibility of a science of nature in the *rational* sense of 'science'—in order to show the need for a careful *experimental* science of nature—that he takes frequent opportunity of stressing the point. While discussing universal propositions, he takes several sections again to point out that 'we can never, from consideration of the *ideas* themselves, with certainty affirm or deny, of a body whose complex *idea* is made up of yellow, very weighty, ductile, fusible, and fixed, that it is soluble in *aqua regia*; and so on for the rest of its qualities' (IV, VI, §9). He repeats his denial of any discoverable connexions or repugnancy (the terms he always uses in referring to certain knowledge) in sections 6, 7 and 10 (see also IV, IX, §1; IV, XII, §9). He points out that a proposition like 'all gold is malleable' *is* certain if malleableness is part of our definition of gold, but this certainty is no different from that in the proposition, 'a centaur is four-footed': what we have said is 'that that sound stands for an idea in which malleableness is contained' (§9). Such linguistic truths are common but they should not be mistaken for the *real* certainty Locke is after, of knowing the necessary connexions of qualities, not just of ideas. It is more important to note that this real certainty depends upon our discovering 'that which ties' the insensible particles together, supporting the suggestion above that it is the *understanding* of cohesion and consolidation, not just the *observation* of the particles, which we need and lack.

A rational science of bodies (or of spirits) would give us a knowledge of all the properties of bodies (and likewise of spirits) quite independent of and prior to observation. We would acquire such knowledge by an analysis of our ideas, not by an analysis of things. Such a knowledge would yield universal principles true of body, necessarily true. The connexions between qualities and the connexions between primary qualities of particles and our ideas of both primary and secondary qualities would also be necessary. An analysis of our ideas (starting with the idea of the real essence of any particular object) would reveal to us, by intuition and

189

demonstration, the necessary connexions which must hold among qualities. To reach such a state of knowledge and understanding would be to have 'a perfect *science* of natural bodies (not to mention spiritual beings)' (IV, III, §29). Philosophers before and after Locke have claimed to have produced such a deductive metaphysics of nature. In saying we are incapable of such a knowledge of nature, Locke does not deny that there are necessary connexions in nature. God's deductive knowledge of bodies and their properties presupposes a necessary connexion in bodies. Bodies are such that had we an understanding of their internal constitution, we would also be able to know the qualities and operations of bodies without observation and with certainty. Our knowledge falls short of the nature of things, probability replaces certainty. There are features of body which we do not know.

Locke does not regret this lack in man's knowledge because he does not think we need it for action, action being one of the main concerns for Locke, the second main division of the sciences. We can have a science of action but not of body. Moreover, realizing that such a rational knowledge of nature is beyond man's faculties, we are able to see the importance of studying nature carefully, rather than trying to find some principles from which to derive truths about nature. Experiment and observation become all-important. A probable science of nature is not only possible; Newton and Boyle (and others) were advancing that science. While Locke accepted the corpuscularian hypothesis, as well as the view that there is a necessary connexion between real essences and the observed properties of bodies and their operations and powers, it is observation not theory which he praises as the way of acquiring knowledge of body. Locke thought that a man 'accustomed to rational and regular experiments, shall be able to see further into the nature of bodies and guess righter at their yet unknown properties than one that is a stranger to them' (IV, XII, §10). He also allowed that hypotheses, 'if they are well made, are at least great helps to the memory and often direct us to new discoveries' (*ibid.* §13). Any hypothesis we accept must not be taken up '*too hastily* (which the mind, that would always penetrate into the causes of things and have principles to rest on, is very apt to do) till we have very well examined particulars and made several experiments in that thing which we would explain by our hypothesis and see whether it will agree to them all, whether our principles will carry us quite through and not be as inconsistent with one *phenomenon* of nature, as they seem to accommodate and explain another' (§13). Quite clearly, Locke thought the corpuscularian hypothesis a useful one in explaining the observed properties and operations of body, even though it did not give any insight at all into the nature of cohesion or consolidation. But the aspect of science which interested Locke was not the formation of hypotheses, however carefully they were constructed. There is in the *Essay* no analysis of knowledge by hypotheses, no analysis of the formation of hypotheses; there is extensive material on classification in terms of observable properties. Repeatedly, Locke tells us how to enlarge our knowledge but he never cites the formation or use of hypotheses (see, e.g., IV, XII, §14). The enlargement of our knowledge of bodies is done by noting coexisting qualities.[1]

Neither maxims, principles, hypotheses, nor language analysis can replace the analysis of things as we observe and experience them. Any of these could and has led us astray in our quest for knowledge of things. Certain qualities are observed to be always 'joined and existing together'. The making of ideas of things is not simply a listing and noting of all the qualities that go together, since not all qualities that coexist in things are used in the class-ideas we form of things (III, VI, §32). But those ideas which we do put into our class-concepts or particular ideas of things must

[1] Locke's distrust of hypotheses or general theories appears also in a letter to Molyneux. Locke speaks of general theories as 'a sort of waking dreams'. He stresses again that any useful hypotheses must be built upon 'the established history of diseases' (he was there discussing Sydenham). See letter of 20 January 1692/3, *Works* (1823), IX, 463–4. Laurens Laudan has recently claimed that hypotheses played a much greater role in Locke's philosophy of science than I have allowed here ('The Nature and Sources of Locke's Views on Hypotheses', *Journal of the History of Ideas* (April–June 1967), pp. 211–23). Laudan's article is useful (as is Mandelbaum's book) in directing our attention to Locke's account of the science of nature. (See also R. Harré's *Matter and Method*, London, 1964.) But Laudan seems to me to overstate his case. He says (p. 213) that Locke 'devoted an entire section of the fourth book of his *Essay* (IV, XII, §13) to the "true use of hypotheses"'. That section is one small paragraph. A later paragraph (IV, XVI, §12) speaks of the use of analogy from what is known for understanding what cannot be observed. *One* of the examples refers to the move from observables to insensible particles. But the main bulk of this paragraph is taken up with a statement of the great chain of being, applying analogy to our conceptions of the gradual connexions there must be throughout the chain. Certainly more attention needs to be given to Locke's attitude towards hypotheses in science. It does not seem to me that the philosophy of science in the *Essay* is much concerned with them: it stresses observation and classification. I would not wish to be classed with those commentators on Locke who, according to Laudan, 'have inferred that Locke was an opponent of the Corpuscular philosophy', since Locke explicitly and repeatedly uses and affirms his faith in that philosophy. Laudan does not appear to name anyone who reads Locke in this way, though he appears to run this reading of Locke together with those who say Locke was opposed 'to the use of virtually all hypotheses in science' (p. 211). Laudan fails to separate the question of whether Locke accepts the corpuscular hypothesis (which he surely does) from the question of whether he finds, in his account of the science of nature, a place for hypotheses in general. I do not think Locke finds a place for knowledge by hypothesis in his account of scientific knowledge. Laudan mentions Aaron, Gibson and myself among the anti-hypothesis interpreters of Locke, but none of the three overlooks Locke's acceptance of the corpuscular hypothesis (Aaron stresses Locke's relations with Boyle in this connexion). None of the three authors cited by Laudan does deal with Locke's remarks about scientific method. In my own case (*John Locke and the Way of Ideas*, Oxford, 1956), I was tracing the reception of Locke's epistemology and metaphysics by his contemporaries. It is interesting that his contemporaries did not show an interest in his remarks about scientific method, though his philosophy of nature attracted much attention.

accurately follow the qualities of things. Some observers are better than others. It is only by a patient observation of the nature and properties of things themselves that we can improve our knowledge and remedy the imperfections and abuses of language. When we argue about 'natural bodies and substantial things' it is insufficient to 'have learned, from the propriety of the language, the common...*idea* to which each word is applied' (III, XI, §24). The grammar rules of the language are an improper and untrustworthy guide to the nature of things (cf. III, IX, §8). Instead, we must acquaint ourselves 'with the history of that sort of things' (III, XI, §24).

Locke even proposed by-passing language by constructing a natural-history dictionary consisting of little pictures of the things named. Such a dictionary would be drawn up by 'men, versed in physical inquiries and acquainted with the several sorts of natural bodies' (*ibid.* §25). Locke cites the naturalists who have used this sort of reproduction of the objects named in their vocabulary: 'he that has occasion to consult them will have reason to confess that he has a clear[er] *idea* of *apium* or *ibex*, from a little print of that herb or beast, than he could have from a long definition of the names of either of them. And so, no doubt, he would have of *strigil* and *sistrum* if, instead of a *currycomb* and *cymbal*, which are the English names dictionaries render them by, he could see stamped in the margin small pictures of these instruments as they were in use amongst the ancients' (III, XI, §25). Locke thought that such a *Petit Larousse Illustré* would 'require too much time, cost, and pains to be hoped for in this age, yet methinks it is not unreasonable to propose that words standing for things which are known and distinguished by their outward shapes should be expressed by little draughts and prints made of them. A vocabulary made after this fashion would perhaps, with more ease and in less time, teach the true signification of many terms, especially in languages of remote countries or ages, and settle truer *ideas* in men's minds of several things, whereof we read the names in ancient authors, than all the large and laborious comments of learned critics' (III, XI, §25). It is the outward shapes of observed objects which would be captured in the natural-history dictionary.

In the absence of such a natural-history dictionary, Locke enjoins each of us to check his ideas of things against themselves. '*Experience here must teach me* what reason cannot' (IV, XII, §9). Arguments from the nature of things themselves give us the probability which experience provides (IV, XVI, §6). Those arguments involve the general consent of all men in all ages concurring 'with a man's constant and never-failing experience, in like cases' (*ibid.*). 'For what our own and other men's constant observation has found always to be after the same manner, that we with reason conclude to be the effects of steady and regular causes' (*ibid.*). Propositions like 'fire warms a man', 'fire makes lead fluid and changes the colour or consistency in wood or charcoal', 'iron sinks in water but swims in quicksilver', are propositions about particular facts which agree to our constant experience and hence may be taken as near-certainties (*ibid.*). Experience and history give us the only science of bodies we can have. 'In the knowledge of bodies, we must be content to glean what we can from particular experiments, since we cannot from a discovery of their real essences grasp at a time whole sheaves, and in bundles comprehend the nature and properties of whole species together. Where our inquiry is concerning coexistence or repugnancy to coexist, which by contemplation of our *ideas* we cannot discover, there experience, observation, and natural history must give us by our senses and by detail an insight into corporeal substances' (IV, XII, § 12). In his admiration for Boyle, Newton, and Sydenham, Locke was praising these men for this method of carefully observing and recording the observed coexistence of qualities.[1] In his own scientific interests Locke practised this method also.[2] Theory and hypothesis must find their place in the context of experience and history. The scientists of the day had been making new discoveries and advances by using the method praised by Locke. Locke's role in these methodological changes was equally important though different in kind from the scientists': he exposed the older techniques and claims (for innate principles, maxims as the foundation for knowledge, substantial forms and finite kinds) as unfounded and unfruitful. Moreover, Locke placed the new method of experience and history in the context of philosophical debate. He gave a philosophical foundation for the new science.

[1] Sydenham's diagnostic methods attracted Locke (they were friends and collaborators from 1667) just because they moved away from the traditional attitudes of relying upon maxims and principles. Sydenham insisted upon 'getting as genuine and natural a description, or history of all diseases, as can be procured' (*Works*, ed. John Swan, 1842, p. iii). This historical method will enable the physician to reduce all diseases to 'certain and determinate kinds' (p. 14). The description of diseases must be done 'with the utmost accuracy; imitating in this the great exactness of painters, who, in their pictures copy the smallest spots or moles in the originals' (p. v). Hypotheses are accepted only when they arise out of the careful observation of diseases, their symptoms and circumstances (pp. v, 474). It is 'experience derived from the solid testimony of the senses' that we should seek; all the knowledge of nature we can acquire 'is to be had only from experience', human knowledge being 're-strained to the narrow limits of knowledge, derivable from the senses' (pp. 485–6). Sydenham, in other words, employed what Locke called the argument from the nature of things themselves. Locke praised Sydenham's method to Molyneux in several letters, see *Works*, IX, 459, 461, 464–5.

[2] Locke's own involvement in the science of his day and his close association with the leading scientists is well known, though the details are just now being revealed. See Dewhurst, *John Locke, Physician and Philosopher*; James Axtell, 'Locke, Newton, and The Elements of Natural Philosophy', *Paedagogica Europaea*, I, 235–45; and James Axtell, 'Locke's Review of the *Principia*', *Notes and Records of the Royal Society of London*, XX, 2 (December 1965).

Faith and knowledge in
Locke's philosophy[1]

by RICHARD ASHCRAFT

During a conversation with a young man who had just received his degree in Philosophy, Politics and Economics from Oxford, I mentioned my interest in Locke, particularly my concern with his religious beliefs. The student admitted his ignorance of that subject, explaining that it was primarily Locke's epistemology his studies had emphasized. He had read Locke in the context of a twentieth-century education. In what follows, I propose to discuss Locke's philosophy, and especially his epistemology, in what I believe to be the seventeenth-century context within which the *Essay concerning Human Understanding* was written.

What appears remote and irrelevant to a modern reader of the *Essay*, namely, questions of religious dogma, were of the greatest importance to Locke's contemporaries. Issues long since encrusted over by centuries of philosophical commentary were then matters of lively disputation among men convinced that the fate of their eternal souls rested upon a proper understanding of the world in which they lived. To some of them, such as Edward Stillingfleet, Bishop of Worcester, Locke's *Essay* represented a radical departure from the established paths men were expected to follow in order to gain salvation. The general consensus of opinion among those who have read the *Essay concerning Human Understanding* in the last two centuries would probably agree with the bishop as to the subversive character of Locke's exploration of the foundations of religious belief. This essay, however, will state the case for another view, one which suggests that Locke's primary commitment was to certain principles of the Christian faith, and that it is within that context the *Essay* should be read in order to gain an appreciation of Locke's viewpoint.

[1] I wish to express my gratitude to the University of California at Los Angeles for a grant enabling me to make use of the manuscript materials in the Bodleian Library, Oxford University. Also, I am deeply indebted to Mr Esmond S. De Beer, who kindly allowed me to benefit from his many years of scholarship and to read the Locke correspondence and journals in his possession.

Unless otherwise noted, references in this essay to the unpublished manuscripts, letters, and journals of Locke state the catalogue listing of the Bodleian Library, Oxford.

Faith and knowledge in Locke's philosophy

THE FRAMEWORK OF THE 'ESSAY'

What is striking about the *Essay concerning Human Understanding* is not the claims it advances on behalf of human reason, but rather, its assertion of the meagreness of human knowledge. 'Our knowledge being so narrow' and our ignorance 'being infinitely larger than our knowledge', the 'clearest and most enlarged understandings of thinking men find themselves puzzled and at a loss in every particle of matter'.[1] In fact, Locke insists, 'the intellectual and sensible world...we can reach with our eyes or our thoughts...is but a point, almost nothing in comparison of the rest'.[2] It is not merely that we do not possess that knowledge which, in time, men would attain to. We are not capable of acquiring the knowledge we lack. '[In] experimental philosophy in physical things...we are not capable of scientifical knowledge; nor shall ever be able to discover general instructive, unquestionable truths concerning them. Certainty and demonstration are things we must not, in these matters, pretend to.'[3] Man exists in a state of 'incurable ignorance' facing a universe of 'impenetrable obscurity'.[4] Since it is a 'lost labour' to attempt 'a perfect science of bodies', it is obviously not Locke's intention in the *Essay* to lay the groundwork for the establishment of such a science.[5]

Throughout the work, Locke's denials are much more frequent than his assertions of our knowledge. Thus, we 'have no knowledge of the internal constitution and true nature of things'. That is, we are ignorant of the 'real essences' of sensuous objects.[6] The 'certainty of universal propositions concerning substances is very narrow and scanty'. Indeed, 'these are so few, and of so little moment, that we may justly look on our certain general knowledge of substances as almost none at all'.[7] Since the motion of the minute particles of matter which come into contact with our senses is too subtle to be perceived by us, 'it is impossible for us to have any exact measures of the different degrees' of simple ideas.[8] And,

---

[1] *Essay concerning Human Understanding*, ed. Alexander Fraser (Oxford, 1894), IV, III, §22; III, VI, §§9, 11. 'We do not know the nature of the sun or stars...the consideration of light itself leaves us in the dark, and a thousand other speculations in nature...', *Journal*, 8 February 1677, MS. f. 2.

[2] *Essay*, IV, III, §§23, 24, 29; IV, IV, §14; IV, VI, §11; IV, XVII, §2; *Mr. Locke's Reply to the Bishop of Worcester's Answer to his Letter* (hereinafter referred to as 2BW), *Works of John Locke*, 12th ed., 9 vols. (London, 1824), III, 184; *Journal*, 26 March, 6–10 April 1677, MS. f. 2.

[3] *Ibid.* IV, III, §26. 　　　　　[4] *Ibid.* IV, III, §§25, 27.

[5] *Ibid.* IV, III, §29; IV, XII, §§10, 13. Even if such a science were possible, it 'would be of no solid advantage to us, nor help to make our lives the happier', *Journal*, 8 February 1677, MS. f. 2. But see Maurice Cranston, for example, who refers to the *Essay* as a 'vindication of empiricism', *John Locke, A Biography* (London, 1957), p. 66. Also see Sir Leslie Stephen, *History of English Thought in the Eighteenth Century* (London, 1881), I.

[6] *Essay*, II, XXIII, §32; II, XXXI, §§6, 13; III, III, §17; III, VI, §§6, 9, 19, 21, 27, 49; III, IX, §12; IV, IV, §12. 　　　[7] *Ibid.* IV, VI, §§13, 15. 　　　[8] *Ibid.* IV, II, §§11, 13; IV, III, §26.

Richard Ashcraft

Locke continues, 'if we are at a loss in respect of the powers and operations of bodies, I think it is easy to conclude we are much more in the dark in reference to spirits, whereof we naturally have no ideas'.[1] Similarly, questions relating to the nature of man's soul lie 'out of the reach of our knowledge'.[2] Ultimately, Locke refuses to allow inductive generalizations to be classified as knowledge.[3]

In the 'Epistle to the Reader', Locke rejects the title of 'master-builder', and instead characterizes himself as 'an under-labourer' engaged in 'clearing the ground a little, and removing some of the rubbish that lies in the way to knowledge'. That portrayal, it would seem, considerably understates the accomplishments of the *Essay*. For, in one magnificent sweeping motion, Locke manages to clear away as 'rubbish' what others expected him to defend as 'knowledge'; and the human condition, with respect to 'the great and visible world', is thereby reduced to one of mediocrity and infinite ignorance.

Yet it would be a misreading of Locke's intentions to regard the *Essay concerning Human Understanding* as a manifesto of scepticism.[4] What is important to Locke is not the *amount* of knowledge human beings are capable of amassing, but rather the *kind* of knowledge they may lay claim to. In this, as in many other respects, Locke stands with an older tradition, and apart from the modern preoccupation with the construction of a quantifiably oriented natural or social science. The admission of an almost total ignorance concerning the natural environment of man is of little consequence, provided we are capable of obtaining that kind of knowledge which will most advance our happiness. It is to assure men that such knowledge lies within their grasp that the *Essay* was written. Once we have identified that form of knowledge Locke seeks to defend, we shall have laid out before us the framework of the *Essay concerning Human Understanding*.

For years, commentators have taken judicial notice of the origins of the *Essay* but, invariably, the issue which set Locke to writing down his thoughts has not found its way into their final judgments of his work. Locke himself reveals only that he began writing in response to certain problems that arose out of a series of discussions with 'five or six friends'

---

[1] *Essay*, IV, III, §17.   [2] *Ibid.* IV, III, §6.

[3] *An Early Draft of Locke's Essay*, ed. R. I. Aaron and Jocelyn Gibb (Oxford, 1936), §§34 ff. 'We must not expect a certain knowledge of any universal proposition.' *De Intellectus*, manuscript in the Shaftesbury Papers, Public Record Office, London (PRO/30/24/47/7). Some specific examples offered by Locke illustrative of the general proposition are, 'it is impossible with any certainty to affirm that all men are rational', IV, VI, §4; or, it is only 'highly probable' that other men exist when I am not actually perceiving them, IV, XI, §9.

[4] Sir Leslie Stephen extols the 'cold blast of scepticism' in the *Essay* (*English Thought in the Eighteenth Century*, vol. I, pp. 2, 34 ff.).

during the winter of 1670–1. From one of those present at the meetings, we know that the topic under discussion was how far the 'principles of morality and revealed religion' are capable of directing men's actions.[1] The question, then, as rephrased by Locke, is, what is the state of our knowledge of the principles of morality and revealed religion, and how far and in what ways can each of them be relied upon as a guide to our conduct? That is the interrogative to which the *Essay* directs itself, and although written, as Locke confesses, 'by incoherent parcels', the author never loses sight of his primary objective. Since, as we shall see, Locke believes the principles of morality capable of being *known* with certainty, while the truths conveyed through revelation must be *believed* by men, demarcating the boundaries between faith and knowledge becomes the paramount issue of the *Essay*.

There can be little doubt as to Locke's willingness to grant priority to that knowledge which will lead men to the worship of God and exact from them an obedience to his will. For the sake of guaranteeing certainty in these matters, all other forms of knowledge may be sacrificed to doubt and uncertainty. As he declares in the *Conduct of the Understanding*:

There is, indeed, one science incomparably above all the rest...I mean theology, which, containing the knowledge of God and his creatures, our duty to him and our fellow creatures, and a view of our present and future state, is the comprehension of all other knowledge directed to its true end, i.e., the honour and veneration of the Creator, and the happiness of mankind. This is that noble study which is every man's duty, and everyone that can be called a rational creature is capable of.[2]

In the *Essay* itself, this theme is stated at the outset, and repeated throughout the text. It is 'morality and divinity' which are 'those parts of knowledge that men are most concerned to be clear in'.[3] Hence, Locke directs the reader to 'the main end of these inquiries: the knowledge and veneration of him [God] being the chief end of all our thoughts and the proper business of all understandings'.[4] And, in the concluding book of the *Essay*, the two themes, *viz.* man's ignorance of the visible world, and his need for certainty in matters of religion and morality, are merged in a paragraph summarizing Locke's position:

[1] The notation is that of James Tyrrell; cf. Cranston, *John Locke*, p. 141.
[2] *Conduct of the Understanding*, §23.
[3] *Essay*, 'Epistle to the Reader', p. 16; III, IX, §22; III, X, §12. 'Heaven being our great business and interest, the knowledge which may direct us thither is certainly so too; so that this... ought to take up the first and chiefest place in our thoughts', *Journal*, 29 March 1677, MS. f. 2.
[4] *Essay*, II, VII, §6; II, XXIII, §12. 'For men being all the workmanship of one omnipotent and infinitely wise Maker... sent into the world by His order and about His business...', *Second Treatise on Government*, §6; *A Letter concerning Toleration*, *Works*, V, 41; *Journal*, 8 February 1677, MS. f. 2.

Since our faculties are not fitted to penetrate into the internal fabric and real essences of bodies, but yet plainly discover to us the being of a God, and the knowledge of ourselves, enough to lead us into a full and clear discovery of our duty and great concernment, it will become us, as rational creatures, to employ those faculties we have about what they are most adapted to, and...it is rational to conclude, that our proper employment lies in those inquiries, and in that sort of knowledge which is most suited to our natural capacities, and carries in it our greatest interest, i.e., the condition of our eternal state...[Thus,] *morality is the proper science and business of mankind in general.*[1]

To the Bishop of Worcester's criticism that his 'new way of ideas' undermined the principles of Christianity, Locke replied that 'all the great ends of religion and morality' were secured in his book.[2] The reply is not merely a defence, *ex post facto*. Rather, the point is, Locke wrote the *Essay concerning Human Understanding* in order to secure the 'great ends of religion and morality'.

It is true, of course, that a great number of Locke's contemporaries thought otherwise. They viewed the *Essay* as a challenge to, not a defence of, their religious beliefs. In this they were partially correct. Locke was attacking certain precepts of traditional religion, but he attacked them because he believed they provided an extremely weak defence for the Christian faith, and he was convinced that faith could be reinforced by better reasoning about the nature and source of ideas. Significantly, it is a concluding remark in the most critical book of the *Essay* that expresses this affirmation:

What censure doubting thus of innate principles may deserve from men, who will be apt to call it pulling up the old foundations of knowledge and certainty, I cannot tell—I persuade myself, at least, that the way I have pursued, being conformable to truth, lays those foundations surer.[3]

Locke knew very well the nature of the censure his attack on innate ideas would draw upon him. Even prior to its English publication, the abstract of the *Essay* Locke contributed to Le Clerc's *Bibliothèque Universelle* had come under fire since, 'if innate ideas were not supposed, there would

---

[1] *Essay*, IV, XII, §11. 'Moral philosophy, which in my sense, comprehends religion too, or a man's whole duty...', *Journal*, 6–10 April 1677, MS. f. 2.

[2] *A Letter to the Right Reverend Edward, Lord Bishop of Worcester* (hereinafter referred to as *BW*), *Works*, III, 33–4.

[3] *Essay*, I, III, §24. 'And I doubt not but to show that a man by the right use of his natural abilities, may, without any innate principles, attain a knowledge of a God, and other things that concern him', I, III, §12. Also, for an indication of Locke's general attitude, see his statement: 'I am always for the builders who bring some addition to our knowledge, or at least, some new thing to our thoughts. The finders of faults, the confuters and pullers down, do but only erect a barren and useless triumph upon human ignorance, but advance us nothing in the acquisition of truth', Locke to William Molyneux, 22 February 1697, *Some Familiar Letters Between Mr Locke and Several of his Friends* (London, 1708), p. 177.

be little left either of the notion or proof of spirits'.[1] Locke notes that 'there are men touchy enough to be put into a heat by my little treatise... If they are so concerned for truth and religion as become sober men, they will answer the end of its publication and show me the mistakes in it', and not reject the work 'only because it is not suited to the systems they were taught'.[2] More than once in the *Essay*, Locke refers to the belief in innate ideas as 'an established opinion', one that is 'commonly taken for granted'.[3]

Among whom was such an opinion 'established'? Locke's critique provides the best answer to that query. He condemns those who believe in innate ideas of whatever form, but it is 'especially about matters of religion' that the doctrine is most frequently invoked.[4] Locke complains that 'even they who require men to believe that there are such innate propositions, do not tell us what they are'. The result is that 'different men of different sects' use the theory of innate principles 'to support the doctrines' of their particular church.[5] These are the individuals who 'stamp the character of divinity upon absurdities and errors'.[6]

That men were endowed with innate knowledge of God and of good and evil was a fundamental axiom of religious belief in the seventeenth century. It stood as a rock against the perilous and uncertain forces of political, social, and intellectual change. Locke's suggestion that the forces of change might be so redirected as to increase the solidity of the principles of religion was doubtfully received. John Edwards, later a critic of *The Reasonableness of Christianity*, also objected to Locke's polemic against innate principles in the *Essay concerning Human Understanding*. In his work, *The Socinian Creed* (1697), Edwards argued that 'these natural impressions in all men's minds are the foundation of religion, and the standard of truth as well as of morality'.[7] And, more than a decade after the publication of the *Essay*, Edwards develops his defence of innate ideas in

---

[1] *Essay*, 'Epistle to the Reader', p. 15.
[2] Locke to Lady Guise, 11/21 June 1688, MS. c. 24, folios 51–2. Even Sir Isaac Newton, apparently referring to Book 1 of the *Essay*, at first believed that Locke had destroyed the orthodox defence of religion and morality. Later, he apologized to Locke: 'I beg your pardon...for representing that you struck at the root of morality in a principle you laid down in your book of ideas...and that I took you for a Hobbist', Newton to Locke, 16 September 1693, MS. c. 16, fo. 153.
[3] *Essay*, I, I, §§1, 2; IV, xx, §8.
[4] *An Early Draft*, ed. Aaron and Gibb, §42; IV, XII, §4. 'The argument I was upon there was to show that the idea of God was not innate', *Mr Locke's Reply to the Bishop of Worcester's Answer to his Second Letter* (hereinafter referred to as *3BW*), *Works*, III, 495. For other associations with religion, see *Essay*, IV, x, §1; IV, xx, §§9, 10.
[5] *Ibid*. I, II, §14.　　　　　　[6] *Ibid*. I, II, §26.
[7] John Edwards, *The Socinian Creed: or a brief account of the professed tenets and doctrines of the foreign and English Socinians: wherein is showed the tendency of them to irreligion and atheism...* (London, 1697), p. 122.

Richard Ashcraft

A Free Discourse Concerning Truth and Error. He maintains that, although the original pattern of innate ideas exists in God's mind, 'yet he hath copied it out into the mind of man, and hath imprinted the figure of it on his rational nature...There are in our minds natural impressions and inbred notices of true and false, which are as it were streams issuing forth from the Uncreated and everlasting spring of truth. And these notions are not indifferent and arbitrary, but fixed and indelible.'[1] Edwards then proceeds to satisfy Locke's demand for a list of innate principles, most of them being precisely those cited in Book 1 of the *Essay* as examples to be rejected.

Edwards was not alone in his views. Joseph Glanvill, a writer of some reputation in his time, spoke of 'those inbred fundamental notices that God hath implanted in our souls, such as arise not from external objects, nor particular humours and imaginations, but are immediately lodged in our minds, independent upon other principles or deductions'.[2] These are but a few of the examples that might be cited in order to indicate the vital importance of the theory of innate ideas to the 'established' religious beliefs of the period.[3] 'Those who had the keenest interest' in the *Essay*, according to one writer, 'were theologians and moralists'.[4] And, 'if a representative of the modern spirit, such as Glanvill, could use such expressions, we may be sure that the theory assumed still cruder forms in the pulpit'.[5] The fact is, the doctrine of innate ideas did not want for defenders, and those who defended it most vigorously were theologians. The reasons for this are not difficult to understand. The belief in innate impressions sheltered ideas for which no other source or justification could be found. Whenever a doctrinal explanation was met with a challenge, the clergy retreated to the fortress of innate knowledge. One of Locke's correspondents recounts a theological discussion with his friends, and boasts, 'I have by your help beaten them off from their *innate ideas*... I have taken away their refuge of ideas.'[6] Another friend, James Tyrrell, writes: 'I find the divines much scandalized that so sweet and easy a part

[1] Cited in John Yolton, *John Locke and the Way of Ideas* (Oxford, 1956), p. 62.
[2] Cited in James Gibson, *Locke's Theory of Knowledge and its Historical Relations* (Cambridge, 1917), p. 31.
[3] A more exhaustive account of the history and popularity of the theory of innate knowledge may be found in Professor John Yolton's excellent piece of scholarship, *John Locke and the Way of Ideas.* See especially pp. 1–71.
[4] Yolton, *John Locke and the Way of Ideas*, p. 22.
[5] Gibson, *Locke's Theory of Knowledge*, p. 31. It was the clergy that 'triumphed mightily' when their doctrine of innate ideas was defended by such men as William Sherlock. Anthony Collins to Locke, 20 June 1704, MS. c. 7, folios 47–8. William Molyneux found it 'remarkable' that within a decade after the publication of the *Essay* anyone would dare to express opinions critical of the theory of innate knowledge from the pulpit. William Molyneux to Locke, 26 September 1696, *Some Familiar Letters*, p. 162.
[6] R. Vincent to Locke, 10 May 1690, MS. c. 23, folios 27–8.

of their sermons as that of the Law written in the heart is rendered false and useless.'[1] Sermons were preached against the *Essay concerning Human Understanding*, and Locke was publicly denounced from the pulpit. William Sherlock, 'a man of no small name', preached that Locke's book was 'atheistical' because it rejected innate ideas.[2] The same person, in a discourse published several years later, expressed rather directly the fears of those theologians hostile to Locke's new way of ideas:

For after all, there is not a more formidable objection against religion than to teach that mankind is made without any connate natural impressions and ideas of a God, and of good and evil; for if all the knowledge we have of God, and of good and evil, be made by ourselves, atheists will easily conclude that it is only the effect of education and superstitious fears.[3]

Clearly, Sherlock touched upon the heart of the controversy. The real issue was not whether, philosophically speaking, there were or were not innate ideas in men's minds, but simply, if there were no innate ideas, what else could supply the foundations of our knowledge of religion and morality? Locke's answer, contained in the *Essay concerning Human Understanding*, failed to satisfy many of his contemporaries because they suspected—as David Hume later demonstrated—that it created new problems for the defence of their religious beliefs. Edward Stillingfleet's plaintive observation that 'in an age wherein the mysteries of faith are so much exposed, by the promoters of scepticism and infidelity, it is a thing of dangerous consequence to start such new methods of certainty, as are apt to leave men's minds more doubtful than before' passed unnoticed by Locke.[4] For him, any problems or 'dangerous consequences' traceable to the *Essay* were purely chimerical. Repeatedly, Locke insists in his replies to Stillingfleet that nothing in his book can disturb the true prin-

---

[1] James Tyrrell to Locke, 18 February 1690, MS. c. 22, folios 82–3.
[2] The appraisal of Sherlock is Locke's. Locke to William Molyneux, 22 February 1697, *Some Familiar Letters*, p. 175.
[3] Cited in Yolton, *Locke and the Way of Ideas*, p. 61. Sherlock also asserted that 'the general reason why men are so zealous against these ideas being innate is to deliver themselves from the necessity of believing anything of God or religion', Dr Robert South to Locke, 18 July 1704, MS. c. 18, folios 175–6. Locke's attack on innate ideas, however, was prompted by other aims. He writes: 'by what means could the law of nature and a definite rule of moral rectitude and goodness be known, if it is once admitted that the dictates of nature and the principles of action vary from person to person...Surely, on this admission, it will be nothing, unless we can find a way of knowledge other than by inscription [innateness]', *Essays on the Law of Nature*, ed. Wolfgang von Leyden (Oxford, 1954), III, 139. In other words, Locke had recognized, as early as 1664, the dangers to which Sherlock alludes. The *Essay concerning Human Understanding* is his proposed remedy, i.e. another 'way to knowledge' which will give support to the law of nature. Moreover, Locke would agree with Sherlock that total relativism in religion is conducive to atheism. See his discussion of this point in the *Fifth Essay on the Law of Nature*, p. 175.
[4] *2BW*, p. 121.

ciples of Christianity. Nevertheless, the question put to him by the latter, poignantly, if not forcefully, is, how can Locke claim 'certainty' for the articles of faith he defends, and yet not include those precepts within his category of 'knowledge'?[1]

The *Essay concerning Human Understanding* is a testament of Locke's dilemma. He is personally convinced of the absolute truth of Christianity and the simple demands of faith drawn from the Scriptures, but, at the same time, he is equally certain that the supposed defenders of that faith have been derelict in the performance of their duty, in attempting to support religion with arguments from authority rather than with the evidence supplied by reasoning. Once the old foundation of innate ideas is replaced by a 'surer' one, the superstructure of Christianity will stand mightier than ever. The purpose of the *Essay* is essentially a conservative one: a renovation and reinforcement of the faith by which the men of the seventeenth century lived.

If it seems impossible to raise a *Weltanschauung* from its base and set it down upon another, intact and undisturbed, it is a mark of Locke's intellectual courage that he did not shrink from the task. But this feat should not obscure the more important point: namely, that Locke shares the firm conviction of his contemporaries that the faith must be preserved. Whenever others employed his epistemological principles in an assault on Christianity, Locke renounced them and sought refuge in the safety of his commitment to that faith within which he had confined the arguments of the *Essay concerning Human Understanding*.[2]

GOD, ORDER, AND KNOWLEDGE

Locke's description of the 'huge abyss of ignorance' confronting man is more than the product of philosophical reflexion. It effuses an air reminiscent of the Old Testament prophets, for whom man appears as the lowliest of creatures when the universe is seen through God's eyes. Locke pictures man as 'no more than the meanest creature, in comparison with God him-

---

[1] 'Can we be certain, without any foundation of reason?...[Locke and his followers] should not at the same time assert the absolute necessity of these ideas to our knowledge, and declare that we may have certain knowledge without them. If there be any other method, they overthrow their own principle; if there be none, how come they to any certainty?' *BW*, p. 30.

[2] Stillingfleet did not accuse Locke himself of espousing views antithetical to religion so much as associate him with those who did, specifically John Toland, author of *Christianity Not Mysterious*. Locke, therefore, spends a great deal of time in his replies dissociating himself from Toland, though rarely by naming him. Locke's intentions were clear enough to his friend, William Molyneux, who wrote to congratulate Locke for 'your shaking him off in your letter to the Bishop of Worcester'. William Molyneux to Locke, 27 May 1697, *Some Familiar Letters*, p. 217.

Faith and knowledge in Locke's philosophy

self'.[1] The 'workmanship of the all-wise and powerful God...further exceeds the capacity and comprehension of the most inquisitive and intelligent man, than the best contrivance of the most ingenious man doth the conceptions of the most ignorant of rational creatures'.[2] Frequently, in the *Essay*, Locke draws comparisons between the omniscience of God or the 'enlarged understandings' of spirits and the 'weak and narrow thoughts' of man.[3] On the one hand, 'there is nothing which (God) cannot make exist each moment he pleases', and on the other, there is man, who can but 'compound and divide' the materials presented to his 'dull' and 'not very acute' senses.[4] The contrast is intended to inspire, not scepticism, but reverence. For, in our ignorance, we may take some comfort in the knowledge that the universe is ruled by 'a superior, powerful, wise, invisible Being'.[5] Yet, if we know so little concerning the natural world, how can we claim as 'knowledge' the proposition that it was created and is directed by a Deity?

Locke, of course, responds to this question. But, from the standpoint of philosophical proofs, his argument contains surprisingly little originality or substance. Although he suggests several reasons for the existence of God in his formal treatment of the subject (*Essay*, IV, x), Locke generally relies upon the argument from design. Thus, it is 'naturally deducible' from 'the visible marks of extraordinary wisdom and power' which 'appear so plainly in all the works of the creation' that a Creator exists.[6] 'By a due contemplation of causes and effects', we may arrive at the notion of a God.[7] Yet it is precisely our assurance that a great architect rules the universe which convinces us of the order and regularity in nature. That which man discovers around him is 'regularly and constantly made' according to 'the steady workmanship of nature'.[8] Locke's frequent allusions to the 'settled constitution', the 'stupendous fabric' and the 'magnificent harmony of the universe' are premised upon an unquestioned acceptance of a Deity.[9] On this point, the reader is overwhelmed by

---

[1] *Essay*, II, XV, §12; II, XXIX, §16; III, VI, §12.

[2] *Ibid.* III, VI, §§9, 11.

[3] *Ibid.* II, X, §9; II, XV, §§11, 12; II, XVII, §§1, 15; II, XXIII, §13; III, XI, §23; IV, III, §§6, 23, 25; IV, VI, §12; IV, XVII, §14; *Conduct of the Understanding*, §3.

[4] *Essay*, II, XV, §12; II, XXIII, §§12 ff.; IV, III, §6.   [5] *Ibid.* I, III, §10.

[6] *Ibid.* II, XVII, §20; *An Early Draft*, ed. Aaron and Gibb, §38. 'He has left so many footsteps of Himself, so many proofs of His being...', *Journal*, 8 February 1677, MS. f. 2.

[7] *Essay*, I, III, §§9, 11; I, II, §6; *The Reasonableness of Christianity*, pp. 129, 135.

[8] *Essay*, IV, V, §§8, 9. 'This visible world is constructed with wonderful art and regularity', *Essays on the Law of Nature*, ed. von Leyden, pp. 151 ff. 'The established steady laws of causes and effects', *A Discourse on Miracles*, *Works*, VIII, 256. 'The eternal order of things', *Essays on the Law of Nature*, ed. von Leyden, p. 199. 'I am of [the] opinion, too, that there is one common uniform Reason [which] runs through all things...', MS. b. 3.

[9] *Essay*, II, II, §3; II, IX, §12; III, VI, §12; IV, VI, §11; *Essays on the Law of Nature*, ed. von Leyden, pp. 109 ff., 133, 147–59. 'God has made the intellectual world harmonious and

repetitious, dogmatic assertions, the questioning of which would subvert one's claim to rationality. It is not only that 'we more certainly know that there is a God, than that there is anything else without us', but such a discovery is 'necessary', 'past doubt', and 'unavoidable' for any 'considering, rational creature'.[1] 'There never was any rational creature that set himself to examine the truth of these propositions that could fail to assent to them.'[2] In Locke's philosophy, 'nothing is of absolute necessity but God'.[3] All his writings bear testimony to this fact. Political toleration is a defensible policy only within a community of believers, i.e. where every member professes a belief in the supreme being.[4] The *Essays on the Law of Nature* open with the declaration, 'I assume there will be no one to deny the existence of God'. This assumption, Locke insists, must be 'taken for granted'.[5] And one of the critics of the *Essay concerning Human Understanding* points out that Locke wrote the greater part of that work presuming upon an 'idea of a God which he has not yet introduced'.[6]

Not only is the existence of God necessary, but this structuring of the antinomies is absolutely essential to Locke's argument in the *Essay*. At crucial points in the exploration of human ignorance, Locke suddenly ascends to view the world through the eyes of an omniscient Deity. This ascension is not gainsaid by any demonstrative knowledge, but by a faith that reveals more to Locke than he will warrant for others. At such times, Locke speaks less as a philosopher than as a prophet, deciphering the intentions of God for those who must be reassured against the supposition of chaos and a disordered universe.

Once the presence of God is 'taken for granted', what formerly appeared mysterious to us, relying upon the information of our senses, is now seen as reasonable. What, in so far as it disturbed us, was viewed as disordering, may now be fitted into a grand design and made intelligible. It is the knowledge that we are the 'workmanship' of a supreme intelligence which 'explains' the 'constant and regular succession of ideas' men have. From the perspective of finite beings, pain is disruptive of the peace

beautiful without us', *Conduct of the Understanding*, §38. 'God having made this great machine of the universe...', *Journal*, 8 February 1677, MS. f. 2. The 'order and beauty' of the universe is also noted in his *Journal*, 1 August 1680, MS. f. 4; cf. MS. c. 27, fo. 67.

[1] *Essay*, I, III, §§9, 12, 23; II, XIV, §31; II, XV, §§3, 4; II, XVII, §§17, 20; II, XXVII, §2; III, IX, §23; IV, X, §§1, 6, 8; *3BW*, pp. 289, 291.

[2] *Essay*, I, III, §17. Anyone 'who would pass for a rational creature' must believe in God. *Journal*, 29 July 1676, MS. f. 1.

[3] *A Third Letter concerning Toleration*, *Works*, v, 165.

[4] 'The taking away of God, though but even in thought, dissolves all', *A Letter concerning Toleration*, *Works*, v, 47.

[5] 'It would be wrong to doubt...that some Divine Being presides over the world', *Essays on the Law of Nature*, ed. von Leyden, pp. 109 ff.

[6] Observations by Bishop William King on the *Essay concerning Human Understanding*, MS. c. 28, fo. 100ᵛ.

and comfort they might expect in their lives. For God, however, pain is a preservative of the 'due proportion' and 'order' in nature. It guarantees the 'proper functioning' of the 'delicate instruments of sensation' in man against that 'disorderly motion' contrary to the 'natural state' of harmony of God's creation.[1] But Locke does not stop here. To this teleological, he adds a theological justification for pain, which is that

God hath scattered up and down several degrees of pleasure and pain, in all the things that environ and affect us; and blended them together in almost all that our thoughts and senses have to do with; that we, finding imperfection, dissatisfaction, and want of complete happiness, in all the enjoyments which the creatures can afford us, might be led to seek it in the enjoyment of Him with whom there is a fullness of joy, and at whose right hand are pleasures for evermore.[2]

God might have created a universe without pain, order, or harmony, but *we* cannot imagine what that universe would look like.[3] Instead, we are compelled by the nature of things to recognize the 'gradual connection' between the 'great variety of things we see in the world'. This order ascends upwards 'in degrees of perfection' reaching to 'the infinite perfection of the Creator'.[4] In short, that there is a supreme being presiding over a rationally designed Creation is the bedrock of all our knowledge, moral or intellectual. The circular reasoning of an argument which infers the existence of God from a perceived rational ordering of objects, and which defends the 'rationality' of that order in terms of God's intentions, is never breached in the *Essay*. Indeed, it is as though Locke is engaged in exploring the various radii of knowledge as they touch upon the perimeters of his beliefs, but never does he permit himself to step outside the circle of his faith.

For example, in Book IV of the *Essay* he writes:

The things that, as far as our observation reaches, we constantly find to proceed regularly, we may conclude do act by a law set them; but yet by a law that we know not; whereby, though causes work steadily, and effects constantly flow from them, yet their connections and dependencies being not discoverable in our ideas, we can have but an experimental knowledge of them.[5]

But if we possess only an 'experimental' or probable knowledge of a law of cause and effect operating in nature, how is it possible for us 'by due contemplation of causes and effects' to arrive at a *certain* knowledge of the

---

[1] *Essay*, II, VII, §4; II, X, §3; II, XXI, §§38, 39 ff.; *Journal*, 16 July 1676, MS. f. 1.
[2] *Essay*, II, VII, §5; II, XXI, §34. 'The Deity inflicts evil [pain] with a settled view to some end; and no end worthy of him can be answered by inflicting it as a punishment, unless to prevent other evils', *A Defence of...Personal Identity*, *Works*, II, 306.
[3] *Essay*, II, II, §3; II, XIII, §21, 22; II, XXIII, §13.
[4] *Ibid.* IV, XVI, §12. [5] *Ibid.* IV, III, §29.

existence of a Deity? At one point in the *Essay*, Locke observes that our measurement of motion is not exact, but only yields probabilities. Hence, any objective regularity of the universe will not be detected by humanly created instruments and so is not really a part of our 'knowledge'. Nevertheless, Locke argues, if we did not imagine or impose an order, through the use of our measuring devices, 'all things would be jumbled in an incurable confusion'.[1] Clearly, if it is *our* imposition of order that rescues us from an 'incurable confusion', we cannot then reason from that order to an objectively grounded knowledge of God governing his ordered universe. Much of the debate between Locke and Stillingfleet focuses on the former's denial of our knowledge of 'substance'. Locke's position is that although 'the secret abstract nature of substance in general' eludes our finite understandings, we must suppose that substance is a peculiar and indispensable ingredient of every particular sensible object with which we do come into contact. That is, the supposition of substance is grounded in the assumed universal order, as a necessary condition for the operation of our rational faculties in their exploration of the visible parts of that order.[2] Similarly, Locke concedes our inability to perceive the impulses emitted from the 'insensible particles of matter'. Again, this confession of human ignorance leads not to scepticism, but to the recognition of God's wisdom. For it is in terms of our assurance of the manner that God has structured the world for us that we can assert the existence of insensible objects or beings. Locke reminds the Bishop of Worcester that

a great many things may be and are granted to have a being, and be in nature, of which we have no ideas. For example, it cannot be doubted but there are distinct species of separate spirits, of which we have no distinct ideas at all. It cannot be questioned but spirits have ways of communicating their thoughts, and yet we have no idea of it at all.[3]

But if we have no ideas of such matters, it is certain that our Maker does, and for Locke, 'it is enough to justify the fitness of anything to be done by resolving it into the "wisdom of God" who has done it'.[4] The number of occasions Locke relies upon this 'resolution'—and always at crucial points in his debates with an opponent—is surprising, coming from a thinker so often hailed as the father of empiricism or as a champion of rationalism. I suggest that Locke's statement is not an anomaly in an otherwise 'modern' philosophy, but is, rather, the core of his world-view. It is the

[1] *Essay*, II, XIV, §§ 21, 22; II, XV, §§ 5, 8; *Journal*, 20 January 1678, MS. f. 3.
[2] *Essay*, II, XXIII, § 6.
[3] *BW*, p. 18; *Essay*, II, VIII, § 13; II, X, § 9. Yet we only 'know' of the existence of such spirits through revelation, *ibid*. IV, III, § 27; IV, XI, § 12; IV, XII, § 12.
[4] *The Reasonableness of Christianity*, *Works*, VI, 134, 151. 'I that am fully persuaded that the infinitely wise God made all things in perfect wisdom', *Essay*, I, III, § 22.

sublime and blasphemous task of bringing together man's ignorance and God's wisdom that Locke attempts in the *Essay concerning Human Understanding*.

If the frontiers of human ignorance are to be resigned to the governorship of an omniscient Being, it becomes important to raise certain questions regarding the goodness of God, who exercises so great a control over men's lives. Such questions, however, inescapably lead one into the thicket of controversy. The character of the Deity was one of those hotly debated issues amongst Locke's contemporaries. At one extreme stood Hobbes, who denied man any knowledge of God's attributes, save his irresistible and absolute power. The fear of eternal damnation at the hands of an all-powerful sovereign is a sufficient motive for the religious worship of Hobbesian man.[1] Locke is unwilling to accept this position, though he does not so much deny Hobbes's view as enlarge upon it. At the other extreme, every member of the clergy espoused his own vision of God's nature, and such conceptions readily became the basis for dogmatic religious creeds. This, too, was unacceptable, since the rigidity of doctrines grounded in ignorance discouraged the use of man's rational faculties, which Locke regarded as the life-giving force of true religion. For if men reason rightly they will ultimately arrive at those truths which support their very being. As in the case of innate ideas, Locke's problem is to avoid the pitfalls of total subjectivism, as practised by the clergy, without casting himself into the abyss of scepticism.

Thus, Locke dissociates himself from those whose veneration of God is solely the product of their fear of him. Such a view of the Deity is too primitive; it is, in fact, not religion, but superstition.[2] Religion demands a more positive conception of God. Yet Locke maintains that all the ideas we have of him are derivations of the simple ideas we have of ourselves, to which is added our notion of infinity. However, when we apply the idea of infinity to our attributes and 'see' them in God, we do so in a 'figurative' sense only, since we lack that knowledge of his true nature which would allow us to speak descriptively.[3] This reservation seems to

---

[1] *The English Works of Thomas Hobbes*, ed. Sir William Molesworth, 11 vols. (London, 1839–45): *Leviathan*, III, 345–6; *De Cive*, II, 12, 13, 206–7; *Liberty and Necessity*, IV, 249–50. Locke grants that God possesses absolute power and that 'all obligation leads back to God', but he adds that 'it is reasonable' for us to obey him, because of his goodness, *Essays on the Law of Nature*, ed. von Leyden, pp. 183, 185; *Journal*, 1 September 1676, MS. f. 1. Also see his definition of natural law, *Essays on the Law of Nature*, ed. von Leyden, p. 111.

[2] Superstition is that which sees God as 'dreadful and terrible, as being rigorous and imperious; that which represents him as austere and apt to be angry'. Under such circumstances, man is forced to live in constant fear and under 'an apprehension of evil from God', 'Superstition' (1682), MS. d. 10. Also, Benjamin Furly to Locke, 8/19 February 1704, MS. c. 9, folios 194–5.

[3] *Essay*, III, VI, §11; II, XVII, §1.

Richard Ashcraft

support the conclusion that God is, after all, 'incomprehensively infinite'. But, in the same paragraph, Locke refers to his 'power, wisdom, and goodness', and adds: 'I do not pretend to say how these attributes are in God, who is infinitely beyond the reach of our narrow capacities; they do, without doubt, contain in them all possible perfection.'[1] God's 'perfection' is precisely the point at issue. Where exactly is the bridge between human imperfection and the 'incomprehensively infinite' Creator? Locke simply assumes both ends of the question, i.e. the Deity's attributes are unknowable and he is perfectly wise, just, good, pure, and reasonable. We are even assured that God 'cannot choose what is not good; the freedom of the Almighty hinders not his being determined by what is best'.[2] Questions concerning the conflict between human and divine reason or between man's free will and the Deity's goodness are all phrased from the human perspective, the answers to which 'resolve' themselves into an acceptance of God's wisdom.

Is man's relationship to the world and to other men limited to the small arena of human knowledge, or is it extended according to the infinitely wider horizons of faith? If it is the former, man will feel himself constantly oppressed by the heavy weight of his ignorance. If, however, he places himself within the latter framework, he will recognize the order, rationality, and goodness of God's Creation, of which he is a part. Locke's choice, and the one he recommends to others, is easily discoverable by anyone prepared to put himself in the audience for which Locke wrote the *Essay concerning Human Understanding*.

OPINION AND KNOWLEDGE:
THE CERTAINTY OF PROBABILITY

In the Introduction to the *Essay*, Locke promises to 'search out the bounds between opinion and knowledge, and examine by what measures, in things whereof we have no certain knowledge, we ought to regulate our assent and moderate our persuasion'.[3] We know what kind of knowledge that search will lead to, and that the old way of innate ideas is inadequate to the task. And we have Locke's word that acceptance of a divinely ruled and rational universe is a necessary precondition for knowledge. But we do not yet know wherein lies the difference between opinion and

---

[1] *Essay*, II, XVII, §1. Throughout *The Reasonableness of Christianity*, Locke assumes that the justice, goodness, purity, love, mercy, and wisdom of God support his interpretation of the Scriptures (*Works*, VI, 6, 8, 11, 112); *Second Vindication of the Reasonableness of Christianity*, *ibid.* p. 228. 'Wisdom and goodness *must* be ingredients of that perfect or super excellent being which we call God...' (my italics), *Journal*, 1 August 1680, MS. f. 4.
[2] *Essay*, II, XXI, §§50, 51.
[3] *Ibid.* Introduction, §§2, 3.

Faith and knowledge in Locke's philosophy

knowledge. Commenting on the passage cited from the Introduction, Alexander Fraser writes: 'In Locke's use of words, *knowledge* usually means what is absolutely certain...'[1] In general, this is Locke's view; but on careful examination the firm boundaries between opinion and knowledge dissolve before the reader's eyes.

Locke defines knowledge as nothing but the perception of the agreement or disagreement between any two ideas, which comparison is the product of either intuition or demonstration.[2] Intuition, such as we have in the case of simple ideas, is an absolutely certain means of obtaining knowledge; demonstration, which requires 'pains' and 'intricate proofs', is less reliable, though if properly conducted will lead one to truths no less certain. In either instance, the crucial and determining factor is one's certainty as to the truth of the proposition. What often passes under the label of knowledge 'in popular ways of talking' is but strong probability.[3] However, 'the highest probability', according to Locke, 'amounts not to certainty, without which there can be no true knowledge'.[4] Thus, to know is to be 'infallibly certain'.[5]

It is relevant to recall that there are very few things of which one may claim 'true knowledge', so that, 'in the greatest part of our concernments', we live in 'the twilight of probability'.[6] Indeed, if one were forced to wait upon certainty 'in the ordinary affairs of life', one 'would be sure of nothing in this world, but of perishing quickly'.[7] Therefore, however firm in principle the lines between opinion and knowledge may be, in practice the distinction apparently matters little. For, Locke concedes,

most of the propositions we think, reason, discourse—nay, act upon, are such as we cannot have undoubted knowledge of their truth; yet some of them border so near upon certainty, that we make no doubt at all about them; *but assent to them as firmly, and act, according to that assent, as resolutely as if they were infallibly demonstrated,* and that our knowledge of them were perfect and certain.[8]

Locke assumes that a rational man acts upon his judgment, and that if, in a particular instance, that judgment is based on certain knowledge, it follows that his action could not have been otherwise. Where the individual's judgment depends on probable information, the resulting action

[1] *Essay*, vol. I, p. 26 n.; cf. p. 40 n. (Dover paperback edition).
[2] *Essay*, IV, I, §2; IV, II, §14.
[3] *Third Letter concerning Toleration, Works*, V, 144.
[4] *Essay*, IV, III, §14; *Third Letter concerning Toleration, Works*, V, 143.
[5] *Ibid*. p. 180.
[6] *Essay*, IV, III, §6; IV, XIV, §2. 'Probability, then, being to supply the defect of our knowledge, and to guide us where that fails', IV, XV, §4.
[7] *Essay*, IV, XI, §10; IV, XIV, §1; IV, XVI, §3.
[8] *Ibid*. IV, XV, §2. In some cases the 'probability is so clear and strong that assent as *necessarily* follows it as knowledge does demonstration' (my italics), IV, XVII, §16. Cf. *An Early Draft*, ed. Aaron and Gibb, §34.

might have been different, had the defect of his knowledge been remedied. Notwithstanding the firmness of this dichotomy between knowledge and opinion, we now discover that Locke believes 'some' matters of probability 'naturally determine the judgment, and leave us as little likely to believe or disbelieve as a demonstration does'. In these cases, it must likewise follow that the individual's actions are 'unavoidable'.[1] One might well ask, what has become of the original demarcation between knowledge and opinion?

The section of the early draft of the *Essay* that deals with this subject, after a series of confusing and indeterminate statements relating to the distinctions between faith and knowledge, concludes: 'and therefore knowledge, and faith, too, at last resolve themselves into and terminate somewhere or other in experience'.[2] Although the matter is discussed at greater length in the final published draft, the reader is not for that any more enlightened as to where, precisely, the lines between opinion and knowledge do terminate in one's experience. And, without a certain knowledge of *that*, all other measures of certainty will prove worthless.

Later, we shall return to the problem of boundaries in connexion with Locke's attempt to preserve the differences between faith and knowledge. Thus far, we have considered the formal definitions offered by Locke, but it will prove helpful to say something about the substantive nature of what he regards as certain knowledge. Moral propositions, for example, may be known with a certainty 'as incontestible as those in mathematics'.[3] Assuming this to be true, how do men arrive at such knowledge?

In order to answer that question we must, as Locke did in the *Essay*, manage a slight detour, and take up the matter of words and definitions, 'since a definition is the only way whereby the precise meaning of moral words can be known'.[4] What Locke refers to as 'mixed modes and relations' of which 'the greater part' are moral terms, possess 'no other reality but what they have in the minds of men'.[5] Not only are moral propositions the product of the mind, but they are 'very arbitrarily made without patterns or reference to any real existence' or to any 'sensible standard' provided by nature.[6] Because the 'real essence' and the 'nominal essence' of moral words are identical, we may attain a certain knowledge of them.[7]

---

[1] *Essay*, IV, XVI, §§6–9. 'Evidently strong probability may as steadily determine the man to assent to the truth, or make him take the proposition for true, *and act accordingly*, as knowledge...' (my italics), *3BW*, p. 299.

[2] *An Early Draft*, ed. Aaron and Gibb, §33.   [3] *Essay*, IV, III, §18; III, XI, §16.

[4] *Ibid*. III, XI, §17.   [5] *Ibid*. II, XXX, §4.

[6] *Ibid*. II, XXXI, §§3, 14. 'When we speak of justice or gratitude, we frame to ourselves no imagination of anything existing', III, V, §§3, 5, 6, 12; III, IX, §7; III, XI, §15.

[7] *Ibid*. III, XI, §16.

Faith and knowledge in Locke's philosophy

This argument, which is beset by difficulties of its own creation, is advanced even further by Locke, who thereby exposes himself to a position from which his later retreat is at once more humiliating and more significant. 'Every man', he affirms, 'has so inviolable a liberty to make words stand for what ideas he pleases, that no one has the power to make others have the same ideas in their minds that he has, when they use the same words that he does.'[1] Thus 'words, in their primary or immediate signification, *stand for nothing but the ideas in the mind of him that uses them, how imperfectly soever or carelessly those ideas are collected from the things which they are supposed to represent*'.[2] Obviously, were this all to be said for morality, we should never free ourselves from the morass of total relativism, the consequences of which Locke himself points out.[3] But, having plunged headlong into it, Locke expends a great deal of energy in the *Essay* in an effort to lead the reader back to firmer ground.

In Book II, Locke proposes 'to examine things as they really are'.[4] Implicit in this declaration is Locke's recognition of the 'fallacy' of attaching too great an importance to words by 'taking them for things' because 'names made at pleasure neither alter the nature of things, nor make us understand them'.[5] Therefore, 'it is not enough to have determined ideas' of moral actions, or 'to know what names belong to such and such combinations of ideas. We have a further and greater concernment, and that is, to know whether such actions, so made up, are morally good or bad.'[6] This statement lends itself to at least two interpretations: (*a*) any definition of moral terms 'made up' by the individual is *ipso facto* insufficiently related to 'the nature of things' to inform him of what actions are 'really' morally condemnable or praiseworthy; or (*b*) no definition, however generally accepted by men, provides a sufficient basis on which to premise one's moral judgments, and one must search elsewhere to discover the true standard of morality. As we shall see, the latter is Locke's position.

The hinge of Locke's argument for the existence of an objectively certain truth is 'reality'. 'By *real ideas*', he explains, 'I mean such as have a foundation in nature, such as have a conformity with the real being and existence of things...*Fantastical* or *chimerical*, I call such as have no foundation in nature, nor have any conformity with that reality of being to which

---

[1] *Essay*, III, II, §8.   [2] *Ibid*. III, II, §2 (my italics).
[3] 'Though the names glory and gratitude be the same in every man's mouth through a whole country, yet the complex collective idea which everyone thinks on or intends by that name is apparently very different in men using the same language. And hence we see that in the interpretation of laws, whether divine or human, there is no end', *ibid*. III, IX, §§8, 9; IV, IV, §9.
[4] *Ibid*. II, XI, §15.   [5] *Ibid*. II, XIII, §18.
[6] *Ibid*. II, XXVIII, §4.

they are tacitly referred...'¹ Our knowledge 'is real only so far as there is a conformity between our ideas and the reality of things'. But, Locke asks, what criteria do we depend on for guidance? 'How shall the mind, when it perceives nothing but its own ideas, know that they agree with things themselves?'² Given the fact that moral ideas admittedly do not refer to any standard, rooted-in-sense-experience 'reality', the question is a good one.

As a minimum, one must accept convention as a standard of morality if, as Locke believes, 'knowledge' is something that frequently emerges from a conversation and social interaction with others. Therefore, either the 'reality of things' or the 'proper signification' of names must form the basis for judging what is true or false, right or wrong. 'And so, in referring our ideas to those of other men, called by the same names, ours may be false; and the idea in our minds, which we express by the word *justice*, may perhaps be that which ought to have another name.'³ The individual is granted his liberty to formulate subjective definitions of moral terms, but those definitions may be discounted unless he is able to provide us with a more general rule than his word to determine their value. For a moral action is one performed voluntarily by a person according to 'some law'. Locke identifies three kinds of laws, any one of which might constitute the framework of a systematic morality. Since all that is requisite for the making of moral judgments is a perceived relationship between a concrete act and the general rule, actions may be classified moral or immoral as they conform to one of the laws: (*a*) divine, (*b*) civil, or (*c*) the 'law' of public opinion. However, the possibility can hardly be overlooked that 'measuring an action' by a wrong rule, one will judge amiss of its moral rectitude.⁴ Consequently, one is obliged to determine which is the 'true' rule of morality.

In Book I of the *Essay*, Locke describes a tripartite division of moral rules which parallels that listed at the end of Book II, from which we have just quoted. The question raised in the earlier section is, why should men keep their agreements? To which, Locke gives three replies: the Christian maintains that the law requiring contracts to be kept is a rule given to man by God, and therefore obliging; a 'Hobbist' regards it as a rule because the public 'and the Leviathan' requires it; and 'the old philosophers' accepted the rule because it was 'below the dignity of man' for one to violate one's agreements.⁵ Which of these reflects Locke's position?

Some contemporaries accused Locke of espousing the third view, and of reducing all morality to acting in conformity with the prevailing

¹ *Essay*, II, xxx, §1; *Journal*, 5 November 1677, MS. f. 2.
² *Essay*, IV, IV, §3. Moral propositions 'agree not to the reality of things', IV, V, §11.
³ *Ibid.* II, xxxII, §§10, 12, 17, 26; III, VI, §28; IV, V, §8.
⁴ *Ibid.* II, xxviii, §20.   ⁵ *Ibid.* I, II, §5.

opinion of society. Locke denies the charge, citing the difference between reporting what men generally do adopt as a rule in practice, and the fact that 'the law of Nature is that standing rule by which they *ought* to judge of the moral rectitude and pravity of their actions'.[1] He goes on to describe the law of nature as 'the rule prescribed by God, which is the true and only measure of virtue'.[2] Locke concludes his defence with a personal affirmation that a judgment according to God's will, 'the eternal and unalterable nature of right and wrong', is that which '*I* call virtue and vice'.[3]

If God is the source of morality, clearly our moral judgments must do more than reflect the conventional standards of any particular society. Locke now points out that while definitions are important to any moral system, they are only 'one part' of it.[4] The law of nature is not 'made up' by men, like mathematical terms, nor can God's will be 'altered to comply with [man's] ill-ordered choice'.[5] Some definitions have been unalterably inscribed on the tablets of the universe by the finger of God. And where God 'has defined any moral names', their meaning is clear, and 'it is not safe to apply or use them otherwise'.[6] The corner of Locke's argument is turned when one learns that it is through revelation that men become cognizant of God's definitions of morality. The problem now becomes, how can one be assured that, following the epistemological principles laid down in the *Essay concerning Human Understanding*, one will arrive at moral definitions that do, in fact, conform to the 'reality' of God's unalterable will as revealed in the Scriptures?

Since natural law is the 'decree of a divine will', we are returned once more to the question of the law-maker's nature in order to justify our obedience to a 'law' representing more than 'power irresistible'. As Thomas Burnet put the issue to Locke,

You allow, I think, moral good and evil to be such antecedently to all human laws; but you suppose them to be such (if I understand you right) by the divine

---

[1] 'Epistle to the Reader', p. 19. Locke specifically argues against an identification of natural law with the general practices or consent of men in the *Second Essay on the Law of Nature.* See also *Thoughts concerning Education*, §61.

[2] *Essay*, I, II, §§6, 18; II, XXVIII, §8; IV, III, §18; IV, X, §7.

[3] 'Epistle to the Reader', p. 18; *The Reasonableness of Christianity, Works*, VI, 10, 15, 112, 115, 133.

[4] *Essay*, IV, III, §20.

[5] *Ibid.* II, XXI, §57; *The Reasonableness of Christianity, Works*, VI, 112. 'The nature of good and evil is eternal and certain, and their value cannot be determined either by the public ordinances of men or by any private opinion', *Essays on the Law of Nature*, ed. von Leyden, pp. 121, 199. 'It is every man's duty to be just whether there be any such thing as a just man in the world or no', *Journal*, 26 June 1681, MS. f. 5. 'General consent in matters of morals... by no means proves a natural law', *Essays on the Law of Nature*, ed. von Leyden, pp. 165 ff. *Essay*, IV, IV, §10. 'I allow to the makers of systems and their followers to invent and use what distinctions they please, and to call things by what names they think fit. But I cannot allow to them, or to any man, an authority...to alter that which God has revealed', *The Reasonableness of Christianity, Works*, VI, 101–2.

law. To know your mind farther, give me leave to ask, what is the reason or ground of the divine law? whether the arbitrary will of God, the good of men, or the intrinsic nature of the things themselves... You seem to resolve all into the will of the lawmaker. But has the will of the lawmaker no rule to go by? And is not that which is a rule to his will also to ours, and indeed the original rule?[1]

Locke replies tartly that 'whoever sincerely acknowledges any law to be the law of God, cannot fail to acknowledge also that it has all the reason and ground that a just and wise law can or ought to have, and will easily persuade himself to forbear raising such questions and scruples about it'.[2] In other words, anyone who understands the nature of God cannot seriously question his obligation to obey natural law. But, as Burnet points out, according to Locke's own epistemology, we cannot know anything of the 'real essence' of God, nor can we do more than determine 'figuratively' his moral attributes. Without a knowledge of the Deity's moral nature, how can man have a *moral* obligation to obey his will?

Whether or not he fully comprehended the scope of the dilemma posed by Burnet, it is significant that, in his reply, Locke refers his critic to the 'revelation of the life and immortality of Jesus Christ through the gospel'. That is, Burnet will discover in the Scriptures everything he wishes to know concerning the nature of God and the reasons for man's moral obligation to follow the law of nature. It is a technique frequently resorted to by Locke in his debates with opponents. And it reveals, I suggest, the vital centre of Locke's moral thought, the Holy Scriptures. All the roads of Lockean philosophy lead to the hallowed ground of Christianity.

How do we 'know' that the world is ordered and rational? that God is wise, just, good, etc.? that his will is a discoverable moral law obliging us? that our beliefs and actions conform to the 'reality' of things as established by God? All these and many more questions beg for an answer without a reference to the revealed truth, which Locke accepts unquestioningly. Unlike the Indian philosopher, who ultimately based his knowledge of the world on 'he knew-not-what', Locke's philosophy rises from the catacombs of an unshakeable Christian faith.

FAITH, REASON, AND SALVATION

As in the case of opinion and knowledge, Locke attempts 'to lay down the measures and boundaries between faith and reason'. For until it is 'resolved how far we are to be guided by reason, and how far by faith,

---

[1] Cited in Sterling Lamprecht, *The Moral and Political Philosophy of John Locke* (New York, 1962), p. 108.
[2] Locke's answer to Burnet is appended to his *Second Reply to the Bishop of Worcester* (2BW), p. 188.

Faith and knowledge in Locke's philosophy

we shall in vain dispute and endeavour to convince one another in matters of religion'.[1] We have at last come full circle to meet directly the issue which gave birth to the *Essay*. Since Locke generally identifies faith with opinion, and contrasts both with knowledge, one might expect his distinction between reason and faith in Book IV to be but a restatement of the earlier dichotomy. It is not. Whereas the crucial feature of the opinion/knowledge definition is the certainty associated with the *product*, i.e. the idea or proposition claimed as knowledge, the important difference separating faith from reason relates to the *means* by which the individual acquires the information. That is, opinions and knowledge are both derived from the ordinary contact man has with the sensible world, though only the latter deserves to be called 'certain'. The information we receive through faith, however, is not part of our ordinary experience, and therefore, quite apart from the differences that lie in the degree of certainty which we attach to any proposition so received, there is a difference in kind separating the information transmitted to us by God from that which we receive by any other means.

Locke defines reason as 'the discovery of the certainty *or probability* of such propositions' as the mind receives '*by the use of its natural faculties*; viz., by sensation or reflection', while faith is 'the assent to any proposition not thus made out by the deductions of reason, but upon the credit of the proposer, as coming from God, *in some extraordinary way of communication. This way of discovering truths to men we call revelation.*'[2] It is obvious that Locke has introduced, at the very end of the *Essay concerning Human Understanding*, a new 'way of discovering truths' not formally considered within the boundaries of his epistemological discussion. Revelation stands outside the ordinary compass of human experience, and faith is explicitly associated with revelation.[3] Hence, the certainty or probability of a particular proposition is not really at issue, since in either case it may be the discovery of reason. What is important is an assessment of the source of the information. Is it the product of sense-experience and human reasoning, or is it the word of God? And how shall the priorities be assigned to information from either source?

To this, Locke gives no clear and consistent answer. Sometimes, the certainty of man's knowledge overrides the claims of faith, or at least puts

---

[1] *Essay*, IV, XVIII, §1. 'In matters of religion it might be well if anyone would tell how far we are to be guided by reason and how far by faith...setting down a strict boundary between faith and reason...ought to be the first point established in all disputes of religion', *Journal*, 24 August 1676, MS. f. 1.

[2] *Essay*, IV, XVIII, §2; *Conduct of the Understanding*, §24. 'Revelation is natural reason enlarged by *a new set of discoveries* communicated by God immediately...', IV, XIX, §4. Through the medium of revelation, we are '*advanced in our knowledge*' (my italics), IV, VII, §2.

[3] *Essay*, IV, XVIII, §6.

them aside, while at other times Locke not only insists that faith can itself claim a certainty but also that it is 'above reason'.[1] Whatever the contradictory nature of Lockean statements on this point, in the end there is no escaping the 'unmoved foundation' of faith or the fact that the Scriptures contain 'divine and infallible truth' against which the fluctuating claims of human reasoning cannot contend.[2] Lockean philosophy describes a poetic tragedy elevated to theology; ultimately, no intellectual hero can prevail standing in the shadow of the cross. 'The certainty of faith', Locke declares in his second reply to the Bishop of Worcester, 'has nothing to do with the certainty of knowledge.' Wherever one places the limits of knowledge, 'this shakes not at all, nor in the least concerns the assurance of faith; that is quite distinct from it [and] neither stands nor falls with knowledge'.[3] Thus, Locke denies the possibility that knowledge *of whatever nature* can disturb one's faith. Given this view, it is understandable that he could insist that not one word of the *Essay concerning Human Understanding* was the least damaging to Christianity.

In order to see how Locke applies the distinction between faith and reason, one might consider the problems posed by 'miracles'. Miracles are important to Locke because 'to know that any revelation is from God, it is necessary to know that the messenger that delivers it is sent from God, and that cannot be known but by some credentials given him by God himself'.[4] The 'credentials' are the miracles performed by the messenger, designed to 'satisfy men as rational creatures' as to the validity of the revelation.[5] A miracle, then, is no ordinary phenomenon within the range of man's sense-experience, but is rather 'a sensible operation, which being above the comprehension of the spectator, and in his opinion, contrary to the established course of nature, is taken by him to be divine'.[6]

---

[1] Consider the range of the following statements: Faith 'carries with it an assurance beyond doubt'. It 'absolutely determines our minds and as perfectly excludes all wavering as our knowledge itself; and we may as well doubt of our own being, as we can whether any revelation from God is true. So that faith is a settled and sure principle of assent and assurance, and leaves no manner of room for doubt or hesitation', *Essay*, IV, XVI, §14. The articles of faith are 'as certain and infallible as the very common principles of geometry', *3BW*, p. 275; cf. *The Reasonableness of Christianity*, *Works*, VI, 93, 95. 'For a way proposed to salvation that does not *certainly* lead thither' would leave men 'to wander in darkness and uncertainty' (my italics), *Second Vindication of the Reasonableness of Christianity*, *Works*, VI, 236. Yet 'faith is not faith without believing', *A Letter concerning Toleration*, *Works*, V, 11. Moreover, we are not capable of knowing 'several of those truths which are to be believed to salvation', *Third Letter concerning Toleration*, *loc. cit.* p. 424; *Fourth Letter concerning Toleration*, *loc. cit.* p. 566. 'Faith comes into our assistance where the light of reason fails, but where we have knowledge, there faith interposes not, nor indeed can to contradict it', *Journal*, 26 August 1676, MS. f. 1. That faith is 'above reason', see *Essay*, IV, XVIII, §§7, 9.
[2] *Second Vindication of the Reasonableness of Christianity*, *Works*, VI, 356; *2BW*, p. 147.
[3] *2BW*, pp. 146–7; cf. *3BW*, p. 303.
[4] *A Discourse on Miracles*, *Works*, VIII, 257; MS. c. 27, fo. 74.
[5] *A Discourse on Miracles*, *Works*, VIII, 262, 264; *Essay*, IV, XIX, §15.
[6] *A Discourse on Miracles*, *Works*, VIII, 256.

Faith and knowledge in Locke's philosophy

Locke is cognizant of the objection that what appears to be a miracle to one man may not appear so to another, and he concedes that such disagreement is an 'unavoidable' consequence arising from the diversity of tempers and opinions among men. Yet divine revelation must be rescued from this implied relativism. If there were no objective criteria for determining what is or is not a revelation, everything would be reduced to chaos, and religion would be equated with any man's vision of the truth. But where is one to discover the objective criteria to which men may appeal? From our own store of knowledge or from what we know—or, paradoxically, don't know—about God? Again, Locke straddles both positions, endeavouring to reconcile them, though his final choice is the one we should expect from a Christian believer.

'No man', he asserts, 'can by any revelation communicate to others any new simple ideas which they had not before from sensation or reflection.' Moreover, no revelation can 'shake or overrule plain knowledge'.[1] If this were not so, we would be unable to separate truth from fancy, and so possess no knowledge whatsoever. At the same time, Locke willingly grants that revelation can and should take precedence over our 'probable' knowledge.[2] But since almost everything we 'know' falls under this category, Locke's concession is no small triumph for revelation. We have certain knowledge of our own existence, of God's existence, of mathematical propositions, and very little else. Beyond that narrow island of certainty extends the great ocean of probability, whose waters we may expect at any time to see parted by a revelation from God.

Apparently, God cannot inform us that black is white, or that a triangle is a four-sided figure, because the understanding of finite beings is not prepared to deal with such information. Yet Locke never explains why a Deity capable of holding the sun motionless or raising men from the dead should feel himself bound to operate within the rules of mathematics or the five senses of human beings. In fact, Locke does admit that God *can* make things function 'even contrary to their nature', but he denies that this occurs in practice.[3] That denial is premised on Locke's personal conviction that the Creator is reasonable, just, and good. Indeed, it is impossible for any man to prove otherwise because 'it is not reasonable to deny the power of an infinite being, because *we* cannot comprehend its operation'.[4] Even if God's action, from the standpoint of our 'narrow

---

[1] *Essay*, IV, XVIII, §§3, 5, 6, 10.   [2] *Ibid.* IV, XVIII, §§8, 10.
[3] *The Reasonableness of Christianity*, *Works*, VI, 84–5; *Essay*, IV, XVI, §13. According to Locke, God only performs miracles 'for the *confirmation* of truths' (my italics), *Journal*, 3 April 1681, MS. f. 5; cf. *ibid.* 26 August 1676, MS. f. 1.
[4] *Essay*, IV, X, §19; *3BW*, pp. 461 ff. 'If all things must stand or fall by the measure of our understandings...there will be very little remain in the world...', *Journal*, 8 February 1677, MS. f. 2.

understandings', should 'utterly incapacitate us to see that wisdom and to judge rightly of it', we have no basis for questioning the propriety of the action.[1] The laws of God's world are all reasonable and good, whatever our opinions of them.[2] How, then, can men employ their power of reasoning in the face of the greater power and wonder of God's miracles?

Thus far, the discussion has been confined to the exploration of Lockean philosophy from the inside in order to see how certain problems illuminate the general structure of Locke's thought. But each advance touching the perimeters of that thought reveals the inadequacy of philosophical terms to encompass what is truly important to Locke; namely, those principles which constitute the supreme science, theology. For a final judgment of the interplay between faith and knowledge *within* Lockean philosophy, it will be necessary to step outside that framework and comment upon the relationship *between* philosophy and theology. We shall conclude, that is, by suggesting that those themes we have drawn from the *Essay concerning Human Understanding* are restated in Locke's last major work, *The Reasonableness of Christianity*. Only there are the problems, so intellectually troublesome to a reader of the *Essay*, resolved definitively.

If *The Reasonableness of Christianity* has been less misunderstood than the *Essay*, it is only because less attention has been paid to it. Those who have taken notice of the work have generally agreed that it represents Locke's concession to the need for religion as a guide for the 'vulgar' masses who are incapable of reasoning their way to truth.[3] If a conservative treatise, such as the *Essay concerning Human Understanding*, should be regarded as a radical statement, it is not surprising that Locke's most radical work should be thought the product of his submission to the 'conservative' religious pressure of his times. Both views spring from a commonly shared misunderstanding of Locke's conceptual framework, and his purpose for writing. Locke wrote *The Reasonableness of Christianity*, not to indicate the 'vulgarness' of Christianity, but in order to demonstrate that, ultimately, philosophy fails to secure those 'great ends of religion and morality' which are the concern of all men, whatever their station in society. Without Christianity, men would be cut adrift from the obligations they owe to God. It is nothing less than a total misconception to regard the *Reasonableness* as a denigration of Christianity and a defence of philosophy.

---

[1] *The Reasonableness of Christianity, Works*, VI, 134, 151.

[2] *Second Vindication of the Reasonableness of Christianity, ibid.* 356. What we understand of God's Creation is 'agreeable to His goodness', but 'it is also agreeable to His greatness that it should exceed our capacities and the highest flights of our imagination, the better to fill us with admiration of His power and wisdom', *Journal*, 8 February 1677, MS. f. 2.

[3] Leo Strauss, *Natural Right and History* (Chicago, 1953); Sheldon Wolin, *Politics and Vision* (Boston, 1960), chapter 9; Richard Cox, *Locke on War and Peace* (Oxford, 1960); C. B. Macpherson, *The Political Theory of Possessive Individualism* (Oxford, 1962).

Rather, the precepts of faith are necessary precisely because of the failure of philosophy.

In effect, *The Reasonableness of Christianity* provides a direct response to questions treated ambiguously in the *Essay*. For example, to the query, what may reason claim as knowledge in the area of morality?, Locke now offers a definite historical reply in place of the philosophical manœuvring in the *Essay concerning Human Understanding* between a denial of such knowledge on the one hand and a claim to its possession on the other. He does not abandon the belief that the law of nature is knowable, in principle, through the use of reasoning, but, Locke asks, 'who ever made out all the parts of it, put them together, and showed the world their obligation?' Philosophers since the ancients have found themselves divided on the subject; hence, philosophy is of little assistance in the matters of greatest concern to us. 'Human reason unassisted', Locke argues,

failed men in its great and proper business of morality. It never from unquestionable principles, by clear deductions, made out an entire body of the 'law of nature'. And he that shall collect all the moral rules of the philosophers, and compare them with those contained in the New Testament, will find them to come short of the morality delivered by our Saviour...[1]

To the repeated insistence of his friend, William Molyneux, that he should write a treatise proving the demonstrability of ethics, fulfilling the claim advanced in the *Essay concerning Human Understanding*, Locke replies: 'The Gospel contains so perfect a body of ethics, that reason may be excused from that inquiry, since she may find man's duty clearer and easier in revelation than in herself.'[2] The only certain and complete compilation of ethical principles is contained in the New Testament. And if men are to be instructed in morality, revelation is 'the surest, the safest, and most effectual way of teaching' them.[3] Such a law as we require, 'Jesus Christ has given us in the New Testament...by revelation', thereby reuniting religion and morality, making our knowledge of each of them more certain than it was before.[4]

Reference to Jesus, however, adds a new dimension to Locke's argument, for it is not merely that, at some point in history, man's 'unassisted reason' failed him. That failure is less historical than ontological, since it was necessary that men fall short of a complete knowledge of natural law. Human ignorance once more manifests God's wisdom. As Locke

---

[1] *The Reasonableness of Christianity, Works*, VI, 140–1.
[2] Locke to William Molyneux, 30 March 1696, *Some Familiar Letters*, pp. 143–4; cf. Locke to Reverend Richard King, 25 August 1703.
[3] *The Reasonableness of Christianity, Works*, VI, 147.
[4] *Ibid.* p. 143.

explains, 'It is necessary for the vindication of God's justice and goodness, that those who miscarry should do so by their own fault, and that their destruction should be from themselves, and they be left inexcusable.'[1] If men possessed a complete knowledge of the law of nature, their actions would be 'unavoidable', and the moral obligation they owe to God would not be 'freely' discharged. To the end, Locke insisted upon human free will, although he admitted to being unable to reconcile that with his belief in God's omnipotence.[2] Paradoxically, it is our ignorance of the law of nature that preserves our freedom to act as moral agents. But if no one has heretofore demonstrated the certainty of moral precepts, why does Locke obstinately insist that there is a body of certain moral knowledge not yet discovered by men?

We shall leave that question unanswered momentarily in order to take up a related issue, one which exposes additional facets of the problem. In some matters, 'especially those of religion, men are not permitted' to be wavering and uncertain; 'they must embrace and profess some tenets or other'. Some form of religious belief is absolutely necessary to one's status as a human being.[3] According to Locke, 'everyone has a concern in a future life, which he is *bound* to look after. This engages his thoughts in religion...*men, therefore, cannot be excused from understanding the words, and framing the general notions relating to religion, right.*'[4] If men must depend on their reasoning, or on the reasoning of a few philosophers, how is this requirement to be met? In the first place, the fact that there is a future life is 'established and made certain only by revelation', to which philosophers may claim no special access.[5] Secondly, it is evident both that 'some men's state and condition requires no great extent of knowledge' and that 'knowledge and science in general is the business only of those who are at ease and leisure'.[6] Nevertheless, the obligation to be just and pious lies upon all men, regardless of their condition or status. Even if it

---

[1] *Third Letter concerning Toleration, Works,* v, 160; *Second Vindication of the Reasonableness of Christianity,* p. 235.

[2] 'I own freely to you the weakness of my understanding, that though it be unquestionable that there is omnipotence and omniscience in God our Maker, and I cannot have a clearer perception of anything than that I am free, yet I cannot make freedom in man consistent with omnipotence and omniscience in God, though I am as fully persuaded of both as of any truths I most firmly assent to. And therefore I have long since given off the consideration of that question, resolving all into this short conclusion, that if it be possible for God to make a free agent, then man is free, though I see not the way of it.' Locke to William Molyneux, 20 January 1693, *Some Familiar Letters,* pp. 26–7; cf. *Journal,* 25 August 1676, MS. f. 1.

[3] *Conduct of the Understanding,* §6. Thus, it is religion which 'elevates us, as rational creatures, above brutes', *Essay,* IV, XVIII, §11; cf. *Journal,* 25–6 August 1676, MS. f. 1.

[4] *Conduct of the Understanding,* §§8, 19 (my italics); *A Letter concerning Toleration, Works,* v, 41. We are under 'an obligation...an absolute and indispensable necessity' to study the Scriptures, *Second Vindication of the Reasonableness of Christianity, Works,* VI, 228, 289, 321, 349–50, 356, 407–8. [5] *3BW,* p. 489. [6] *Conduct of the Understanding,* §§7, 37.

were possible for philosophy to discover the full extent of the law of nature, Locke refuses to allow God's egalitarian commandment to be fulfilled by any means which make the many dependent upon the few, however enlightened the few might be. 'Those things that every man ought sincerely to inquire into himself, and by meditation, study, search, and his own endeavours, attain the knowledge of, cannot be looked upon as the peculiar profession of any one sort of men.'[1]

At this juncture, the same question is raised in both the *Essay concerning Human Understanding* and *The Reasonableness of Christianity*: namely, can God be supposed to have placed men under an obligation which the vast majority of them cannot fulfil? If so, individuals denied the privilege of leisure would become the victims of a life of 'unavoidable sinning'.[2] In defending his negative reply to the question, Locke argues that no man is so occupied with his daily affairs as to have no time to read and study the Holy Scriptures. However ignorant he may be of philosophy, or of sophisticated demonstrations of God's existence, simple belief in divine revelation is all that God requires of him.[3] But if God has given men a commandment of strict obedience to his will, why does he accept from them less than that? The answer to this and to the previous question (p. 220) expresses the central theme of *The Reasonableness of Christianity*. God gave man a severe law to follow, a law of absolute good, because it was in conformity with his nature to do so.[4] Since he 'cannot choose' other than what is good, God could do nothing less. In other words, moral knowledge must be certain, and men must be subject to absolute obedience to the law of nature because God's qualities dictate such a structuring of the universe.

Still, the fact remains that men are not able to live in 'exact conformity' to the divine law, and their violation of any part of it must be regarded

---

[1] *A Letter concerning Toleration, Works*, v, 25. In fact, 'it is plain that the teaching of philosophy was no part of the design of divine revelation', *A Paraphrase of St. Paul's Epistles*, Preface (*Works*, vol. vii). Samuel Bold writes to Locke that the authors of the Scriptures 'used such words as the common sort of people did ordinarily use and in the sense they generally understood them, and did not send their hearers to the Rabbis, nor philosophers to learn the meaning of the words in which they delivered to them the mind of God. And if the first Fathers of the Church...had waived the mixing of the philosophical notions they had imbibed with the Christian doctrines...I am inclined to think their writings would have done religion more service...', Samuel Bold to Locke, 11 April 1699, MS. c. 4, folios 28–9. Locke replies: 'What you say about critics and critical interpretations, particularly of the Scriptures, is not only in my opinion true...', Locke to Samuel Bold, 16 May 1699.

[2] *Essay*, iv, xx, §§2, 3; *The Reasonableness of Christianity, Works*, vi, 6. 'I cannot imagine that God...would put poor men...under almost an absolute necessity of sinning perpetually against Him...', *Journal*, 20 March 1678, MS. f. 3.

[3] *Conduct of the Understanding*, §§3, 8; *3BW*, pp. 291, 299; *Second Letter concerning Toleration, Works*, v, 82; *Third Letter concerning Toleration, Works*, v, 157; *The Reasonableness of Christianity, Works*, vi, 147.

[4] *The Reasonableness of Christianity, Works*, vi, 11.

as a sin. Now, if God damned men for the least transgression of the law, he would be a cruel and malicious being for having created men as weak creatures and then punishing them for a weakness they could not avoid. Fortunately, this is not the situation. Rather, Locke argues, 'God, who knows our frailty, pities our weakness, and requires of us no more than we are able to do, and sees what was and what was not in our power, will judge as a kind and merciful Father'.[1] Therefore, he gave man the law of faith, promising salvation through man's belief in him. 'By the law of faith,' Locke writes, 'faith is allowed to supply the defect of full obedience; and so the believers are admitted to life and immortality as if they were righteous.'[2] Locke never implies that faith alone is sufficient, for 'unless we also obey His laws' we have no claim to salvation. But any man who believes in the Scriptures has 'all the faith necessary to a Christian and required to salvation', and Locke assumes that he will naturally 'show his faith by his works'.[3] Thus, even if men do not gain a certain knowledge of morality through the use of their reasoning faculties, they may still discover those 'infallible' principles of right action necessary to the securement of their 'eternal estate', provided they accept the basic principles of Christianity as set forth in the New Testament. Since the end is the same whether one follows the path of philosophy or theology, and since the latter is not only the 'easier' and 'surer' path, but also the only one that is *necessary*, there can be no question as to the priority, given a choice between faith and knowledge.[4]

There are 'a great many things', Locke observes, 'we take for unquestionable obvious truths, and easily demonstrable', of which we would be ignorant 'had revelation been silent'. The fact is, 'many are beholden to revelation who do not acknowledge it'. Moreover, 'it is no diminishing to revelation that reason gives its suffrage, too, to the truths revelation has discovered.[5] But it is our mistake to think that, because reason *confirms* them to us, we had the first certain knowledge of them from thence.'[6] Precisely the reverse is true. Reason 'confirms' what we believe, even as our faith is 'confirmed' by performing good works. The 'main end' of both the *Essay concerning Human Understanding* and *The Reasonableness of Christianity* is 'the honour and veneration of the Creator'. According to

---

[1] *Essay*, II, XXI, §54; *Works*, II, 316. 'The whole covenant and work of grace is the contrivance of God's infinite wisdom. What it is, and by what means He will dispense His grace, is known to us by revelation only...', *Third Letter concerning Toleration*, *Works*, V, 493.

[2] *The Reasonableness of Christianity*, *Works*, VI, 14.

[3] *3BW*, p. 299.

[4] 'Faith only, and inward sincerity, are the things that procure acceptance with God', *A Letter concerning Toleration*, *Works*, V, 28, 30.

[5] Note that the deference is paid to revelation, i.e. it is no 'diminishing' of revelation for men to consult reason, not the reverse.

[6] *The Reasonableness of Christianity*, *Works*, VI, 145 (my italics); cf. *Essay*, IV, I, §2.

the former, man successfully 'honours' God by exercising his powers of reasoning, thereby 'confirming' the rationality and goodness of the Creation. According to the latter, man 'honours' God through his faith and, by virtue of that faith, he is raised to a special, i.e. a truly religious, relationship to his Maker, one which sets him apart from all other of God's works. Locke writes: 'As men, we have God for our King, and are under the law of reason; as Christians, we have Jesus the Messiah for our King, and are under the law revealed by him in the gospel.'[1] It is a glorious thing to be a rational animal, but human rationality is only a part of the divine framework; and in the last analysis it is not the most important part of that framework. Faith is the essential ingredient of human salvation, a point Locke takes special pains to emphasize throughout his writings. As he assures Stillingfleet,

The Holy Scripture is to me, and always will be, the constant guide of my assent; and I shall always hearken to it, as containing infallible truth, relating to things of the highest concernment...and I shall presently condemn and quit any opinion of mine, as soon as I am shown that it is contrary to any revelation in the Holy Scripture.[2]

It is within such a context that the *Essay concerning Human Understanding* ought to be read, a context that makes the work a 'confirmation' of Locke's faith. At those crucial points in Locke's thought, when knowledge, reason, philosophy, and history disclose the ignorance and failings of men, and one is led to the brink of the abyss, it is faith that is 'allowed to supply the defect', providing a bridge to the immanent order and the wisdom of God. Locke's resolution of the philosophical problems discussed in the *Essay* parallels what he believed was God's own resolution of the human dilemma, as stated in the writings of Christianity. If, ultimately, the epistemological views of Locke, the Christian, cannot be satisfactorily reconciled with those of Locke, the philosopher, it is the faith of the former which ensures the salvation of the latter.

---

[1] *Second Vindication of the Reasonableness of Christianity, Works*, vi, 229.
[2] *BW*, p. 96. 'I read the revelation of the holy scripture with a full assurance that all it delivers is true', *3BW*, p. 341. 'I know no other infallible guide but the Spirit of God in the Scriptures', *Second Vindication of the Reasonableness of Christianity, Works*, vi, 356, 357, 359.

What is a nominal essence the essence of ?

by W. VON LEYDEN

One of Locke's original and important contributions to philosophy is his study of the nature of words and definition in Book III of his *Essay*, which he himself expected to lead to a new 'sort of logic and critic'.[1] Leibniz, otherwise one of his strictest censors, was the first to commend him for this particular interest.[2] Certainly, Locke's merit was to have attempted to sort out some of the issues involved in traditional philosophical doctrines and to introduce a number of clear definitions and relevant distinctions. Throughout, his chief project was to 'weigh distinctly' ideas as well as words—those 'great instruments of knowledge'[3]—and to deliver the human mind from fallacies caused by taking ambiguous or empty metaphysical words for things.[4] His underlying purpose of course was to inquire into the nature and extent (and hence the limits) of human knowledge. On this basis he was able to scrutinize effectively the different kinds of evidence or corroboration that can be legitimately advanced in support of different types of statement or different types of inquiry.[5]

In spite of his commendable intentions, however, Locke's new 'logic and critic' is far from perfect. It suffers from some remaining ambiguities, chiefly in his doctrine concerning substance and essences. As a result, there is much vacillation and even inconsistency in his thought.

Consider his treatment of the concept of substance first. He still adhered to the traditional ontology according to which there are such things as substances, each of which must be granted a 'real' essence. At the same time he believed that our idea of substance is obscure and perplexing. Though his distinction here between being and thought is appropriate, his views concerning the assumption that our idea of substance is im-

---

[1] *Essay concerning Human Understanding*, IV, XXI, §4.
[2] See Leibniz's second letter to Thomas Burnet of 22 November 1695, in C. I. Gerhardt (ed.), *Die philosophischen Schriften von G. W. Leibniz* (Berlin, 1875–90), III, 165. Cf. also H. Aarsleff, 'Leibniz on Locke on Language', *American Philosophical Quarterly*, I (1964), 165–88.
[3] *Essay*, IV, XXI, §4.   [4] *Ibid.* II, XIII, §18.
[5] Gilbert Ryle, 'John Locke on the Human Understanding' (Tercentenary Address, October 1932), London, 1933, pp. 24 and 38.

perfect oscillate between two rather different theories. At times he asserts that the difficulties concerning this notion can, in theory at least, be removed. His argument is that, though our idea of substance may be imperfect and often 'fail of being exactly conformable to things themselves',[1] it must ultimately be derivable from the real characteristics of things and to that extent perfectible. What he had in mind was the possibility of rendering inquiries into 'the nature and properties of the things themselves', their 'natural history',[2] more and more detailed and accurate. If it were argued that the problem concerning substance could never be solved empirically, Locke would have replied that the problem is logically soluble and in this sense reasonable and genuine. For he seriously assumed that 'spirits of a higher rank than those immersed in flesh may have as clear ideas of the radical constitution of substances as we have of a triangle, and so perceive how all their properties and operations flow from thence'.[3]

Evidently, then, 'substance' for Locke is a descriptive word, not unlike 'tree' or 'animal', except that it stands for the *ultimate* nature of things. On the other hand, his empiricism made him realize that the manner in which anyone (including 'angels') could arrive at the knowledge of the 'real essences' of things and think of substances at all clearly exceeded our conceptions. 'For whensoever we would proceed beyond these simple ideas we have from sensation and reflection, and dive further into the nature of things, we fall presently into darkness and obscurity, perplexedness and difficulties, and can discover nothing further but our own blindness and ignorance.'[4] This recognition together with the fact that both Locke's traditionally minded adversary, Bishop Stillingfleet, and also his more radically minded adversary, Bishop Berkeley, thought that he had gone so far as to 'discard' or 'banter' the idea of substance (at least in regard to matter),[5] shows him to have been one of the first to become sceptical of the traditional notion itself. Indeed, it is possible to suggest that occasionally Locke treats this notion as a 'fiction'. To the extent that he does, the traditional problem concerning substance could no longer have remained a genuine problem for him, nor could he have defended the view that 'substance' is in any sense a descriptive word.

Let us now consider the various aspects which Locke thought are involved in the concept of substance. The tangle of ambiguities in his own theory stems precisely from his failure to draw the distinctions in question as clearly as possible and to keep to them consistently.

---

[1] *Essay*, IV, IV, §11.
[2] *Ibid.* III, XI, §§24-5; cf. also II, XXIII, §§11-13.
[3] *Ibid.* III, XI, §23.
[4] *Ibid.* II, XXIII, §32.
[5] Cf. *ibid.* II, XIII, §§ 19-20; Edward Stillingfleet, *A Discourse in Vindication of the Doctrine of the Trinity* (London, 1696), pp. 233-4; Berkeley, *Philosophical Commentaries (Commonplace Book)*, ed. A. A. Luce (London, 1944), fo. 113, entry 89.

W. von Leyden

One way in which, according to Locke, we talk of substance is derived from the notion of pure substance in general. His claim is that we would find it impossible to do without this abstract notion, since the idea of something underlying and supporting the several distinct qualities that go to make up an individual object and causing them to be united in that thing always and necessarily forms part of our perceptions and thoughts of things. The word 'substance' then stands for a logical presupposition, i.e. the notion that the qualities characterizing an object require an owner, some peg or hook from which they may be supposed to hang. On Locke's view the presupposition is as necessary as the assumption, on the part of a certain legendary Indian philosopher,[1] that the earth requires something to support it in mid-air, 'something, he knew not what'. It is evident that, not unlike Aristotle's concept of matter, the Lockean concept of substance, though necessary, represents something featureless which as such cannot be descriptive of the physical world.

Another way in which, according to Locke, we talk of substance is when we perceive or think of a *particular* man, horse, or gold nugget and refer to it as one distinct entity, however much it may resemble any other individual thing. The idea of any such particular substance is, in terms of Locke's empiricist epistemology, a compound of several simple ideas like redness, hardness, fusibility, reasoning, willing, etc., which he thinks are found constantly together whenever we perceive or think of a given material object or mind. In this sense, then, a substance is constituted by a certain number of coexisting and constantly conjoined properties which belong to the particular thing which supports and unites them. While the idea of certain coexisting qualities is comparatively clear, the notion that there is something underlying these but unknown to us is again obscure.

Locke uses the word 'substance' in yet another way. He points out that we can think of particular *sorts* of substances such as gold (not a particular gold nugget), man, or horse, and even of more general, in fact ultimate sorts, viz. God, finite spirits, and body.[2] He raises the question whether, when we apply the word 'substance' to these three main classes of things, the word denotes one and the same idea of substance throughout or three different ideas. He suggests no answer to this question, except that he rejects the idea of one common nature of substance (as was in Spinoza's mind) and also that of two or three different kinds of substance (as suggested by Descartes). What he concedes is that the name of any given sort of substance conjures up the idea of something that, though it may never be adequately definable, can nevertheless be investigated and, if fully discovered, described.

[1] *Essay*, II, XIII, §19; II, XXIII, §2.   [2] *Ibid.* II, XIII, §18; II, XXVII, §2.

226

What is a nominal essence the essence of?

A new difficulty now arises. In using the name of a sort of substance such as man, horse, or gold, we might be thought to indicate that we know from experience what this kind of thing is. However, some sorts of substance, for example dragons, do not exist and therefore do not describe anything in reality. The nature of others which exist offers an endless scope for scientific inquiry and may never be finally determined. Hence, though in either of these two cases some definition of a sort of substance is possible, this would not be a 'real' definition: in the former case because there is nothing in reality to which the name of the sort of substance applies; in the latter because no investigation, not even a very full one, can ever elicit what a given class of things is really like, or whether there are in fact any fixed natures or unalterable species in reality. The difficulty is the basis of Locke's distinction between the 'real' and 'nominal' essences of things.

This celebrated distinction is itself by no means free from confusion. As Locke himself points out,[1] it is possible to speak of 'real essences' in two different senses. The resulting ambiguity, as I shall attempt to show, interferes with a clear understanding of the issues involved in the Lockean distinction.

One meaning of the phrase 'real essence' which Locke has in mind refers again to particular substances; the other to kinds or classes of substance. By the real essence of a particular substance such as a gold nugget he means the internal constitution of its imperceptible parts on which its sensible and discoverable qualities, e.g. its shape, weight, and colour, depend. His opinion is that this kind of real essence, i.e. the internal atomic constitution of a physical object, is necessarily unknown.[2] The reason for this agnosticism was not only that the real nature of atoms happened to be imperceptible in his day, but also that no empiricist would have accepted an *a priori* argument concerning the nature of atoms as a possible basis for scientific discovery. In spite of the fact that on Locke's own showing the real essence of a particular thing is unknown, he regards the idea of such an individual essence as wholly legitimate and as the primary meaning of the word 'essence'. He claims that this word is 'still used' when we 'speak of the essence of *particular* things, without giving them any name'.

On the other hand, when Locke speaks of the real essence of any of the several *species* of substances, what he has in mind is the traditional theory of 'genus' and 'species', i.e. something like Aristotle's natural kinds or even the Platonic 'forms or moulds, wherein all natural things

[1] *Essay*, III, III, §§15 ff.
[2] *Ibid.* IV, III, §§16 and 25; IV, VI, §14; IV, XVI, §12.

that exist are cast, and do equally partake'.[1] However, Locke looks upon the supposition that such 'sortal'[2] substances have themselves real essences as 'wholly useless and unserviceable to any part of our knowledge'.[3] He goes so far as to consider the assumption not only obscure but 'wholly unintelligible'.[4] One of his reasons for rejecting it is that, as in the case of the primary meaning of 'essence', it stands for something 'they know not what'. Secondly, the notion of the real essence of a species represents something that is *necessarily* imperceptible and not only happens to be so as a result of our imperfect sense-organs (so that, if our senses were more acute, we might be able to perceive the nature of a species of things more or less accurately).

Thirdly, and Locke was the first to recognize this, the notion is not only conceptually problematic but also factually erroneous. In a celebrated passage of the *Essay*[5] he counters the theory that the meanings of general words are common properties with the vigorous challenge: 'And I demand what are the alterations which may, or may not be made in a *horse* or *lead*, without making either of them to be of another species?...if any one will regulate himself herein by supposed *real* essences, he will, I suppose, be at a loss: and he will never be able to know when anything precisely ceases to be of the species of a *horse* or *lead*.' The challenge is unanswerable.[6] It indicates that (*a*) there are no fixed essences or common properties of things, (*b*) our knowledge of what an object is or how it will behave can never be certain or necessary, and (*c*) it is experience only which enables us to say what the behaviour of an object is likely to be and whether it is more conveniently classified as belonging to one species rather than another, or whether it is possibly falling between two classes of things as in the case of borderline cases such as 'monsters and changelings'.[7] On Locke's view, then, the so-called essence of, for example, horse, has no sharp lines of demarcation. With the discovery of a rather different race of horses we should either have to modify our description of horse and our definition of the word 'horse', or alternatively use the word so as to exclude its applicability to the newly discovered race.

Though the first of the two meanings of the phrase 'real essence' discussed by Locke, i.e. that relating to an individual's substance, appears to him 'more rational', there is no doubt that the second, i.e. that relating to a species, cannot have been so unintelligible to him as he tries to make

---

[1] *Essay*, III, III, §17.   [2] Locke's own expression, *ibid.* III, III, §15.
[3] *Ibid.* III, III, §17.   [4] *Ibid.* III, VI, §10.
[5] *Ibid.* III, III, §13. See also IV, IV, §§13–14.
[6] See M. Lazerowitz, 'The Existence of Universals', *Mind*, LV (1946), 12; also R. I. Aaron, *The Theory of Universals* (Oxford, 1952), pp. 24–5.
[7] *Essay*, III, III, §17; III, VI, §§16–17; III, VI, §23; IV, IV, §§13–14; IV, IV, §16.

out.[1] He concedes that, when speaking of the essences of several sorts of things, we have in mind something of an objective and truly scientific criterion whereby to decide what these essences are; that therefore they might well be thought to have a *real* foundation in nature. 'I would not here be thought to forget, much less to deny, that Nature, in the production of things, makes several of them alike: there is nothing more obvious, especially in the races of animals, and all things propagated by seed.'[2] It appears then that both the foundation and criterion of the essence of a natural kind or of a sort of substance is the 'similitude of things': that resemblances, or better still 'relevant' resemblances, are the device by which God or nature has more or less precisely delimited the boundaries between the several species and kinds of things. This concession to the Platonic or Aristotelian approach to the problem caused a certain vacillation and lack of precision in some of Locke's pronouncements about real essences. That is to say, it is not always clear whether, when speaking of a real essence, he has in mind an individual object or a class of objects.

I will now explain what Locke means by the nominal essences of things and then point to a similar ambiguity arising in this part of his doctrine.

A nominal essence, Locke claims, is the 'most familiar' use of the word 'essence'. By it he understands a man-made, abstract idea of groups of sensible qualities or powers consistently found together in objects which resemble one another and which bear the same general name such as 'man', 'horse' or 'gold'. The reason for saying that men make the species or sorts of things is that it is men's understanding which 'frames' any of the abstract general ideas denoted by a general word. In Locke's opinion the process of abstraction leading to the general idea of a kind of thing consists in this: in imagination one strips off or eliminates from among the simple empirical qualities that characterize a given object those in respect of which it differs from objects which in other respects resemble it closely.[3] As the final product of this process of abstraction there emerges a general idea of a sort of thing, in which all the characteristics common to a given set of resembling objects are combined. For instance, Locke believes that one can frame a concept or abstract general idea of gold. In this there would be combined the ideas of qualities consistently found together in any lump of gold, i.e. yellowness, weight, fusibility, solubility in *aqua regia*, etc. Details of the difficulties besetting Locke's conceptualism need not concern us here. I want to concentrate on the ambiguity mentioned before, which is characteristic of Locke's whole treatment of the

[1] See particularly *Essay*, III, VI, §6.
[2] *Ibid.* III, III, §13; III, VI, §28; also Locke's letter to William Molyneux, 20 January 1692/3 (*The Works of John Locke*, 10 vols., London, 1823, VIII, 305–6).
[3] *Essay*, III, III, §6.

issues under discussion. The ambiguity arises if we ask: what is a nominal essence the essence of?

The answer to this question is by no means obvious nor does Locke himself provide one that is clear-cut. Possible answers are that a nominal essence is the essence *either* (a) of the finished product of Locke's alleged process of abstraction, i.e. a general *idea* or class concept, *or* (b) of individuals, *or* (c) of both a class concept and the individuals that fall under this concept. In my view, Locke's approach to the problem is ambiguous in that he appears to be in favour now of this and now of that answer. I believe there are at least two explanations for this uncertainty. First, there is a corresponding, though by no means frequent, lack of certainty on his part with regard to the question 'what is a real essence the essence of?' Secondly, Locke sometimes talks of the nominal essence of a particular thing rather than of a species, because when talking of real essences it is usually that of a particular thing and not that of a species which he has in mind.

In recent years Professor P. T. Geach has maintained, rightly it would seem, that there is a nominal essence of individuals. The point of his argument is that there cannot be such a thing as *being the same* without being the *same such-and-such*.[1] That is to say, the continued use of a proper name '*A*' always presupposes a continued reference to an individual as being the same *x*, where *x* is some common noun (for example, 'man', 'river' or 'city') and expresses the nominal essence of the individual called '*A*'. Hence, being the same individual means being the same *x*, so that an individual belongs to a kind such as *x* or alternatively the kind is predicable of the individual. Geach's point can also be expressed, in a way contrary to modern existentialist doctrine, by asserting that no existing thing can be considered uncombined with essence, since existent particulars are left void of content if their essence is abstracted or omitted. In other words, a particular man cannot be a completely undefined being, something which might be or become anything else. There is, after all, some truth in Aristotle's teaching that a thing is not at all times potentially any or every other thing.[2] Nor can it be denied that there are reasons (though perhaps not always very definite ones) why a man is called a *human* being.

Now Geach also maintains that Locke held the opposite view, i.e. that one can identify a particular thing without identifying it as *a such-and-such*,

---

[1] Cf. P. T. Geach, 'Good and Evil', *Analysis*, XVII, 2 (December, 1956), 34; *Mental Acts* (London, 1957), chapter 16; (with G. E. M. Anscombe) *Three Philosophers* (Oxford, 1961), pp. 8, 10, 86, 87; *Reference and Generality* (Ithaca, New York, 1962), pp. 43 ff.; G. E. M. Anscombe and S. Körner, symposium on 'Substance', in *Aristotelian Society*, supp. vol. XXXVIII (1964), pp. 70 and 80 ff.

[2] *Metaphysics*, Θ, VII, 1049 a 1–2; Λ, II, 1069 b 28–31.

and that therefore there is no nominal essence of individuals. In this interpretation of Locke's view, I believe, Geach is only partially right. True, Locke often speaks of 'the nominal essences of species or kinds', of abstract ideas as the 'essences of sorts or species of things', of 'properties belonging only to species, and not to individuals'.[1] Similarly, he holds that 'universality belongs not to things themselves',[2] and that the qualities or properties that represent a nominal essence are not so annexed to any particular object as to be essential to it or inseparable from it.[3] Also, in his view nominal essences, unlike real essences, are incorruptible and therefore independent of individuals.[4]

On the other hand, just as he speaks of the 'real essence' of *a* thing, Locke speaks of the colour, weight, fusibility, etc. of 'that parcel of matter which makes the ring on my finger' as '*its* nominal essence'.[5] He also says 'I have often mentioned a real essence, distinct in substances from those abstract ideas of them, which I call *their* "nominal essence"'.[6] Accordingly he holds that '*having* the essence of any species' is that 'which makes *anything* to be of that species', so that nothing can be a man 'but what *has* the essence of that species'.[7] Or again, 'between the *nominal essence* and the *name* there is so near a connexion, that the name of any sort of things cannot be attributed to any particular being but what *has* this essence'.[8] And finally, 'why do we say, "This is a horse, and that a mule"? ...How comes any *particular thing* to be of this or that sort, but because *it has that nominal essence*?'[9] To judge by all the latter quotations, it does not seem right to follow Geach in charging Locke with denying that there are nominal essences of individuals, nor to accuse Locke of assuming that one can identify a thing without identifying it as a man, horse, river, or plant respectively.

It is of course true that for Locke nominal essences are independent of individuals, i.e. there can be nominal essences regardless of whether there are any individuals in the world to which we would attribute the names of the sorts of things to which the nominal essences belong. For instance, there are nominal essences of unicorns and mermaids, and these are as intelligible, complete, and permanent as those of men or triangles.[10] But this only means that a nominal essence is an idea, not a fact, and that therefore no nominal essence is a sufficient condition of the existence of any particular thing. It does not mean that it is not true that a nominal essence is the necessary condition, if not of the existence of the particular thing which falls under it, at least of its identification.

[1] *Essay*, III, VI, §6.
[2] *Ibid.* III, III, §11.
[3] *Ibid.* III, VI, §6.
[4] *Ibid.* III, III, §19.
[5] *Ibid.* III, III, §18 (my italics).
[6] *Ibid.* III, VI, §6 (my italics).
[7] *Ibid.* III, III, §12 (my italics).
[8] *Ibid.* III, III, §16.
[9] *Ibid.* III, VI, §7 (my italics).
[10] *Ibid.* III, III, §19.

W. von Leyden

In sum, then, it would seem that on Locke's own view the nominal essence of any given individual object is that which we impose on it by giving it a name such as 'cat', 'river' or 'city'. The name would be *its* name, just as the nominal essence would be *its* nominal essence.[1] Alternatively, we might say that Locke's theory of nominal essences implies that, if we were to change the general idea of cat, or river or city, we could not then say of *everything* that we now call 'cat', 'river' or 'city' that it is still a cat, river or city. This, too, would seem to show that on Locke's view nominal essences are of *particulars*. If, on the other hand, it is urged that a nominal essence is, after all, an abstract idea and that an abstract idea cannot belong to an individual object, it may be said in reply that what the doctrine concerning nominal essence, on Locke's as well as on Geach's view, amounts to is merely that there are substantial predicates which apply necessarily to the individuals to whom they apply: Stalin could not have been Stalin without being a man and an animal.

Two last points may be considered. Suppose one were to argue against Geach's view of individuals having nominal essences. The case which comes to mind is when the word 'same' is applied and a name given to a particular object, even if it is by no means clear what 'sort' of a particular it is one is observing or talking about. For instance,[2] I might say that I saw today the same figure of a man on the top of the hill, which I have come to call '*A*', as I saw yesterday and the day before, although it is by no means clear whether what I saw is a real man, a large anthropoid ape, a robot, or a scarecrow fluttering in the wind. In dealing with this by no means ill-conceived example of a lack of precise connexion between an individual's proper name and the assignment of a classificatory scheme one might say that the uncertainty involved is the result of partial ignorance and could be removed as soon as a (putatively) correct classification has been ascertained. Alternatively, it may be perfectly clear *to me*, although perhaps not to others, that '*A*' is the name of a man rather than of an orang-utan or a scarecrow. In this case, as Locke himself points out,[3] the proper name applied by me to the particular thing in question would be connected *in my mind* with certain ideas, and hence my calling the object '*A*' would imply that I had classified it as a man and that for me at least it has this particular nominal essence rather than another.

Secondly, the confusion in Locke's doctrine of nominal essences which I have discussed is not altogether unpardonable. The use of such words

---

[1] *Essay*, III, III, §16.
[2] Cf. Körner, 'Substance', *Aristotelian Society*, supp. vol. xxxviii, p. 81.
[3] *Essay*, III, III, §3.

What is a nominal essence the essence of?

as 'same' or 'our' can be equally confusing. The word 'same' is ambiguous in that to speak of identity may mean either that there is one and the same particular, or alternatively that there is one and the same sort, or kind, or type of particular thing.[1] Pointing to a Ford Convertible on the motorway and exclaiming 'this is the same car as the one I bought early this year' I may mean to say either that the two are the same in kind, i.e. that both are of the same make and type of body, though the one on the motorway belongs to a Mr X and is brand-new and the other is in my garage at home and was bought second-hand ten months ago. Alternatively, my statement may mean that the car on the motorway is numerically identical with my own particular car and is the one that was stolen from me last week. The personal pronoun 'our' allows of similar differences of use. Referring to the car on the motorway as the same as 'our' car, I may tell my children either that it is of the same make and type of body as our own car at home, or alternatively that they are now face to face with the particular car which we reported missing last week.

The bearing of all this on the topic of this essay is that the ambiguity in Locke's doctrine of nominal essence arises precisely to the extent that he left it undetermined whether on his view essences belong to particulars or alternatively to a species or sort of thing. Despite his distinctions between real and nominal essences and between different senses of 'substance', there thus remains in Locke's doctrine a good deal of confusion. But then throughout the seventeenth century the same ambiguity attached to the word 'substance'. For it is by no means always clear whether the concept of matter for Descartes or that of a monad for Leibniz is meant to stand for something particular and individual or alternatively for something generic and universal.

[1] Cf. O. R. Jones, 'Identity and Countability', *Analysis*, xxiv (June 1964), 201 ff.

The essayist in his *Essay*

by ROSALIE COLIE

I

Nowadays, when Locke is so out of favour with philosophers of great analytic rigour and so much a favourite of historians of philosophy and of ideas, it might be profitable to look at his major work with an eye to its powers of attraction, or lack of them. If, as I have been variously informed, Locke's thought was so often muddled and muddling, his style so awkward, how does it happen that his ideas, of all the thinkers' ideas in an age distinguished for its philosophers, were so widely read by his contemporaries and by educated men, European as well as English, for a good hundred years? It is all very well to say loftily that since most men are not philosophers, they will naturally choose the easiest way to what they hope or suppose is philosophical enlightenment, and that Locke's easy style and sloppy thinking offered them such a primrose path. Very well: but in that case, the aspiring reader had to get through long passages of grim impersonality, such as the major part of Book II, on ideas, without the rewards of folksy style or friendly encouragement from the author. Or one might venture, in a twentieth-century crypto-insight, the suggestion that most people prefer medium to message, and since Locke's medium was relatively attractive, his message was got over by that means. A corollary to this axiom is that if the message is trivial, the medium must be attractive, to seem thereby the more significant. Unfortunately, such paradigms of packaging information do not help us much in the case of Locke, whose packaging has often been unfavourably compared to his philosophical contemporaries' skilful manipulations of style. By comparison with the magnificence of Bacon's architectonics and clarity, with the incisive duplicities of Hobbes, and with the witty fluency of Hume, Locke's style can seem as trivial as his thoughts seem to some. Neither medium nor message appears to be worth much ink or paper.

History tends to redeem Locke from such dismissal; his publishers and his readers used up much paper and ink on his works, in particular on *An Essay concerning Human Understanding*. We know that the book was widely read by men in the Republic of Letters, and by women and children

The essayist in his Essay

as well: two of Locke's most enthusiastic devotees and defenders were seventeenth-century bluestockings, Lady Masham and Catherine Cockburn; and Lady Masham's son was only one of the many children, known and unknown to the philosopher, brought up on Lockean principles. The *Essay* was translated into French under the author's supervision and into Latin as a commercial venture by the Churchills, Locke's publishers.[1] For its initial appearance, the *Essay* had been epitomized and that epitome separately published for distribution among Locke's friends and acquaintances—and, it appears, among their friends and acquaintances as well.[2] In Locke's lifetime, the *Essay* went into four editions (1690, 1694, 1695, 1700), and the posthumous 1706 edition carried the alterations and improvements he had made between the 1700 edition and his death. There are many copies of the *Essay* in public collections bearing evidence of their owners' efforts to understand as directed; no copy attests to such devotion as James Tyrrell's magnificent attempt at a variorum,[3] but many copies have been scrupulously brought up to date by marginal notation, and many copies of an early edition have sheets of emendations and errata bound in from a later. Library and auction catalogues give some indication of the range of persons who thought they had to own, if not to read, Mr Locke's *Essay*; his collected works, first published in 1714, went into edition after edition in the eighteenth and nineteenth centuries; even to-day, for all its defects, Locke's work does a brisk business, under the care of more or less devoted editors.[4]

It was not simply middling men untrained in systematic thinking who read Locke's *Essay*. In England, as Mr Yolton's study has shown, the ideas expressed in the book met with immediate and widespread interest and criticism, much of it trivial but some of it intelligent in the highest degree.[5] Stillingfleet, King, and Norris were considerable critics; Collins, Burthogge, and Toland were no negligible advocates. What finally justifies Locke's philosophical existence, I suppose, is the part his ideas played in the development of the thought of Berkeley and Hume; but considerable as this effect was, it was by no means his only claim to attention. Locke's

---

[1] *Essai philosophique concernant l'entendement humain*, trans. Pierre Coste (Amsterdam, 1700); *De intellectu humano*, trans. E. Burridge (London, 1701).

[2] *Bibliothèque universelle*, VIII (1688), 44–142; *Abrégé d'un ouvrage intitulé Essai philosophique touchant l'entendement*, trans. J. LeClerc (Amsterdam, 1688); John Wynne, *An Abridgement of Mr. Locke's Essay concerning Human Understanding* (London, 1696); other abstractions, syllabuses, contractions, and condensations of the *Essay* were made through the nineteenth century.

[3] British Museum, shelfmark C.122.f.14.

[4] Of the devoted editors, mention in particular must be made of W. von Leyden, ed., *John Locke: Essays on the Law of Nature* (Oxford, 1954); Peter Laslett, ed., *John Locke: Two Treatises, of Government* (Cambridge, 1960); Philip Abrams, ed., *Two Tracts on Government* (Cambridge, 1967); and of Dr E. S. de Beer's forthcoming edition of Locke's correspondence.

[5] John W. Yolton, *John Locke and the Way of Ideas* (Oxford, 1956).

Rosalie Colie

works crossed national boundaries in a remarkable way: Leibniz and Bayle read and criticized elements of the *Essay*; Barbeyrac and the natural lawyers for whom he provided the text had to take Locke into account in their redefinitions of their subject; the partisanship of Diderot and Voltaire is well known. The Lockean psychology made its way into teaching, and into stranger places, as the fiction of Richardson, Sterne, and Diderot all testifies.[1] His political ideas, adapted to various local conditions and purposes, made their mark in the New World as well as the Old.[2] As Christianity became more and more reasonable, Mr Locke's authority was cited for that purifying process.

In the context of the discursive writing of his own age and of the next great age of prose, where he had formidable competition, Locke's work was strikingly effective. This paper attempts to examine some of the reasons for that effectiveness in the case of the *Essay*, simple-mindedly beginning at the beginning. This beginning is, I think, the book's title; *An Essay concerning Human Understanding*. Locke's titles, published and unpublished, are interesting—though he certainly published a book definitively named *Two Treatises of Government*, his tendency was toward more tentative titles—*Some Considerations of the Lowering of Interest, and Raising the Value of Money*; *Further Considerations concerning Raising the Value of Money*; *A Letter on Toleration*, and *A Second Letter*, and *A Third*; *Some Thoughts concerning Education*—and the headings of his notes, too, indicate that Locke worked in terms of exploration, heading his notes *Adversaria*, *Commonplacebooks*, and so on. In contrast to the titles of some of the other major philosophical works of the period—*A Discourse upon Method*; *Principia Philosophiae* or *Mathematica* or whatever; *Leviathan*; *Ethica*—Locke's titles rarely sound the note of self-confident definition characteristic of contemporary philosophical usage. A shrewd critic might unsympathetically observe that Locke was trying to escape from justified criticism of his work by giving it a title indicating work-in-progress: we know from his own utterances, indeed, that this *was* one of Locke's intentions. But a title indicating a degree of tentativeness does not automatically protect an author from serious consideration, nor did Locke expect it to do so. He knew very well, on the contrary, that to publish at all implied an author's seriousness as well as his right to be taken seriously. Taken seriously he has been ever since the *Essay* was first launched into the world.

It is not my purpose to defend Locke's untidiness, which offers great

---

[1] See Dr A. R. Standley's forthcoming work on this subject.

[2] For a brief survey of Locke's importance in the colonies, see Caroline Robbins's *The Eighteenth Century Commonwealthman* (Cambridge, Mass., 1959); also J. R. Pole, *Political Representation in England and the Origins of the American Republic* (London and New York, 1966).

inconvenience to scholars without much rigour, like myself; nor do I attempt to contort his sprawling thoughts into a pure and classical consistency: I am not equipped for such exercise, even if I would undertake it.[1] Rather, I wish to try to understand some of that untidiness, by looking at the *Essay* as an *essay*, by examining some of the ways Locke managed to make his book readable for so many readers. To this end, I shall stress some of the literary elements of his remarkable book, especially its exploitations of the generic and rhetorical possibilities in the essay form itself.

First of all, a word about the word: a weighing, a trial, an attempt, an experiment. The term's literary currency in the Renaissance derived from Montaigne's brilliant choice of title to his collection of meditations and *pensées*, his disquisitions and discourses, his self-examinations and self-measurements. That he meant his readers to recognize the meanings implicit in the title is evident from his emphasis on his own *impresa*, the hanging-scale everlastingly taking the weight of his successive thoughts and emotions, of his personality and of his total life. Bacon extended the range of style possible in the essay, a style which, taken together with his influence as a thinker, had particular meanings for men of Locke's generation; furthermore, in his nominalist way, Bacon observed that though the title was a modern invention, the thing itself had existed in antiquity, in Seneca's Epistles. In the seventeenth century, the word was also used to mean a draft of a piece of writing, customarily discursive or informal rather than poetic or dramatic. All these meanings help us somewhat to understand Locke's peculiar choice of the word *Essay* for the title of a philosophical discourse: the essay weighed things, assayed and tested notions and ideas.[2] In those essays derived chiefly from Montaigne's model, emphasis tended to lie upon process, development, growth, and change; as Morris Croll's pioneering studies indicated, that emphasis was reflected in the shifting, variable style of Montaigne and his imitators, concerned to show a man thinking rather than the finished thoughts of a writer.[3] Locke of course knew Montaigne, whose works he possessed;[4] by the late 1680s, or whenever he finally settled upon a title for his great work, however, he would not have needed direct knowledge of Montaigne's work to realize some of the advantages and possibilities of the essay form for his kind of philosophy. What is remarkable is that he *did* realize some of

---

[1] In any case, I have argued for different criteria of consistency elsewhere, 'John Locke and the Publication of the Private', *Philological Quarterly*, XLV (1966), 24–45.
[2] Henry Peacham's title to his book of very personal essays offers these notions in a cluster: *The Truth of our Times: Revealed out of one Mans Experience by Way of Essay* (London, 1638).
[3] Morris Croll, *Style, Rhetoric, and Rhythm* (Princeton, 1966), especially chapters II, IV, V.
[4] See John Harrison and Peter Laslett, *The Library of John Locke*, The Oxford Bibliographical Society, n.s. XIII (Oxford, 1965), 191.

those possibilities, which meant that he chose to step down from the high chair of philosophy to ask his questions in an informal genre requiring an informal style: in Locke's effort to laicize philosophy, his choice of title and mode were of major importance.

The essayist had a certain choice in rhetorical strategies; at one end of the spectrum (for example Bacon), he could formulate considerable and even ponderous thoughts into neat aphorisms; at the other (for example Montaigne), he was permitted considerable randomness, allowed to juxtapose notions and ideas in a manner later to be christened, by Locke himself, the association of ideas. Whichever his dominant style, the essayist was allowed deviations from it: as Croll's analyses of the great essayists of the late sixteenth and early seventeenth centuries demonstrate, flexibility, humility, liveliness were the criteria of such form and style. In writers like Pierre Nicole, some of whose *Essais* Locke indeed translated,[1] he could have found something of the elegance and the freshness of the ideal essay style. Crisp and aphoristic or loose and rambling, the essayist spoke directly and personally to his readers; in exchange for the frankness with which the essayist appeared to present his thinking self, he was allowed certain liberties from logical rigour; there was, furthermore, a screen of formality conventionally thin between the essayist and his readers, so that vernacular language and syntax could alternate with passages of remarkable balance and aphoristic detachment. Though dialectic is often present in essays, characteristically it is truncated or played down; logical steps are taken, but the system of logic followed is more likely to be personal than scholastic. By the exercise of a cunning rhetoric of disarming informality, the essayist gets his way; by a show of anti-rhetorical panache, the essayist's *genus humile* tends to conceal his concentrated effort to attract others to his point of view—conceals, then, his own concern for and reliance upon the devices of rhetoric and style.

The seventeenth century witnessed the coming of age of the essay form, so well suited to secular and religious meditation and speculation. In England, the 'honesty' proclaimed by theorists of 'Attic' prose style, and demonstrated largely in essays, was reinforced from other directions than the merely stylistic. Plain-style prose took some of its impetus from the Protestant preachers' insistence upon direct transcription of religious experience and the clear exposition of scriptural cruces; their contributions to the formation of an 'empirical' style in hortatory prose ran parallel to the scientists' insistence upon unvarnished descriptive exactness as the proper medium for their kind of work; both religious thinkers and

[1] For Locke's translations of Nicole, see Pierre Nicole, *Discourses* (London, 1828); and von Leyden, ed., *John Locke: Essays on the Law of Nature*, pp. 252–7.

The essayist in his Essay

scientists tended to write in essay form and even to entitle their works, from time to time, 'Essays'.[1] In Locke's background lay Bacon and the stylistic programme of the Royal Society, of which he was a nearly silent member, as well as the rigorous simplifications of the Protestant preachers; he knew, also, the work of Montaigne, Charron, Bacon, Lipsius, Attic-style theorists of the early Renaissance, as well as their descendants into his own generation, Guez de Balzac, Antoine Arnauld, and Pierre Nicole.[2]

One of the interesting things about Locke's *Essay* accounted for by the genre is the range of styles Locke employed in his work, even in its first edition. His *Essay* is an anthological document, somehow managing to accommodate within its irregular boundaries many different tones, from a reduced factual or formulaic style to a loose anecdotal one; passages of extended formal analysis, of words, ideas, and principles, alternate with passages of easy exposition, with pseudo-dialogue, with canny variations upon traditional rhetorical commonplaces, with interior monologues, *pensées*, and self-analyses. Some of the charm, as well as much of the difficulty, of the *Essay* lies in this variety and unevenness; one cannot tell, from one section to the next, what tone the author will take, or how he will direct his readers to conduct themselves in response to him.[3]

On the whole, Locke adopted the apologetic pose, with its attendant false modesty, hallowed in the rhetorical tradition generally and particularly appropriate to the middle-style essayist, always casting his work to his readers before it had been polished to perfection. Locke's work, he assures his readers, was composed only at broken intervals and across decades of his life (facts which in his case can be documented); it was published only after his friends had persuaded him into it (again, sufficiently true to be said, if not the entire truth): in this case, the official apologetics of rhetoric coincide with the truth of the matter. But Locke is by no means rhetorical only when his biography justifies it; again and again, extended metaphors break through the prosaic surface of his expositions, the great light metaphors, the *camera obscura* metaphor, the *tabula rasa* itself, to show his command over 'style'.[4] But surely the sense one carries away from the *Essay* is that it is largely anti-rhetorical, that long passages of unrelieved exposition and analysis must be got through before one is offered the occasional refreshment of a green thought in a green shade. Locke of course overtly repudiates style—'I am not nice about

---

[1] For comments on both the pulpit and the scientific efforts to simplify the English language, see R. F. Jones, *The Seventeenth Century* (Palo Alto, 1951).

[2] See Harrison and Laslett, pp. 75 (Arnauld), 78 (Bacon), 79 (Balzac), 91–2 (Boyle), 105–6 (Charron), 175 (Lipsius), 195 (Nicole).

[3] I hope elsewhere to remark on the various styles and strata of the *Essay*.

[4] See R. S. Crane, 'Notes on the Organization of Locke's "Essay"', *The Idea of the Humanities* (Chicago and London, 1966), I, 288–301.

Rosalie Colie

phrases' (*Essay*, II, XXI, §71)[1]—and rhetoric, which he polemically treats as sophistry:

> I confess, in Discourses, where we seek rather Pleasure and Delight, than Information and Improvement, such Ornaments as are borrowed from them, can scarce pass for Faults. But yet, if we would speak of Things as they are, we must allow, that all the Art of Rhetorick, besides Order and Clearness, all the artificial and figurative application of Words Eloquence hath invented, are for nothing else, but to insinuate wrong *Ideas*, move the Passions, and thereby mislead the Judgment; and so indeed are perfect cheat: And therefore however laudable or allowable Oratory may render them in Harangues and popular Addresses, they are certainly, in all Discourses that pretend to inform or instruct, wholly to be avoided; and where Truth and Knowledge are concerned, cannot but be thought a great fault, either of the Language or Person that makes use of them. (III, x, §34, 2nd edition, 1694.)

Let us examine some passages in the *Essay*, to see to what extent they are used to insinuate right ideas, and to win his audience to the way of those ideas.

II

That Locke was capable of performing from well within the rhetorical tradition, his two prefatory epistles make entirely clear. Both observe the requisite modesty-trope,[2] graduated to suit the different persons to whom they are addressed. In the 'Epistle Dedicatory', unchanged throughout the editions, Locke spoke to Thomas Herbert, Earl of Pembroke, whose patronage had indeed been of considerable service to him and who, because of his private studies, was a suitable recipient of a book on the subject of human understanding. Locke presents himself, as decorum demanded, in the role of Pembroke's social and intellectual inferior. Pembroke is mightily praised: he is

> allowed to have got so intimate an Acquaintance with her [truth], in her more retired recesses. Your Lordship is known to have so far advanced your Speculations in the most abstract and general Knowledge of Things, beyond the ordinary reach or common Methods, that your Allowance and Approbation of the Designe of this Treatise, will at least preserve it from being condemned without reading; and will prevail to have those Parts a little weighed, which might otherwise, perhaps, be thought to deserve no Consideration, for being somewhat out of the common road.

Locke appeals to Pembroke's authority as a thinker and as the appropriate patron for such a thesis, in order to bolster his argument for the publica-

[1] Unless otherwise specified, all quotations from the *Essay* are from the first edition of 1690.
[2] E. R. Curtius, *European Literature of the Latin Middle Ages* (Harper Torchbook, 1963), pp. 83–9, for the 'affected modesty trope' and 'things never thought before trope'.

tion of the book; the *Essay* is derogated, very gently, by being treated as the forerunner of the greater thoughts of the earl himself. When Pembroke shall 'please to oblige the Publick with some of those large and comprehensive Discoveries, you have made, of Truths hitherto unknown, unless to some few, to whom your Lordship has been pleased not wholly to conceal them', then truth herself shall be unveiled in her purity, and all other assays of truth, including the present one, shall become supererogatory.

This alone were a sufficient Reason, were there no other, why I should Dedicate this piece to your Lordship; and its having some little Correspondence with some parts of that nobler and vast System of the Sciences, your Lordship has made so new, exact, and instructive a Draught of, I think it Glory enough, if your Lordship permit me to boast, that here and there I have fallen into some Thoughts not wholly different from yours.

This compliment is twisted yet another way: Locke urges his *Essay* as a guide to Pembroke's conduct, so that he shall himself be willing to publish his own, by definition far greater, speculations in due course.

If your Lordship think fit, that by your encouragement this should appear in the World, I hope it may be a Reason, some time or other, to lead your Lordship farther; and you will allow me to say, That you here give the World an earnest of something, that, if they can bear with this, will be truly worth their expectation.

Should the sentiment in this sentence prove too insubordinate in a client, it finds its proper qualification in the next sentence, where Pembroke's superior position is made clear in language particularly suited to the proprietor of a great house, in imagery used again and again by poets in praise of their patron's generosity, as Ben Jonson praised his patrons at Penshurst:

just such as the poor Man does to his rich and great Neighbour, by whom the Basket of Flowers, or Fruit, is not ill taken, though he has more plenty of his own growth, and in much greater perfection.

Under the aegis, then, of a grandee intellectual the *Essay* makes its entry on the world—and this in spite of the fact that, as Locke says in the second sentence of the 'Epistle Dedicatory', ''Tis not that I think any Name, how great soever, set at the beginning of a Book, will be able to cover the Faults that are to be found [in] it.' The book must stand alone; this assertion turns out to emerge from an otherwise unlikely sentence to contain it, a passage of classical compliment to the earl:

Worthless Things receive a Value, when they are made the Offerings of Respect, Esteem, and Gratitude: These you have given me so mighty and peculiar

Reasons to have in the highest degree for your Lordship, that if they can add price to what they go along with, proportionable to their own Greatness, I can with Confidence brag, I here make your Lordship the richest Present you ever received.

This looks at first like a typical abasement-*topos*, the value of the gift depending entirely on the earlier generosity of the patron; but the more one looks at the idea hidden in the rhetoric, the clearer it becomes that Locke thinks very well of his *Essay*, and knows, for example, that it is unlikely that Pembroke would ever receive a richer present from any client, or from anyone. In the roster of works dedicated to the members of a family distinguished for the munificence of its patronage, of course *An Essay upon Human Understanding* stands high: the conventional hyperbole blinks unexpectedly into fact. With this in mind, as one looks afresh at the dedication, one recognizes the author's consistent self-regard running beneath the obeisance of the surface prose.

'Things in print must stand or fall by their own Worth, or the Reader's Fancy', he announces, to prepare himself and his readers for the fact that the essay, 'being somewhat out of the common road', may get short shrift from the public.

The Imputation of Novelty, is a terrible charge amongst those who judge of Men's Heads, as they do of their Perukes, by the Fashion; and can allow none to be right, but the received Doctrines. Truth scarce ever yet carried it by Vote any where, at its first appearance: New Opinions are always suspected, and usually opposed, without any other Reason, but because they are not already common. But Truth, like Gold, is not the less so, for being newly brought out of the Mine. 'Tis Trial and Examination must give it price, and not any antick Fashion: And though it be not yet current by the publick stamp; yet it may, for all that, be as old as Nature, and is certainly not the less genuine.

Not only are various notions in Locke's philosophy covertly assumed as the basis for these observations—received opinion, so drubbed in Book I, is taken as read for wrong-headedness; in the gold-reference, much of Locke's utility-theory is hidden—but also the rhetoric itself leads us to the author's position. Perukes—which Locke characteristically declined to wear for his last and most impressive portrait, by Kneller—are here taken as foolish adornments of foolish men. Truth is understood to suffer in the world of opinionated human beings; but she is like gold, able to stand all assaying and to emerge as pure and unchangeable, just as, for instance, the elements of nature, however little understood, are in fact pure and unchangeable from the beginning. Also insensibly the author brings his reader to realize that his treatise is to be identified with truth. Even Pembroke's 'long Train of Favours' shown to Locke is somehow made to seem justified by the truth the author represents, which so intelligent and discriminating a man as Pembroke must have recognized. We are not surprised, at the end, when the client hints at a relation with his patron more like equality than clientage—'you vouchsafe to continue me in some degrees of your Esteem and allow me a place in your good Thoughts, I had almost said Friendship'. The friendship justifies the little joke between the two philosophers with which the dedication closes:

This I am sure, I should write of the *Understanding* without having any, if I were not extremely sensible of them [your favours], and did not lay hold on this Opportunity to testifie to the World, how much I am obliged to be, and how much I am, *My Lord,*
Your Lordships
Most Humble, and
Most Obedient Servant,
JOHN LOCKE

In the first epistle, to Pembroke, Locke insisted that he had published his incomplete treatise at Pembroke's behest—'This Treatise, which is grown up under your Lordship's Eye, and has ventured into the World by your Order'; in the second epistle, 'To the Reader', he did not insist that he published only to quiet importunate friends, though he was careful to make plain that there were 'those who advised me to publish it'; the constant approbation of the half-dozen original friends is implied, certainly. In the 'Epistle to the Reader' Locke plays a delicate tonal game, presenting himself as a plain, stolid, slow man sincerely concerned to define some steps toward truth; he is, he implies, a man like the men his readers might be assumed to think themselves, a man who, with the goodwill of those readers in hand, ventures to risk his opinions in print. To this end, he manipulates the modesty-trope with an appearance of bluff frankness:

For though it be certain, that there is nothing in this Treatise of whose Truth I am not persuaded; yet I consider my self as liable to Mistakes, as I can think thee...I pretend not to publish this Essay for the information of Men of large Thoughts and quick Apprehensions; to such Masters of Knowledge I profess my self a Scholar, and therefore warn them before-hand not to expect any thing here, but what being spun out of my own course [*sic*] Thoughts, is fitted to Men of my own size, to whom, perhaps, it will not be unacceptable, that I have taken some Pains to make plain and familiar to their Thoughts some Truths, which established Prejudice, or the Abstractions of the Ideas themselves, might render difficult.

Small wonder that readers, finding themselves so naturally assimilated to the character and mental powers of the author, responded to the

Essay's hospitality, so unmistakably offered at the work's entrance. Locke is a man among men, busy, intermittently curious, lazy, concerned for human welfare and for truth, but often the reluctant servant of these high mistresses. Who does not see himself so? Who can fail to be won to an author who continually makes disclaimers for his book, for his industry, for his mental capacity?

> Mistake not this, for a Commendation of my Work; nor conclude, because I was pleased with the doing of it, that therefore I am fondly taken with it now it is done...It was not meant for those that had already mastered this Subject, and made a thorough Acquaintance with their own Understandings; but for my own Information, and the Satisfaction of a few Friends, who acknowledged themselves not to have sufficiently considered it.

In a famous passage, he sets the limits of his own endeavour, comparing himself, it seems, unfavourably to those giants among his thoughtful contemporaries:

> But every one must not hope to be a *Boyle*, or a *Sydenham*; and in an Age that produces such Masters, as the Great — *Hugenius*, and the incomparable Mr. *Newton*, with some other of that Strain; 'tis Ambition enough to be employed as an Under-labourer in clearing the Ground a little, and removing some of the Rubbish, that lies in the way to Knowledge...

Modesty, certainly, but an odd kind of modesty that insists that such masters of thought have not sufficiently clarified knowledge so that an under-labourer of the sort Locke makes himself out to be, is still needed. All the same, by reason of his tone, there is no breath of pretentiousness in Locke's self-presentation at this point; any reader might fearlessly undertake the quest of—of all things!—human understanding, under the guidance of so plain a man as this.

Locke manages great intimacy with his readers, from the epistle's very first sentence, addressed as to a companion in the room:

> I here put into thy Hands, what has been the Diversion of some of my idle and heavy Hours: If it has the good luck to prove so of any of thine, and thou hast but half so much Pleasure in reading of it, as I had in writing it, thou wilt as little think thy Money, as I do my Pains ill-bestowed.

The reader is 'thou', an accustomed companion, as it were, to be addressed without formality or flurry; the relation between them is assumed to be such that the author may wryly refer to the reader's expenditure for the book, assimilating that pain to the long and pleasurable pain of his composition. With this closeness, though, an injunction to independence is slipped in, naturalized by Locke's seeming to acknowledge the cluster of feelings the reader must have:

The essayist in his Essay

This, Reader, is the Entertainment of those, who let loose their own Thoughts, and follow them in writing; which thou oughtest not to envy them, since they afford thee an Opportunity of the like Diversion, if thou wilt make use of thy own Thoughts in reading.

One notices, here as later in the *Essay*, that Locke urges independence of mind on his readers, not so much from him as from received opinion and authority: rather, he ranges himself and his readers together against those enemies to truth, confident of his readers' support as they are made confident of his: ''Tis to [thy Thoughts], if they are thine own, that I refer myself.' 'If thou judgest for thy self, I know thou wilt judge candidly; and then I shall not be harmed or offended, whatever be thy Censure.'

The reader's good faith assured, the author may then acknowledge the ticklish truth that he has elsewhere occasionally deplored, that his book must ultimately stand by the good opinion of its readers: I 'know that this Book must stand or fall with thee, not by any Opinion I have of it, but thy own'.

After this insinuation of himself into the readers' favour, he then tells of the book's genesis, or at least gives a version of its genesis which is by no means untrue. A group of friends met to discuss matters of common interest, and fell out over what Locke took to be a disagreement simply about method and about words. In that anecdote itself, a fellowship is established, for what reasonably intelligent and sensible man has not had the same experience? In the highly clubbable world out of which and into which the *Essay* was born, the collective pursuit of learning meant a great deal. Locke himself, as he relates it, undertook to define certain epistemological foundations to the common discussion, the substantive questions of which were to be postponed until the group could agree on fundamentals. These proving as difficult to define as in fact they are, it took Locke rather longer than he had expected to formulate his thoughts. In a sentence matching the historical discontinuity of his application to the problem, Locke apologizes for such confusions as are still to be met with in the argument, style, and tone of the book as it finally appeared, almost twenty years after the date Tyrrell, another member of the group, set into the margin of his 'variorum' copy:

Some hasty and undigested Thoughts, on a Subject I had never before considered, which I set down against our next Meeting, gave the first entrance into this Discourse, which having been thus begun by Chance, was continued by Intreaty; written by incoherent parcels; and after long intervals of neglect, resum'd again, as my Humour or Occasions permitted; and at last, in a retirement, it was brought into that order that thou now seest it.

The order itself, however, is far from ideal; Locke's assessment of his defects in argumentation is accurate, if rather broadly stated—'This discontinued way of writing may have occasion'd, besides others, two contrary Faults, *viz.* that too little, and too much may be said in it.' He has his excuses for both—'too little' does not greatly matter in a treatise which the author designs as a stimulus to other people's thinking, who can be trusted to fill in the gaps he must leave; 'too much', simply, must be excused. In a charming description of philosophical naïveté, he wrote,

If it seems too much to thee, thou must blame the Subject; for when I first put Pen to Paper, I thought all I should have to say on this Matter, would have been contained in one sheet of Paper; but the farther I went, the larger Prospect I had: New Discoveries led me still on, and so it grew insensibly to the Bulk it now appears in.

Locke never denies that his *Essay* might profit by contraction, though his excuse for prolixity is calculated to charm an audience accustomed to philosophical austerity: 'But to confess the Truth, I am now too lazie, or too busie to make it shorter.' For his frequent use of the same examples, he adduces his own principle of relation:

the same Notion, having different Respects, may be convenient or necessary, to prove or illustrate several parts of the same Discourse...I shall frankly avow, that I have sometimes dwelt long upon the same Argument, and expressed it different ways, with a quite different Design...Some Objects had need to be turned on every side; and when the Notion is new, as I confess some of these are to me; or out of the ordinary Road, as I suspect they will appear to others, 'tis not one simple view of it, that will gain it admittance into every Understanding, or fix it there with a clear and lasting Impression.

The principle of reinforcement, called on so often by Locke in the psychological sections of the *Essay*, is here called into play before the reasons for it are given the reader. One notices also how readily the novelty-trope, here given in terms of modesty ('as I confess some of them are to me'), is assimilated to the readers' philosophical inexperience ('as I suspect they will appear to others').[1]

It is always difficult for an author to turn his own tediousness into a virtue. Locke manages to disarm critics of his long-windedness by attributing to them peculiar capacities of intellect:

I had much rather the speculative and quick-sighted should complain of my being in some parts tedious, than that any one, not accustomed to abstract Speculations, or prepossessed with different Notions, should mistake, or not comprehend my meaning.

[1] For an example of the novelty-trope, see *Essay*, IV, XVII, §7.

The essayist in his Essay

By managing, then, to associate himself with plain men of good sense and to assimilate their views to his own, Locke on the whole makes excuse for faults of construction in his book and dismisses potential objections to his philosophical simplicity. By insisting both covertly on the novelty of his ideas and overtly on the sturdy independence of his readers, he manages to square himself and those readers against a restrictive and always nameless authority, against conventional men of received opinion, and against flighty followers of philosophical fashion. None the less, for all this comradeship, he is not invariably cosy with his readers—'I plainly tell my Readers, except half a dozen, this Treatise was not at first intended for them; and therefore they need not be at Trouble to be of that number'. With this, we are returned to the initial intimacy of the little discussion group from which the *Essay* sprang: readers who penetrate to the core of the book are, simply, joining that colleagual audience fit and few. Locke gets it both ways with this play; he takes refuge in a commonplace of indifference, and he draws his readers into a circle of independent amateurs of thought.

Getting it both ways is one gift of rhetoric. As he managed to do in his dedication and in his 'Epistle to the Reader', Locke at once disclaimed any originality of thought, any skill in composition, any particular justification for claiming attention, and asserted his conviction of the worth and importance of his treatise:

I have so little Affectation to be in Print, that if I were not flattered, this Essay might be of some use to others, as I think, it has been to me, I should have confined it to the view of some Friends, who gave the first Occasion to it. My appearing therefore in Print, being on purpose to be as useful as I may, I think it necessary to make what I have to say as easie and intelligible to all sorts of Readers as I can...

It will possibly be censured as a great piece of Vanity, or Insolence in me, to pretend to instruct this our knowing Age, it amounting to little less, when I own that I publish it with hopes it may be useful to others. But if it may be permitted to speak freely of those, who with a feigned Modesty condemn as useless what they themselves write, methinks it savours much more of Vanity or Insolence, to publish a Book for any other end; and he fails very much of that Respect he owes the Publick, who prints, and consequently expects Men should read that, wherein he intends not they should meet with any thing of Use to themselves or others: and should nothing else be found allowable in this Treatise, yet my Design will not cease to be so; and the Goodness of my intention ought to be some Excuse for the Worthlessness of my Present.

The affable self-confidence, concealed under a show of courtesy and modesty, is quite different from the real tentativeness apparent in the

Rosalie Colie

'Epistle to the Reader' and carried throughout the rhetorical programme of the *Essay*, a tentativeness which reminds us always of the tonal value implied in the title; this enterprise is an experiment in thinking and in thinking about thinking. Some of the metaphors and much of the personal reference in the second Epistle bear out the theme of experiment:

Its *searches* after Truth, are a sort of *Hawking* and *Hunting*, wherein the very *pursuit* makes a great part of the Pleasure.

For though it is certain, that there is nothing in this Treatise of whose Truth I am not persuaded; yet I consider my self as *liable to Mistakes*, as I can think thee.

...but the farther I went, the *larger Prospect* I had.

...to such Masters of Knowledge I *profess* my self a *Scholar*...

...if I *were not flattered*..., I *should have confined it*...

But *if it may be permitted*..., *methinks* it savours much more of Vanity or Insolence...

...'tis Ambition *enough* to be employed as an *Under-labourer*... (My italics.)

In the second edition, the 'Epistle to the Reader' carried certain alterations and additions, notably Locke's lengthy answer to one of his critics, a stiff and closely argued passage hardly calculated to endear Locke or his *Essay* to the readers he had coaxed, cajoled, and manipulated in the original epistle; still less could his new readers, whom, he said, his bookseller so hoped to attract, have been encouraged by that additional matter. The additions to the various versions of the second epistle do carry, however, another evidence of the developmental nature of the treatise: Locke was from the beginning aware that he would have critics and might have to answer them; in the first edition, he promised temperance on his part—'But yet if any one thinks fit to be angry, and rail at it, he may do so securely: For I shall find some better way of spending my time, than in such kind of Conversation.' By the second edition, he was prepared to go on record that his hostile critics advanced his understanding not at all—

But what forwardness soever I have to resign any Opinion I have, or to recede from any thing I have Writ, upon the first evidence of any error in it; yet this I must own, that I have not had the good luck to receive any light from those Exceptions, I have met with in print against any part of my Book, nor have, from any thing has been urg'd against it, found reason to alter my Sense, in any of the Points have been question'd. (Epistle to the Reader, 1694.)

Indeed, so far was Locke from accepting criticism with good grace that he ignored specific criticisms which, had he answered them, might greatly have strengthened his own arguments.[1] From his readers, Locke expected indulgence; with them, he shared his irritation at his critics' misunderstanding his own intentions, believed fully shared by the readers for whom he was writing. In a revealing passage, he attacks his critics for not realizing the functions of the essay form:

If any other Authors, careful that none of their good thoughts should be lost, have publish'd their censure of my *Essay*, with this honour done to it, that they will not suffer it to be an *Essay*, I leave it to the publick to value the obligation they have to their critical Pens, and shall not wast my Readers time in so idle and ill natur'd an employment of mine, as to lessen the satisfaction any one has in himself, or gives to others in so hasty a confutation of what I have Written. (Epistle to the Reader, 1694.)

This is undercutting with a vengeance: in one sentence to suggest that the work of critics who did not recognize the experimental character of an essay was negligible, because the nature of essays is to be carelessly written, stretches fairness to the breaking point: one way or another, some criticism ought to have been tolerable.

The third edition carried the 1694 'Epistle to the Reader' unaltered; the fourth added a page on an alteration Locke rightly felt to be major, the substitution in this edition of the words 'determinate or determined' for the words 'clear and distinct' with respect to ideas. In view of the drubbing Locke's use of the word 'idea' has come in for,[2] it is well to remember that he was himself uneasy with his formulations and made some effort to specify his own meaning and to subject his notions to improvement. The fourth edition of the *Essay* carried two notable new chapters: in Book II, 'On the Association of Ideas', and in Book IV, 'Of Enthusiasm'. The connexion between these two topics, clear enough to men of Locke's generation, may seem a little less obscure to us when we realize that they come from the same stratum of the author's developing thought.

The various additions of matter to the 'Epistle to the Reader' show tendencies already manifest in Locke's rhetoric—that is, they often sort ill with material before and after them, seem to be interruptions to the readers' convenient thought. They tend undeniably to lessen the insinuating and winning persuasion of the first epistle, although some have the same frank charm of the first, most polished version. One such is Locke's comment in 1694 on his enlargement of his chapter on Power:

What I had there Writ concerning *Liberty* and the *Will*, I thought deserved as accurate a review, as I was capable of...Upon a closer inspection into the

---

[1] As Mr Yolton's analyses of several of Locke's critics' works demonstrate.
[2] Gilbert Ryle, *John Locke: Tercentenary Essays* (Oxford, 1933); for a sympathetic view of Locke's appeal in his own time and since, see Ryle, 'John Locke', *Critica*, I (1967), 3–16.

Rosalie Colie

working of Men's Minds, and a stricter examination of their motives and views, they are turn'd by, I have found reason somewhat to alter the thoughts I formerly had concerning that, which gives the last determination of the *Will* in all voluntary actions. This I cannot forbear to acknowledge to the World, with as much freedom and readiness, as I at first published, what then seem'd to me to be right, thinking my self more concern'd to quit and renounce any opinion of my own, than to oppose that of another, when Truth appears against it. For 'tis Truth alone I seek, and that will always be welcome to me, when or from whencesoever it comes.

This is noble, but far from true: though there are traces of amendment in the *Essay* as a result of the friendly help of Molyneux, Collins, and even Coste, Locke never acknowledged an improvement from the correction of a foe. Indeed, as time went on, he seems to have felt it imperative to denigrate and question the motives of hostile readers of his book; for all his insistence upon the negligence of his style, he never allowed that its faults might have misled his critics—and this in spite of the fact that so devoted a student of Locke's utterances as Pierre Coste found that after considerable attention to a given passage, he often misunderstood it.[1] The following passage, from the 1694 epistle, comes with ill grace from a man so critical of the loose and equivocal use of words as Locke:

But what forwardness soever I have to resign any Opinion I have, or to recede from any thing I have Writ, upon the first evidence of any error in it; yet this I must own, that I have not had the good luck to receive any light from those Exceptions, I have met with in print against any part of my Book... Whether the Subject, I have in hand, requires often more thought and attention, than Cursory Readers, at least such as are prepossessed, are willing to allow? Or whether any obscurity in my expressions casts a cloud over it, and these notions made difficult to others apprehensions in my way of treating them? So it is, that my meaning, I find, is often mistaken, and I have not the good luck to be rightly understood.

Locke's impatience and irritation is betrayed by his sloppy syntax, which even by the standards of staccato essay-writing is jumpy, awkward and confusing. Simply, Locke could be wayward, and his prose shows that unphilosophical defect in his nature: one must wonder, further, at this negligence in a man as impatient as he at 'those, who will not take Care about the meaning of their own Words, and will not suffer the Significancy of their Expression to be inquired into'.

Through the various versions of his epistle, Locke took less and less care with rhetoric. If this demonstrates his decreasing attention to the legitimate expectations and demands of his readers, it at least sorts with

[1] Coste, 'Avertissement du Traducteur', *Essai philosophique.*

his attitude toward his own work—he wanted to get on with it, was impatient with interruptions, however well-meant; and he no longer felt that he had to woo his readers to follow him through his book. After all, by the second edition, they could be expected to know what they were in for. The *Essay* was sufficiently successful that the bookseller wanted attention drawn to the additions and alterations in the second edition, because they were regarded as inducement enough to print another edition. To some extent, Locke's cavalier treatment of readers in his later additions to their epistle is a record of his own increasing security with them: in his mind at least, the *Essay*'s importance was established and needed little apology for its faults, so manifest were its merits.

III

Locke was writing, not about metaphysics or ontology, but about epistemology; or, as he chose to put it, about *understanding*. He was concerned with the process of thinking, not simply with the thoughts men formulated: to set out his findings on this subject, he chose the form of the essay. Furthermore, he flaunted his own processes of finding his formulations; as he tells us in the 'Epistle to the Reader' and throughout the *Essay*, this was his own lifelong assaying of himself and of the human understanding, the record of his own experiment in understanding. To describe human understanding he himself had to understand and to recognize the fact: he had to understand how he came to that understanding. One result of his lifelong inspection of his mind's workings, on which so often his own opinion altered, was a certain attitude apparent in the verbs he used about himself. Often Locke seems quite unconsciously, as a matter of habit, to present himself to his readers as a thinker with no secure holdfast on truth, as a man groping and reaching out for what he cannot fully grasp, does not expect ever fully to grasp. He makes tentatives, both toward truth and (an equally difficult task) toward expressing that truth intelligibly to other men.

One manifestation of this is in locutions like these—'I must here *beg pardon*' (I, I, §8); 'I *imagine* that anyone will easily grant' (I, II, §1); ...which I *presume* may be done' (I, II, §3); '*But*...this argument... seems* to me...' (I, II, §4); '*But yet* I *take the liberty* to say...' (I, II, §4); 'This I *hope* to make plain...' (I, II, §12); 'I *would fain* know' (I, II, §23); ...it is, *in my opinion*, a strong *presumption*...' (I, II, §27); 'I must therefore *beg a little truce*' (I, II, §28); 'I *confess*' (I, III, §3); and so on. My examples all come from early in the *Essay*, from a section, moreover, rewritten several times and by the date of the first edition known by the author to need defence; but these locutions of caution can be duplicated from any part of the whole work, from sections less often revised and from others added late in the book's development. 'I think' and 'I imagine' introduce many different sorts of proposition; not infrequently Locke's use is disingenuous, for he appears to have been quite certain of some of the formulations so entered upon. At other times—more often, I think—he seems genuinely unsure, as in I, III, §19, where he doubles his tentatives ('I *think* it is very much *to be doubted*'; 'I *imagine* it will *scarce seem possible*'). Locke habitually 'confesses', 'appeals', 'allows', 'agrees', and 'grants'; certainly this habit is an encouraging one for readers wrestling with the ideas he introduces this way; in particular, though, his allowances, grants, and agreements tend to be followed by 'but' (e.g. I, II, §§1, 14, 18; I, III, §§2, 3, 6, 21, etc.). For all his humility, Locke does not cede everything by any means. Qualifications are always present, both in the direction of scepticism and away from it; his regular use of 'I doubt not' is a case in point, an assertive prelude to a statement which at the same time implies that Locke has gone through the obligatory process of doubting before he has arrived at his formulation. The locution itself is the earnest of the author's having thought.

The style itself implies in many ways continued processes of thinking. One way is that in which Locke, by continually siding with his readers against inimical strawmen, manages to give them, and to give us at this long remove, the impression of the reader's active part in the *agon* of ideas. As an actor in this drama, he continually manipulates himself, sidling up to readers to get them to take over from him, derogating himself, asking for correction, keeping before his readers' attention the fact that human understanding is both a collective and an endless enterprise. Some of the ways he does so are illustrated in the brief extracts that follow:

And since I *impartially search* after Truth, I *shall not be sorry* to be convinced that I *have been too fond* of *my own Notions*; which I *confess we are all apt* to be, when Application and Study have warmed *our Heads* with them. (I, II, §28.)

...I *desire to know* how first and innate Principles can be tried; or at least it is reasonable to demand the marks and characters, whereby the genuine, innate Principles, may be distinguished from others; that so, amidst the great variety of Pretenders, I *may be kept from mistakes*, in so material a point as this. When this is done, I *shall be ready to embrace* such welcome, and useful, Propositions; and till then I *may with modesty doubt*... (I, III, §27.)

...I *would gladly be resolved*, by one of Seven, or Seventy, Years old... (I, IV, §4.)

I *must own*, as far as I *can observe*, I *can find none*, and *would be glad to be informed* by another. (I, IV, §17.)

The essayist in his Essay

If they have any innate Ideas, *I would be glad to be told*, what, and how many they are. (I, IV, §19.) (My italics.)

This sequence illustrates very neatly the progression from genuine humility to absolute irony: as the intervening argument has strengthened Locke's position, he is safe in asking for evidence of innate ideas, since he persuaded himself and his readers there can never be any. It is perhaps worth noting that Book I, so long worked over, has more such disingenuously modest requests for correction than the later books.

The first-person pronouns appear again and again in this work; Locke clearly had no intention of hiding, as for example Bacon does in the *Advancement of Learning*, behind a pose of monumental impersonality. Taking three passages as guides, I should like to suggest some merits and defects in his ways of presenting his own person and his *personae* in order to move and direct readers' reactions. The first is taken from the second paragraph of Book I, and may be assumed to represent his most polished efforts:

> This, therefore, being my *Purpose* to inquire into the Original, Certainty, and Extent of humane Knowledge; together, with the Grounds and Degrees of Belief, Opinion, and Assent; I shall not at present meddle with the Physical Considerations of the Mind; or trouble my self to examine, wherein its Essence consists...These are Speculations, which, however curious and entertaining, I shall decline, as lying out of my Way, in the Design I am now upon. It shall suffice to my present Purpose, to consider the discerning Faculties of a Man, as they are employ'd about the Objects, which they have to do with: and I shall imagine I have not wholly misemploy'd myself in the Thoughts I shall have on this Occasion, if, in this Historical plain Method, I can give any Account of the Ways, whereby our Understandings come to attain those Notions of Things we have...and yet asserted somewhere or other with such Assurance and Confidence that he that shall take a view... (I, I, §2.)

The writer as himself dominates the paragraph: *My* purpose; *I* shall not at present meddle...or trouble *my self*; *I* shall decline as lying out of *my* way in the design *I* am now upon; It shall suffice to *my* present purpose; *I* shall imagine *I* have not wholly misemployed *my self* in the thoughts *I* shall have...if...*I* can give any account...of those notions of things *we* have; *he* that takes a view... The manly self-assertions gradually shade off into a single 'we', until a lone 'he' emerges to formulate two subversive propositions ('That either there is no such thing as Truth at all; or that Mankind hath no sufficient Means to attain to a certain Knowledge of it'), which the *Essay* exists to examine and to refute. Locke moves from preoccupation with his particular purpose, on which he is now engaged and expects to continue to be engaged in ('the Design I am now upon'; 'the Thoughts I shall have'); he states it first negatively, then positively, to identify his own thoughts with those of 'our Understandings'. 'Those Notions of Things which we have' sets him and his readers solidly together, so that he can afford to loose from the consensus of humankind the single 'he' who offers opportunity for dialogue.

A quite different example is the last paragraph of Book 1; here Locke lays out his intentions anew, covers for his possible faults, appeals to the good nature and good sense of his readers to test and, by implication, to corroborate the accuracy of his findings.

But in the future part of this Discourse, designing to raise an Edifice uniform, and consistent with it self, as far as my own Experience and Observation will assist me, I hope, to lay the foundation so, that the rest will easily depend upon it: And I shall not need to shore it up with props and buttrices, leaning on borrowed or begg'd foundations: Or at least, if mine prove a Castle in the Air, I will endeavour it shall be all of a piece, and hang together. Wherein I tell you before-hand, you are not to expect undeniable, cogent demonstrations, unless you will suffer me, as others have done, to take my Principles for granted; and then, I doubt not, but I can demonstrate too. All that I shall say for the Principles I proceed on, is, that I can only *appeal* to Mens own unprejudiced *Experience*, and Observations, whether they be true, or no; and this is enough for a man who professes no more, than to lay down candidly and freely his own Conjectures, concerning a Subject not very obvious, without any other design, than an unbiass'd enquiry after Truth. (I, IV, §24.)

The modesty is classically present—'as far as my own experience and observation will assist me, I hope to raise'; 'I shall not need to shore it up'; 'I will endeavour'; 'I tell you before-hand'; 'unless you will suffer me'; 'I can only appeal'; 'this is enough for a man who professes no more'— but the confidence shows through as well—'I doubt not, but I can demonstrate too'; 'without any other design, than an unbiassed enquiry after Truth'. Interestingly enough, there are certain changes in the style, simply, of this passage in the second edition, one of which is rhetorically important, if not otherwise. What had been simply 'a Subject not very obvious' in 1690 became 'A Subject lying in the dark' in 1694; the alteration recalls the great light metaphor of the *Essay*'s introductory paragraph:

But whatever be the Difficulties, that lie in the way of this Enquiry; whatever it be, that keeps us so much in the Dark to our selves; sure I am; that all the Light we can let in upon our own Minds; all the Acquaintance we can make with our own Understandings, will not only be very pleasant; but bring us great Advantages, in directing our Thoughts in the search of other Things.

The essayist in his Essay

My third example, far less rhetorically elegant than the first two, illustrates quite a different element of the *Essay*, as Locke presents his own processes of thinking. Occasionally his thinking overrode his need to express that process clearly to his readers, and certainly overcame his pretensions to prose style. In the passage following, precisely because of its awkwardness, the man seems actually to be working out his ideas, struggling to set right his recalcitrant, repetitious, and intermittent notions. At this level of thought, the author disappears beneath his language, able to hack out from his linguistic resources only the crudest frame for his developing ideas:

Though it be hard, I think, to find any one so absurd, as to say he has the positive *Idea* of an actual infinite Number; the Infinity whereof lies only in a Power of still adding any Combination of Unites to any former Number, and that as long, and as much as one will; the like also being in the Infinity of Space and Duration, which Power leaves always to the Mind room for endless Additions; yet there be those, who imagine they have *positive* Ideas *of infinite* Duration and Space. It would, I think, be enough to destroy any such positive *Idea* of infinite, to ask him that has it, whether he could add to it or no; which would easily show the mistake of such a positive *Idea*. We can, I think, have no positive *Idea* of any Space or Duration, which is not made up of, and commensurate to repeated Numbers of Feet or Yards, or Days and Years, which are the common measures whereof we have the *Ideas* in our Minds, and whereby we judge of the greatness of these sort of quantities. And therefore, since an *Idea* of infinite Space or Duration must needs be made up of infinite Parts, it can have no other Infinity, than that of Number capable still of farther Addition; but not an actual positive *Idea* of a Number infinite. For, I think, it is evident, that the Addition of finite things together (as are all lengths, whereof we have the positive *Ideas*) can never otherwise produce the *Idea* of infinite, than as Number does; which consisting of Additions of finite Unites one to another, suggests the *Idea* of Infinite, only by a Power we find we have, of still increasing the Sum, and adding more of the same kind, without coming one jot nearer the end of such Progression. (II, XVII, §13.)

This thought is admittedly difficult, the subject leading to confusion, but Locke slogs on—'though it be hard *I think* to find'; 'It would, *I think*, be enough'; 'We can, *I think*, have no positive idea'; 'For *I think*'—to reiterate in his last sentence the thought contained in the first. Infinity does not lend itself to a clear and distinct, or to a determined or determinate idea, but neither did Locke manage a plain statement of it; his whole chapter on infinity is full of coils and recoils of thought, as well as of syntactical infelicities such as this paragraph presents. Locke's pronouns slip away from him—'those who imagine they have positive ideas of infinite duration and space' become 'him that has it'; and point of view shifts uncontrolledly through a passage seeking to regain its direction by 'I think'. But we veer after him, through such shifts as these: '*it* be hard'; '*it* would be enough'; '*we* can have'; 'an *idea*...can have'; '*it* is evident that'; 'a power *we* find *we* have of still increasing' creates a surface turbulence to engulf the poor thinking 'I'.

In some ways, the developmental character of the *Essay* limits its effectiveness; Locke's constant use of phrases indicating neglect of a subject or its enlargement in another place is distracting, because also he does not always tell us why he neglects or where the enlargement can be found:

The Reason of this I shall show in another Place. (II, IV, §6.)

...of which, of how vast an extent it is, I shall have occasion to consider hereafter. (II, IX, §4.)

...which we shall have occasion hereafter to consider more at large, when we come to speak of Words. (II, XVII, §7.)

...whether that which we call *Extasie*, be not dreaming with the eyes open, I leave to be examined. (II, XIX, §1.)

I do not pretend to enumerate them all, nor to treat at large of this set of *Ideas* which are got from Reflection, that would be to make a volume. (II, XIX, §2.)

But this by the bye. (II, XIX, §4.)

This might carry our thoughts further, were it seasonable in this place. (II, XX, §6, 1694 edition.)

But that these are wrong ways of judging were easie to shew in every particular, if I would examine them at large singly; but I shall only mention this in general ... (II, XXI, §66, 1694 edition.)

I shall not now enlarge any further on the wrong judgments, and neglect of what is in their power, whereby Men mislead themselves. This would make a Volume, and is not my business. (II, XXI, §70, 1694 edition.)

Though I shall have occasion to consider this more at large, when I come to treat of Words, and their Use, yet I could not avoid to take this much notice here... (II, XXII, §8.)

Again and again Locke cuts off speculation, to return to his own chief avenue of thought; we recognize, then, an elasticity to the book which is borne out by the way in which the book took its shape, in which its author dealt with its problems. For Locke found his own order often needed alteration as his thinking developed and refined. As he tells us at the end of his second book, he had not originally intended to treat of language:

Having thus given an account of the original, sorts, and extent of our *Ideas*, with several other Considerations, about these (I know not whether I may say)

The essayist in his Essay

Instruments, or Materials, of our knowledge, the method I at first proposed to my self, would now require, that I should immediately proceed to shew, what use the Understanding makes of them, and what Knowledge we have by them. This was that which, in the first general view I had of this Subject, was all that I thought I should have to do: but upon a nearer approach, I find, that there is so close a connexion between *Ideas* and Words...that it is impossible to speak clearly and distinctly of our Knowledge...without considering, first, the Nature, Use, and Signification of Language; which therefore, must be the business of the next Book. (II, XXXI, §27, 1690 edition; later II, XXXIII, §19.)

The subject, however, required an entire book, and attracted his attention again and again. Sometimes Locke's remarks about his additions and alterations are quite disarming, as in his apology for altering 'Of Power' in the second edition:

In the former Edition of this Treatise, I gave an account of my thoughts concerning them, according to the light I then had: And now as a Lover of Truth, and not a Worshipper of my own Doctrine, I own some change of my Opinion, which I think I have discover'd ground for. In what I first writ, I with an unbiassed indifferency followed Truth, whither I thought she led me. But neither being so vain as to fansie Infallibility, nor so disingenuous as to dissemble my mistakes for fear of blemishing my reputation, I have, with the same sincere design for truth only, not been asham'd to publish what a severe enquiry has suggested. (II, XXI, §72, 1694 edition.)

But he not only altered already existing chapters; he also added whole chapters, some of them of major importance, such as the chapter in the second edition on 'Identity and Diversity', and the chapter on the 'Association of Ideas' still later. Again, the essay form did Locke good service here. His chapters, like most of Montaigne's and all of Bacon's essays, are called 'Of something-or-other'—'Of Simple Ideas', 'Of Complex Ideas', 'Of Knowledge in General', 'Of Maxims', 'Of Reason', 'Of Enthusiasm'. Though of course most of them depend upon what has gone on in the preceding chapter and lead to the chapter succeeding, a surprising number of Locke's chapters can be read independently as essays. His method, though far from haphazard, was that of the essayist, to address himself as much as possible to his subject problem by problem, dividing aspects of his inquiry into the parcels prescribed by Descartes, and proceeding in the Cartesian and Baconian way from simpler to more complex aspects of his investigation. Though of course his reasoning was supposed to be read sequentially, he also hoped that the segments of his experiment in thought would stand as valid alone. In the case of the curious fourth book, this essayist's organization might help us to understand the disorderly, disconnected, unexplained sequence of the latter part of the book. Indeed, the whole *Essay* seems disastrously to shelve off into nowhere, with the last sentence of the last chapter, 'Of the Division of the Sciences':

All which three, *viz.* Things as they are in themselves knowable; Actions as they depend on us, in order to Happiness; and the right use of Signs in order to Knowledge, being *toto coelo* different, they seemed to me to be the three great Provinces of the intellectual World, wholly separate and distinct one from another. (IV, xx, §5.)

Such disconcerting open-endedness is, however, perfectly characteristic of books of essays, which also tended to have additional chapters, additional sections, additional subjects added throughout their authors' publishing lives; books of essays do not characteristically wind up their coils neatly in a knot at the end, but let them trail, to be grasped by whoever comes after. Or, to alter my metaphor, the scale is left half-empty at the end of the series of assays, the reader to make the next test and to carry on the process the *Essay* began.

One last technique remains to be examined, the author's use of his own experience directly transcribed into the work. Sometimes he speaks as if actually present, to be overheard by the unembarrassed and unembarrassing reader—'It is not impossible, but that some may think my former notions right, and some (as I have already found) these later; and some neither' (II, XXI, §72, 1694 edition). Again, he interrupts himself as to answer an actual remark the reader might have made: 'This...is the foundation of the greatest, I had almost said, of all the Errors in the World...' (II, XXXIII, §18); 'For our *Idea* of Substance, is equally obscure, or none at all, in both, it is but a supposed, I know not what, to support those *Ideas*, we call Accidents' (II, XXIII, §15). Occasionally a half-dialogue with the reader is carried over several paragraphs, as in II, XXIII, §§13–14;) sometimes the reader is forcibly jerked into the foreground and made to speak:

Knowledge, say you, is only the perception of the agreement or disagreement of our own *Ideas*; but who knows what those *Ideas* may be?...And so, by your Rules, he will be the more knowing...
To which I answer, That if... (IV, IV, §§1–2.)

Another trick is his use of his own observations, as in his references to the cassowaries in St James's Park (II, XXV, §8; III, VI, §34), or the winter-flood of the Thames (II, XXVI, §16); or the dating in IV, XI, §11, presumably the day on which Locke wrote that sentence in its final form, 10 July 1688. Sometimes an example of his own is translated into the common experience: 'How frequently do we, in a day, cover our eyes with our eye-lids, without perceiving that we are in the dark?' (II, IX, §20.) As he takes

The essayist in his Essay

himself for his own example, so he urges his readers into the habit of doing the same for themselves: 'Anyone may observe this in his own thoughts, who will take the pains to reflect on them' (II, IX, §10); 'almost every one has Experience of in himself, and his own Observation without difficulty leads him thus far' (II, XIX, §4). This is philosophy not only laicized, but domesticated: grown men are asked to watch in their developing children the growth of mind, intellect, and understanding, by which Locke's hypotheses can be checked in every family. The thinking man is invited to make himself his own subject; a gentle blueprint is given for heightening self-consciousness in such a way as also to assist the common enterprise. A man can observe himself in almost all his mental activities, even those going on while he is asleep; he can become his own epistemological student and critic, with nothing too remote for observation. Locke illustrates this in a particularly immediate way when he uses himself writing his *Essay* as an example for the arguments that *Essay* communicates:

Had I the same consciousness, that I saw the Ark and *Noah*'s Flood, as that I saw an overflowing of the *Thames* last Winter, or as that I write now, I could no more doubt that I, that write this now, that saw the *Thames* overflow'd last Winter, and that view'd the Flood at the general Deluge, was the same *self*... that I that write this am the same *my self* now whilst I write (whether I consist of all the same Substance, material or immaterial, or no) that I was Yesterday. (II, XXVII, §16, 1695 edition.)

His *Essay*, then, becomes part of him and part of the proof of his identity, however skewed this particular proof turns out to be; further, his *Essay* is a part of all of his experience, not just a particular or isolated or special relation of himself. The mere fact of his writing is part of his perception, part of his thinking:

...Whilst I write this, I have, by the Paper affecting my Eyes, that *Idea* produced in my Mind; which, whatever Object causes, I call *White*...I can no more doubt, whilst I write this, that I see White and Black, and that some thing really exists, that causes that Sensation in me, than that I write or move my Hand... (IV, XI, §2.)

Hidden away in the chapter 'Of Our Knowledge of the Existence of Other Things' is a passage about the *Essay* which asserts its own reality and the reality of communication.[1] Locke begins with his own process of writing, which he thinks about as he does it: 'Thus I see, whilst I write this, I can change the Appearance of the Paper; and by designing the

[1] See my 'Social Language of John Locke', *Journal of British Studies*, IV (1965), 29-51.

Letters, tell before-hand what new *Idea* it shall exhibit the very next moment, barely by my drawing the Pen over it: which will neither appear (let me fansie as much as I will) if my Hand stand still; or though I move my Pen, if my Eyes be shut...' This is an experiment in thought, but no thought-experiment: one can see the author actually testing his facts as he goes. Moreover, once he has designed his letters, chosen his words, he is bound by their existence: 'Nor when those Characters are once made on the Paper, can I chuse afterwards but see them as they are; that is, have the *Ideas* of such letters as I have made.' His book actually comes into existence before our eyes, to live its life independent of its author. 'Whence it is manifest, that they are not barely the Sport and Play of my own Imagination, when I find, that the Characters that were made at the pleasure of my own Thoughts, do not obey them; nor yet cease to be, whenever I shall fansie it, but continue to affect my Senses constantly and regularly, according to the Figures I made them.' Furthermore, the book's reality must work on the minds that take it up and in: 'To which if we will add, that the sight of those shall, from another Man, draw such Sounds, as I before-hand design they shall stand for, there will be little reason left to doubt, that those Words, I write, do really exist without me, when they cause a long series of regular Sounds to affect my Ears, which could not be the effect of my Imagination, nor could my Memory retain them in that order.' (IV, XI, §7.) That is, when Locke's secretary reads his words back, they must still occur in the order in which he set them down: the secretary can read them no other way, because the order has become their mode of existence, and in that order they must go forth to other men. Simple, immediate, domestic, intelligible as this is, it also epitomizes in a practical example the high hopes Locke had for his book and that book's place in the continuous essay upon human understanding. To think is part of all men's existence; to think about thinking, and to try to communicate one's conclusions on that subject, is to begin at the beginning, in an effort to understand one's own understanding in such a way that other men can more fully comprehend their own processes of understanding—and can, by that enlightenment, in their turn extend the area of human understanding.

In the process, men must cooperate, and know that they are doing so— by the fluidity, the flexibility of his language, by the variety in his style, now austere and magisterial, now hesitant and searching, now friendly and even insinuating, Locke set himself to involve his readers in the endeavour he believed the common responsibility of mankind. To do so, he had to translate philosophy into the vernacular, so that no man need be intimidated either by the difficulty or the remoteness of the subject.

Philosophy, then, must be naturalized to the human understanding and, when possible, domesticated to the human condition. In many different ways, the *Essay* invites men to partake of its enterprise, appealing now to this mood in a reader, now to that one: its hospitable author makes the process of thinking about thinking so engaging that men naturally took up his book, and took him, so generously recorded in his *Essay*, as a model for self-experiment, for self-assaying.

Some observations
on recent Locke scholarship*

by HANS AARSLEFF

On the whole recent Locke scholarship has been much too concerned with pseudo-problems which may appear striking, in some cases even sensational, but which have diverted attention from the core and substance of Locke's thought. There has been much concern over pretended conflicts between the early *Essays on the Law of Nature* and the *Two Treatises*, though the publication of the former would clearly not have illuminated the concept of natural law in the latter; between the *Two Treatises* and the *Essay*, though the law of nature, like all other knowledge, is not innate; between the early political doctrine and the later doctrine, though Locke's rejection of the possibility that the law of nature could be known from the general consent of men was as firm in the beginning as it was in the end—men's general consent did indeed tend to gather round a common understanding of natural law, but its truth depended not on that consent but on 'the conduct of reason';[1] between the pretended hedonism and the law of nature, though both belong intimately together in the later development of Locke's thought after the years in France; between a 'voluntaristic' concept of law and the law of reason, though within man's view of God's creation and dispensation there can be no conflict. At the bottom of these supposed oppositions lies the mistaken view that Locke was a rationalist in his political philosophy while he was an empiricist in his natural philosophy. Reason plays the pre-eminent role in Locke's entire account of the foundations of knowledge, whether natural or moral, and if Hume can be considered the typical empiricist, then Locke is better considered a rationalist. Only the candle of the Lord, the light of nature,

---

* *Editor's Note:*
   The following was originally written as part of Professor Aarsleff's essay in the volume. The points he is making in these pages, and the plea he makes at the very end, seemed to me to make an excellent conclusion for this volume. I prevailed upon Professor Aarsleff to allow me to print these pages here, even though these remarks emerged from his work on the state of nature and the nature of man.

[1] See M. Cranston, *John Locke, A Biography* (London, 1957), p. 67 for a view also found in other writers. Thus in 1660 and 1661, Locke was no more and no less 'a man of the Right, an extreme authoritarian', than he was later.

gives knowledge by the play of reason on sense-experience, those two inborn faculties which the great Creator and law-maker put into man as sufficient guides to his conduct. There may be minor inconsistencies in Locke's thought—and in which philosopher are they not to be found?— but the overall tenor of his dominant principles and ideas is not inconsistent. There is, as Professor Mandelbaum says in an essay that is surely the most balanced and distinguished analysis of Locke in recent years, 'simply a working out of them in greater detail'.[1] Development and refinement are very different from conflict and opposition. We have had too many hypotheses, based on slender or local evidence, raised almost to the status of fact.

Still, it is only fair to admit that some explanation is required to account for this tendency to find so much confusion and contradiction in Locke, leaving aside what can be put down to inadequate knowledge of his writings at large and their plain arguments as well as to faulty readings, which are surprisingly common. I think two general factors go a long way toward explaining the unnecessary difficulties that have been raised: Locke's own way of writing and the deplorable state of the text of Locke, indeed of the whole canon. As to the former, I think everyone will agree that there are firm grounds for admitting that Locke's works lack the precision, polish, and ordered structure we generally expect in writing of that sort—or at least have come to expect. A full reading of the *Essay* offers abundant evidence, and Locke himself was acutely aware of it as he openly admitted both in the 'Epistle to the Reader' and repeatedly in correspondence. He had a private way of writing (by which I do not mean a concealed or devious way) for himself and a few friends, and the external circumstances of his life precluded long stretches of steady, undisturbed application. In place of the quiet leisure of a studentship at Christ Church, he chose active participation in the affairs of his day. During the better part of his active, adult life he was busy in the risky and demanding politics of his day, travelled much, was often without his books, spent years of exile abroad to escape what would almost certainly have meant severer restriction of his freedom at home, and increasingly suffered physical infirmities that stole away his time and capacity for work.[2] The *Essay* was

---

[1] Maurice Mandelbaum, 'Locke's Realism', *Philosophy, Science, and Sense Perception: Historical and Critical Studies* (Johns Hopkins Paperbacks, 1966), p. 14.

[2] From the middle of the 1690s, Locke's asthmatic condition is frequently mentioned in the letters, for instance in these letters from the Limborch correspondence: 'Hæc ego raptim inter urbis negotia & laborantium pulmonum anhelitus' (Locke to Limborch, 11 December 1694); 'Inter negotia publica & privatam valetudinem tam parum mihi conceditur otii literarii ... Ego nuper Londinum profectus post octidui incommodam & anhelosam moram præpropero reditu huc me recipere coactus sum. Hæc pulmonum imbecillitas me brevi spero restituet pristino otio' (Locke to Limborch, 4 March 1696/7); 'Prælegit mihi hisce diebus Guenellonus

Hans Aarsleff

written by 'incoherent parcels, and after long intervals of neglect resumed again, as my humour or occasions permitted'. The result was 'this discontinued way of writing', and the shapelessness and length of the work, which he was, however, 'to confess the truth...too lazy, or too busy' to remedy. There is every reason to believe that the *Two Treatises* were written under equally unfavourable conditions (indeed the two works seem largely to have been written concurrently); the result was the same, again evident upon a first reading.[1] It is as true of the *Treatises* as of the *Essay* and the other works that Locke would have good reason to be grateful to readers who do not 'stick barely in the words', but observe 'the design and foundation' of the whole.[2] The difficulty then is primarily with the way of writing and the conditions of work, not with the arguments and the thought. In the 'Epistle to the Reader' Locke spoke directly to this point with a certain resignation: 'So it is that my meaning, I find, is often mistaken, and I have not the good luck to be everywhere rightly understood.'

This quality in Locke is so evident that it is incumbent upon writers who make assumptions to the contrary to prove their case. It has two important consequences. It becomes meaningless to argue, as has often been done, that Locke's failure to publish this or that after encouragement to do so, to revise this or that, or to complete something he had talked about, proves that he was unwilling to do so or unable to make a promised argument come out. This goes for instance for the much-debated demonstrability of ethics, which has been seen, by his failure to provide it, as proof of some basic fault in his entire system. The general principle is very simple: It is much safer and infinitely more useful to argue from what a man does and says than from our opinion of the suspected reason for our view of his omissions. The same factor strikes at the root of the caution or concealment hypothesis, first advanced by Professor Strauss and repeated with ornamentations by Professor Cox—though much else tells against that hypothesis, chiefly the very arguments and 'evidence' that are propounded in its favour. That hypothesis is forced to assume that Locke was an exceptionally careful writer, who deliberately involved his sense in meticulously phrased and precisely placed ambiguous locutions, that his discourse is a tissue of the most intricate and no doubt time-

noster epistolam tuam, quæ te cum asthmate graviter conflictari nuntiabat' (Limborch to Locke, 18 February, 1701), in *The Works of John Locke*, 9 vols. (London, 1794), IX, 42, 58–9, and 102.

[1] This is clearly shown by Mr Laslett in his edition, both in the Introduction and in the dates assigned to the composition of the different parts.

[2] *Works*, VIII, 303 (Locke to Molyneux, 20 January 1692/3); cf. IX, 285 (Locke to Anthony Collins, 21 March 1703/4). See also p. 129, n. 2 above.

consuming subterfuges. This procedure would require enough concealment not to be found out by everyone, yet not so much as not to be
understood at all, at least by a few, and presumably first of all by those
who might be swayed to accept the argument, that is by those, among
others, who were potentially the very enemies whose wrath Locke should
have wished to escape. For it is surely not enough to believe that Locke
wrote for a small coterie who already had the message. Thus this method
would seem to offer little hope of success without also having the sup-
posedly dangerous heterodoxy and even heresy come out in the open.
One might as well argue that the Bible was not only read but indeed also
written by the devil for his own purposes.

In support of the claim that Locke was the careful writer the concealment hypothesis demands, we are told that he did not publish till he was
in his fifties; that his journals, workbooks, and letters show 'prodigious
activity'; and that he wrote several versions of the *Essay*.[1] But these facts
may just as well be used to support the opposite claim. It is surely within
everyone's observation that people who have amassed notes, even careful
notes, through half a lifetime have in the end written carelessly or not at
all, just as others have been known to write with care and precision with
few notes and short years of preparation. Locke's journals, notes and
correspondence are not particularly voluminous or careful: the letters
especially are on the whole disappointingly sparse in their philosophical
content when compared with the letters of, for instance, Marin Mersenne,
Descartes or Leibniz. The early versions of the *Essay* do not prove that
the finished product was a model of compactness and clarity. The proof
is in the pudding, not in assurances about the excellence of the recipe.
We have Locke's own statement, the remarks of his contemporaries, and
our own observation to tell us that his writings do not have the qualities
claimed for them to support the concealment hypothesis.

If the sense is deliberately concealed, we might expect to be provided
with a key, and this we are told that Locke also did. The pretended advice
says that we must read with 'stubborn attention, and more than common
application' in order to find the true meaning. The passage is drawn from
Locke's Preface to his *Paraphrase and Notes on the Epistles of St. Paul*, from
which we are told we can learn 'to apply to the reading of his work the
same rigorous and demanding standards which he set for himself in inter-
preting other writings'. What we learn is, for instance, in Cox's words,
'that an author of stature—and Locke himself certainly was such an
author—presumably has some purpose in writing as he does, and that
therefore the obscurities and perplexities which may appear at first reading,

[1] Richard H. Cox, *Locke on War and Peace* (Oxford, 1960), pp. 28–9, 207.

or even after several readings, are not easily to be presumed as due to want of coherence, perspicacity or consistency on the part of the author. They may, in fact, be part of the author's plan or method.' There is only one very great difficulty with this argument: the 'author of stature' is St Paul, who—as Locke repeatedly insists in the very paragraph from which Cox is quoting—'was miraculously called to the ministry of the gospel, and declared to be a chosen vessel...he had the whole doctrine of the gospel from God, by immediate revelation...God himself had condescended to be his instructor and teacher.' On these grounds, Locke was persuaded that St Paul 'was not a man of loose and scattered parts, incapable to argue, and unfit to convince those he had to deal with'. Professor Cox's 'author of stature' is in fact the Holy Ghost. Hence, in the familiar tradition of scriptural exegesis, Locke could rest assured that the Epistles did contain profound meaning and truth, and nothing but truth, no matter how difficult it might be for a man to comprehend all. This claim can be made for no other writing in history than the Scriptures. I think many may share my hesitancy to take Locke's words in the Preface to the *Paraphrase* as a statement of 'the principles of interpretation which are to be applied to the *Treatises*'. We are further told that Locke in his remarks on Filmer's style and discourse early in the *First Treatise* left directions for the reading of his own writing. Here Locke had remarked that Filmer had a 'peculiar way of writing', had deliberately 'scattered' his meaning 'up and down in his Writings' and often huddled 'several suppositions together and that in doubtful and general terms'. This, we are told, is Locke's own method and his remarks on Filmer are designed to make the reader understand that Locke himself deliberately followed the same method and must be read accordingly.[1] The argument is surely unique, in print. The whole matter rises to comic proportions when a reviewer comments with approval that the entire hypothesis gains support 'from following Locke's own advice as to how political tracts should be read in order to extract the author's intentions from the subterfuges the times may require'.

Exactly what subterfuges the time may have required is never very clear, except that Locke is said to have been inordinately cautious about revealing pretended minor points of unorthodoxy or heterodoxy, while the major point is not touched that Locke presumably never destroyed the part of the *Second Treatise* in which he, without the slightest caution or ambiguity, stated the same seditious doctrine for which Algernon Sidney was executed—though we know that the agents of James sought to reach Locke even during the years of his exile in Holland. The evidence

---

[1] Cox, *Locke on War and Peace*, pp. 35, 64.

that is offered is not reassuring. During his diplomatic mission to Cleves as secretary to Sir Walter Vane in 1665, Locke wrote back to his friend John Strachey in England: 'What private observations I have made will be fitter for our table at Sutton than a letter.'[1] I wonder if there is any letter writer who has not himself made similar remarks—it may not even imply caution but merely that some things are better in conversation than in writing. Locke was on official business, and letters might well be opened to the embarrassment of the cause he was employed to serve. If this is caution, then it is both trivial and common.[2] Further evidence is drawn from Locke's directions to Limborch in a letter from the early months of 1698. At Limborch's urging, Locke had agreed to discuss 'l'unité de Dieu', both for Limborch's benefit and for that of 'cette excellent homme, & aux autres personnes, qui se trouvèrent dans votre conference'.[3] Locke added three conditions: That they should promise to communicate their opinion of his argument, that they should communicate their own arguments, and that no copy of the letter should be given to anybody and the letter burnt if Locke so requested. This certainly seems a reasonable and not over-cautious request, for who wants to run the risk of being dragged into public controversy over the contents of a private letter? Limborch had previously irked Locke by his indiscretion about the *Epistola de Tolerantia*, the matter had already come up in the Stillingfleet controversy, and Locke said both in this letter and in a previous one that his thoughts were not settled on the subject but that he might in the next edition of the *Essay* please Limborch and satisfy the wish 'd'aucun de vos amis en y inserant les preuves de l'unité de Dieu qui se presentent à mon esprit'.[4] Thus the caution or concealment hypothesis collapses, and even if caution were detected it does not follow that Locke's discourse was designed to be an elaborate tissue of deliberate ambiguities, hidden meanings, and cabbalistical obscurities. Even on general grounds, there is the strong objection against the hypothesis that it cannot be tested: If it were claimed that all the divines of seventeenth-century England were really atheists

---

[1] *Ibid.* p. 8.

[2] Most of the evidence cited for Locke's caution has to do with political matters, where the reasons for caution are altogether different from any that might apply to his published writings, e.g. the matter mentioned in *Essays on the Law of Nature*, ed. von Leyden (Oxford, 1954), pp. 249–50, and cited by Cox, *Locke on War and Peace*, pp. 8–9 in favour of his opinion.

[3] *Works*, IX, 70 (Locke to Limborch, 2 April 1698, but the correct date seems to be 21 February 1697/8, as given in Henry Ollion, *Lettres inédites de John Locke* (La Haye, 1912), pp. 211–12, which also prints an additional page not in the *Works*).

[4] *Works*, IX, 63 (Locke to Limborch, 29 October 1697). With reference to the letter cited in the previous note, Cox says (*Locke on War and Peace*, p. 10) that Locke 'forbids Limborch even to mention his name in connexion with the views expressed', but I do not see that it says so anywhere in the published version, whether in *Works* or in the additional matter printed in Ollion.

18-2

who for the sake of caution and clever concealment continued to perform their duties as if they were not, I do not see how it could be disproved, which surely is no reason to accept it.[1]

It will still be argued that Locke's decision not to put his name to several of his published works is proof of a certain caution and perhaps even secretiveness, but I think Locke had quite a different motive. With all the great men of his century, he believed that truth was the result of steady, disinterested search; that it was available to many more than had commonly been imagined, and that the chief obstacle to agreement and peace was controversy and men's self-interested commitment to sectarian belief. With his contemporaries he was strongly impressed by the disasters of the Thirty Years War, and he wished to find objective evidence, open and convincing to all, of the greatness and design of the Creator. Neither

---

[1] Professor Cox gives several instances of how he, on the advice he took from Locke, pursues his readings with 'more than common application'. On p. 61, he mentions Locke's doctrine that 'in the State of Nature, everyone has the executive Power of the Law of Nature' (Cox says 'all men have a natural right to execute', which is not what Locke says); he goes on to say that Hooker never said so but forgets to cite the sentences preceding the quotation, which indeed show that Hooker said just that: 'Men always knew that when force and injury was offered they might be defenders of themselves; they knew that howsoever men may seek their own commodity, yet if this were done with injury unto others it was not to be suffered, but by all men and by all good means to be withstood; finally they knew [here begins the Cox quotation] that no man might in reason take upon him to determine his own right, and according to his own determination proceed in maintenance thereof, inasmuch as every man is towards himself and them whom he greatly affecteth partial; and therefore that strifes and troubles would be endless, except they gave their common consent...' (Richard Hooker, *Of the Laws of Ecclesiastical Polity*, 2 vols. (London, 1907), I, x, §4). Thus Hooker says the same as Locke, and the emphasis lies on the phrase 'in reason', i.e. man knew that it is contrary to reason, without the sanction of reasonable procedures, for man to be a (potentially partial) judge in his own case. To Locke this is also the fundamental weakness in the state of nature, the weakness that makes consent and civil society necessary. Here, incidentally, Professor Cox must assume that Hooker is talking about the state of nature, whereas two pages earlier he has blamed Locke for quoting Hooker on that state though 'Hooker never once used the expression "state of nature"'. Here, at the bottom of p. 58, Cox would also have lost his point if he had continued the quotation from Locke after 'naturally in that state'. Cox often has difficulty with Locke's plain words, thus managing to find support for his thesis; on p. 89 he refers to 'what Locke at times chooses euphemistically to call "inconveniences" of the natural state'. This use is not euphemistic. Locke uses both 'inconvenience' and its antonym 'convenience' throughout his writings in this sense. Hooker (e.g. *ibid.* I, x, §4) and Hume also use it in this sense; it is a translation of the Latin *incommodum*, which has a long history in this meaning, so also used by Pufendorf and by Locke in the Latin *Essays on the Law of Nature*. Similarly, on pp. 86–7, he conducts a strange argument which, among other errors, depends on the remarkable misunderstanding that 'to use the creatures' means 'to eat animals of flesh and blood'. 'To use' is of course not the same as 'to eat', and 'creatures' include all created things, such as water, soil, rain, sunshine, oxen, dogs, streams, and 'every herb bearing seed, which is upon the face of all the earth, and every tree, in the which is the fruit of a tree yielding seed; to you it shall be for meat' (Gen. i. 29, which is very relevant to the argument). Locke is following traditional scriptural exegesis, such as might be found in the 'learned and judicious Ainsworth', who offers many insights into Locke's readings, especially in the *First Treatise* and on the very points Cox is arguing about. Locke owned and carefully used Ainsworth—it will also do a great deal for the Cain passage in *Two Treatises*, II, §11.

the interpreters of the Bible nor official religion had promoted the cause of peace. For Locke and for Boyle, for Bacon and the men of the Royal Society, the basic motive for the study of nature was to overcome dissension and strife by finding objective truth open to the senses and reason, above private opinion, enthusiasm, or particular men's doctrines. Natural philosophy served natural theology. As early as the treatise of the civil magistrate, Locke had observed that 'all those flames that have made such havoc and desolation in Europe, and have not been quenched but with the blood of so many millions, have been at first kindled with coals from the altar'.[1] To have put his name to those works would have involved him in public controversy, and Locke did not believe that such controversy advanced truth:

Truth, I hope, I always shall be fond of, and so ready to embrace, and with so much joy, that I shall own it to the world, and thank him that does me the favour. So that I am never afraid of any thing writ against me, unless it be the wasting of my time, when it is not writ closely in the pursuit of truth, and truth only.[2]

But once controversy was forced upon him, he was not sorry for it, which could not have been the case if fear and caution were his motives. He did not hesitate to call the *Essay* heterodox and was so fond of truth that he would take it wherever he found it.[3] Locke's grand, passionate thought and motive was labour for the public good—'I think every one, according to what way Providence has placed him in, is bound to labour for the public good, as far as he is able, or else he has no right to eat.'[4] The public good was peace and toleration, the means objective truth and knowledge. Controversy did not serve that cause, and he would rather abstain from it than give cause for disorder and contention, 'mais j'aime la paix, & il y a des gens dans le monde, qui aiment si fort les criailleries

[1] Philip Abrams, *John Locke: Two Tracts of Government* (Cambridge, 1967), pp. 160–1. Cf. also the Latin tract, *ibid*. pp. 185–7. It is still commonly though erroneously believed that there was a conflict between religion and science in the seventeenth century. There was not, they were allies. The conflict is between sectarian belief and unreason (as for example in enthusiasm) on the one hand and objective truth on the other. There is complete harmony between special and manifest revelation. The intention of Boyle's will, often cited in this context, was not to defend faith and science against scientific doubt, but to combat sectarian division and its destructive consequences. The motto on his portrait reads, 'Ex rerum causis supremam noscere causam'.

[2] *Works*, VIII, 417 (Locke to Molyneux, 3 May 1697). Locke often makes similar statements in the Molyneux and Limborch correspondences, e.g. *Works*, VIII, 294, 314, 351, 354, 355.

[3] *Works*, IX, 39 (Locke to Limborch, 26 October 1694): 'Libri mei de Intellectu Humano secunda editio distrahitur, celerius quam credere possem, nec adhuc invenit dissertatio illa, utcunque heterodoxa, oppugnatorem.' *Ibid*. pp. 6–7 (Locke to Limborch, 6 October 1685): 'Ego, qui ubique solam quæro veritatem, eamque, quantum capere possum, sive inter orthodoxos reperio, sive heterodoxos, pariter amplector.' Cf. *Works*, VIII, 313, 332, 408, 431.

[4] *Works*, VIII, 332 (Locke to Molyneux, 19 January 1693/4).

Hans Aarsleff

& les vaines contestations, que je doute si je dois leur fournir de nouveaux sujets de dispute'.[1]

If inadequate awareness of Locke's particular way of writing has caused so many difficulties, it is obvious that the deplorable state of the text has created further obstacles. A reliable and well-edited text is the first requirement for reasonably correct and efficient scholarship. At present, among the great British philosophers, only four are or will be available in good editions. We have Sir William Hamilton's superb and still unsurpassed edition of Dugald Stewart (now over a hundred years old), the recent edition of Berkeley, and the editions of John Stuart Mill and Bentham now being published. This record compares very poorly with the good, complete editions of French and German philosophers, both the big standard editions and new ones that have been coming out in recent years. We also have the serviceable, though by no means remarkable, nineteenth-century editions of Bacon, Hobbes, and Bentham. For Locke, however, we have nothing but a succession of jumbled editions which ultimately go back to the early eighteenth century, without the barest minimum of editorial apparatus, except for scanty indexes. Until a recent reprint, the last edition was over a hundred years old. For seventy years the standard text of the *Essay* was Fraser's wretched and misleading edition. No edition gives ready access to the revisions Locke made in the five editions he prepared for the press. Though of the first importance to an understanding of his thought, this information can be gathered only by painstaking comparison of the editions themselves, a task that can only be undertaken in a few major libraries. It is true that British philosophy has shown a strong antipathy to historical studies during the last generation, but it is also true that its chief concern has been the analysis of philosophical language. In so far as older philosophers come into the picture at all—and on occasion they do—the reliability of the text would seem to matter. Printer's errors and the whims of anonymous editors are hardly the admitted objects of philosophical analysis, but with our present texts there is no guarantee that they do not become so.

Since the opening of the Lovelace Collection, we have seen a profusion of piecemeal and often inaccurate and incomplete publication from the papers, almost to the point where we stand in need of something similar to what Ravier's *Bibliographie des œuvres de Leibniz* does for Leibniz, a situation which for Locke has largely arisen within the last generation compared to more than two hundred years of scattered Leibniz publication. Even recent editions of the longer, previously unpublished writings leave something to be desired—really good indexes, precise information

[1] *Works*, IX, 63 (Locke to Limborch, 29 October 1697).

about dating clearly stated, lists of works cited, and precise listings of biblical citations. In spite of the usefulness they may have, the introductions have tended to raise obstacles between the reader and his free view of the text.

We may soon hope to see a good edition of the correspondence. The magnificent edition of Leibniz that is now being published—and will be coming out for at least another thirty years—supplies all we can wish to have for Locke's great contemporary, with whom he had so much in common. The question concerns not only Locke, but our view of the entire seventeenth century and of England's and even America's position in what Leibniz was the first to call 'notre Europe'. The tercentenary of Locke's death is now some thirty-five years away. It would be a fitting goal for the completion of a new, up-to-date edition of the entire works, both those that have been printed before and the papers. Without it, Locke scholarship will be as uncertain in the future as it has been in the past.

Index

Aaron, R. I., 81n. 4, 191n. 1, 228n. 6
Aaron and Gibb, 99n. 1, 104n. 3, 106n. 6,
 111n. 1, 118n. 1, 119n. 1, 123n. 3, 124nn.
 2–4, 196n. 3, 199n. 4, 203n. 6, 209n. 8,
 210n. 2
Aaronson, Janson, 60n. 1
Aarsleff, Hans, 224n. 2
Abrams, Philip, 23n. 5, 82n. 5, 83n. 2,
 104n. 3, 119n. 2, 127n. 3, 239n. 4, 269n. 1
action, 2, 190
Acton, Lord, 20, 32
Adair, Douglass, 79n. 1
Adams, John, 78
Adams, Samuel, 75n. 3, 76
Ainsworth, Henry, 268n. 1
Akzin, B., 19n. 1, 30n. 4
America, 21, 23, 31, 48, 65 ff., 137 ff., 148
anarchism, 17, 53
Andrews, Charles McLean, 138n. 1, 139n. 2,
 140nn. 1–2, 141n. 1, 157n. 2 and 4
Andros, Sir Edmund, 160, 161, 162
Anscombe, G. E. M., 230n. 1
Arieli, Y., 31n. 2
Aristotle, 8, 32, 78n. 5, 89, 166, 172, 226, 227,
 229, 230
Arnauld, Antoine, 239n. 2
Asgill, John, 149, 150n. 2
Ashley, Maurice, 146, 175n. 2
atheism, 16, 17, 40, 170, 201
Atwood, Sir William, 57n. 1
Avineri, S., 31n. 1
Axtell, James, 193n. 2

Babington, Dr, 171
Backus, Isaac, 74n. 2
Bacon, Francis, 105, 141, 183, 234, 237, 238,
 239, 257, 269, 270
Bailyn, Bernard, 45n. 1, 46n. 2, 79n. 1
Balzac, Guez de, 239
Barbeyrac, Jean, 236
Barker, Sir Ernest, 94n. 2
Barnes, Harry E., 88n. 1
Barrow, Isaac, 175n. 2
Bayle, Pierre, 236
Becker, Carl L., 46n. 1
Becker, Howard, 88n. 1
being, great chain of, 64
Belcher, Governor, 70

Benn, S. I., 93n. 5
Bentham, J., 60, 62, 270
Bentley, Richard, 170, 171
Berkeley, Bishop G., 61, 62, 69, 126, 225, 235,
 270
Blackall, Offspring, 61
Blackstone, Sir William, 58
Blair, James, 157, 160, 161, 162, 163
blasphemy, 65, 74
Blathwayt, William, 140n. 1, 153n. 3, 155,
 161, 162–3
Boas, Marie, see Hall, M. B.
Bodin, Jean, 69n. 4
Bold, Samuel, 40, 221n. 1
Bolingbroke, Lord, 60
Boorstin, Daniel, 45n. 1, 46
Boucher, Jonathan, 61n. 2, 63, 76–7
Boyle, Robert, 36n. 2, 105, 129n. 2, 139,
 170–2, 173, 183, 186, 190, 191n. 1, 193,
 239n. 2, 244, 269
Brewster, David, 171n. 1, 177n. 2
Brounower, Sylvester, 35, 83, 155
Brown, Louise Fargo, 138n. 1, 139n. 2,
 140n. 2, 143n. 3, 144n. 4
Bulkley, John, 71–2
Burgh, James, 58
Burke, Edmund, 24, 61n. 3, 67n. 2, 68, 142,
 164
Burnet, Bishop Gilbert, 142
Burnet, Thomas, 132n. 1, 213–14, 224n. 2
Burthogge, Richard, 235
Bushman, Richard L., 72n. 1

Campbell, Colin, 169
Care, Henry, 39
Carlyle, Thomas, 78n. 5
Carolina (colony), 21, 28, 143
Carritt, E. F., 93n. 4, 96n. 2
Cary, John, 58, 67n. 1, 76, 144n. 1, 157,
 158
Chamberlain, Charles, 148n. 4, 150n. 1
Chamberlain, Judge Mellen, 80n. 1
Chamberlayne, Edward, 38, 39
Charron, Pierre, 239
Chatham, Earl of, 59
Checkley, John, 71
Chesterfield, Philip Dormer Stanhope, 4th
 Earl of, 58

Index

Child, Sir Josiah, 144n. 1, 147n. 3, 149, 150n. 1, 151n. 2
Chilton, Edward, 162n. 5
Churchill, Awnsham, 35, 155n. 1, 174, 235
Clarendon, Edward Hyde, 1st Earl of, 37–8, 39, 41, 42, 47, 69n. 4
Clarke, Edward, 35, 146, 147, 154, 158nn. 1 and 3, 164, 174
Clarke, Samuel, 153n. 3, 154n. 1
Clarke, Dr Timothy, 173
Clement, Simon, 58
Clerke, Gilbert, 170
Cobban, A., 19n. 1, 20n. 1
Cockburn, Catherine, 235
Colbourn, H. Trevor, 79n. 1
Collins, Anthony, 235, 250
consent, 8, 10–13, 20–8, 32, 39, 50, 75, 83, 87, 90, 92–4, 103, 160, 192, 213, 268n. 1
constitutionalism, 38
contractualism, 24, 25, 31, 50, 81
Cook, Thomas I., 92nn. 1 and 2
Cooper, A. A., see Shaftesbury, Earl of
Copernicus, 166, 178
corpuscularianism, 183–4, 186, 190–1
Coste, Pierre, 57n. 2, 111n. 3, 117n. 3, 129n. 2, 235n. 1, 249n. 2, 250
Cox, R. H., 26n. 2, 88nn. 1 and 3, 96n. 2, 107n. 3, 108n. 2, 130n. 1, 133n. 1, 136n. 1, 218n. 3, 264–8
Cox, Sir Richard, 66n. 5
Craig, Sir John, 144n. 2, 150n. 2, 156n. 2, 168, 171
Crane, R. S., 239n. 4
Cranston, Maurice, 81n. 1, 140n. 1, 143n. 2, 152n. 1, 175n. 4, 195n. 5, 197n. 1, 262n. 1
Croll, Morris, 237, 238
Croune, Dr William, 173
Crowley, Hannah, 181
Curtius, E. R., 240n. 2

Danby, Thomas, Earl of, 146n. 3
Davenant (d'Avenant), Charles, 140, 144nn. 1 and 2, 149, 150, 151, 153, 155n. 3
De Beer, E. S., 66n. 1, 194n. 1, 235n. 4
Defoe, Daniel, 48
deism, 170
De Maistre, J., 63
democracy, 19, 20
De Moivre, Abraham, 169
Denham, Sir John, 139
Derham, William, 168
Desaguliers, J. T., 171n. 2, 177, 182n. 1
Descartes, 166, 167, 172, 174, 176, 226, 233, 257, 265
Desmaizeaux, Pierre, 41n. 1, 178n. 1, 179n. 2

Deutsch, K. W., 20n. 2, 30
Dewhurst, Kenneth, 172n. 1, 174n. 1, 193n. 2
Diderot, D., 236
Dijksterhuis, E. J., 168n. 2
Duillier, Fatio de, 169
Duniway, C. A., 71n. 3
Dunn, John, 93n. 4, 159n. 1

Ebenstein, William, 81n. 1
Edwards, John, 163n. 3, 199–200
Edwards, Jonathan, 70
Eisinger, Chester E., 72n. 3
Elibank, Lord, 62n. 3
Eliot, Jared, 73
Elrington, Thomas, 58
empiricism, 1, 139, 179, 206, 226, 262
Ent, Dr George, 173
Erskine, Thomas, 67n. 2, 68
Euclid, 175
Evelyn, John, 139, 170n. 3

faith, 16, 51, 63, 194–223
Farish, Hunter Dickinson, 162n. 5
Fay, C. R., 155n. 3
Feaveryear, A. E., 144n. 2
Figgis, John Neville, 81n. 1
Filmer, Robert, 3, 21, 24, 34–5, 40–2, 49–51, 55–6, 59, 60n. 1, 61n. 2, 63, 78n. 5, 81–2, 84–7, 91–4, 98, 266
Fitzhugh, George, 78
Folkes, Martin, 166n. 2
Fontenelle, Bernard de, 166, 167, 168, 169n. 4
Forbes, R. J., 168n. 2
Fox Bourne, H. R., 102n. 1, 119n. 1, 127n. 1, 135n. 1, 140n. 1, 152n. 1, 161n. 4, 172n. 1
Franklin, Benjamin, 70, 77
Fraser, A. C., 1n. 1, 111n. 3, 117n. 5, 195n. 1, 209, 270
freedom (see also liberty), 1–18, 86, 87, 92, 94, 97, 100, 108, 112
Freke, John, 146, 147, 151nn. 2 and 3, 153n. 3
Friedrich, C. J., 30
Furley, O. W., 48n. 1
Furly, Benjamin, 175, 207n. 2

Galileo, 166
Geach, P. T., 230–2
Gerhardt, C. J., 224n. 1
Gibb, Jocelyn, see Aaron and Gibb
Gibson, James, 191n. 1, 200nn. 2 and 5
Givner, David, 179n. 3
Glanvill, Joseph, 200
God, 1–8, 15, 16, 17, 40, 41, 42, 45, 49, 50–6, 64, 83, 84, 87, 89, 105, 107–9, 110n. 2, 117, 118n. 2, 120, 122n. 1, 123, 126n. 2, 127, 128, 130, 134, 166, 170, 183, 187,

Index

God (cont.)
  190, 197, 198, 199, 200, 202–8, 212, 213,
  215, 217–20, 226, 262, 266, 267
Goddard, Dr Jonathan, 173
Godfrey, Michael, 148
Godolphin, William, 150n. 2, 151
Goldsmith, Oliver, 178
Gordon, John, Dean of Salisbury, 59
Gough, J. W., 88n. 2, 94n. 2, 95n. 1, 138n. 2
Grattan, Henry, 66
Greene, Jack P., 75
Gregory, David, 167–9, 174, 175, 181
Greig, J. Y. T., 62n. 3
Grey, Forde, Earl of Tankerville, 153n. 1, 164
Grotius, Hugo, 69n. 4, 70
Guenellon, P., 36
Guericke, Otto von, 173
Guise, Lady, 199n. 2

Haddow, Anna, 70n. 5
Hagan, William T., 72n. 3
Halévy, Elie, 60n. 1
Hall, Marie Boas, 179n. 4, 185n. 1, 186n. 1
Hall, Rupert, 167, 179n. 4
Halley, Edmond, 168, 177n. 3
Hamilton, Sir William, 270
Hampton, John, 57n. 3
happiness, 4, 5, 112, 114, 115, 116, 119, 123,
  124–6, 128, 133, 134, 196
Hardy, Thomas, 67
Harré, Rom, 191n. 1
Harrington, James, 69n. 4, 79n. 1, 80n. 1, 141
Harrison, John, 144n. 1, 149n. 2, 175n. 2,
  237n. 4, 239n. 2
Hartz, Louis, 72n. 3
Hawkins, Sir John, 57n. 4, 58, 75
Heathcote, Gilbert, 148n. 4, 149, 150n. 2,
  151n. 2
hedonism, 111, 121, 122n. 1, 127
Hegel, G. W. F., 6, 30, 31n. 1, 69
Herbert, Thomas, Earl of Pembroke, 145, 146,
  147, 174, 176, 240–3
Herne, Joseph, 150n. 1
Hill, Abraham, 137, 150, 153n. 3, 156n. 1
Himmelfarb, G., 20n. 1, 32nn. 1 and 2
Hiscock, W. G., 167n. 2, 168n. 4, 181n. 3
historicism, 19, 94
historiography, 46
Hoadly, Benjamin, 59, 63, 64
Hobbes, Thomas, 10, 12, 37, 51–2, 55–6, 63n. 1,
  69n. 4, 78n. 1, 81, 96n. 2, 100, 103, 104n. 3,
  136n. 1, 141, 199n. 2, 207, 212, 234, 270
Hodgskin, Thomas, 69
Hooke, Robert, 129n. 2, 173, 185n. 1
Hooker, Richard, 41, 60, 103, 108n. 5, 268n. 1
Horne, George, 61n. 2
Horsefield, John Keith, 150n. 2

Houblon, Sir James, 148n. 4
Houblon, Sir John, 148n. 4, 150nn. 1–2
Hovey, Alvah, 74n. 2
Hume, David, 60, 62, 94n. 2, 126, 201, 234,
  235, 262, 268n. 1
Hunt, Leigh, 46
Hunter, Philip, 40
Hutcheson, Francis, 62, 70
Hutchinson, Lieutenant-Governor Thomas,
  74, 75–6
Huygens, Christiaan, 168, 177, 179n. 2, 244
Hyde, Edward, see Clarendon, Earl of

Indians, American, 23, 36, 72, 104, 135, 157
  Canadian, 84n. 6, 97
individualism, 15, 16, 51, 52, 56, 74, 78
innatism, 1, 101, 102, 104, 127, 129, 130–1,
  132n. 1, 134, 198, 199–202, 208, 253, 262
irredentism, 26, 27

Jacobsen, Gertrude Ann, 140n. 1, 155n. 2
Jefferson, Thomas, 77, 78
Jeffreys, Judge, 35 n. 1
Jenkins, J. J., 88n. 3
Jenyns, Soame, 64–5
Johnson, Samuel, 57n. 4, 61
Jones, J. R., 47n. 1
Jones, O. R., 233n. 1
Jones, R. F., 239n. 1
Jones, Rev. William, 45, 61n. 2
Jonson, Ben, 241
Jouvenel, Bertrand de, 60n. 1
judgment, 2–5, 15–17, 73, 115, 116, 118n. 2,
  123, 124, 209, 213

Kant, I., 3, 5
Kearney, H. F., 66nn. 1, 3 and 5, 159n. 2
Kedourie, E., 20n. 1
Keill, John, 169
Kelly, Patrick, 137n. 1, 139n. 2, 143n. 3,
  144nn. 2 and 4, 147n. 2, 152n. 3, 155n. 2,
  156n. 2, 158n. 3, 161n. 4
Kepler, J., 132
King, C. S., 66n. 5
King, Peter, 104n. 3, 106n. 5, 107n. 3,
  117n. 1, 118n. 2, 119 nn. 1 and 4, 121n. 1,
  126n. 2, 127n. 3, 128n. 1, 136n. 1,
  140n. 1, 152n. 1
King, Richard, 219n. 2
King, Bishop William, 66n. 5, 204n. 6, 235
Kneller, Sir Godfrey, 242
knowledge, 52, 101, 108, 110, 112, 114,
  118n. 2, 120, 123–5, 129, 132, 183, 184,
  189–91, 193, 195, 202–23, 224, 225, 228,
  240, 244, 258, 262
  moral, 106, 107, 220
  natural, 106

Index

Koebner, Richard, 66n. 7
Kohn, H., 19nn. 1–3, 30n. 3
Körner, S., 230n. 1, 232n. 2
Kramnick, Isaac, 60n. 1
Kuhn, Thomas S., 166n. 1

Lakoff, Sanford A., 92n. 1
Lamprecht, Sterling P., 82n. 1, 88n. 1, 214 n. 1
language, 20–2, 29, 41, 120n. 2, 191, 192
Lansdowne, Marquis of, 141n. 3, 170n. 1
Laski, Harold, 81n. 1
Laslett, Peter, 35–6, 81, 135n. 1, 237n. 4, 239n. 2, 264n. 1
Laudan, Laurens, 191n. 1
Lavoisier, 160
law, common, 39
  divine, 48, 117, 127, 211, 214, 221
  moral, 17
  Mosaic, 130n. 3
  natural, 7, 24, 29, 40, 42, 72, 88n. 3, 109–10, 119, 121, 127–9, 133, 214, 219
  philosophical, 120n. 2
  positive, 7, 9, 13, 14, 110, 130, 133, 134
law of nations, 39
  of nature, 7, 9, 10, 14, 23, 25, 39, 41, 42, 72n. 2, 84, 88n. 3, 90, 92, 96n. 2, 99, 100, 101, 102, 106, 108, 110, 111, 114, 117n. 5, 118, 120–2, 125–8, 130, 131, 134, 136, 201n. 3, 203nn. 8 and 9, 204, 207n. 1, 213, 219–21, 238n. 1, 262, 267, 268n. 1
  of opinion, 117, 119, 120n. 2, 133, 212
  of reason, 7, 11, 23, 96n. 2, 100, 102, 114, 134, 262
Lawson, George, 69n. 4
Lazerowitz, M., 228n. 6
LeClerc, Jean, 35, 57n. 2, 175, 198, 235n. 2
Lee, Henry, 129n. 2
Lees, R. M., 140nn. 1–2, 141n. 3, 142nn. 3–4, 148n. 4, 150n. 2, 153n. 3, 157nn. 2 and 4
Leibniz, G. W. von, 110n. 2, 117n. 3, 126, 129n. 2, 167, 168, 175n. 3, 224, 233, 236, 265, 270–1
Leslie, Charles, 61n. 1, 63–5, 71
Letwin, William, 144n. 4
L'Hermitage, 154, 156
liberalism, 17, 18, 19–33, 34–44
liberty (see also freedom), 2–8, 17, 28, 29, 32, 36, 38, 74n. 1, 80, 83, 94, 112, 115, 116, 117n. 1, 207n. 1, 211, 249
Lieber, Francis, 78
Limborch, Franz van, 36, 263n. 2, 267, 269n. 3, 270n. 1
Lincoln, Abraham, 60
Linus, 168
Lipsius, Justus, 239

Lowde, James, 111n. 3, 114n. 2, 117n. 5
Lowndes, William, 149, 151, 155
Lucas, Charles, 66
Luther, Martin, 130n. 3

Macaulay, Thomas Babington, Lord, 142n. 3, 149n. 2
McDowell, R. B., 58
Machiavelli, N., 69n. 4, 79n. 1
Machin, John, 169, 171
McIlwain, Charles Howard, 159n. 2
Macpherson, C. B., 88n. 1, 218n. 3
Madison, James, 77
Malebranche, P., 174
Mandelbaum, M., 187n. 1, 191n. 1, 263
Manley, Thomas, 144n. 4
Marsilio, 32
Marvell, Andrew, 154
Marx, Karl, 69
Masham, Lady Damaris, 151, 177, 235
Masham, Sir Francis, 146, 177
Masham, Francis Cudworth, 177
Maston, T. B., 74n. 2
Mauduit, Jasper, 74
Meadows, Sir Philip, 153n. 3, 156n. 1
Mellon, Paul, 35
Mersenne, M., 265
Methuen, John, 153n. 3
Meyer, R. W., 126n. 1
microscopes, 185, 186
Mill, J. S., 31–2, 160, 270
Miller, Perry, 71nn. 1 and 3, 73n. 2
Milton, John, 59
Molesworth, Sir William, 207n. 1
Molyneux, William, 57n. 1, 58, 66–7, 76, 101, 104n. 3, 111, 116n. 1, 117n. 1, 124n. 4, 129, 158n. 3, 159–60, 191n. 1, 193n. 1, 198, 200n. 5, 201n. 2, 202n. 2, 219, 220n. 2, 229n. 2, 250, 264n. 2, 269nn. 2 and 4
Monmouth, James, Duke of, 147, 152, 156n. 2, 158, 161
Montagu, Charles, 137, 139, 145, 151n. 2, 156n. 2
Montaigne, Michel de, 237, 239
Montgomery, T. H., 70n. 6.
morality, 1, 5, 8, 119, 120, 122n. 1, 128, 135, 197–9, 201, 211, 212, 213, 218, 219
Mordaunt, Charles, 146, 180n. 1
More, Thomas, 72n. 3
Morrison, Samuel Eliot, 80n. 1
Mossner, E. C., 62n. 3
Moyle, Walter, 57n. 1, 58
Munter, Robert, 66n. 7

Nedham, Marchamont, 78n. 1
Newton, Humphrey, 171

Index

Newton, Sir Isaac, 68, 78n. 2, 79, 104, 132, 140, 144n. 2, 149, 150, 151n. 2, 155n. 3, 156, 165–82, 190, 193, 199n. 2, 244
Nicholson, Francis, 156n. 4, 160, 162
Nicole, Pierre, 109n. 5, 123, 134–5, 238, 239
Nolte, E., 29n. 2
Norris, Isaac, 69n. 3
Norris, John, 235

obligation, 5, 7, 8, 10, 11, 12, 13, 17, 18, 26, 41, 51, 53, 62, 71, 77, 85, 87, 93, 95, 96n. 2, 97, 98, 101, 104, 107, 118, 119, 120, 207n. 1, 214, 219, 220, 221
Ogg, David, 142n. 3
Ollion, Henry, 267nn. 3 and 4
order, 3, 9, 17, 18, 50, 53, 54, 64, 65, 73, 75, 77, 98, 107, 133, 134, 184, 202–8, 223
Otis, James, 74n. 5, 77
Ovid, 3

Paine, Thomas, 68n. 3
Paley, William, 60, 62
papacy, 17
Park, Sir James Allan, 61n. 2
Parry, Geraint, 89n. 6
Pascal, Blaise, 174, 175
patriarchalism, 63, 81, 83, 86, 90, 91, 92, 94, 97, 98
Pawling, Robert, 162, 163
Paxton, Peter, 41
Peacham, Henry, 237n. 3
Pell, John, 174
Pemberton, Henry, 167n. 4, 179n. 1
Pembroke, Earl of, see Herbert, Thomas
Peterborough, Lady, 40
Peters, R. S., 93n. 5
Petty, Sir William, 141, 144n. 1, 169–70
Pettyt, William, 41
Pitkin, Hanna, 93n. 5
Pitt, Thomas, 59n. 1
Pitt, William, 67n. 2, 68
Plamenatz, J. P., 82n. 1
Plato, 32, 227, 229
Plumb, J. H., 47n. 1, 62n. 3, 139n. 1, 153n. 2, 161n. 2
Pocock, J. G. A., 41n. 2, 79n. 1
Pole, J. R., 75n. 1
Polin, Raymond, 110n. 4
Pollexfen, John, 153n. 3, 156n. 1
Pollock, Sir Frederick, 81n. 1
Pollock, J., 66
popish plot, 39
Popple, William, 17, 154–5, 161
Power, Henry, 185n. 1
power, 1–3, 5, 6, 8, 14
Price, Richard, 58
Prior, Matthew, 164

probability, 115, 116, 118n. 2, 123–5, 128, 192, 206, 208–14, 215, 217
property, 6, 7, 8, 11, 38, 68, 69, 72, 82n. 1, 85, 86, 92
Pufendorf, Samuel, 41, 62, 69n. 4, 70, 268n. 1

Randolph, Thomas Mann, jr., 78n. 3
Ravier, Émile, 270
reason, 2, 3, 5, 6, 7, 13, 17, 24, 101, 106, 108, 109, 112, 114, 116, 126, 127n. 3, 131, 133, 134, 195, 203n. 8, 216n. 1, 219, 222
Renan, E., 24
revelation, 105–8, 110, 114, 117, 118n. 2, 127, 213, 215, 217, 219, 220, 221, 222
revolution, 26, 50, 54, 59, 60, 146
   American, 31, 47, 70, 77–80
   French, 19, 31
   scientific, 165, 166, 181
   Whig theory of, 80
revolutionary settlement, 142
Richardson, S., 236
Richmond, Duke of, 67n. 2, 68
right(s), 8, 15, 23, 24, 26, 29, 37, 39, 41, 42, 53, 68, 69, 72, 78n. 1, 82n. 1, 86, 87, 89, 92, 96, 98
Ritchie, David G., 82n. 1
Robbins, Caroline, 79n. 1, 160n. 1, 236n. 2
Rossiter, Clinton, 46n. 2
Rousseau, J.-J., 9–10, 78n. 1, 89, 92, 94n. 2
Rush, Benjamin, 78
Russell, Rev. M., 181n. 2
Ryle, Gilbert, 224n. 5, 250n. 1

Sabine, George H., 81n. 1, 88n. 1
Sagard, Gabriel, 97
Sainsbury, W. N., 161n. 1
salvation, eternal, 4–5, 7, 16
Sargent, John, 187n. 1
Schlatter, Richard, 82n. 1
science, 79, 174, 175, 189
Seliger, M., 88n. 3, 91n. 1
Seneca, 237
sense experience, 108, 109, 133, 134
Shaftesbury, Anthony Ashley Cooper, Earl of, 36, 37n. 1, 43, 47, 48, 60, 63, 138n. 1, 139, 143, 144n. 4, 146, 172, 175n. 2
Shaw, W. A., 144n. 2
Sherlock, William, 61, 200n. 5, 201
Shipton, Clifford K., 74n. 1
Shores, Louis, 70n. 1
Shrewsbury, Earl of, 147–8, 150n. 2
Sidney, Algernon, see Sydney, Algernon
Slafter, Edmund F., 71n. 1
slavery, 8, 13, 22, 26, 28–9, 38, 157
Smith, William, 70
Snow, C. P., 165, 181
social contract, 10, 13, 22, 23, 63, 94

277

society, civil, 10, 11, 20, 25, 32, 33, 87, 88, 100–4, 107, 134, 268n. 1
  political, 15, 16, 20–2, 24, 87, 88, 90n. 3, 93, 134
  religious, 16
Somers, John, 59, 137, 139, 144–7, 148n. 1, 149, 151–8, 164
South, Robert, 201n. 3
Southwell, Sir Robert, 170n. 1
sovereignty, 6, 14, 17, 21, 37, 40, 67, 159
Spence, Thomas, 68
Spencer, Herbert, 32
Spinoza, B., 226
Stanhope, P. D., *see* Chesterfield, Earl of
state of nature, 6, 8, 15, 37, 43, 63, 87–92, 96n. 2, 97–136, 268n. 1
Stephen, Sir Leslie, 86, 195n. 5, 196n. 4
Sterne, Laurence, 236
Stevens, W., 45
Stewart, Dugald, 104, 135, 270
Stillingfleet, Edward, Bishop of Worcester, 104n. 1, 170, 194, 195n. 2, 198, 199n. 4, 201, 202n. 2, 206, 214n. 2, 216, 223, 225, 235, 267
Stock, J., 61n. 3
Stoics, 2, 3, 15
Straka, Gerald M., 61n. 3
Strauss, Leo, 88n. 3, 115n. 4, 128n. 3, 136n. 1, 218n. 3, 264
substance, 184, 188, 195, 206, 224–33, 258
substratum, 183, 184, 187n. 1
Swammerdam, Jan, 185n. 1
Swan, John, 193n. 1
Swift, Jonathan, 66
Sydenham, Thomas, 191n. 1, 192, 241
Sydney (Sidney), Algernon, 41, 59, 78, 80n. 1, 266

Tacquet, André, 174, 175
Talmon, J. L., 20n. 1, 29n. 1
Tankerville, Forde Grey, Earl of, *see* Grey, Forde
Telescope, Tom (= Oliver Goldsmith?), 178
theology, 51, 55, 105, 156n. 3, 182, 216, 218, 269
Thierry, A., 31
Thomson, Mark A., 142n. 3
Toland, John, 202n. 2, 235
toleration, 16, 73, 74, 156n. 3, 174, 204nn. 3–4, 209n. 4, 216n. 1, 220nn. 1 and 4, 221n. 1, 222nn. 1 and 4
Tolles, Frederick B., 69n. 3
Tone, Wolfe, 66
Tönnies, F., 22
treason, 67, 68
Treitschke, Gotthard Heinrich von, 20
Trenchard, John, 59

Trumbull, Sir William, 145n. 2, 149n. 1, 152, 153, 161
Tucker, Josiah, 61, 62
Tucker, Louis L., 74n. 3
Turner, B. N., 64n. 2
Tussman, Joseph, 93n. 5
Tyrrell, James, 40–2, 111n. 3, 127–9, 197n. 1, 200, 201n. 1, 235, 245

understanding, 1, 4, 5, 15, 41, 108n. 5, 112, 178, 183, 190, 244, 251
uneasiness, 2, 4, 110, 113, 116, 117, 123
unitarian, 161n. 2
United Nations, 30
Usher, Abbott P., 144n. 2, 150n. 2, 151n. 1, 155n. 3
utilitarianism, 86, 111

Vane, Sir Walter, 267
Van Schaack, Peter, 77
Vaughan, Alden T., 72n. 3
Vaughan, C. E., 26n. 2, 130–1
Vincent, R., 200n. 6
Voltaire, F. M. A. de, 175n. 3, 236
von Leyden, W., 119n. 4, 122n. 1, 123

Walcote, Robert, 146n. 3
Waldman, Theodore, 93n. 4
Waller, Edmund, 139
Wallis, Dr John, 140, 149, 150n. 2, 181n. 1
Washburn, Wilcomb E., 72n. 3
Watson, Richard, 59, 64n. 2
Watson, Robert, 58
Watts, Isaac, 80n. 1
Whiston, James, 141, 148
Whitaker, John, 61n. 2, 63
will, 2, 4, 5, 6, 12, 14, 24, 108, 112, 113, 116, 119, 123n. 3, 124, 129, 249, 250
William III, King, 142, 145, 148
Williams, Elisha, 73, 74
Winthrop, Governor, 73
Wise, John, 73, 74
Wish, Harvey, 78n. 5
Wolcott, Roger, 71, 72n. 1
Wolin, Sheldon S., 88n. 1, 218n. 3
Woodward, C. Vann, 78n. 5
Worcester, Bishop of, *see* Stillingfleet, E.
Wordsworth, Christopher, 181nn. 1 and 4
Wormely, Ralph, 69
Worsley, Benjamin, 143n. 3
Wotton, William, 171n. 1
Wren, Sir Christopher, 140, 149, 150
Wynne, John, 235n. 2

Yolton, J. W., 88n. 3, 132n. 1, 200nn. 1 and 3, 201n. 3, 235, 249n. 1
Yonge, Sir Walter, 146
Yorke, Henry, 67n. 2